The Shia: The Real Followers of the Sunnah

Muhammad al-Tijani al-Samawi

Translated by
Hasan Muhammad Najafi

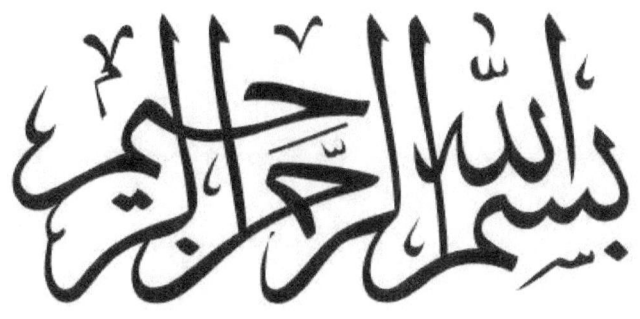

IN THE NAME OF ALLAH

THE BENEFICIENT, THE MERCIFUL

CONTENTS

Publisher's Preface.. 1
Introduction and Foreword by the Author............................. 7
Identifying the Shi'as.. 17
Identifying Ahlul Sunnah...25
The First Incident that Divided Muslim Ummah into Shi'as and Sunnis.......31
Second Incident that led ro Divergence from the Prophet's Sunnah........... 35
Third Incident that Juxtaposed the Shi'as Versus the Sunnis.................... 37
1. Isolation of the Opposition and its Economic Paralyzation..................38
2. Isolating the Opposition and Paralyzing it Socially........................... 39
3. Isolating the Opposition Politically... 42
Ahlul Sunnah are not Familiar with the Prophet's Sunnah...................... 44
The Proof:... 47
Ahlul Sunnah and the Obliteration of the Sunnah...............................55
The Attitude of Ahlul Sunnah towards the Shi'as................................ 71
Shi'as' Attitude towards Ahlul Sunnah wal Jama'ah............................ 77
Introducing the Imams of the Shi'as.. 81
Imams of Ahlul Sunnah wal Jama'ah... 87
The Prophet Appointed the Imams of the Shi'as................................. 97
Oppressive Rulers Appointed the Imams of Ahlul Sunnah....................107
The Secret Why Sunni Sects are in the Majority............................... 113
Malik Meets Abu Ja`Far Al-Mansour..121
Unavoidable Commentary Serving the Research............................... 125
The Abbaside Ruler Tests the Scholars of His Time...........................131
Hadith Al-Thaqalayn According to Shi'as.. 141
Hadith Al-Thaqalayn According to Ahlul Sunnah.............................. 145
Is it "The Book of Allah and My Progeny" or "The Book of Allah and My Sunnah"?.. 147
Shi`a Sources of Legislation.. 161
The Sources of Shari`a According to "Ahlul Sunnah wal Jama'ah"............165
1. The "Sunnah" of the "Righteous Caliphs".....................................167
2. The "Sunnah" of the Sahabah *En Masse*...171
3. The "Sunnah" of the Tabi`in or "Ulema Al-Athar"......................... 173
4. The "Sunnah" of the Rulers.. 175
5. The Rest of Sources of Legislation According to Ahlul Sunnah............179
A Comment Necessary to Complete the Research............................. 183

Taqlid and Maraji' According to Shi'as..191
Taqlid and Islamic Authorities According to Ahlul Sunnah wal Jama'ah......195
The Righteous Caliphs According to the Shi'as................................199
The Righteous Caliphs According to Ahlul Sunnah wal Jama'ah............. 203
The Prophet Rejects the Legislation of Ahlul Sunnah wal Jama'ah........... 207
A Necessary Post Script... 209
Enmity of Ahlul Sunnah Towards Ahlul Bayt Reveals their Identity..........211
How Ahlul Sunnah wal Jama'ah Distort the Blessing of Muhammad and His Progeny...217
Allegations Refuted by Facts.. 223
Imams and Pillars of Ahlul Sunnah wal Jama'ah.................................225
1. Abu Bakr "Al-Siddiq" Ibn Abu Quhafa.......................................227
2. Umar Ibn Al-Khattab "Al-Farooq".. 233
3. Uthman Ibn Affan "Dhul-Noorayn"..238
4. Talhah Ibn Ubaydullah.. 247
5. Al-Zubayr Ibn Al-Awwam... 255
6. Sa'd Ibn Abu Waqqas.. 265
7. Abdul-Rahman Ibn Awf.. 276
8. Ayesha Daughter of Abu Bakr "Mother of the Faithful".................. 283
9. Khalid Ibn Al-Waleed... 291
10. Abu Hurayra Al-Dawsi.. 305
11. Abdullah Ibn Umar.. 317
Violations of Abdullah Ibn Umar of the Book and the Sunnah...............330
12. Abdullah Ibn Al-Zubayr..335
According to Shi'as, Prophet's Sunnah does not Contradict the Qur'an....... 341
The Sunnah and the Qur'an According to Ahlul Sunnah wal Jama'ah........ 345
Prophet's Ahadith Reported by Ahlul Sunnah Contradict one Another......359
Muhammad Ibn Abu Bakr's Letter to Mu'awiyah...............................369
Mu'awiyah Answers Muhammad Ibn Abu Bakr's Letter...................... 373
The Sahabah According to the Followers of Ahlul Bayt...................... 383
The Sahabah According to Ahlul Sunnah wal Jama'ah........................ 389
The Final Word in Evaluating the Sahabah..................................... 397
How Ahlul Sunnah wal-Jama'ah Contradict the Prophet's Sunnah.......... 407
1. Islam's Government System...409
2. To Call all the "Sahabah" Equitable is to Contradict the Clear Sunnah....415
3. The Prophet Orders the Muslims to Emulate His `Itrat while Sunnis Oppose Him... 419
4. "Ahlul Sunnah wal Jama'ah" and Love for Ahlul Bayt......................423

5. "Ahlul Sunnah Wal Jama'ah" and the Curtailed Prayer..................... 430
Prophet's Infallibility and its Impact on Ahlul Sunnah wal Jama'ah.......... 435
With Dr. Al-Musawi and his "Authentication"................................439
Glossary.. 455
Bibliography.. 463
Index... 469

PUBLISHER'S PREFACE

This book[1] can best be described as an inquiry of an explorer of the truth into the delicate yet essential question of: "Who is better qualified to the claim of being a follower of Islam's Prophet in spirit and in practice?" Just as it is mandatory to follow the Qur'an, it is equally essential to follow the Prophet, peace be upon him. While the Qur'an is the Almighty's revelation, the Prophet's statements and actions, without any doubt, are also guided by the Almighty, and he cannot err:

"Nor does he speak out of desire. It is naught but revelation that is revealed" (*Qur'an, 53:3-4*), hence the importance of taking the Sunnah (the Prophet's traditions and statements) very seriously.

Both major schools of Islamic law, the Sunni and the Shi`a, differed with regard to the important issue of the spiritual as well as the temporal succession of the Prophet of Islam. This difference resulted in the Muslims' ideological division after the Prophet's death. Here is an interesting fact for your consideration:

Both Sunni and Shi`a groups agree all along with regard to the importance of the Qur'an and of the Sunnah, accepting them as the bases upon which they establish the implementation of their faith. Despite this fact, however, the Sunnis arrogated to themselves the title of "Ahlul Sunnah," or "the people of the Path," and the rest of the world passively gave in to this assumption and accepted it as a fact.

---

[1] This book is available at: https://www.al-islam.org/shiah-are-real-ahlul-sunnah-muhammad-al-tijani-al-samawi

In his *Dictionary of Islam*, Thomas Hughes[2] points out: "... hence it comes to pass that although the Shi'as, even to a greater degree than the Sunnis, rest their claims upon traditional evidence, they have allowed their opponents to claim the title of traditionists, and consequently Mr. Sale[3] and many European writers have stated that the Shi'as reject the tradition."

In our times, the freedom of thought and expression, coupled with a spirit of independent inquiry, has helped men and women to free themselves from misbeliefs, whims, and superstitions.

Amazingly, the distinct task of separating the truth from the myth on an issue of such a great importance, namely the question of who the genuine followers of the Sunnah of the Prophet are and who followed in his footsteps, Ali and his friends, or the *sahabah* (the friends of the Prophet) who opposed the Prophet's cousin after his death had to be pioneered by the author of this book who grew up as a Sunni.

After several years of independent inquiry as to who was right, Ali or his opponents, he gave up the beliefs of his ancestors and accepted the Twelve Imams of the Shi'as as his "rightly guided" leaders after the Prophet. The author of four previously published books (Pyam-e-Aman had published the English translation of his

---

[2] Born in Berkshire on October 20, 1822 and died in Brighton, England, on March 22, 1896, Thomas Patrick Hughes was a jurist, reformer, and novelist. He attained fame following the publication in 1857 of his novel Tom Brown's School Days. His other famous works include: Tom Brown at Oxford (which he wrote after studying at Oxford from 1842 to 1845 and which was published in 1861), A Layman's Faith (1868), and The Manliness of Christ (1879). His Dictionary of Islam was published by Rupa & Co. of Calcutta, India, in 1885.

[3] Rev. George Sale is the British scholar, traveler and Arabist who, in 1734, produced one of the earliest English translations of the Holy Qur'an, a translation which remained in circulation for 127 years. Tr.

first book titled *Then I was Guided*), Dr. Muhammad al-Samawi al-Tijani is a great scholar and Arabist.

As a student of comparative religion, he has tirelessly pursued his quest for the truth, and he continues to write what he calls, in the beginning of his first book, "a story of a journey..., a story of a new discovery... in the field of religious and philosophical schools."

The question of who Ahlul Sunnah are and who are not is critical to any believer, both in the context of history as well as in the practice of religion today. It is also important because those who labelled themselves as the "traditionists" viewed all others as "heterodox" in contrast to their claiming themselves to be the "orthodox."

This resulted in violence and coercion as the rulers of the time used such accusations to oppress the masses as they demonstrated their power and ruthless control over their destiny. Western Islamists picked up the jargon from the writers of the "majority sect" and divided the Muslim world in their writings into "Orthodox" and "Heretical," referring to the Sunnis and the Shi'as respectively.[4]

This hypothetical dichotomy is misleading and completely baseless. It is also due to the lack of understanding about the world of Islam. Western writers fail to observe that, other than the belief

---

[4] The Western Islamists misjudged, in fact exploited, the differences in the Islamic world. They tried to apply the dichotomous division of Christianity between the "Orthodox" and "Heretical" to the Muslim world. Needless to say that the Christian sects maintain totally divergent views in respect of their basic beliefs viz: Oneness of God, Sonship of Jesus and Divine Trinity. In sharp contrast, the Muslims, notwithstanding their differences on certain issues, have consensus with regard to their basic beliefs such as *"Tawhid"*, Oneness of God, the Prophethood of Muhammad and the Finality of his Prophethood, and the Day of Judgment.

in the issue of Imamate, the Sunnis have far greater differences within their own four sects (or schools of thought) system compared to their differences with the Shi'as.

The views of the Hanafis regarding theological questions, for example, may well coincide with those of the Shi'as while remaining in an uncompromising contradiction to many doctrines espoused by, say, the Hanbalis, the Shafi'is, or the Malikis.

In sharp contrast to the evidence of "irreconcilable differences" between the four Imams who had established the afore-mentioned Schools of Sunni Thought, even with regard to issues of minor as well as major importance, a total consensus exists among the Twelve Imams of Ahlul Bayt (People of the Prophet's House) on each and every doctrinal aspect of the faith.

In his celebrated treatise titled *Kitab al-milal wal nihal* (the book of religions and religious sects), al-Shahristani,[5] a Muslim thinker who lived during the Medieval times, gives an account of the Muslim sects (*firaq*, singular: *firqa*) and their disagreements on four fundamental issues: *Tawhid* (Oneness of God and His Divine Attributes), *Adl* (justice), *Iman* (faith or conviction), and lastly Revelation, the Prophetic mission, and the right to be the leader (Imam) of the Muslim community.

A revealing picture that emerges from his work shows that, unlike the usual European concept of a religious sect, the Muslim *firaq*, with their different views on issues, allow a dialogue between scholars and followers of different theological persuasions. This offers hope that in the new "information era," with people coming

---

[5] Nicknamed "Abul-Fath," Muhammad ibn Abd al-Kareem al-Shahristani was born in Shahristan, Khurasan, in 469A.H./1076 A.D. and died in 548 A.H./1153 A.D. He was the most prominent Sunni historian of religions and philosophical trends in the Middle Ages. His famous book Kitab al-milal wal nihal was published in Cairo, Egypt, in 1288 A.H./1871 A.D.

closer to and eager to communicate with one another and ready to adapt to change, the Muslim world may achieve its homogeneous synthesis, notwithstanding the minor variants, in a not too distant future, *InshaAllah*.

Dr. Tijani's book, written in Arabic, is a voluminous work. We had to selectively though discreetly omit certain parts of it both to ensure economy and to make it more palatable to the English speaking readers. The first two chapters have been rewritten by Br. Yasin T. al-Jibouri in order to incorporate full accounts of important events that took place just before the Prophet's death to provide the reader with the context of the author's comments.

We are grateful to Br. Yasin T. al-Jibouri (P.O. Box 5132, Falls Church, VA 22044) for translating the original Arabic text of this book into English. He, by the way, has translated, written, or edited as many as twenty-three books and is a great asset to our community. Without his help, the publication of this book may not have become possible. Our special thanks to Br. Nasir Shamsi who has so far edited fifteen of the books published by Pyam-e-Aman and persevered in reviewing and editing this book. May Allah *Ta`ala* reward them both on behalf of all those who will *InshaAllah* benefit from this book, and on our own.

Pyam-e-Aman
P.O. Box 390
Bloomfield, New Jersey 07003, U.S.A.
Rabi` II 1, 1416 A.H./August 27, 1995

INTRODUCTION AND FOREWORD BY THE AUTHOR

All Praise is due to Allah, Lord of the Worlds, and peace be upon the greatest among the prophets and messengers, our master and leader Muhammad, and upon his righteous and pure progeny.

The Messenger has said, "To Allah, the ink of the scholars is superior to the blood of the martyr." It is, therefore, incumbent upon every scholar or writer to write for people what he sees as beneficial for their guidance, what socially binds them together, and what unites them for a common cause and takes them out of the darkness into the light. A martyr seeking Allah's Pleasure invites to the truth and sets the foundations of justice.

Yet he may not bear any impact except on his contemporaries. A reader, however, may be influenced by his contemporary scholar whose book remains a beacon of guidance, generation after generation, till Allah sends His Guardian for the earth and of everyone on it. Everything diminishes through spending except knowledge: it multiplies by giving.

The Messenger of Allah has also said, "If Allah were to guide through you even one man, it surely is better for you than everything upon which the sun and the moon shine," or "better than the life of this world and everything in it." How many writers died centuries ago, and whose bones turned into ashes, yet their thoughts and knowledge survived through their books which are printed hundreds of times across the centuries, guiding people to success?!

Since a martyr is alive with his Lord, receiving sustenance, a scholar who causes people to receive guidance is likewise alive with his Lord and with the servants of the Lord who think well of him, praying and seeking Allah's forgiveness for him. As far as I am concerned, I am not among the scholars, nor do I put forth such a claim, and I seek refuge with Allah against being conceited. Rather, I am a servant of the scholars, relishing their legacy, savoring it, following in their footsteps like a servant following his master.

Since Allah inspired me to write my book *Then I Was Guided*[1], I received a great deal of encouragement from many readers and researchers, so I followed it with my second book *To be with the Truthful*[2], which was also well received. I was, hence, encouraged to continue my research and investigation; therefore, I wrote the third volume, namely *Ask Those Who Know*[3], in defense of Islam and the prophet of Islam to dispel the allegations against him, and to uncover the plot against him and his pure progeny.

I received many letters from the Arab and Islamic world carrying the readers' affection, loyalty, love and expressions of brotherhood. I was invited to attend many intellectual conferences throughout the world organized by Islamic establishments in the United States of America, the Islamic Republic of Iran, Britain, India, Pakistan, Kenya, West Africa and Sweden.

Whenever I met a group of educated youths and intellectuals, I found them appreciating my works and seeking more knowledge. They asked me, "Do you have anything new forthcoming? Are you writing any new book?" I praised Allah, therefore, and thanked Him for this success. I implored to Him to grant me more of His Attention and Guidance. I solicited His help to write this book

---

[1] https://www.al-islam.org/then-i-was-guided-muhammad-al-tijani-al-samawi

[2] https://www.al-islam.org/be-with-truthful-muhammad-al-tijani-al-samawi

[3] The translation of Tijani's book *Fas'aloo Ahlul Dhikr* (Ask those who have with them the knowledge of the Qur'an) has been published under the title *Ask Those Who Know* by Ansariyan Publications, P.O. Box 37185/187, Qum, Islamic Republic of Iran. Tr. https://www.al-islam.org/ask-those-who-know-muhammad-al-tijani-al-samawi

which I now place before Muslim researchers and which revolves in the same orbit circled by the three previous books.

I hope it will benefit some educated people and those who seek the truth: perhaps they will come to know that the party being targeted for attacks, the one referred to as "Imamite Shi`ites," is the one that will attain salvation, and that they, i.e. the Shi'as, are followers of the true and authentic Sunnah, that is, the Sunnah with which Muhammad was entrusted to convey according to the revelation of the Lord of the Worlds.

He surely does not say anything out of his own desire; rather, his is only a revelation. I will explain to the readers the fact that the identification label used by those who oppose and disagree with the Shi'as, that of "Ahlul Sunnah wal Jama'ah," i.e. followers of the Sunnah and consensus, has little to do with the Sunnah of Prophet Muhammad.

How often have people lied and attributed their lies to the Messenger of Allah? How often were his traditions, statements, and actions prohibited from reaching the Muslims on the pretext it may not be taken as Allah's speech a pretext more feeble than a spider's cobweb?! And how many authentic traditions were discarded, disregarded, and neglected?

How many fantasies and hoaxes made to appear as injunctions were wrongly attributed to the Prophet after his demise? How many of the noble personalities, whose nobility are testified by history were after him ignored, neglected, unheeded, even accused of apostasy and punished for their noble stands?! How many are the shiny and attractive labels that hide behind them apostasy and misguidance?!

The Lord of Honors and Dignity has described the above in the very best way when He said,

"And among men is one whose speech about the life of this world causes you to wonder, and he (even) calls upon Allah to testify to what is in his heart, yet he is the most violent of adversaries. And when he turns back, he runs along in the land in order to cause mischief and to destroy the tilth and the stock, and Allah does not love mischief-making. And when it is said to him: Guard (your soul) against (the punishment of) Allah, pride carries him off to sinning; so, hell suffices him, and it certainly is an evil abode" (Holy Qur'an, 2:204-206).

I may not exaggerate if I act upon the axiom saying, "If you reverse (an equation), you will then be right. 'An investigative researcher must not take anything for granted; rather, he has to reverse and remain most of the time skeptical in order to reach the hidden truth. It was in such politics that all dirty roles were played. He must not be deceived by appearances or numerical superiority, for Allah, the Most Exalted, has said in His great Book,

"And if you obey most of those on earth, they will surely cause you to stray from Allah's Path; they only follow conjecture, and they only lie." (Holy Qur'an, 6:116).

Falsehood may appear in the garb of truth to falsify and mislead, and this may often succeed either due to the naivety of the general public, or because of the worldly position or influence of the scheming individual(s). Falsehood may at times also appear to prevail because of the number of those who support it. The truth is patient and waits for Allah to fulfill His promise by making falsehood appear as false. Surely falsehood is often defeated in the long run.

The best testimony to the above is the Qur'anic narrative relevant to the story of Jacob and his sons. The latter

"Came to their father in the early part of the night weeping; they said: `O father! We went racing with one another and left Joseph with our belongings, so the wolf devoured him, but you will

never believe us even though we tell the truth'" (Holy Qur'an, 12:16-17).

Had they indeed been truthful, they ought to have said, "And you will never believe us because we are liars." Our master Jacob, who was a prophet of Allah receiving His revelation, had no choice except to give in to their falsehood, seeking help from Allah through patience, despite his knowledge that they were liars. Said he,

"Rather, your minds have made up a tale; so, patience is most fitting (for me); it is Allah (alone) Whose help can be sought (against your scheme)." (Holy Qur'an, 12: 18).

What more could he have done especially since he was facing eleven men who unanimously agreed to say the same thing and who performed the hoax of the shirt and the false blood, weeping over their "missing" brother? Could Jacob reveal their lies, refute their falsehood, and rush to the well to get his beloved young son out then penalize them for their abhorrent action? No; such will be the doing of the ignorant who are not guided by Allah's wisdom. As for Jacob, he is a prophet who behaves as a wise man of knowledge about whom Allah has said:

"He was, by Our instruction, full of knowledge, but most men do not know" (Holy Qur'an, 12:68).

He was bound by his knowledge and wisdom to distance himself from them and say,

"How great my grief for Joseph is! And his eyes became white with sorrow, and he fell into silent melancholy" (Holy Qur'an, 12: 84).

Had Jacob behaved otherwise, that is, by getting his son out of the well, rebuking the others for their lies, and penalizing them for their crime, their hatred towards their brother would have intensified, and they might have even gone as far as assassinating their father, too. They might have implied the same when they said to their father,

"By Allah! You will never cease remembering Joseph till you reach the last extremity of illness, or till you die!" (Holy Qur'an, 12:85).

From this we may deduct that at times silence is commendable when confronting falsehood that may result in harm or an imminent peril, or when keeping quiet rather than revealing the truth serves the public's interest, even if such a service is deferred. This helps in understanding the *hadith* of the Prophet saying:

"One who keeps silent rather than saying the truth is a silent Satan."

Such understanding conforms to reason and Allah's Book. And if we probe the biography of the Messenger of Allah, we will find out that there were times when he took to silence in the interest of Islam and Muslims as *Sahih* books narrate to us with regard, for example, to the peaceful treaty of Hudaybiyyah, and to other such instances.

May Allah be Merciful to the Commander of the Faithful Ali who kept silent after the death of his cousin. Referring to the same, he made this famous statement: "I kept pondering whether I should fight with an amputated hand, or take to patience regarding a blind calamity wherein the adult ages and the child grows gray hair and a believer struggles till he meets his Lord; I saw that patience regarding both options was wiser; therefore, I took to patience though the eye was sore and the mouth was choking with grief."

Had the father of al-Hasan not taken to silence rather than demanding his right of caliphate, thus advancing the cause of Islam and Muslims rather than that of his own, Islam, as Allah and His Messenger had outlined it, would not have survived after the demise of Muhammad.

This is the fact with which most people, who always argue with us that the caliphate of Abu Bakr and Umar was right, are not familiar. They say that Ali kept silent about such caliphs, adding, as they always enjoy doing, "Had the Messenger of Allah appointed Ali as his successor in leading the Muslim masses, he would not have been right in remaining silent, since doing so would not have been appropriate at all, and one who takes to silence rather than saying the truth is a silent Satan." Such is their argument, and such is their often-played record.

This clearly is an error in comprehension. Such is one who recognizes only the truth with which his whims and desires agree. Such is one who fails to realize the wisdom resulting from the outcome of that silence and its invaluable deferred benefits, were one to compare the latter with the temporal interest resulting from a revolt against falsehood supported by a great many supporters and promoters.

During the incident of the Hudaybiyyah, the Messenger of Allah remained silent and accepted the terms of the Quraysh and the Pagans of Mecca, so much so that Umar ibn al-Khattab could not control his outrage; he asked the Messenger of Allah, "Are you not truly the Messenger of Allah?! Are we not right while they are wrong? If so, then why should we sell our religion so cheap?"

Had the silence of the Prophet been negative, as it was conceived by Umar ibn al-Khattab and most *sahabah* who were present there and then, the truth of the matter would not have proven beyond any doubt that it was, in fact, positively in the best interest of Islam and Muslims even when such interest was not immediately served.

Its positive outcomes surfaced one year later when the Messenger of Allah conquered Mecca without fighting any war or meeting any resistance: it was then that people joined the ranks of the Muslims in large numbers. It was then that the Messenger of

Allah called upon Umar ibn al-Khattab and showed him the result of his having remained silent rather than demanding what was right; he showed him the underlying wisdom of his silence at the Hudaybiyyah.

We provide such arguments only to highlight the truth which cannot be avoided: Assisted by supporters and helpers, falsehood will triumph over truth. Although Ali was with the truth, and the truth was inseparably on his side, he found neither supporters nor helpers to oppose Mu`awiyah and his lies, and because the latter had found a great many supporters to defeat the truth and subdue it. People, Imam Husayn said, are slaves of the life of this world; they give religion only their lip-service. They do not love the truth, and they incline to falsehood; the taste of the truth is bitter and hard, whereas falsehood is easy and accessible. Allah has surely said the truth when He said,

"Rather, he brought the truth, but most of them hate the truth." (Holy Qur'an, 23:70).

Yazid's falsehood won an apparent "victory" over Husayn's truth for the same reason. Likewise, the falsehood of Umayyad and Abbaside rulers trampled upon the truth regarding the Imams from among Ahlul Bayt who were all martyred while remaining silent, preferring the interest of Islam and Muslims to that of their own. And Allah made the Twelfth Imam disappear go into occultation to protect him from the mischief of the promoters of falsehood.

He took to silence and will continue to do so till the truth finds helpers and supporters. It is only then that Allah will permit him to come out to the open so that the revolution of the truth against falsehood may become universal; it will then, and only then, fill the world with justice and equity just as it is being constantly filled with injustice and iniquity. In other words, he will fill it with the truth after its being filled with falsehood.

Since most people hate the truth, they become the natural supporters of falsehood. Only a small number of people remain faithful to the truth. They cannot overcome the supporters of falsehood without Allah's help manifested through divine miracles. This is recorded in the Glorious Book of Allah during all wars and battles where the supporters of the truth had to fight those who supported falsehood:

"How often has a small force, by Allah's will, vanquished a big one?." (Holy Qur'an, 2:249).

Those who, despite their small number, persevere while supporting the truth will be assisted by Allah, Glory to Him, with miracles. He will send them powerful angels to fight on their side. Without such a direct interference from Allah, the truth can never subdue falsehood.

We nowadays are living through this painful reality: Truthful believers, those who support the truth wherein they believe, are helpless, vanquished, exiled, victimized, while the supporters of falsehood, those who disbelieve in Allah, are the rulers who hold in their hands the reins of government, wreaking havoc with the destiny, with the life and death, of their subjects.

The downtrodden among the believers can never score victory in their battle against the arrogant disbelievers except with the help of Allah, the most Exalted One. This is why many traditions indicate that miracles will take place upon the reappearance of al-Mahdi.

Yet this is not an invitation to apathy or idle anticipation: how can it be so while I have already indicated saying that he will not appear except when he has supporters and helpers? Suffices the truthful believers to uphold the true Islamic ideology embodied in the *wilaya* (authority) of Ahlul Bayt, I mean their upholding the Two Weighty Things: the Book of Allah and the Progeny of the

Prophet, so that they may be the supporters and helpers of the Awaited al-Mahdi, the best of peace and salutations be upon him and his forefathers.

My success relies only on Allah; upon Him do I rely, and to Him shall I return.

Muhammad al-Tijani al-Samawi (of Tunisia)

IDENTIFYING THE SHI'AS

If we wish to discuss the Shi'as without fanaticism or affectation, we would say that they are the adherents of the Islamic School of Thought which respects and follows the twelve Imams from the family (Ahlul Bayt) of the Prophet. They are Ali and eleven of his offspring. The Shi'as refer to the Prophet and the Twelve Imams regarding all *fiqh* (jurisprudence) issues and public dealings.

They do not prefer anyone over the Twelve Imams with the exception of their grandfather, the bearer of the Message, Muhammad, the Messenger of Allah. This is briefly the true definition of the Shi'as. Disregard the allegations circulated by scandal mongers and fanatics who claim that the Shi'as are the enemies of Islam, that they believe in the "prophethood" of Ali, and that he is the one who bears the prophetic Message, or that they belong to Abdullah ibn Saba, the Jew, and that they are this and that...

I have read many books and articles written by those who try very hard to "prove" that the Shi'as are *kafirs* (apostates), trying to excommunicate them from the Islamic creed altogether. Yet their statements are no more than sheer calumnies and obvious lies which they cannot prove or document except by quoting what their predecessors among the enemies of Ahlul Bayt have said, in addition to the statements of the Nasibis who forced their authority on the Islamic world and ruled it by force and intimidation, pursuing the Prophet's progeny as well as those who follow them, killing and expelling them, calling them by all bad names.

Among such bad names, which are often repeated in books written by the enemies of the Shi'as, is the misnomer "Rafidis," rejectionists. Any uninformed reader will instantly consider the possibility that they are the ones who rejected the Islamic principles and who did not act upon them, or that they rejected the Message of Prophet Muhammad. But the truth of the matter is quite different.

They were called "Rafidis" simply because early Umayyad and Abbaside rulers, as well as evil scholars who always tried to please them, wanted to misrepresent them by attaching such a misnomer to them. Early Shi'as preferred to remain loyal to Ali, rejecting the caliphate of Abu Bakr, Umar, and Uthman, and they rejected the caliphate of all other Umayyad and Abbaside rulers.

Such folks may have misled the Islamic *Ummah* through the help of a number of fabricators from the *sahabah* (companions of the Holy Prophet), claiming that their caliphate was legitimate because it was mandated by Allah, Praise be to Him. Thus did they promote the allegation that the verse saying:

"O you who believe! Obey Allah, and obey the Messenger and those charged with authority among you." (Holy Qur'an, 4:59)

was revealed in their regard, especially since they were the ones charged with the authority of government and obedience to them, hence, was the obligation of all Muslims. They hired those who attributed to the Messenger of Allah the following tradition: "None abandons the authority of the ruler even in as little as an inch then dies except that he dies the death of *jahiliyya* (pre-Islamic period of ignorance)."

We thus come to realize that the Shi'as were oppressed by the rulers because they refused to pay allegiance to them and rejected their authority, regarding it as the usurpation of the right which belonged to Ahlul Bayt. Hence, rulers across many centuries duped their commoners into believing that the Shi'as rejected Islam and desired no less than its annihilation and demise, as stated by some past and present writers and historians who claim to be men of knowledge.

If we return to the game of making wrong look right, we will realize that there is a difference between those who wished to annihilate Islam and those who tried to put an end to the oppressive and corrupt governments whose norm of conduct is anti-Islamic. Shi'as never abandoned Islam; rather, they opposed unjust rulers, and their objective has always been the returning of the trust to its rightful people and thus erect the foundations of the type of Islam that rules with justice and equity.

Anyway, the conclusion we reached in our past researches, as outlined in *Then I was Guided, To be with the Truthful,* and *Ask Those Who Know*, is that Shi'as are the ones who will attain salvation because they are the ones who have always upheld the Two Weighty Things: the Book of Allah, and the Progeny of His Messenger.

For the sake of fairness, some scholars from those referred to as "Ahlul Sunnah wal Jama'ah" (followers of the Sunnah and consensus) admit this same fact. For example, Ibn Manzur says the following in his lexicon *Lisan al-Arab* where he defines the Shi'as:

The Shi'as are the people who love what the Prophet's Progeny loves, and they are loyal to such Progeny.[1]

Commenting on this statement, Dr. Sa`id Abd al-Fattah `Ashoor says, "If the Shi'as love whatever the Prophet's Progeny loves and are loyal to such Progeny, who among the Muslims would refuse to be a Shi`a?!"

The age of fanaticism and hereditary enmity has gone by, and the age of enlightenment and intellectual freedom has dawned; therefore, the educated youths have to open their eyes and read the literature published by the Shi'as. They ought to contact them and

---

[1] Refer to p. 189, Vol. 8, of *Lisan al-Arab* lexicon by Abul-Fadl Jamal ad-Din Muhammad Ibn Manzur (630 - 711A.H./1233 - 1311 A.D.).

talk to their scholars in order to know the truth first-hand, for how often have we been deceived by honey sweet talk and by calumnies which do not withstand any proof or argument?

The world nowadays is accessible to everyone, and Shi'as are present in all parts of the world. It is not fair that researchers studying the Shi'as should ask their enemies and opponents, those who hold different religious views from the Shi'as, about them. And what does an inquirer expect other than being told by such opponents what has always been said since the beginning of the Islamic history?

Shi'as are not a secretive cult that does not reveal its beliefs except to its members; rather, their books and beliefs are published throughout the world, their schools and religious circles are open to all seekers of knowledge, their scholars hold public discussions, lectures, debates, and conferences, and they call for common grounds and try to unite the Islamic *Ummah*.

I am convinced that fair-minded individuals in the Islamic nation who seriously research this subject will find out the truth beyond which there is nothing but falsehood. Nothing stops them from reaching such truth except biased propaganda media, false rumors circulated by the enemies of the Shi'as, or a particular erroneous practice by some Shi`a commoners.[2] Sometimes it suffices an enemy of the Shi'as to remove one false claim, or wipe out one erroneous myth, to join their ranks.[3]

I recollect in this regard the incident of a Syrian man who was misled by the propaganda machine of that time. Having entered

---

[2] We will conclude, when we come to the end of this book, that the conduct of some Shi`a commoners discourages educated Sunni youths from continuing their research to discover the truth.

[3] As did, indeed, happen to the author of this book and to many others. Tr.

Medina to visit the grave site of the greatest Messenger of Allah, he happened to see a rider on horseback whose dignity and awe were captivating, and who was accompanied by some of his followers surrounding him from all directions, eagerly awaiting his commands. The Syrian man was quite astonished to find a man besides Mu`awiyah surrounded with such a halo of reverence. He was told that the rider was al-Hasan ibn Ali ibn Abu Talib. "Is he the son of Abu Turab, the Kharijite?!" asked he.

Then he went to extremes in cursing and taunting al-Hasan, his father, and his Ahlul Bayt. Al-Hasan's companions took their swords out of their scabbards and rushed to kill that Syrian, but they were stopped by Imam al-Hasan who alighted from his horse, welcomed the Syrian, and with noble manners asked him, "It seems to me that you are a stranger in these quarters, O brother of the Arabs, are you?" "Yes," the Syrian answered, "I am from Syria, and I am a follower of the commander of the faithful and the master of the Muslims Mu`awiyah ibn Abu Sufyan." Al-Hasan again welcomed him and said to him, "You are my guest," but the Syrian rejected the invitation, yet al-Hasan kept insisting to host him till he agreed.

The Imam, and for the entire (three-day customary) hospitality period, kept serving him in person and being extremely nice to him. On the fourth day, the Syrian showed signs of regret and repentance on account of his past conduct towards al-Hasan ibn Ali ibn Abu Talib; he remembered how he had cursed and taunted him, while here he was so kind to him and so generous. He asked al-Hasan and pleaded to him to forgive his past conduct, and the following dialogue resulted in the presence of some of al-Hasan's companions:

AL-HASAN: "Have you recited the Qur'an, O brother of the Arabs?"

SYRIAN: "I have memorized the entire text of the Qur'an."

AL-HASAN: "Do you know who Ahlul Bayt from whom Allah removed all abomination and whom He purified with a perfect purification are?"

SYRIAN: "They are Mu`awiyah and the family of Abu Sufyan." Those present there were very surprised to hear such an answer.

AL-HASAN smiled and said to the man, "I am al-Hasan ibn Ali; my father is the cousin and brother of the Messenger of Allah; my mother is Fatima, Mistress of the ladies of all mankind; my grandfather is the Messenger of Allah and the master of all prophets and messengers. My uncle is al-Hamza, master of martyrs, and so is Ja'far al-Tayyar.

We are Ahlul Bayt whom Allah, Praise to Him, has purified and kindness to whom He required of the Muslims. We are the ones whom Allah and His angels blessed, ordering the Muslims to bless us. I and my brother al-Husayn are the masters of the youths of Paradise."

Then Imam al-Hasan enumerated some virtues of Ahlul Bayt, acquainting him with the truth, whereupon the Syrian could see the light, so he wept and kept kissing al-Hasan's hands and face, profusely apologizing to him for his misconduct, saying, "By Allah Who is the One and Only God! I entered Medina and none on the face of earth I hated more than you, while now I seek nearness to Allah, Praise to Him, through loving you, obedience to you, and dissociation from those who antagonize you."

It was then that Imam al-Hasan turned to his companions and said, "And you wanted to kill him though he was innocent! Had he known the truth, he would not have been our opponent. Most Muslims in Syria are like him. Were they to know the truth, they would follow it." Then he recited the verse saying,

"The good deeds and the bad deeds are not alike; repel (evil) with what is best, so one between whom and you there is enmity will be as if he were a warm friend." (Holy Qur'an, 41:34).

Yes, this is the reality with which most people, unfortunately, are not familiar. How many are those who oppose the truth and reject it for a good portion of their lives till one day they find out that they were wrong, so they rush to repent and seek forgiveness? Everyone is obligated to seek the truth: it is said that reverting to the truth is a virtue.

The problem is with those who see the truth with their very eyes and who touch it with their very hands, yet they still stand in its face and fight it for the achievement of low ends, for the sake of a fleeting life, and because of hidden grudges. About such people has the Lord of Honors and Dignity said,

"It is the same whether you warn them or not; they will never believe" (Holy Qur'an, 36:10).

So there is no sense in wasting time with them; rather, it is our obligation to sacrifice everything for those who are fair-minded and who truly seek the truth and exert a genuine effort to reach it. Such are the ones about whom the Lord of Honor and Dignity has said,

"You can only warn one who follows the Reminder and fears the Beneficent God in secret; so announce to him forgiveness and an honorable reward." (Holy Qur'an, 36:11).

Those endowed with awareness from the Shi'as everywhere are obligated to spend their time and wealth to introduce the truth to all members of the Islamic Ummah. The Imams from Ahlul Bayt are not the exclusive privilege of the Shi'as; rather, they are the Imams of guidance of everybody.

They are the light that shatters for all Muslims the darkness of ignorance. If the Imams from Ahlul Bayt remain unknown to most Muslims, especially the educated among the "followers of the

Sunnah and consensus," the Shi'as will bear the burden of such a responsibility before Allah.

If there are still among people those who are apostates or atheists who are not familiar with the straight religion of Allah as brought by Muhammad, the master of all messengers, the responsibility falls upon the shoulders of all Muslims.

IDENTIFYING AHLUL SUNNAH

These are members of the largest Muslim community; they represent three-quarters of the total population of the Muslims of the world, and they are the ones who refer for religious verdicts (*fatawa*) and for religious following of the Imams of the four sects, namely Abu Hanifah, Malik, al-Shafi`i, and Ahmad ibn Hanbal.

Later in time, those called Salafis branched out of them; the characteristics of their beliefs were later revived by Ibn Taymiyyah whom they call "the one who revived the Sunnah," then by the Wahhabis whose ideology was invented by Muhammad ibn Abd al-Wahhab; theirs is the sect of the present rulers of Saudi Arabia.[1]

All these call themselves "Ahlul Sunnah," sometimes adding the word "Jama`ah" so they may be identified as "Ahlul Sunnah wal Jama'ah."

Were one to research history, it will become evident to him that anyone who belonged to what they term as "al-khilafa al-rashida," the righteous caliphate, or "al-khulafa al-rashidoon," the righteous caliphs, namely Abu Bakr, Umar, Uthman, and Ali[2], and who recognized their Imamate during their life-time, or in our contemporary time, such person belongs to "Ahlul Sunnah wal Jama'ah." Anyone who rejects the said caliphate or considers it illegitimate, advocating the texts which prove that only Ali ibn Abu Talib was worthy of it, is a Shi`a.

---

[1] According to informed Saudi citizens, the population of Wahhabis in Saudi Arabia does not exceed 8%, whereas the majority are Maliki Sunnis. Tr.

[2] It will become evident to us from forthcoming researches that "Ahlul Sunnah wal Jama`ah" did not add the name of Ali ibn Abu Talib to the three "righteous caliphs" except at a very late period in history.

It will also become clear to us that the rulers, starting from Abu Bakr and ending with the last Abbaside ruler, were pleased with the "followers of the Sunnah" and in total agreement with them, and that they were angry with, and were seeking revenge against, all those who opted to follow the leadership of Ali ibn Abu Talib as well as those who swore the oath of allegiance to him and to his offspring thereafter.

Based on these premises, Ali ibn Abu Talib and his followers, according to them, were not counted among "Ahlul Sunnah wal Jama'ah," as if this term, i.e. "Ahlul Sunnah wal Jama'ah," was coined to confront and juxtapose Ali and his followers. This is the major reason for the division which afflicted the Islamic Ummah following the demise of the Messenger of Allah into Sunnis and Shi'as.

If we go back to analyze the underlying factors and remove the curtains, relying on the authentic historical references, we will then find out that such a distinction surfaced immediately after the death of the Messenger of Allah. Abu Bakr soon took control, having ascended to the seat of government with the help of the vast majority of the *sahabah*. Ali ibn Abu Talib and Banu Hashim in addition to a very small number of the *sahabah* who were politically weak did not accept him.

It goes without saying that the ruling authority expelled the latter and banished them, regarding them as dissenting from the Islamic mainstream. It did its best to paralyze their opposition by all economic, social, and political means.

It is also a well-known fact that our contemporary followers of "Ahlul Sunnah wal Jama'ah" do not realize the political dimensions of the roles played during those periods and the extent of enmity and hatred those vicious periods brought forth to isolate and expel the greatest personality in the history of humanity after the Messenger of Allah Muhammad.

Our contemporary "Ahlul Sunnah wal Jama'ah" believe that everything went in the very best possible way, and that everything still revolves in full agreement with the Book of Allah (the Holy Qur'an) and the Sunnah since the time of the "righteous caliphs," and that the latter were like angels; therefore, they respected one another, and there were no ill feelings among them nor ambition nor bad intentions. For this reason, you find them refusing all what the Shi'as say about the *sahabah* in general and the "righteous caliphs" in particular.

It is as if "Ahlul Sunnah wal Jama'ah" never read the history books written by their own scholars, feeling satisfied with only the praise, compliments, and admiration their ancestors lavished on the *sahabah* in general and on the "righteous caliphs" in particular. Had they opened their minds and vision and turned the pages of their history books, as well as the books of *hadith* (traditions of the Prophet [P]) available with them, seeking the truth and getting to know who is right and who is wrong, they would have changed their mind not only about the *sahabah*, but also about many injunctions which they regard as correct while they are not.

Through this humble effort, I am trying to clarify for my brethren among "Ahlul Sunnah wal Jama'ah" some facts which fill the books of history, and to briefly highlight for them the clear texts which refute falsehood and show the truth, hoping that doing so may heal the Muslims' disunity and division and bring about their unity.

Contemporary "Ahlul Sunnah wal Jama'ah," as I know them, are not fanatics, nor are they against Imam Ali or Ahlul Bayt; rather, they love and respect them, but they, at the same time, also love and respect the enemies of Ahlul Bayt and follow in their footsteps, thinking that "they all sought nearness to the Messenger of Allah."

"Ahlul Sunnah wal Jama'ah" do not act upon the principle of befriending the friends of Allah and dissociating themselves from the enemies of Allah; rather, they love everyone and seek nearness to Mu`awiyah ibn Abu Sufyan just as they seek nearness to Ali ibn Abu Talib.

The shiny term "Ahlul Sunnah wal Jama'ah" has dazzled them, and they are not familiar with the implications and insinuations which the most shrewd Arabs had embedded therein. If they one day come to know that Ali ibn Abu Talib is the personification of Muhammad's Sunnah, and that he is the gate leading to such Sunnah, and that they have contradicted him and he has contradicted them..., they will surely renounce their stand and research this issue very seriously, and there will be no Ahlul Sunnah except those who followed Muhammad's and Ali's Sunnah.

In order to come to such a conclusion, we have to unravel for them the greatest plot which played the most serious role in setting Muhammad's Sunnah aside, and in substituting it with Jahili innovations which caused the Muslims' setback and their deviation from al-Sirat al-Mustaqeem (the Straight Path), and their disunity and dissension. It also caused them at a later time to call each other apostate, and even fight one another. It thus caused their scientific and technological backwardness which led to their being invaded and occupied then subjugated, humiliated, and assimilated.

Having concluded this brief survey identifying the Shi'as and the Sunnis, we have to take note of the fact that the proper noun "Shi`a" (or Shi`ites) does not imply that its adherents oppose the Sunnah, as most people are misled into thinking when they brag and say: "We are the followers of the Sunnah," implying that others are opponents of the Sunnah.

This is something which the Shi'as do not accept at all; rather, the Shi'as are convinced that they, and only they, are the ones who uphold the authentic Sunnah of the Prophet especially since they have approached such Sunnah through its gate, namely Ali ibn Abu Talib; there is no gate to it other than his and, according to them, nobody can reach the Prophet except through him.

We, as usual, seek neutrality in order to reach the truth while taking the dear reader from one stage to another so that we may together review some historical events. We will thus provide him with the proof and argument showing the Shi'as to be the true followers of the Sunnah as this book's title suggests, leaving to him after that the freedom to make up his mind and to comment as he pleases.

THE FIRST INCIDENT THAT DIVIDED MUSLIM UMMAH INTO SHI'AS AND SUNNIS

It is the stunningly sad stand taken by Umar ibn al-Khattab and a number of other *sahabah* against an order by the Messenger of Allah to bring him something to record a testament for them. He promised that this would prevent their backsliding into error.[1]

This Thursday Calamity[2] is, indeed, a most tragic one. It is narrated by all authors of *sahihs* and *sunan* and is documented by all traditionists and historians. In a section dealing with the statement of the ailing Messenger (pbuh): "Get away from me," al-Bukhari records it in his *Sahih*,[3] relying on the authority of 'Ubaydullah ibn Abdullah ibn 'Utbah ibn Mas'ud. Abdullah quotes Ibn 'Abbas saying that when death approached the Messenger of Allah, his house became full of men including Umar ibn al-Khattab.

The Messenger of Allah said: "Let me write you something that will forever protect you against straying after me." Umar said: "The Prophet is in a state of delirium, and you have with you the Qur'an; so, the Book of Allah suffices us." Those who were present there argued among themselves, and their argument developed into a dispute.

Some of them said: "Come close to the Prophet so that he may write you something that will safeguard you against straying after

---

[1] It is the famous "Thursday Calamity" recorded in both al-Bukhari's and Muslim's *Sahih* books.

[2] The author has written another book '*Black Thursday*' that describes this incident in detail. https://www.al-islam.org/black-thursday-muhammad-al-tijani-al-samawi

[3] Al-Bukhari, *Sahih*, Vol. 4, p. 4.

him," while others repeated what Umar had said. When the argument and dispute intensified in the presence of the Prophet, the Messenger of Allah said to them: "Get away from me." Ibn Abbas used to say: "The calamity, the real calamity, is what discouraged the Messenger of Allah from writing what he wished to write on account of their argument and dispute."

The authenticity of this *hadith* is not questioned, nor is the occasion whereupon it came to be. Al-Bukhari quotes it in his treatise on knowledge on page 22, Vol. 1, of his *Sahih*, and it is recorded in many other books. He quotes it in several places of his *Sahih*. Muslim, too, quotes it at the conclusion of the Prophet's will in his *Sahih* on page 14, Vol. 2. Ahmad narrates Ibn Abbas's hadith on p. 325, Vol. 1, of his *Musnad*. It is narrated by all authors of traditions and books of history, each writer editing it yet retaining its gist, reiterating the fact that the Prophet was described as "hallucinating," or "delirious."

But they also mentioned that Umar had said: "The Prophet has been delirious" just to sanitize the statement and undermine the sentiments of those who found it abominable. Supporting this fact is what Abu Bakr Ahmad ibn Abdul-Aziz al-Jawhari has said in his book *Al-Saqifa* where he relies on the authority of Ibn Abbas.

Ibn Abbas has said,

When death approached the Messenger of Allah, there were many men present at his house. One of them was Umar ibn al-Khattab. The Messenger of Allah said: "Bring me ink and a tablet so that I may write you something that will safeguard you against straying after me."

Those present at his house disputed among themselves. Some of them said, "Come close and watch the Prophet write you something," while others repeated what Umar had said. When the argument and dispute intensified, the Messenger of Allah, became crossed and said: "Get away from me."[4]

This proves that the traditionists who did not wish to state the name of the person who went against the Prophet's wish had nonetheless quoted his statement *verbatim*. In a chapter on rewarding the envoys, in his book *Al-Jihad wal Siyar*, page 118, Vol. 2, al-Bukhari states:

Qabsah narrated a tradition to us from Ibn Ayeenah, Salman al-Ahwal, and Saeed ibn Jubayr. They consecutively quote Ibn Abbas saying: "On a Thursday, what a day that Thursday was...." He burst sobbing then went on to say, "...the pain of the Messenger of Allah intensified; so, he ordered us to bring him some writing material so that he might write us something whereby we would be protected against straying after him, but people disputed, knowing that nobody should dispute in the presence of any Prophet.

They said: 'The Messenger of Allah is delirious.' He, therefore, said: 'Leave me alone, for the pain I am suffering is more tolerable than what you are attributing to me.' He left in his will three orders: to get the polytheists out of the Arab land, to reward the envoys the same way whereby he used to reward them,' and I forgot the third one."

The same hadith is narrated by Muslim at the conclusion of a chapter dealing with the will in his *Sahih*, and by Ahmad in Ibn Abbas's *ahadith* on page 222, Vol. 1, of his work, and by all other traditionists. It is obvious from this incident that Umar ibn al-Khattab was of the view that he was not bound by the Prophet's Sunnah.

This explains the edicts which he issued when he became the caliph and in which he employed his own view even when it

---

[4] Ibn Abul-Hadid, *Sharh Nahjul Balagha*, Vol. 2, p. 20.

contradicted the Prophet's statements. Actually, he followed his own personal views when he contradicted clear divine texts. He thus prohibited what Allah had permitted, and *vice versa*.

It is only natural to see that all his supporters among the *sahabah* harbor the same attitude with regard to the Prophet's Sunnah. The next chapters will prove to the reader that those *sahabah* had in fact, and to the great misfortune of the Islamic Ummah, forsaken the Sunnah of the Prophet and adopted the Sunnah of Umar ibn al-Khattab instead.

SECOND INCIDENT THAT LED TO DIVERGENCE FROM THE PROPHET'S SUNNAH

That was their refusal to join Usamah's army which was personally raised by the Messenger of Allah who ordered them, two days before his demise, to enlist under Usamah's leadership. They went as far as casting doubt about the wisdom of the Messenger of Allah and criticizing him for having appointed a 17 year old young man, who did not even grow a beard, as the army's leader.

Abu Bakr and Umar, as well as many other *sahabah*, refused to join the army in the pretext of taking care of the issue of caliphate despite the Prophet's curse upon all those who would not join Usamah.[1]

As for Ali and his followers, they were not assigned by the Messenger of Allah to join Usamah's army in order to circumvent dissension, and in order to thus remove the obstacle of the presence of the stubborn ones who opposed Allah's Commandment, so that they might not come back from Mu'tah before Ali was in full control of the reins of government, as Allah and His Messenger wanted him to, as a successor to the Prophet.

But the shrewd Arabs among Quraysh anticipated the Prophet's plan and refused to get out of Medina. They waited till the Messenger went back to his Lord. It was then that they carried out their own scheme as they had planned, going against what Allah and the Messenger of Allah had willed; in other words, they rejected the Prophet's Sunnah.

Thus does it become obvious to us, and to all researchers, that Abu Bakr, Umar, Uthman, Abdul-Rahman ibn Awf, and Abu

---

[1] Read on p. 29, Vol. 1, of al-Shahristani's book *Kitab al-milal wal nihal* the Prophet's statement: "Allah curses whoever lags behind Usamah's army."

Ubaydah Amir al-Jarrah always refused to be bound by the Prophet's Sunnah, preferring to follow their own views. They always pursued their worldly interests and desired to attain political dominance even if the price of doing so was transgression against Allah and His Messenger.

As for Ali and the *sahabah* who followed him, they always upheld the Prophet's Sunnah and acted upon implementing it to the letter as much as they could. We have seen how Ali during that crisis carried out the Prophet's will to give him his funeral bath, prepare the coffin, perform the funeral prayers for him, and to lay him to rest in his grave.

Ali carried out all these orders without being diverted by anything even though he knew that the others were racing to Banu Sa`ida's *Saqifa* (shed) in order to promote one of them as the caliph. He could do the same and sabotage their plan, but his respect for the Prophet's Sunnah, and his implementation thereof, dictated that he remain by the side of the Prophet.

Here we have to pause, though for a short while, to observe such great manners which Ali had learned from the Prophet. While sacrificing his position as the caliph in order to carry out the injunctions of the Sunnah, he witnessed the others rejecting the Sunnah as they sought the caliphate.

THIRD INCIDENT THAT JUXTAPOSED THE SHI'AS VERSUS THE SUNNIS

This was the very serious stand taken by most of the *sahabah* at Banu Sa`ida's shed which clearly contradicted the Prophet's statements appointing Ali as the caliph and which they all witnessed on the Day of the Ghadeer[1] following Hijjatul Wada`.

Despite the differences of views among the Muhajirs (Meccan immigrants) and the Ansars (Medenite helpers) with regard to the issue of caliphate, they all impudently raced with one another to forsake the Prophet's binding statements by advancing Abu Bakr to the caliphate even if it cost them perdition, thus demonstrating their readiness to kill anyone who even remotely considered opposing them, and even if he were the closest person to the Prophet.[2]

This incident also underscored the fact that the vast majority of the *sahabah* assisted Abu Bakr and Umar in rejecting the Sunnah of their Prophet and replacing it with their own *ijtihad*, personal viewpoints, for they surely were in favor of *ijtihad*. It also distinguished from the rest of the community a Muslim minority that upheld the Prophet's statements and boycotted the allegiance to Abu Bakr, namely Ali and his Shi'as, supporters and followers.

Yes; the distinct identity of each of these two groups, or parties, became apparent in the Muslim society immediately following the incidents stated before. One party attempted to respect and implement the Prophet's Sunnah, whereas the other attempted to defeat it, obliterate it, and replace it with *ijtihad*, a

---

[1] For details of this incident, pls visit: https://www.al-islam.org/ghadir/

[2] The most glaring testimonial is Umar ibn al-Khattab's threat to burn the house of Fatima and everyone inside it. This incident is quite famous in history chronicles.

concept which attracted the majority, tempting it to be hopeful of reaching the seat of government or at least participating in it.

The first Sunni party was headed by Ali ibn Abu Talib and his Shi'as, whereas the other party which advocated *ijtihad* was headed by Abu Bakr and Umar and most of the *sahabah*. The second party, led by Abu Bakr and Umar, took upon itself to crush the first one, and many measures were planned to wipe out the other opposition party such as the following:

1. ISOLATION OF THE OPPOSITION AND ITS ECONOMIC PARALYZATION

The first attempt undertaken by the ruling party was to exclude its opponents from having a free access to the sources of livelihood and finance. Abu Bakr and Umar dismissed the farmers who had been hired by Fatima to cultivate the land of Fadak[3], considering it a Muslim commonwealth rather than the sole property of Fatima as her father had stated.

They also deprived her of all the rest of her father's inheritance, claiming that prophets left no inheritance. They terminated her share of the *khums* which the Messenger of Allah had assigned for himself and his family because they were prohibited from receiving charity.

Thus did Ali become paralyzed economically: the land tract of Fadak, which used to yield excellent profits for him, was confiscated from him; he was deprived of his cousin's inheritance

---

[3] Fadak's story is well known in history books and so is al-Zahra's dispute with Abu Bakr. She died angry with him. This is a famous incident recorded by both Bukhari and Muslim.

which, at the same time, was also the legitimate right of his wife; moreover, his share of *khums* was also cut-off.

Ali and his wife and children suddenly found themselves in need of those who could feed and clothe them, and this is exactly what Abu Bakr meant when he said to Fatima al-Zahra once: "Yes; you have the right to receive the *khums*, but I will fare with it just as the Messenger of Allah had fared, so that I do not let you be without food or without clothes."

As we have already indicated, the companions who sided with Ali were mostly slaves who had no wealth; so, the ruling party did not fear them or their influence, for people incline to the rich and despise the poor.

2. ISOLATING THE OPPOSITION AND PARALYZING IT SOCIALLY

In order to discard the opposition party headed by Ali ibn Abu Talib, the ruling party also isolated it socially. The first thing which Abu Bakr and Umar did was the removal of the psychological and emotional barrier which obligated all Muslims to respect and revere the relatives of the Greatest Messenger of Allah.

Since Ali is the cousin of the Prophet and the master of the Purified Progeny, there were some among the *sahabah* who hated him and envied him for the favors which Allah had bestowed upon him, not to mention the hypocrites who were waiting in ambush for him. Fatima was the only offspring of the Prophet who survived him.

She was, as the Messenger of Allah said, the leader of all the ladies of the world; therefore, all Muslims respected and revered her due to the status which she had earned with her father and because of the traditions which he stated about her virtues, honor, and purity.

But Abu Bakr and Umar deliberately tried to remove such respect and regard from the hearts of the public. Umar ibn al-Khattab once approached Fatima's house bearing a torch of fire and threatened to burn the house and everyone inside it if its residents refused to come out to swear the oath of allegiance to Abu Bakr. In his *Al-'Iqd al-Fareed*, Ibn Abd Rabbih says,

As regarding Ali, al-Abbas, and al-Zubayr, these stayed at Fatima's house till Abu Bakr sent them Umar ibn al-Khattab to get them out of Fatima's house. He said to him: "If they refuse, fight them." So he came bearing a torch of fire in order to burn the house on them. Fatima met him and asked him, "O son of al-Khattab! Have you come to burn our house?" "Yes," said he, "unless you accept that regarding which the Ummah has agreed."[4]

If Fatima al-Zahra is the Leader of the women of all the world, as indicated in the *Sahih* books of "Ahlul Sunnah wal Jama'ah," and if her sons al-Hasan and al-Husayn are the masters of the youths of Paradise and the Prophet's fragrant flower in this nation are thus humiliated and demeaned to the extent that Umar swears in front of everyone to burn them and their house if they refused to swear the oath of allegiance to Abu Bakr, can anyone expect others to retain any respect for Ali ibn Abu Talib when most of them hated and envied him? After the Prophet's demise, Ali became the leader of the opposition, yet he did not have any wealth to attract people to him.

Al-Bukhari indicates in his *Sahih* how Fatima demanded that Abu Bakr return what she had inherited from the Messenger of

---

[4] This is stated in Volume Four of *Al-'Iqd al-Fareed* where the author discusses those who refused to swear the oath of allegiance to Abu Bakr.

The Shi'a: The Real Followers of the Sunnah

Allah, whatever Allah had allocated for him in Medina in addition to Fadak and the spoils of Khaybar, but Abu Bakr refused to give anything to her.

Fatima, therefore, became very angry with Abu Bakr whom she boycotted and to whom she did not say a word after such unfair confiscation till she died only six months after the death of her father the Prophet. When she died, her husband Ali buried her at night. Abu Bakr did not perform the funeral prayers for her.

And Ali used to be held in high esteem by the public so long as Fatima was alive, so when she died, Ali saw how people turned away from him; therefore, he sought reconciliation with Abu Bakr and allegiance to him, whereas he never did so during all those months.[5]

Thus did the ruling party score a big success in isolating Ali ibn Abu Talib economically and socially, and in removing the respect people used to have for him, for they did not maintain any respect or regard for him especially following the death of Fatima al-Zahra, so much so that he was surprised to see how people's attitude towards him had changed.

He, therefore, felt forced to reconcile with Abu Bakr and give his allegiance to him according to the narration of al-Bukhari and Muslim. In other words, the phrase "Ali was surprised to see how people's attitude towards him had changed," borrowing al-Bukhari's own words, provides us with a clear indication of the extent of grudge and animosity the father of al-Hasan had to face after the death of his cousin then of his wife. Some *sahabah* may have even

---

[5] Al-Bukhari, *Sahih* (original Arabic text), Vol. 5, p. 82 in the discussion of the Battle of Khaybar, and it is also recorded in the "Book of Itjihad" in Muslim's *Sahih*.

taunted and ridiculed him upon seeing him in public places; this is why he was surprised and resented such an abomination.

This chapter is not meant to narrate history or detail the injustices inflicted upon Ali in as much as we would like to demonstrate the bitter and painful fact: The standard-bearer of the Prophet's Sunnah, and the gate of the Prophet's knowledge, became a pariah. Ironically, those who supported the concept of deriving their own personal religious views, from those who rejected the Prophet's Sunnah, became the rulers whom the vast majority of the *sahabah* supported.

3. ISOLATING THE OPPOSITION POLITICALLY

Despite enforcing a severe blockade, the confiscation of the monetary rights, and the isolation of Ali ibn Abu Talib from the society, which turned people's attention away from him as we have explained, the ruling party was not satisfied with all these measures, so it resorted to isolating Ali politically, excluding him from all apparatuses of the state and not permitting him to participate in any official position or any responsibility.

Although they appointed permissive Umayyads who fought Islam during the life-time of the Prophet, such rulers kept Imam Ali away from the stage of political activity for one quarter of a century during the life-time of Abu Bakr, Umar, and Uthman. While some *sahabah* who were appointed governors were hoarding wealth and treasuring gold and silver at the Muslims' expense, Ali ibn Abu Talib was watering the palm trees owned by the Jews in order to earn his livelihood with the sweat of his brow.

Thus did the gate of knowledge, the nation's scholar, and the standard-bearer of the Sunnah remain confined inside his house not appreciated except by a handful of the downtrodden who remained loyal to him, receiving guidance from him, and upholding his rope.

During his own caliphate, Imam Ali tried in vain to bring people back to the Qur'an and the Prophetic Sunnah because they became fanatical in their support of the *ijtihad* which Umar ibn al-Khattab had invented, and some of them even publicly cried out: *Waa Sunnata Umarah!* ("O what a great Sunnah Umar has brought us!").

This is not an allegation but the fact agreed upon by the consensus of all Muslims and which they recorded in their *Sahih* books and with which every researcher and man of fairness is familiar. Imam Ali used to know the entire text of the Holy Qur'an by heart and was familiar with all its injunctions. He was the first person to compile it as al-Bukhari himself testifies, whereas neither Abu Bakr nor Umar nor Uthman knew it by heart, nor did they know its injunctions.[6]

Historians went as far as counting as many as seventy instances when Umar said: *Lawla Ali la halaka Umar* (Had it not been for Ali, Umar would have surely perished), and his own telling Abu Bakr: "May I not live in any period of time without al-Hasan's father."

---

[6] Umar's ignorance regarding the distribution of the legacy of a man who leaves neither parents nor offspring behind, and who has no will, is quite famous in the books of Sunnah. The same is true about his ignorance of the injunctions relevant to tayammum; these are all known to everyone as al-Bukhari indicates on p. 90, Vol. 1, of his *Sahih*.

AHLUL SUNNAH ARE NOT FAMILIAR WITH THE PROPHET'S SUNNAH

Do not let this heading intimidate you, dear reader, for you are, by the Grace of Allah, walking on the path of righteousness so that you may in the end reach what pleases Allah, Glory and Exaltation to Him. Do not, therefore, let Satan's whispering, or your own conceit, or any abominable fanaticism control you or divert you from arriving at the anticipated goal, at the lost right, at the Garden of Eternity.

As we have already indicated, those who call themselves "Ahlul Sunnah wal Jama'ah" are the ones who believe in the legitimacy of the four "righteous caliphs," namely Abu Bakr, Umar, Uthman, and Ali. This is known to everyone in our time. But the sad fact is that Ali ibn Abu Talib was not originally counted by "Ahlul Sunnah wal Jama'ah" among the "righteous caliphs;" they did not even recognize the legitimacy of his caliphate; rather, his name was added to the list at a very late time in history: in 230 A.H./844 A.D., during the lifetime of Imam Ahmad ibn Hanbal.

As for the *sahabah* who were not Shi'as, as well as the caliphs, kings, and princes who ruled the Muslims from the time of Abu Bakr and till the reign of the Abbaside caliph Muhammad ibn al-Rasheed al-Mu`tasim, they never recognized the caliphate of Ali ibn Abu Talib at all. Moreover, some of them used to curse him and regard him non-Muslim; otherwise, how did they justify cursing him from their pulpits?!

We have already come to know how Abu Bakr and Umar treated him with excluding and expelling him from their government, then Uthman came after them to go to extremes in demonstrating his contempt for him, more than both of his friends, underestimating him to the extent that he once threatened to banish him just as he had banished Abu Dharr al-Ghifari.

The Shi'a: The Real Followers of the Sunnah

When Mu'awiyah became the ruler, he went to the extreme limits in cursing him and ordering people to do likewise. Umayyad rulers, therefore, were consistent in every town and village in doing so for as long a period as eighty years.[1]

Actually, the cursing, charging, and dissociation from him and his Shi'as, went on beyond that. The Abbaside caliph al-Mutawakkil, for example, went as far in his hatred for Ali as desecrating his grave and the grave of his son Imam al-Husayn ibn Ali in the year 240 A.H./854 A.D.

Al-Waleed ibn Abd al-Malik, who was the "commander of the faithful" of his time, delivered a sermon one Friday in which he said, "The *hadith* saying that the Messenger of Allah once said (to Ali, as): `Your status to me is like that of Aaron to Moses' was altered from: `Your status to me is like that of Qarun to Moses' because the listener became confused."[2] Such was the malice of these rulers against the brother of the Prophet.

During the reign of al-Mu'tasim, when there was a substantial increase in the number of atheists, apostates, and fabricators of *hadith*, who ascended the seat of the "righteous" caliphate, and when people were distracted during al-Mu'tasim's time by marginal problems, in addition to the dilemma caused by Ahmad ibn Hanbal labelling the Holy Qur'an as being infinite in its pre-existence..., people blindly followed the creed of their kings, believing that the Holy Qur'an was "created."

When Ahmad ibn Hanbal withdrew his theory regarding the Holy Qur'an, being apprehensive of al-Mu'tasim, he became after

---

[1] They all did so with the exception of Umar ibn Abd al-Aziz, may Allah be Merciful to him.

[2] *Tarikh Baghdad*, Vol. 8, p. 266.

that quite famous among scholars of *hadith*[3] like a shining star. It was then decided to add the name of Ali ibn Abu Talib to the list of the "righteous caliphs."

It is quite possible that Ahmad ibn Hanbal was dazzled by the authentic *ahadith* enumerating Ali's virtues which surfaced against the wish of the rulers of the time, especially since he is the one who has said, "Nobody among all people has received as many *ahadith* in his favor as Ali ibn Abu Talib." It was then that the number of the "righteous caliphs" was increased to four, and Ali's caliphate was regarded as "legitimate" after being rejected due to its "illegitimacy."

---

[3] That is to say, such scholars belonged to "Ahlul Sunnah wal Jama`ah."

THE PROOF:

In the *Tabaqat*, regarded by the Hanbalis as their main reference, Ibn Abu Ya`li quotes Wadeezah al-Himsi as saying:

I visited Ahmad ibn Hanbal after having added the name of Ali, Allah be pleased with him,[1] to the list of the three ["righteous caliphs"]. I said to him, "O Abu Abdullah! What you have done discredits both Talhah and al-Zubayr!" He said, "What a foolish statement you have uttered! What do we have to do with those folks' war, and why do you mention it now?" I said, "May Allah lead you to righteousness, we have mentioned it only after you added the name of Ali and mandated for him (of honors because) of the caliphate what is mandated to the Imams before him!" Said he, "And what stops me from doing so?" I said, "One tradition narrated by Ibn Umar." He said to me, "Umar [ibn al-Khattab] is better than his son, for he accepted (i.e. recommended) Ali's caliphate over the Muslims and listed him among the members of the (consultative) council of *shura*, and Ali referred to himself as the Commander of the Faithful; am I the one to say that the faithful did not have a commander?!" So I left.[2]

This incident clarifies for us the fact that the narrator is the leader of "Ahlul Sunnah wal Jama'ah" and their spokesman, and that they rejected Ali's caliphate because of what Abdullah ibn Umar, the Sunnis' *faqih*, says, a statement which al-Bukhari records

---

[1] Notice how the speaker says: "Allah be pleased with him," yet he refuses to accept his name to be added to the list of "righteous caliphs" and protests to Ahmad ibn Hanbal for having done so. Notice also how he says: "We have mentioned it, etc.," implying his speaking on behalf of Ahlul Sunnah who had sent him to Ahmad ibn Hanbal to register their protest.

[2] *Tabaqat al-Hanabila*, Vol. 1, p. 292.

in his *Sahih*. Since they claim that al-Bukhari's *Sahih* is the most authentic book next to the Book of Allah, it is mandatory on them to reject Ali's caliphate and not to recognize it.

We have discussed this "tradition" in our book *So Ask the People of Remembrance*, and there is no harm in repeating it here in order to make the benefit general.

In his *Sahih*, al-Bukhari quotes Abdullah ibn Umar saying, "During the lifetime of the Prophet, we used to regard Abu Bakr most, then Umar ibn al-Khattab, then Uthman ibn Affan, may Allah be pleased with them."[3]

Al-Bukhari quotes another tradition narrated by Ibn Umar which is more frank than this one. In it, Abdullah ibn Umar says:

During the lifetime of the Prophet, we did not regard anyone as being the peer of Abu Bakr, then Umar, then Uthman, then we leave the rest of the Prophet's companions without making any distinction among them.[4]

Upon the premises of this "tradition," which the Messenger of Allah neither mandates nor endorses, but one which is no more than the brainchild of Abdullah ibn Umar and his biased views and well known grudge and animosity towards Ali, do "Ahlul Sunnah wal Jama'ah" base their sect and justify their attitude as to why they did not recognize Ali's caliphate.

It is through "traditions" such as this one that Banu Umayyah permitted cursing, condemning, taunting, and belittling Ali. Their rulers since the reign of Mu`awiyah and till the days of Marwan ibn

---

[3] Al-Bukhari, *Sahih*, Vol. 4, p. 191, Vol. 4, in the book of the genesis of creation in a chapter dealing with Abu Bakr's merits being next only to those of the Prophet.

[4] Al-Bukhari, *Sahih*, Vol. 4, p. 203, in a chapter dealing with the merits of Uthman ibn `Affan in the book of the genesis of creation.

Muhammad ibn Marwan in 132 A.H. ordered the cursing of Ali from the pulpits. All those who supported him or did not endorse such animosity were killed.[5]

Then the Abbaside government started in 132 A.H./750 A.D. with the reign of Abul-Abbas al-Saffah [the blood-shedder]; it was then that dissociation in various means from Ali and from those who supported him continued, and the means of this dissociation varied according to the then prevailing conditions and circumstances because the Abbaside dynasty was erected on the ruins of Ahlul Bayt and those who followed their line. Some rulers, if the government's interest demanded, did not publicly curse Ali but were secretly doing more than what the Umayyads did.

They learned from the historic experience which highlighted the oppression to which Ahlul Bayt and their supporters were subjected: such oppression drew the sympathy of people to them; therefore, the rulers cunningly tried to tilt the situation in their favor.

They, therefore, sought to be close to the Imams from Ahlul Bayt not out of love for them, nor recognizing their confiscated rights, but in order to contain the public uprisings which broke out near the borders and which threatened the government's very existence.

This is what al-Ma'mun son of Haroun al-Rasheed had done to Imam Ali ibn Musa al-Rida. But when the government was in full control, and internal dissent was contained, it went to extremes in insulting these Imams and their Shi'as as the Abbaside caliph al-Mutawakkil did. He became quite famous for his hatred of Ali and

---

[5] The only exception is the couple of years during which Umar ibn Abd al-Aziz ruled. He stopped the nefarious custom of cursing, but after his murder, they resumed the cursing and went beyond that to desecrate his grave. They went as far as prohibiting anyone to be named after him...

for cursing him and even desecrating his grave and the grave of his son al-Husayn.

It is because of these facts that we have said that "Ahlul Sunnah wal Jama'ah" refused to recognize the legitimacy of Ali's caliphate till many years after Ahmad ibn Hanbal.

It is true that Ahmad ibn Hanbal was the first person to promote this notion, but he could not convince the scholars of *hadith*, as we have pointed out to adopt his view due to their following in the footprints of Abdullah ibn Umar. A long time was needed to convince people of it and to let them accept Ahmad ibn Hanbal's view, a view which might have presented the Hanbalis as seeking justice and nearness to Ahlul Bayt. This distinguished them from other Sunni sects such as the Malikis, Hanafis, and Shafi'is who were vying to gain supporters. They, therefore, had no choice except to accept the view and adopt it.

As time passed by, "Ahlul Sunnah wal Jama'ah" became unanimous in endorsing Ahmad ibn Hanbal's view, and they agreed to make Ali the fourth of the "righteous caliphs," requiring the faithful to respect him as much as they respected the other three.

Is this, then, not the greatest proof that "Ahlul Sunnah wal Jama'ah" were Nasibis who hated Ali and tried their best to belittle and disrespect him?

One may ask the following question: "How can this be true while we nowadays see 'Ahlul Sunnah wal Jama'ah' loving Imam Ali and seeking Allah to be pleased with him?"

We say: Yes, after the passage of time, and the death of the Imams from Ahlul Bayt, the rulers had no worry, nor did they face any threat against their government, and when the dignity of the Islamic government disappeared and the Mamlukes, Moguls, and Tatars took control of it, and when the creed weakened and many Muslims were diverted with arts, singing, amusement, promiscuity, wine and concubines..., and when one generation succeeded another that lost the prayers, followed its own low desires..., when right seemed wrong and wrong seemed right, when corruption prevailed on the land and the sea..., it was then and only then that Muslims eulogized their ancestors and sung the praise of their glory.

It was then that they yearned for their past history and legacy, calling them their "golden ages." The best of times, from their viewpoint, is the age of the *sahabah* who conquered many lands, expanded the Islamic kingdom in the east and the west, subduing the Kaisers and Caesars.

It was then that they started praying to Allah to be pleased with all of them, including Ali ibn Abu Talib, became acceptable. Because "Ahlul Sunnah wal Jama'ah" believe in their justice, all of them, they could not exclude Ali from their list of *sahabah*.

Had they excluded him, their scheme would have become evident to everyone who is wise and who researches, so they misled the public into believing that the fourth caliph was the gate of knowledge Ali ibn Abu Talib, Allah glorified his countenance. We ask them, "Why do you then refuse to emulate him with regard to your religious and secular matters if you truly believe that he was the gate of knowledge? Why did you deliberately forsake that gate and prefer to emulate Abu Hanifah, Malik, al-Shafi`i, and Ibn Hanbal, as well as Ibn Taymiyyah, those who do not even come close to the loftiness of Ali's deeds, merits, and honorable descent, for what is the distance between the earth and Pleiades, or how can one compare the sword with the sickle, or how can one compare Mu`awiyah to Ali, if you only follow reason?"

All this can be said were one to set aside all the *ahadith* narrated about the Messenger of Allah mandating upon all Muslims to follow Imam Ali after the Prophet and to emulate him. Someone among Ahlul Sunnah may say, "Ali's merits, his being the foremost in embracing Islam, his *jihad* in the cause of Islam, his deep knowledge, his great honors, and his asceticism are known to all people; rather, Ahlul Sunnah know and love Ali more than Shi'as do."

Such is the statement repeated by many of them these days. To these we say: Where were you[6], and where were your ancestors and scholars when Ali was being cursed from the pulpits for hundreds of years? We never heard, nor does history document any fact, that even one single person among them resented it or prohibited it or was killed because of his loyalty and love for Ali.

Nay! We will never come across even one name among all the scholars of Ahlul Sunnah who did so. Instead, they were close to the monarchs, rulers, and governors because of the allegiance they had sworn to them, because of being pleased with them, and because they issued for them verdicts legalizing the killing of all "rejectionists" who were loyal to Ali and his progeny, and such people are present even in our own time.

Christians have for many centuries borne enmity towards the Jews whom they regarded as criminals. They accused them of being responsible for killing Jesus Christ son of Mary. But these Christians weakened, and the tenets of their creed disappeared, and many of them became apostates. The Church was consigned to the waste basket due to its opposing stand towards science and scientists.

---

[6] I have deliberately said "Where were you?" to address contemporary Muslims from "Ahlul Sunnah wal Jama`ah" for they read in Muslim's *Sahih* that Mu`awiyah used to curse Ali and order the *sahabah* to do likewise, and they do not find it objectionable. Rather, they plead to Allah to be pleased with their master Mu`awiyah to whom they refer as "the revelation's scribe." This proves that their love for Ali is not genuine at all and unworthy of being taken seriously.

In contrast, the Jews gained power, and such power gained momentum when they occupied Arab and Islamic lands by force. Their influence spread in the east and the west, and they established the "state of Israel..." It was only then that Pope John Paul II met Jewish rabbis and cleared them of the crime of killing Jesus, for such are some people, and such is our time.

AHLUL SUNNAH AND THE OBLITERATION OF THE SUNNAH

In this chapter, we would like to explain something very important which researchers ought to deeply investigate in order to find out, beyond any shadow of doubt, that those who call themselves Ahlul Sunnah in all reality have very little to do with the Sunnah of the Prophet.

This is so because they, or rather their predecessors among the *sahabah* and "righteous caliphs," whom they emulate, and through loving for and allegiance to whom they seek nearness to Allah, took a negative stand towards the Prophetic Sunnah to the extent that they burnt that Sunnah and prohibited anyone from recording it or narrating its *ahadith*.[1]

Moreover, we have to unveil the mean plot woven against the pure Prophetic Sunnah in order to prohibit its dissemination, and in order to kill it in its infancy and substitute it with innovations, personal views, and interpretations of the rulers and the *sahabah*. Early rulers did the following:

FIRST: They fabricated false *ahadith* to support their stand to prohibit the recording of the Prophet's Sunnah and the *sacred ahadith*. Imam Muslim, for example, records in his *Sahih* what is quoted by Haddab ibn Khalid al-Azdi who cites Humam citing Zayd ibn Aslam citing Ata ibn Yasar citing Abu Sa`id al-Khudri saying that the Messenger of Allah has said, "Do not record anything which I say, and whoever quotes what I tell you besides the Qur'an should erase what he writes, and [orally] narrate about

---

[1] Read in this regard from page 200 and beyond in my book *Ask Those Who Know*.

me without any hesitation."² The purpose of fabricating this alleged "*hadith*" is to justify what Abu Bakr and Umar did to the Prophet's *ahadith* written down and recorded by a number of companions of the Prophet. This "tradition" was fabricated many years after the end of the period of the "righteous caliphs," and the fabricators, professional liars, overlooked the following issues:

1. Had the Messenger of Allah actually said so, the *sahabah* would have acted upon his orders (not to write traditions down), and they would have erased all traditions many years before Abu Bakr and Umar had burned them.

2. Had this tradition been authentic, Abu Bakr would have first cited it, and then Umar, in order to justify their prohibition of recording *hadith*, and they would have erased them, and those who had recorded them would have sought an excuse for having done so either due to their ignorance [of such a "tradition"] or to their lapse of memory.

3. Had this tradition been authentic, Abu Bakr and Umar would have had to erase all traditions, not burn them.

4. Had this "tradition" been authentic, the Muslims, who were contemporary to Umar ibn Abd al-Aziz, till our time, would have been committing the sin of disobeying the Messenger of Allah, particularly their chief, namely Umar ibn Abd al-Aziz who had ordered the scholars of his time to record *hadith*, in addition to al-Bukhari and Muslim who regarded this tradition as authentic yet they did not act upon it but wrote thousands of the Prophet's *ahadith*.

5. Finally, had this "tradition" been authentic, it would not have been missed by the gate of knowledge Ali ibn Abu Talib who compiled the *ahadith* of the Prophet in one *saheefa* the length of

---

² Muslim, *Sahih*, Vol. 8, p. 229, "Kitab al-Zuhd" (Book of Asceticism) in a chapter dealing with verification of hadith and the injunction regarding the recording of knowledge.

whose pieces reached seventy yards which he called *al-jami`a*, the one that includes everything, and which we will discuss later by the help of Allah.

SECOND: Umayyad rulers spared no efforts to underscore their theory that the Messenger of Allah was not protected by Allah against falling into error as is the case with all other human beings who sometimes are right and sometimes are wrong, fabricating several "traditions" to support their claim.

The purpose of fabricating such "traditions" was to make sure that the Prophet used to follow his own personal views; therefore, he often erred to the extent that some of his companions had to correct him, as indicated in the incidents of palm tree pollination, the revelation of the verse referring to the issue of *hijab* (veil), the case of accepting *fidya* (ransom) from the captives seized after the Battle of Badr, in addition to many such incidents claimed by "Ahlul Sunnah wal Jama'ah" and included in their *Sahih* books in support of such an attitude towards the Messenger of Allah, peace and the best of blessings be upon him and his progeny.

We argue with "Ahlul Sunnah wal Jama'ah" thus:

If such is your creed and attitude towards the Messenger of Allah, how do you claim to be upholding his Sunnah, believing that you and your predecessors regarded such Sunnah as unprotected from Allah from error, even unknown and unrecorded?![3] Yet we

---

[3] This is so due to the fact that recording the Sunnah was postponed till the time of caliph Umar ibn Abd al-Aziz or even thereafter. As for the caliphs and rulers who preceded him, they burnt it and prohibited anyone from writing it down or quoting it.

reject these claims and false charges and are able to refute them by quoting your own references and *Sahih* books.[4] Examples:

In a chapter on recording knowledge in his *Kitab al-`Ilm* (Book of Knowledge) of his *Sahih*, al-Bukhari quotes Abu Hurayra saying, "None among the companions of the Prophet narrates more *hadith* than me except Abdullah ibn Umar, for he can write whereas I cannot (i.e. I am illiterate)."[5]

This statement clearly indicates that there were among the Prophet's *sahabah* those who wrote his *ahadith* down. Since Abu Hurayra narrated more than six thousand traditions of the Prophet orally (because he could not write), Abdullah ibn Umar quoted more traditions of the Prophet because of his ability to write them down.

Undoubtedly, there were among the *sahabah* those who could write the Prophet's traditions and whom Abu Hurayra did not mention because they were not famous for being so prolific. Add to the above Imam Ali ibn Abu Talib who used to spread out from the pulpit a scroll which he used to call *al-jami`a* in which he compiled all what people need of the Prophet's traditions, and which was inherited by the Imams of Ahlul Bayt who often referred to it. Examples:

Imam Ja`far al-Sadiq has said, "We have the *saheefa*; it is seventy yards long: it is the dictation of the Messenger of Allah written down in the hand-writing of Ali. Nothing permissible or prohibitive the knowledge thereof is needed by people, nor any

---

[4] What is strange is that Ahlul Sunnah often narrate one hadith and its antithesis in the same book. Yet even more strange is that they quite often follow false traditions and neglect authentic ones.

[5] Bukhari, *Sahih*, Vol. 1, p. 36, "Kitab al-`Ilm" (Book of Knowledge).

other issue, except that it is in it, even the penalty for inflicting an offense as minor as a tiny scratch on someone's cheek."[6]

Al-Bukhari himself has referred to this *saheefa*, which was in Ali's possession, in many chapters of his book, but he, as was quite often his habit, curtailed a great deal of information about its nature and contents. In his *Kitab al-`Ilm*, al-Bukhari records the following:

Al-Sha`bi has quoted Abu Juhayfa saying, "I asked Ali: `Do you have a book in your possession?' He said, `No, except the Book of Allah, or some knowledge bestowed upon a Muslim man, or what this *saheefa* quotes of the Prophet.' I asked him, `And what is in this *saheefa*?' `It contains reason,' he said, `the ransoming of the captives, and that no Muslim should kill another Muslim.'"[7]

In another place, al-Bukhari quotes Ibrahim al-Taymi quoting his father quoting Ali saying, "We have nothing except the Book of Allah and this *saheefa* which quotes the Prophet."[8] In yet another place in al-Bukhari's *Sahih*, the author quotes Ibrahim al-Taymi quoting his father saying, "Ali delivered a sermon once to us in which he said, `We have no book to read except the Book of Allah and what is recorded in this *saheefa*.'"[9]

In another place of his *Sahih*, al-Bukhari quotes Ali saying, "We did not write down from the Prophet except the Qur'an and this *saheefa*."[10] In yet another place of his *Sahih*, al-Bukhari says, "Ibrahim al-Taymi quotes his father saying, `Ali, may Allah be pleased with him, delivered a sermon to us once from a pulpit built of baked bricks, and he was carrying a sword from which a *saheefa*

---

[6] *Usul al-Kafi*, Vol. 1, p. 239, and also on p. 143 of *Basair al-Darajat*.
[7] Al-Bukhari, *Sahih*, Vol. 1, p. 36, [original Arabic text].
[8] Al-Bukhari, *Sahih*, Vol. 2, p. 221.
[9] Al-Bukhari, *Sahih*, Vol. 4, p. 67, and Muslim, *Sahih*, Vol. 4, p. 115.
[10] Al-Bukhari, *Sahih*, Vol. 4, p. 69.

was draping and said, 'By Allah! We do not have any book to read except the Book of Allah and what is recorded in this *saheefa*."[11]

Al-Bukhari, however, did not indicate that Imam Ja`far al-Sadiq had said that this *saheefa* was called "*al-jami`a*" due to the fact that it contained all what is permissible and prohibitive, and it had all what people need, even the penalty for scratching one's cheek, that it was dictated by the Messenger of Allah and handwritten by Imam Ali ibn Abu Talib.

Instead, he only made a casual reference to it. He has said once that it has reason, the ransoming of the captives, and that no Muslim man should be killed on account of a non-Muslim. And once he says, "Ali spread it out, and it had a reference to camels' teeth, that Medina is not to be entered by non-Muslims, that the Muslims' security is their collective responsibility, and that if someone followed certain people without the permission of his masters..., etc."

This is nothing but forgery and the adulteration of facts; otherwise, does it make sense to say that Ali wrote only those four statements on it then draped it to his sword to the extent that it was with him even whenever he preached from the pulpit, making it second only to the Holy Qur'an as his reference, telling people, "We have not quoted of what the Prophet has said except the Qur'an and what this *saheefa* contains"?!

Was Abu Hurayra's mind greater than that of Ali ibn Abu Talib to the extent that he learned by heart one hundred thousand traditions from the Messenger of Allah without having written a single one of them down?!

Strange, by Allah, is the case of those who accept one hundred thousand traditions narrated by Abu Hurayra who did not

---

[11] Al-Bukhari, *Sahih*, Vol. 8, p. 144.

accompany the Prophet except for three years, the illiterate that he was, while claiming that Ali was the gate of the city of knowledge from whom the *sahabah* learned various branches of knowledge.

Yet, according to them, Ali was carrying a scroll containing only four *ahadith* that remained with him during the Prophet's lifetime till his own caliphate, so he ascended the pulpit and it was draping from his sword...! What a big statement they make, and what lies they fabricate...

Yet what al-Bukhari has recorded suffices the researchers and any discreet person especially since he mentioned that that *saheefa* contained many topics relevant to the human mind and to the Islamic intellect. Our point is not to prove or disprove what the *saheefa* contained, for the residents of Mecca best know its valleys, and the family members know best what their house contains, but what concerns us in this research is the fact that the *sahabah* were indeed writing down the traditions of the Prophet.

Abu Hurayra's statement that Abdullah ibn Umar used to record the Prophet's traditions, in addition to the statement of Ali ibn Abu Talib saying, according to al-Bukhari's *Sahih*, "We have not quoted of what the Prophet has said except the Qur'an and what this *saheefa* contains," irrevocably proves that the Messenger of Allah never prohibited anyone from recording his *ahadith*; rather, it proves the opposite.

The tradition recorded in al-Bukhari's *Sahih* quoting the Prophet saying, "Do not quote me, and anyone who quotes anything from me other than the Qur'an must erase it" is a false tradition fabricated by those who supported the caliphs so that they might support them. It was fabricated in order to justify what Abu Bakr and Umar and Uthman had done: the burning of Prophet's *ahadith* and the prohibition of the Sunnah from being disseminated.

What increases our conviction is the fact that not only did the Messenger of Allah refrain from prohibiting the writing of his *ahadith*, but that he even ordered them to be recorded. Imam Ali, who was the closest person to the Prophet, said: "We have not quoted of what the Prophet has said except the Qur'an and what this *saheefa* contains." This statement is quoted by al-Bukhari in his *Sahih*.

If we add to the above what Imam Ja`far al-Sadiq has said, that is, that *al-saheefa al-jami`a* was the dictation of the Messenger of Allah in the hand-writing of Ali, we will conclude by saying that the Prophet had ordered Ali to quote him.

In order to dispel any doubt which may still linger in the mind of the dear reader, I would like to shed more light and state the following:

Al-Hakim in his book *Al-Mustadrak*, Abu Dawood in his *Sahih*, Imam Ahmad in his *Musnad*, and al-Darimi in his *Sunan* have all quoted a very important *hadith* regarding Abdullah ibn Umar to whom Abu Hurayra referred and whom he described as having written down a larger number of the Prophet's *ahadith* than he himself had quoted; it is as follows:

Abdullah ibn Umar has said: "I used to write down whatever I heard from the Messenger of Allah, so Quraysh prohibited me from doing so saying, `Do you write everything you hear from the Messenger of Allah who is a human being talking in anger or when pleased?' So I stopped writing, then I told the Messenger of Allah about it, whereupon he pointed to his mouth and said, `Keep writing, for by the One Who holds my soul do I swear that nothing comes out of it except the truth."¹²

This tradition clearly tells us that Abdullah ibn Umar used to write down everything he heard from the

Messenger of Allah who did not prohibit him from doing so; rather, such a prohibition came from Quraysh. Abdullah did not want to identify those who prohibited him from writing what he was writing, for their prohibition contradicted what the Messenger of Allah had told him.

It is also quite clear that his generally ambiguous reference to "Quraysh" means the leaders of Quraysh [who were then present in Medina], that is, the *Meccan Muhajirs*, immigrants, led by Abu Bakr, Umar, Uthman, Abdul-Rahman ibn Awf, Abu Ubaydah, Talhah, al-Zubayr, and all those who followed their line.

We also notice that their prohibiting Abdullah took place while the Prophet was still alive: this by itself emphasizes the depth of the conspiracy and its gravity; otherwise, why should these men prohibit Abdullah from writing *hadith* without first consulting with the Prophet himself in this regard? This can also be understood from their statement that the Messenger of Allah was an ordinary human being who talked when angry and when pleased. It indicates how weak their belief in the Prophet was to the extent that they expected him to say something wrong, or pass an erroneous verdict, especially in the state of anger.

The fact that the Prophet said the following when Abdullah ibn Umar mentioned to him Quraysh's prohibition and what they said about him, he pointed to his mouth and said, "By the One Who

---

[12] Al-Hakim, *Mustadrak*, Vol. 1, p. 105. Also Abu Dawud, *Sunan*, Vol. 2, p. 126. Also al-Darimi, *Sunan*, Vol. 1, p. 125, and Imam Ahmad ibn Hanbal, *Musnad*, Vol. 2, p. 162.

holds my soul do I swear that nothing comes out of it except the truth" is another proof of the Prophet's knowledge of their doubting his justice, and that they expected him to err and to utter falsehood (*Astaghfirullah!* [We seek forgiveness of Allah]); therefore, he swore by Allah that he said nothing except the truth. This is the accurate interpretation of the verse saying,

"Surely he does not utter anything of his own desire; it is but a revelation revealed" (*Holy Qur'an, 53:3-4*), and that he was protected against erring or uttering falsehood.

Because of all the above, we emphatically state that all "traditions" fabricated during the time of the Umayyads which implied that he was not divinely protected against erring are not authentic at all. The tradition cited above also gives us the impression that their influence on Abdullah ibn Umar was so great that he stopped writing *hadith* down as he himself admitted when he said, "... so I stopped writing..."

He remained so till an occasion came wherein the Messenger of Allah interfered in person to dispel the doubts circulated against his infallibility and equity, the doubts which were quite often articulated even in his own presence such as their asking him: "Are you *really* a prophet?!"[13] or: "Are you the one who claims to be a prophet?!"[14] or: "By Allah, he did not seek in this distribution the Pleasure of Allah!"[15] or Ayesha's statement to the Prophet: "Your

---

[13] This statement was made by Umar ibn al-Khattab during the Treaty of Hudaybiyyah, and it is recorded on p. 122, Vol. 2 of al-Bukhari's *Sahih*.

[14] This statement was made by `Ayesha daughter of Abu Bakr; see p. 29, Vol. 2, of al-Ghazali's book *Ihya al-`Ulum*.

[15] This was the statement made to the Prophet by an Ansar companion as recorded on p. 47, Vol. 4, of al-Bukhari's *Sahih*.

God is sure swift in fulfilling your desires!"[16] or her asking the prophet once to be fair..., up to the end of the list of impertinent statements which demonstrate the fact that they doubted his infallibility, believing that he was liable to be unfair, to oppress, to err, to lie...; we seek Allah's protection.

He, indeed, possessed sublime morals; he was kind and compassionate as he tried to dispel such doubts by saying once, for example, "I am only a servant receiving orders from his Master," and once, "By Allah! I am kind for the sake of pleasing Allah Whom I fear," and at another time he said, "By the One Who controls my life! It utters nothing except the truth." He used quite often to say: "May Allah have mercy on my Brother Moses! He was subjected to more afflictions than this, yet he persevered."

Those impertinent statements which cast doubts about the Prophet's infallibility and about his Prophethood were not made by those who were outcasts or hypocritical; rather, they were unfortunately made by very prominent companions of the Prophet, and by the Mother of the Believers, and by those who are still regarded by "Ahlul Sunnah wal Jama'ah" as role models of conduct; so, there is no power nor might except in Allah, the Sublime, the Great.

What confirms our conviction that the tradition which supposedly prohibited the recording of *hadith* is fabricated and was baseless, and that the Prophet never said so at all, is the fact that Abu Bakr himself used to write down the traditions of the Prophet during his lifetime. Yet when he ascended to the post of caliph, he decided to burn them for a reason with which the researchers are familiar.

---

[16] Al-Bukhari, *Sahih*, Vol. 6, p. 24, and also Vol. 6, p. 128, of the same reference.

Here is his daughter Ayesha saying, "My father gathered the ahadith of the Messenger of Allah, and they totalled five hundred, then he spent his night sleeplessly turning on his sides. I thought that he was upset because of someone's complaint, or because of some news which he had heard. The next morning, he said to me, 'Daughter! Bring me the ahadith in your possession,' so I brought them to him, and he set them on fire."[17]

And here is Umar ibn al-Khattab, also upon becoming caliph, delivering a sermon one day to people in which he said, "Anyone who has in his possession a book must bring it to me so that I may tell him what I think of it." People thought that he simply wanted to verify their contents to remove from them any discrepancy, so they brought him their books whereupon he set them on fire.[18] Then he dispatched his orders to Islamic lands ordering people thus: Anyone who has any *ahadith* written down has to erase them.[19]

This is the greatest evidence testifying to the fact that all the *sahabah*, had they lived in Medina or in the rest of Muslim lands, had in their possession books in which they compiled sacred *ahadith* of the Prophet which they had recorded during the Prophet's lifetime. They were all burnt according to the orders first of Abu Bakr then of Umar. All other books found in other lands were erased during Umar's caliphate as he had ordered.[20]

---

[17] See p. 237, Vol. 5, of *Kanz al-`Ummal*. Refer also to Ibn Kathir's book *Al-Bidaya wal-Nihaya* as well as p. 5, Vol. 1, of al-Dhahabi's *Tadhkirat al-Huffaz*.

[18] Ibn Sa`ad, *Al-Tabaqat al-Kubra*, Vol. 5, p. 188. It is also recorded in *Taqyeed al-`Ilm* by al-Khateeb al-Baghdadi.

[19] Refer to Ibn Abd al-Birr's book *Jamai` Bayan al-`Ilm*.

[20] Look, may Allah protect you, at such a horrible act committed by the caliphs Abu Bakr and Umar towards the Prophetic Sunnah! Imagine the greatly immeasurable loss which they inflicted upon the Islamic Ummah which very badly needed such ahadith in order to understand the Holy

Based upon the above, we cannot, nor can any sane person, believe that the Messenger of Allah had prohibited them from writing them down, having come to know that most *sahabah* possessed books containing traditions especially the *saheefa* with which Imam Ali never parted, and whose length reached seventy yards, and which he used to call *al-jami`a* [literally meaning: the university] because it contained all sorts of knowledge.

Since the interests of the ruling authority and the dominant political line dictated the obliteration and the burning of the Sunnah and the prohibition of quoting *hadith*, the *sahabah* who supported such caliphate obeyed those orders and burnt such Sunnah and ceased quoting *hadith*.

Thus, they left themselves and their followers no option except resorting to personal views expressed as *ijtihad*, or following the "sunnah" of Abu Bakr, Umar, Uthman, Mu`awiyah, Yazid, Marwan ibn al-Hakam, al-Waleed ibn Abd al-Malik, Sulayman ibn Abd al-Malik.... This continued till [Umayyad caliph] Umar ibn Abd al-Aziz came to power and asked Abu Bakr al-Hazmi to write down what he remembered of the *ahadith* and Sunnah of the Messenger of Allah or the "sunnah" of Umar ibn al-Khattab.[21]

Thus does it become clear to us that even during the circumstances that permitted the recording of the Sunnah, a hundred years after the obliteration and prohibition of the Sunnah,

---

Qur'an and the commandments of Allah, the Most Glorified One. They were, by my life, authentic ahadith because they were direct quotations from the Prophet recorded in the absence of a second narrator. As for the "traditions" which were compiled after that period, these were mostly fabrications because dissension had already taken place, and Muslims killed one another, and they were manufactured according to the specifications provided by various oppressive rulers...

[21] Malik, *Al-Muwatta'*, Vol. 1, p. 5.

we can see the moderate Umayyad caliph whose name was added by "Ahlul Sunnah wal Jama'ah" to the list of the "righteous caliphs" ordering the compilation of the Sunnah of the Messenger of Allah in addition to the "sunnah" of Umar ibn al-Khattab, as if Umar ibn al-Khattab was a partner of Muhammad in his Prophetic mission and prophethood...!

And why did Umar ibn Abd al-Aziz not ask the Imams from Ahlul Bayt, who were his contemporaries, to give him a copy of *al-saheefa al-jami`a*? And why did he not put them in charge of collecting the Prophet's *ahadith* especially since they knew best what their grandfather had said? But verifiers and researchers know the secret.

Can those traditions which were compiled by "Ahlul Sunnah wal Jama'ah" be taken for granted especially since those who compiled them belonged to Banu Umayyah and their supporters who represent Quraysh's caliphate? Can we rely on them after having already come to know the truth about Quraysh and its attitude towards the Messenger of Allah and his purified Sunnah? It remains obvious, having come to know all of that, that the ruling authority across the centuries acted only upon the principles of *ijtihad*, analogy, and mutual consultation...

Since the said authority had expelled Imam Ali from the stage of public life and ignored him, it had nothing against him to require him to burn what he had recorded during the Prophetic Message according to the dictation of the Prophet himself.

Ali remained in possession of that *saheefa* in which he compiled everything people need, even the penalty for slightly scratching one's cheek. When he became caliph, he was still letting it drape from his sword as he ascended the pulpit to deliver a sermon to people to acquaint them with its importance.

Consecutive stories told by the Imams of Ahlul Bayt kept indicating that their sons inherited that *saheefa* from their fathers, chronologically one from another, and that they used to refer to it in order to issue religious decisions (*fatawa*) with regard to questions raised to them by their contemporaries who were guided by the light of their guidance. For this reason, Imam Ja`far al-Sadiq, Imam al-Rida, and many other Imams, used to always repeat the same statement in its regard.

They used to say, "We do not issue verdicts to people according to our own views; had we been issuing verdicts to people in the light of our own views and according to the dictates of our own inclinations, we would surely have been among those who perish. Rather, they are legacies of the Messenger of Allah of knowledge which sons inherit from their fathers, and which we treasure as people treasure their gold and silver."[22] Imam Ja`far al-Sadiq said once,

'My hadith is my father's, while my father's hadith is my grandfather's, and the hadith of my grandfather is that of al-Husayn; al-Husayn's hadith is that of al-Hasan; al-Hasan's hadith is that of the Commander of the Faithful; the hadith of the Commander of the Faithful is the hadith of the Messenger of Allah, and the hadith of the Messenger of Allah is the speech of Allah, the Lord of Dignity and Greatness.'[23]

Based on such premises, the tradition of the Two Weighty Things (al-Thaqalayn) becomes consecutively reported (*mutawatir*), and its text is as follows:

---

[22] `Allama al-`Askari, *Ma`alim al-Madrasatayn*, Vol. 2, p. 302.
[23] Al-Kulayni, *Al-Kafi*, Vol. 1, p. 53.

I have left among you the Two Weighty Things: the Book of Allah and my Progeny; so long as you (simultaneously) uphold both of them, you shall never stray after me.[24]

---

[24] Muslim, *Sahih*, Vol. 5, p. 122, also al-Tirmidhi, *Sahih*, Vol. 5, p. 637.

THE ATTITUDE OF AHLUL SUNNAH TOWARDS THE SHI'AS

If we exclude some contemporary scholars who have written with fairness about the Shi'as as dictated to them by their Islamic norms of conduct, most others, in the past and the present, have been writing about the Shi'as in the mentality of hateful Umayyads.

Hence, you see them in every valley frantically going around saying what they do not do, taunting and cursing, piling false charges and calumnies against the innocent followers of Ahlul Bayt. They call them *kafirs* (apostates). They yell bad names at them, following in the footsteps of their "al-salaf al-salih," socalled "good predecessors," namely Mu`awiyah and his likes who took control of Islamic caliphate by force, oppression, cunning and conniving, treachery and hypocrisy.

Once they say that the Shi'as are a group founded by Abdullah ibn Saba', the Jew, and once they say that they descended from Zoroastrian origins, or that they are Rafidis, and that their danger against Islam is more than that of the Jews and the Christians.

They also write that they are hypocrites, that they follow the principle of *taqiyya*, that they are permissive folks who legitimize illegitimate marriages, permitting the *mut`a* which, in their view, is nothing but adultery... Some of them write saying that they have a Qur'an different from that of their own, that they worship Ali and the Imams among his offspring and hate Muhammad and Gabriel..., and that they do this and that, etc.

Hardly one year passes without the publication of a book or a group of books written by "scholars" who lead "Ahlul Sunnah wal Jama'ah," as they call themselves, filled with charges of apostasy and insults towards the Shi'as. They have neither justification nor motive except pleasing their masters who have a vested interest in tearing the Islamic Ummah apart and shattering its unity even its total annihilation.

Moreover, they have no proof nor argument except blind fanaticism, veiled hatred, contemptible ignorance, and the blind imitating of their predecessors without any discerning of facts, nor scholarly research, nor any evident argument. They are, hence, like parrots: They are ever repeating what they hear, copying what the Nasibis from the Umayyads' henchmen, and those who are still making a living praising and glorifying Yazid son of Mu`awiyah.[1] So do not be surprised at those who glorify Yazid son of Mu`awiyah when you see them cursing the enemies of this Yazid, calling them *kafirs*.

Has the Prophetic Sunnah not stated that: "Each Muslim to another Muslim is like a strong building: each one strengthens the other," and, "A Muslim relates to another Muslim like one body: if one part thereof agonizes, the rest of the body will responds with vigilance and fever"?

Has not the Prophet said, "Cursing a Muslim is a sin, and fighting him is *kufr*"? Had these writers who claim to be among "Ahlul Sunnah wal Jama'ah" really come to know the Prophetic Sunnah, they would never have permitted themselves to throw the charge of *kufr* at anyone who testifies that: *La ilaha illaAllah, Muhammadun Rasool-Allah* (There is no god except Allah, Muhammad is the Messenger of Allah), and who uphold the prayers, pay the *zakat*, fast during the month of Ramadan, perform the pilgrimage to the Haram House, enjoin what is right, and forbid what is wrong.

---

[1] The Ministry of Education in Saudi Arabia has published a book titled *Haqaiq an Ameer al-Mumineen Yazid ibn Mu'awiyah* (facts about the commander of the faithful Yazid son of Mu`awiyah) to be taught as a curriculum text book at its public schools.

But since they are in fact followers of the "sunnah" of the Umayyads and some leaders of Quraysh, they talk and write in the same mentality that prevailed during the period of *jahiliyya* (pre-Islamic period) when tribalism and racist arrogance prevailed. Whatever comes from its source surprises none, and every pot drips of its contents.

Has the Messenger of Allah not said just as the Holy Qur'an states:

"Say: O People of the Book! Come to an equitable proposition between us and you: that we shall not worship anyone except Allah and not associate aught with Him and that we shall not take others for lords besides Allah" (Holy Qur'an, 3:64)?

If they are true followers of the Sunnah, then they should invite their Shi`a brethren to a common agreement between them.

Since Islam calls upon its enemies among the Jews and Christians to come to a common agreement of understanding and brotherhood between them, what would you say about those who worship only one God, and whose Prophet is one and the same, and so is their Book, *qibla*, and destiny?! Why don't the scholars among Ahlul Sunnah invite their brethren Shi`a scholars and sit with them at the discussion table and argue with them in the best manner so that they may "mend" their beliefs which they claim to be "corrupt"?

Why don't they hold an Islamic conference of scholars from both sides where all disputed issues are discussed and heard and seen by all Muslims so that they may distinguish the truth from falsehood? We say so knowing that "Ahlul Sunnah wal Jama'ah" comprise three-quarters of the Muslims of the world, and they have the financial potential and the political clout which make the achievement of the above easy, for they even own satellites...

"Ahlul Sunnah wal Jama'ah" do not attempt to do anything like this at all, nor do they desire any scholarly debate like the one called for in the Glorious Book of Allah in the verse saying,

"Say: Bring your proof if you tell the truth" (Holy Qur'an, 2:111), and also in this one:

"Say: Do you have any knowledge with you so you should bring it forth to us? You only follow conjecture, and you only tell lies" (Holy Qur'an, 6:148).

For this reason, you see them resorting to cursing, taunting, lying and false charges, while they know fully well that the argument and the proof are with their Shi`a opponents! I think that they fear lest most Muslims should embrace Shi`ism if the facts are revealed as actually took place to some Egyptian scholars who graduated from al-Azhar and who permitted themselves to seek the truth. They did, indeed, find the truth. They did, indeed, see the light. And they did, indeed, abandon the beliefs they were nurtured by the "good predecessors."

Scholars among "Ahlul Sunnah wal Jama'ah" realize this danger which threatens their entity with dissolution. When they run out of tricks, therefore, some of them go as far as prohibiting their followers and imitators to be with the Shi'as, or to debate with them, or to marry their daughters, or to give their own daughters to them in marriage, or even to eat the meat of what they slaughter...

Such a stand is indicative of the fact that they are further from the Prophet's Sunnah than anything and closer to the "sunnah" of the Umayyads who exerted their efforts to mislead the nation of Muhammad at any cost because their hearts never really feared the mentioning of Allah's Name nor the truth which He revealed. Rather, they accepted Islam against their free will.

This is admitted by their "Imam" Mu`awiyah ibn Abu Sufyan who killed the best of *sahabah* only to become ruler; in the very first *khutba* which he delivered, he said, "I did not fight you so that you may pray, fast, or perform the pilgrimage; rather, I fought you in order to take charge of you, and Allah [?!] has granted it to me while you hate it." Allah has surely spoken the truth when He said,

"Surely when the kings enter a town, they ruin it and make the most noble of its people the very lowest, and thus do they (always) do" (Holy Qur'an, 27:34).

SHI'AS' ATTITUDE TOWARDS AHLUL SUNNAH WAL JAMA'AH

If we exclude some Shi`a fanatics who regard all "Ahlul Sunnah wal Jama'ah" to be Nasibis, the vast majority of their scholars in the past and the present believe that their brethren "Ahlul Sunnah wal Jama'ah" are the victims of Umayyad intrigues and cunning. This is so because they thought well of the "good predecessors," emulating them without researching or verifying their conduct.

The latter, hence, misled them from discerning al-Sirat al-Mustaqeem (the Straight Path) and distanced them from al-Thaqalayn, i.e. the Book of Allah and the Purified Progeny that safeguard whoever upholds them from misguidance and guarantee for him sure guidance.

For this reason, we find them defending themselves and informing others about their beliefs, calling for justice and equity and for unity with their brethren "Ahlul Sunnah wal Jama'ah." Some Shi`a scholars even toured various countries looking for means to establish Islamic organizations and institutions to close the gap between the sects and to bring about unity. Others went to al-Azhar al-Shareef, the lighthouse of knowledge and scholarship for "Ahlul Sunnah," and met with its scholars with whom they debated in the best manner, trying to remove the grudges.

One such scholar was Imam Sharaf al-Din Sadr ad-Din al-Musawi who met Imam Saleem al-Din al-Bishri, and the outcome of that meeting and the correspondence between both great men was the birth of the precious book titled *Al-Muraja`at*, a book which has played a significant role in narrowing Muslims' ideological differences.

The efforts of those scholars were also crowned with success in Egypt where Imam Mahmud Shaltut, the then grand *mufti* of

Egypt, issued his brave *fatwa* granting full legitimacy to adherence to the Shi`a Ja'fari sect, a sect the *fiqh* (jurisprudence) of which is now among the topics taught at al-Azhar al-Shareef.

Shi'as in general and Shi`a scholars in particular have been trying their best to introduce the Imams of the Purified Ahlul Bayt to others and to acquaint them with the Ja'fari sect which represents Islam in all what this word implies, writing volumes of books and articles, holding sessions, especially after the victory of the Islamic revolution in Iran, conducting numerous conferences in Tehran under the banner of the Islamic unity and the bridging of the gap between the Islamic sects. All these are sincere calls for the renunciation of enmity and animosity, and to instill the spirit of Islamic brotherhood, so that Muslims may respect one another.

In every year, "Mutamar al-Wahdah al-Islamiyya" (Islamic Unity Conference) invites Shi`a and Sunni scholars and thinkers to live one week under the shade of a sincere fraternity, to eat and drink together, to pray, supplicate, and exchange views and ideas, to give and take.

Had the only achievement of these conferences been creating unity and narrowing the gaps between Muslims so that they may know one another and remove their grudges, their good would be great, and their benefit overwhelming. They will, by the Will of Allah, the Lord of the Worlds, in the end bear the anticipated fruits.

If you enter the house of any ordinary Shi`a family, let alone the houses of their scholars and the educated among them, you will find in it a library containing, besides Shi`a works, a large number of books written by "Ahlul Sunnah wal Jama'ah," contrary to the case with the latter who very seldom keep a Shi`a book.

They, therefore, remain ignorant about the facts relevant to these Shi'as, not knowing anything but the lies written by the enemies of Shi'as. Even any ordinary Shi`a individual is most often familiar with the Islamic history in all its stages, and he may even celebrate some of its occasions.

As for the Sunni scholar, you will find him very seldom expressing interest in history which he regards among the tragedies he does not wish to dig up in order to be familiar with them; rather, he is of the view that neglecting them and not looking into them is a must because they will undermine the good impression held about the "good predecessors."

Since he has convinced, or misled, himself of the "justice" of all the *sahabah* and their integrity, he no longer accepts what history has recorded against them. For this reason, you find him unable to withstand any constructive discussion based on proof and argument. You will find him either running away from such a research due to his prior knowledge that he will be defeated, or he may overcome his feelings and emotions and force himself into researching; it is then that he rebels against all his beliefs, embracing, in the end, the faith of the Ahlul Bayt of the Prophet.

Shi'as are, indeed, the adherents to the Prophetic Sunnah because their first Imam after the Prophet is Ali ibn Abu Talib who lived and breathed the Prophetic Sunnah. Look at him and see how he reacted when they came to him seeking to swear the oath of allegiance to him as the new caliph on the condition that he should rule according to the "sunnah" of the *shaykhain* (the two shaykhs, namely Abu Bakr and Umar ibn al-Khattab), whereupon he said, "I shall not rule except according to the Book of Allah and the Sunnah of His Messenger."

Ali had no need for the caliphate if it was at the expense of the Prophetic Sunnah, for he is the one who had said, "Your caliphate to me is like a goat's sneeze except when I uphold one of the commandments of Allah." His son, Imam al-Husayn, has made his famous statement which is still ringing in the ears of history: "If

Muhammad's faith is to be straightened only if I am killed, then O swords! Take me!"

For this reason, Shi'as look at their brethren from "Ahlul Sunnah wal Jama'ah" with eyes of love and affection, desiring nothing for them except guidance and salvation. To them, the price of guidance is recorded by authentic traditions better than this life and everything in it.

The Messenger of Allah has said to Imam Ali upon sending him to conquer Khaybar, "Fight them till they testify that There is no god except Allah, and Muhammad is the Messenger of Allah; so if they utter it, their lives and wealth will be protected against your might, and Allah will judge them. If Allah guides through you even one single person, it is better for you than everything on which the sun shines (or better than all red camels)."[1]

Ali's main concern was, after all, to guide people and to bring them back to the Book of Allah and the Sunnah of His Messenger. For this reason, his Shi'as nowadays are mostly concerned about refuting all the charges and lies piled up against them, and about introducing to their brethren from "Ahlul Sunnah wal Jama'ah" the truth about Ahlul Bayt and, hence, guide them to the Straight Path.

Surely in the tales there is a lesson for men of understanding. It is not a narrative that could be forged but a verification of what is before it and a distinct explanation of all things, and a guide and mercy to those who believe. (Holy Qur'an, 12:111)

---

[1] Muslim, *Sahih*, Vol. 7, p. 122 "Kitab al-Fadail" (Book of Virtues), the chapter dealing with the merits of Ali ibn Abu Talib.

INTRODUCING THE IMAMS OF THE SHI'AS

Shi'as have confined their loyalty to the twelve Imams from Ahlul Bayt, peace be upon them, the first of whom is Ali ibn Abu Talib followed by his son al-Hasan then his son al-Husayn then the nine infallible ones among al-Husayn's offspring, peace and blessings of Allah be upon all of them.

The Messenger of Allah had named all these Imams in many of his statements either explicitly or implicitly, and he had mentioned them by name according to some traditions transmitted by the Shi'as and others transmitted by "Sunni" scholars.

Some of Ahlul Sunnah may object to these traditions, expressing astonishment at how the Messenger could have talked about issues related to the unknown which were enshrouded with non-existence. The Holy Qur'an states:

"Had I known the unseen, I would have had much of good and no evil would have touched me" (Holy Qur'an, 7:188).

To counter this argument, we say that this sacred verse does not exclude the Messenger from knowing the unseen at all; rather, it was revealed in response to some polytheists who asked him to inform them when the Hour would come, and the time of the Hour is the sole knowledge of Allah, Glory to Him, which He shares with nobody. The Holy Qur'an, on the other hand, clearly states:

"The One Who knows the unseen! So He does not reveal His secrets to anyone except to whomsoever He chooses (such) as an apostle" (Holy Qur'an, 72:26-27).

The exception to which this verse refers indicates that He, Glory to Him, acquaints His messengers whom He chooses with the knowledge of the unseen. For example, read what Joseph (Yusuf), peace be upon him, said to his prison inmates:

"No food shall come to you except that I will inform you of it before it reaches you; surely this is of what my Lord has taught me" (Holy Qur'an, 12:37).

Another example is this verse:

"Then they found one of Our servants whom We had granted mercy and whom We had taught knowledge from Us" (Holy Qur'an, 18:65).

This is a reference to the story of al-Khidr who met Moses and whom he taught of the knowledge of the unseen, the knowledge which he could not wait to know in time.

Muslims, be they Shi'as or Sunnis, did not dispute the fact that the Messenger of Allah used to know the unseen, and many incidents have been recorded in this regard such as his statement to Ammar: "O Ammar! The oppressive party shall kill you," and his statement to Ali: "The worst wretch among the generations to come is a man who will strike you (with the sword) on your head, so he will drench your beard (with your blood)."

He had also said to Ali, "My son al-Hasan will be the one through whom Allah will bring peace between two large parties." Another is his statement to Abu Dharr al-Ghifari in which he told him that he would die alone in banishment, and the list of such numerous incidents goes on and on. Among them is the famous tradition which al-Bukhari and Muslim and all those who succeeded them states: "The Imams after me are twelve: all of them will belong to Quraysh," and according to another narration, "all of them will be the offspring of Hashim."

In both our previous books *To be with the Truthful* [*Ma`a al-Sadiqin*] and *Ask Those Who Know* [*Fas'aloo Ahlul Dhikr*], we proved that Sunni scholars themselves have referred in their *Sahih* and *Musnad* books to the traditions relevant to the Imamate of the Twelve Imams, admitting their authenticity.

Someone may ask, "Why did they, then, set those traditions aside and followed the Imams of the four sects if they actually admitted the existence and the authenticity of those traditions?" The answer is: All the "good predecessors" were supporters of the three caliphs who reached caliphate through the *Saqifa* (the shed of Banu Sa`ida), namely Abu Bakr, Umar, and Uthman, so it was only natural that they should turn away from Ahlul Bayt and become enemies of Imam Ali and his offspring.

They, therefore, tried very hard to obliterate the Prophetic Sunnah and substitute it with their own *ijtihad*, personal viewpoints. This caused the division of the nation into two groups immediately following the death of the Messenger of Allah. Those among the "good predecessors" and those who followed them and adopted their attitudes represented "Ahlul Sunnah wal Jama'ah," who are the vast majority of the Muslim *Ummah*. A small minority which included Ali and his Shi'as boycotted the allegiance (to Abu Bakr) and rejected it, becoming the outcasts and the condemned. They were called Rafidis, rejectionists.

Due to the fact that "Ahlul Sunnah wal Jama'ah" were the ones who controlled the destiny of the Ummah across the centuries, the rulers from Banu Umayyah as well as those from Banu al-Abbas were all supporters and followers of the school of caliphate founded by Abu Bakr, Umar, Uthman, Mu`awiyah[1] and Yazid.

When that caliphate failed, its dignity was lost, ending in the hands of the Mamlukes and non-Arabs, and there were those who were heard calling for the documenting of the Prophetic Sunnah...,

---

[1] We have deliberately made no reference to the caliphate of Ali ibn Abu Talib because "Ahlul Sunnah wal Jama`ah" did not recognize it except during the time of Ahmad ibn Hanbal, as we have already indicated above; so, refer to the chapter with the heading "Ahlul Sunnah Are Not Familiar with the Prophetic Sunnah" in this book.

it was only then that such traditions, which former generations tried very energetically to obliterate and hide but could not do so, in addition to those particular traditions persisted as puzzles mystifying them: they contradicted their beliefs at that time.

Some of them tried to reconcile those traditions with their beliefs, so they pretended to love Ahlul Bayt; therefore, whenever the name of Imam Ali is mentioned, they would say, "May Allah be pleased with him," or "Allah glorified his countenance," so that people might get the impression that they were not the enemies of the House of Prophethood.

None among the Muslims, not even the hypocrites among them, can demonstrate his enmity towards the Prophet's family because the enemies of Ahlul Bayt are the enemies of the Messenger of Allah, and such enmity will eject them from the Islamic fold altogether as is obvious.

What we can understand from all of this is that they, in reality, are, indeed, enemies of the Prophet's family, and by "they" we mean the "good predecessors" who adopted the label of, or who were labelled by their supporters as, "Ahlul Sunnah wal Jama`ah." Another proof is that you can find all of them following the four sects which were created by the ruling authority (as we will soon prove), and they have nothing in their religious injunctions to which they can refer such as the *fiqh* of Ahlul Bayt, or of any of the Twelve Imams.

The truth mandates that Imamite Shi'as are actually the followers of the Sunnah of Muhammad because they upheld in all their juristic injunctions the teachings of the Imams of Ahlul Bayt who inherited the authentic Sunnah from their grandfather the Messenger of Allah without mixing it with their own personal views, opinions, or the statements of the caliphs.

The Shi'a: The Real Followers of the Sunnah

Shi'as remained across the centuries upholding these texts and rejecting the concept of *ijtihad* in the presence of clear traditions, believing in the caliphate of Ali and his offspring because the Prophet had clearly indicated so.

They, therefore, call them the caliphs of the Messenger of Allah although only Ali had the chance to be the actual caliph. They reject and refuse to recognize the rulers who held the caliphate from the beginning to the end because such caliphate was [in the words of Umar ibn al-Khattab himself] based on "a grave mistake from the evil of which Allah protected us," and because it came as a rejection and a renunciation of the texts stated by Allah and His Messenger. All those who came after that made such caliphate hereditary; each caliph ruled only because he was nominated by his predecessor or by fighting and winning the battle.[2]

Because of all this, "Ahlul Sunnah wal Jama'ah" were obligated to say that obedience was obligatory to both a good and a bad Imam; they accepted the caliphate of all their rulers, including the sinners among them.

Imamite Shi'as are characterized by preaching the necessity of the infallibility of the Imam; so, no major Imamate nor the leadership of the nation can be right except to an infallible Imam, and there is no human being in this nation who is infallible except those from whom Allah removed all abomination and whom He purified with a perfect purification [according to verse 33, Chapter 33, of the Holy Qur'an].

---

[2] The only exception is the caliphate of Ali ibn Abu Talib. Only he was not appointed by his predecessor, nor did he achieve it by fighting others and subduing them. Rather, Muslims chose him out of their free will to be their caliph, and they insisted on it when they invited him to rule.

IMAMS OF AHLUL SUNNAH WAL JAMA'AH

"Ahlul Sunnah wal Jama'ah" have followed the four Imams after whom their sects are known, namely Abu Hanifah, Malik, al-Shafi`i, and Ahmad ibn Hanbal.

These four Imams were never among the *sahabah* of the Messenger of Allah, nor did they know him, nor did he see them, nor did they ever see him. Their senior in age is Abu Hanifah whose time is separated from that of the Prophet by more than a hundred years: he was born in 80 A.H./699 A.D. and died in 160 A.H./777 A.D. Their youngest is Ahmad ibn Hanbal: he was born in 165 and died in 241 A.H. (782 – 855 A.D.). All this is in reference to the religion's branches (*furu` al-din*).

As for the roots of the creed (*usul al-din*), "Ahlul Sunnah wal Jama'ah" refer to Imam Abul-Hasan Ali ibn Isma`eel al-Ash`ari who was born in 270 A.H. and died in 335 A.H. (883 - 946 A.D.)

These are the Imams of "Ahlul Sunnah wal Jama'ah" to whom the latter refer with regard to the roots and branches of their creed. Do you find any of the Imams of Ahlul Bayt among them? Or do you find among them anyone who was a companion of the Messenger of Allah, or about whom the Messenger of Allah said that he is the most wise person to lead the nation? Of course not! There is nothing like that at all.

If "Ahlul Sunnah wal Jama'ah" claim that they uphold the Prophet's Sunnah, why did these sects appear so late in time after the Prophet's demise, and where were "Ahlul Sunnah wal Jama'ah" before the existence of these sects, and what religion were they following, and to whom were they referring?!

Having asked these questions, let us add this one: "How can they be so dedicated to men who were neither contemporary to the Prophet nor did they ever know him but who were born after the dissension had already taken place, and after the companions fought and killed one another, charging one another with apostacy, and after the caliphs treated the Holy Qur'an and the Sunnah according to their own *ijtihad*, their own personal views?"

Having taken control of the reins of government, Yazid violated the sanctity of sacred Medina, giving his army permission to wreak whatever havoc it desired in it, so the said army inflicted death and destruction in it, killing the best among the *sahabah* who refused to swear the oath of allegiance to him, raping chaste women to the extent that there were many who were born thus illegitimately.

How can any wise person place his trust in these imams who belong to such type of human beings who waded in the mud of dissension, who were colored by its various hues, who grew up mastering its cunning and cunniving, vesting upon themselves the false medals of knowledge and scholarship? Indeed, no scholar ever rose to distinction except one with whom the government was pleased and who was pleased with the government.[1]

How can anyone who claims to adhere to the Sunnah forsake Imam Ali, the gate of knowledge, or Imams al-Hasan and al-Husayn, masters of the youths of Paradise, or other purified Imams from the progeny of the Prophet who had inherited the knowledge of the Messenger of Allah, and prefer to follow "Imams" who were not knowledgeable of the Prophetic Sunnah but were the product of Umayyad politics?

How can "Ahlul Sunnah wal Jama'ah" claim that they follow the Prophetic Sunnah while neglecting those who safeguard it? How can they abandon the recommendations and explicit orders of

---

[1] In the coming researches, you will *InshaAllah* come to find out that Umayyad and ʾAbbaside rulers were the very people who brought those sects to existence and forced people to follow them.

the Prophet to uphold the Purified Progeny then claim to be the ones who follow the Sunnah?!

Can any Muslim individual who is familiar with the Islamic history, the Holy Qur'an, and the Sunnah, doubt the fact that "Ahlul Sunnah wal Jama'ah" are followers of the Umayyads and Abbasides?

And can any Muslim who is familiar with the Holy Qur'an and Sunnah, and who has come to know the Islamic history, deny the fact that the Shi'as who emulate and pay homage to the Progeny of the Prophet are, indeed, followers of the Prophetic Sunnah, whereas nobody else can claim to do so?

Have you seen, dear reader, how politics turns matters upside down, making right look wrong and *vice versa*?! Those who remained loyal to the Prophet and his Progeny came to be called Rafidis and people of innovations, while those who excelled in inventing innovations and renounced the Sunnah of the Prophet and his Progeny, following the *ijtihad* of their oppressive rulers, came to be called "Ahlul Sunnah wal Jama`a"?! This is truly strange.

As for me, I firmly believe that Quraysh was behind this label, and it is one of its secrets and riddles.

We have already come to know that Quraysh was the one that prohibited Abdullah ibn Umar from writing the Prophetic Sunnah down in the pretext that the Prophet was not infallible. Quraysh, in fact, is comprised of specific individuals who wielded a great deal of influence, and who were known for their fanaticism and powerful influence over Arab tribes. Some historians call them "the most shrewd Arabs" due to their reputation in cunning and conniving and superiority in managing the affairs, whereas others call them "the people who tie and untie."

Among them are: Abu Bakr, Umar, Uthman, Abu Sufyan and his son Mu`awiyah, Amr ibn al-As, al-Mugheerah ibn Shu`bah,

Marwan ibn al-Hakam, Talhah ibn Ubaydullah, Abdul-Rahman ibn Awf, Abu Ubaydah Amir ibn al-Jarrah, and many others.[2]

These "shrewd men" used to meet to discuss and decide something upon which they would eventually agree, then they would make up their mind to propagate it among the people so that it might become thereafter a matter of fact and a followed reality, without most people knowing how it came to be.

One such scheme, which they plotted, was their claim that Muhammad was not infallible, and that he was as human as anyone else: he could err, they claimed, so they would belittle him and argue with him about the truth while fully knowing it. And among such schemes was their cursing Ali ibn Abu Talib and using a misnomer for him, calling him "Abu Turab" (father of dust), portraying him to people as the enemy of Allah and His Messenger.

Another is their taunting and cursing the highly respected *sahabi* Ammar ibn Yasir, using for him a borrowed name: "Abdullah ibn Saba'" simply because Ammar opposed the caliphs and was calling people to the Imamate of Ali ibn Abu Talib.[3]

---

[2] We have excluded from this list Imam Ali because he distinguished between shrewd judgment and good management, between the shrewdness of cunning, deception and hypocrisy. He has said more than once, "Had it not been for deception and hypocrisy, I would have been ranked the most shrewd person among the Arabs," as stated in the Holy Qur'an: "They plan, and Allah plans, and surely Allah is the best of planners." Allah's plans mean wisdom and good management. As for the polytheists' plans, they are nothing but deception, hypocrisy, swindling, forgery, and falsehood.

[3] For more details, refer to *Al-Sila bayn al-Tasawwuf wal Tashayyu`* by Dr. Mustafa Kamil al-Shibeebi, an Egyptian author. By bringing ten strong arguments, al-Shibeebi proves that Abdullah ibn Saba', the Jew, or "Ibn al-Sawdaa'" (son of the black woman) was a pseudonym and title maliciously given to Ammar ibn Yasir because he was a follower of Imam Ali.

Another was their calling the Shi'as who were loyal to Ali "Rafidis" in order to mislead the public by giving them the impression that the latter had rejected Muhammad and followed Ali.

Another is calling themselves "Ahlul Sunnah wal Jama'ah" in order to mislead sincere believers into thinking that only they are the ones who uphold the Prophet's Sunnah *versus* the Rafidis who reject it.

They, in fact, mean by their "Sunnah" the infamous innovation which they invented: the custom of cursing and condemning the Commander of the Faithful and the Prophet's Progeny from the pulpits in every mosque throughout the Muslim world and in all other lands, cities, and villages where Muslims lived. This innovation lasted for eighty years. Whenever one of their preachers descended from the pulpit before leading the prayers, he would curse Ali ibn Abu Talib, and if he did not, everyone at the mosque would yell at him: *Tarakatal Sunnah! Tarakatal Sunnah!* ("You left out the Sunnah!).

When caliph Umar ibn Abd al-Aziz wanted to change that "Sunnah" with the Qur'anic verse saying,

"Surely Allah enjoins the effecting of equity and of goodness (to others) and the giving (in charity) to the kindred" (Holy Quran, 16:90),

they plotted against him and killed him for killing their "Sunnah" and taking lightly the statements of his predecessors who had brought him to caliphate. They poisoned him when he was only thirty-eight years old, having ruled no more than two years. He became the victim of his reform because his cousins, the Umayyads, did not agree to his laying their "Sunnah" to rest and thus raising the status of "Abu Turab" and the Imams among his offspring.

After the fall of the Umayyad government, the Abbasides came and persecuted the Imams from Ahlul Bayt and their followers till the reign of Ja`far son of al-Mu`tasim, who was titled "al-Mutawakkil," came, and he proved to be the most bitter enemy of Ali and his offspring. His hatred and animosity caused him to desecrate the grave of Imam Husayn in Karbala. He prohibited people from visiting it[4], and he never gave anything nor was he generous to anyone except to those who cursed Ali and his offspring.

The incident involving al-Mutawakkil and the famous scholar of linguistics `*Allama* Ibn al-Sikkeet is well known. He killed him in the very worst manner, cutting his tongue off when he discovered that he was a follower of Ali and his Ahlul Bayt, although he was the tutor of both of his [al-Mutawakkil's] sons.

Al-Mutawakkil's animosity towards Ali and his adherence to Nasibism went as far as killing any new born named "Ali" because it was the most hateful name to him. When Ali ibn al-Jahm, the poet, met al-Mutawakkil, he said, "O commander of the faithful! My parents have done me a great deal of injustice." Al-Mutawakkil asked him, "How so?" He said, "They named me Ali although I hate this name and anyone named by it." Al-Mutawakkil laughed and ordered him to be richly rewarded.

One man used to live inside al-Mutawakkil's meeting house. He was an entertaining buffoon who used to mimic Ali ibn Abu Talib and thus make fun of him. Upon seeing him, people would laugh and say, "Here comes the bald man, the man with the big

---

[4] If the caliph went that far in meanness and lowliness to the extent that he dug up the graves of the Imams from Ahlul Bayt, especially that of the master of the youths of Paradise, do not ask beyond that what they did to the Shi`as who used to seek Allah's blessings by visiting that grave. The Shi`as suffered the ultimate pain and tribulation.

stomach!" So he would be ridiculed by everyone meeting there to the delight and amusement of the caliph.

We must not forget in this regard to point out to the fact that this al-Mutawakkil, whose animosity towards Ali revealed his hypocrisy and promiscuity, was very much loved by the scholars of *hadith* who vested upon him the title of "Muhyyi al-Sunnah," the one who revived the Sunnah. And since those scholars of *hadith* were themselves "Ahlul Sunnah wal Jama'ah," it is proven by the evidence which has no room for any doubt that what they meant by the "Sunnah" was simply hating Ali ibn Abu Talib and cursing him and dissociating themselves from him; it is, in a word, Nasibism.

What makes this matter more clear is that al-Khawarizmi says the following on p. 135 of his book: "Even Haroun ibn al-Khayzaran and Ja`far al-Mutawakkil *alal-shaitan* (the one who relies on Satan), rather than on al-Rahman (the Merciful One), used not to give any money or wealth except to those who cursed the family of Abu Talib and who supported the sect of the Nasibis."

Ibn Hajar has quoted Abdullah ibn Ahmad ibn Hanbal saying, "When Nasr ibn Ali ibn Sahban narrated a tradition saying that the Messenger of Allah took the hand of al-Hasan and al-Husayn and said, `Whoever loves me and loves both of these men and their parents will be in my level on the Day of Judgment,' al-Mutawakkil ordered him to be whipped one thousand lashes. He almost died had Ja`far ibn Abd al-Wahid not kept interceding on his behalf with al-Mutawakkil, saying to him, `O commander of the faithful! He is one of Ahlul Sunnah,' and he persisted in doing so till he (Nasr) was left alone."[5]

---

[5] This is quoted in Ibn Hajar's *Tahdhib al-Tahdhib*, in his biography of Nasr ibn Ali ibn Sahban.

Any wise person will understand the statement made by Ja`far ibn Abd al-Wahid to al-Mutawakkil that Nasr was among "Ahlul Sunnah," in order to save his life, to be an additional testimony to the fact that Ahlul Sunnah are the enemies of Ahlul Bayt who are hated by al-Mutawakkil. The latter used to kill anyone who mentioned even one of their merits even if he was not a Shi`a.

Ibn Hajar indicates in the same book that Abdullah ibn Idris al-Azdi was a man of "al-Sunnah wal Jama'ah," that he was very strict in upholding the "Sunnah," pleasing others, and that he sympathized with Uthman.[6]

About Abdullah ibn Awn al-Basri, the [same Sunni] author says: "He is held as reliable, and he used to be consistent in his worship, very firm in upholding the Sunnah, and in being tough against the people who invent innovations; Ibn Sa'd says that he was a supporter of Uthman."[7] He has also indicated that Ibrahim ibn Ya`qub al-Jawzjani used to follow the Hareezi sect (i.e. the sect founded by Hareez ibn Uthman al-Dimashqi), who was well known for adhering to the beliefs of the Nasibis, and Ibn Hayyan has said, "He was very zealous in adhering to the Sunnah."[8]

All this makes us draw the conclusion that Nasibism and hatred towards Ali and his offspring, the cursing of the descendants of Abu Talib, the condemning of Ahlul Bayt..., is regarded by them as "zeal in adhering to the Sunnah." We have also come to know so far that the supporters of Uthman are the ones who promoted Nasibism and hatred towards Ahlul Bayt, and they are the ones who

---

[6] Ibn Hajar, *Tahdhib al-Tahdhib*, Vo. 5, p. 145. It is a well-known fact that those who sympathized with Uthman used to curse Ali and accuse him of killing Uthman ibn Affan.

[7] Ibn Hajar, *Tahdhib al-Tahdhib*, Vol. 8, p. 348.

[8] *Ibid.*, Vol. 1, p. 82.

were very tough with anyone who was loyal to Ali and his offspring.

The label of "innovators" was attached by them to the Shi'as who called for the Imamate of Ali because, to them, that was an innovation, since it disagreed with the policies of the "righteous caliphs" and the "good predecessors," the policy of expelling the Imam and not recognizing his Imamate and Wisayat.

Historical facts supporting this statement are quite abundant, but what we have already stated here should suffice those who wish to research this issue further and investigate it on their own. We have, as has always been our habit, tried to be brief, and researchers have to keep in mind that they can find many times this much if they wish.

(As for) those who struggle hard for Us, We will most certainly guide them in Our ways, and Allah is most surely with the doers of good. (Holy Qur'an, 29:69)

THE PROPHET APPOINTED THE IMAMS OF THE SHI'AS

No researcher who has studied the biography of the Prophet, and who become familiar with the Islamic history, doubts the fact that the Prophet was the one who appointed the Twelve Imams, clearly stating so in order that they might succeed him and take charge of his nation.

Their number is mentioned in the *Sahih* books of Ahlul Sunnah together with the fact that they were twelve in number, and that all of them descended from Quraysh; this is what al-Bukhari and Muslim, as well as many others, have confirmed. Some Sunni references indicate that the Prophet named all of them, saying that the first of them was Ali ibn Abu Talib, followed by his son al-Hasan then al-Hasan's brother al-Husayn, followed by nine from the offspring of al-Husayn the last of whom is al-Mahdi.

The [Sunni] author of *Yanabi' al-Mawaddah*[1] narrates the following incident in his book:

---

[1] Abul-Qasim Mahmud ibn Muhammad ibn Ahmad al-Khawarizmi al-Zamakhshari was a great scholar and instructor in exegesis, hadith, Arabic grammar, and logic. He was born on a Wednesday in the month of Rajab, 367 A.H./978 A.D. in the village of Zamakhshar in the area of Khawarizm. He died in Jurjan on the eve of Arafat, Thul Hijjah 9, 538 A.H./June 20, 1144 A.D. He was a Mu`tazilite who followed the Hanafi sect. He wrote more than a hundred excellent books some of which are still in manuscript form waiting to be published. He was characterized by his love for justice and equity and renunciation of any type of fanaticism. Though Hanafi in his beliefs, he wrote an excellent book in which he compiled numerous statements made by Imam al-Shafi`i titled Shari al-`Ay (healer of mental blocks). May Allah have mercy on the soul of this great man and on the souls of all great men, Allahomma, Ameen. __ Tr.

A Jew named al-A'tal came to the Prophet and said, "Muhammad! I wish to ask you about certain things which I have been keeping to myself; so, if you answer them, I shall declare my acceptance of Islam before you." The Prophet said, "Ask me, O father of Imarah!"

So he asked him about many things till he was satisfied and admitted that the Prophet was right. Then he said, "Tell me about your *wasi* (successor): who is he? No prophet can ever be without a *wasi*; our prophet Moses had appointed Yusha` [Joshua] son of Noon as his successor." He said, "My *wasi* is Ali ibn Abu Talib followed by my grandsons al-Hasan and al-Husayn followed by nine men from the loins of al-Husayn." He said, "Then name them for me, O Muhammad!"

The Prophet said, "Once al-Husayn departs, he will be succeeded by his son Ali; when Ali departs, his son Muhammad will succeed him. When Muhammad departs, his son Ja`far will succeed him. When Ja`far departs, he will be succeeded by his son Musa. When Musa departs, his son Ali will succeed him. When Ali departs, his son Muhammad will succeed him.

When Muhammad departs, his son Ali will succeed him. When Ali departs, his son al-Hasan will succeed him, and when al-Hasan departs, al-Hujjah Muhammad al-Mahdi will succeed him. These are the twelve ones." That Jew, therefore, embraced Islam and praised Allah for having guided him.[2]

If we wish to turn the pages of Shi`a books and discern the facts they contain with regard to this subject, we will surely find many times as many *ahadith* as this one, but this suffices to prove

---

[2] This is recorded on p. 440 of *Yanabi` al-Mawaddah* by the Hanafi author al-Qandoozi. It is also recorded by al-Hamawayni [another Sunni scholar] who quotes Mujahid quoting Ibn Abbas.

that the scholars of "Ahlul Sunnah wal Jama'ah" admit that the number of the Imams is twelve, and there are no such Imams besides Ali and his purified offspring.

What strengthens our conviction that the Twelve Imams from Ahlul Bayt were never tutored by any of the Ummah's scholars is the fact that no historian, nor traditionist, nor biographer, has ever narrated saying that one of the Imams from Ahlul Bayt learned what he knew from some *sahabah* or *tabi'in* as is the case with all the Ummah's scholars and Imams.

Abu Hanifah, for example, was a student of Imam Ja'far al-Sadiq; Malik was a student of Abu Hanifah; al-Shafi'i learned from Malik and so did Ahmad ibn Hanbal. As for the Imams from Ahlul Bayt, their knowledge is gifted by Allah, Glory and Exaltation to Him, and they inherit such knowledge son from father, for they are the ones to whom the Almighty specifically refers when He says,

"Then We gave the Book for an inheritance to those whom We chose from Our servants" (Holy Qur'an, 35:32).

Imam Ja'far al-Sadiq has expressed this fact once when he said, "How strange some people are! They say that they derived all their knowledge from the Messenger of Allah, so they acted upon it and were guided! And they narrate saying that we, Ahlul Bayt, did not learn any knowledge, nor were we thereby guided, while we are his family and offspring: in our homes did the revelation descend; from us was knowledge imparted to people! Have they really learned and were guided while we remained in ignorance and misguidance?!"

How can Imam al-Sadiq not wonder at those who claimed to have learned from the Messenger of Allah while they bear grudge and animosity to his Ahlul Bayt and the gates of his knowledge which lead to such knowledge?! How can he help expressing such amazement at calling themselves Ahlul Sunnah while they do the opposite of what this Sunnah contains?!

If the Shi'as, as history testifies, have chosen Ali to support and defend against his enemies, fighting with him, concluding peace whenever he concluded it, learning all what they knew from him, "Ahlul Sunnah wal Jama'ah," contrariwise, were never his supporters, followers, or helpers.

Rather, they fought him and desired to put an end to him. Having killed him, they pursued his sons in order to kill, jail, or expel them. They oppose him in most *ahkam* (religious rulings) by following those who held views different from his, and who followed their own *ijtihad* with regard to Allah's commandments, changing them according to their wishes and to serve their own interests.

How can we nowadays help wondering about those who claim to adhere to the Prophet's Sunnah while they testify against themselves that they, indeed, abandoned the Prophet's Sunnah because it became the identification mark of the Shi'as?![3] Is this not strange?!

How can we help wondering about those who claim to be "Ahlul Sunnah wal Jama'ah" (people who follow the path of the Prophet [P] and who follow the consensus) while there are many Maliki, Hanafi, Shafi'i, and Hanbali groups, each opposing the other with regard to the jurisdic injunctions, claiming that such differences are mercy to them? Is it merc to change Allah's religion to fit certain people's wishes, views, and desires...?!

---

[3] For more details on this matter, refer to pp. 159-160 of my book *To be with the Truthful* where you will come to know that Ibn Taymiyyah calls for abandoning the Prophet's Sunnah because it became the banner of the Shi`as. Yet they call him mujaddid al-Sunnah, the one who revived the Sunnah!

Yes, they are various groups who disagreed among themselves in interpreting the commandments of Allah and His Messenger, yet they are united in endorsing the injustice that took place at the *Saqifa* of Banu Sa`ida, and in abandoning and isolating the Purified Progeny of the Prophet.

How can we help wondering about those who boast of being Ahlul Sunnah while they have abandoned the order of the Messenger of Allah to uphold the Two Weighty Things: the Book of Allah and his Progeny, despite their documentation of this particular tradition and their admission of its authenticity?!

They, indeed, upheld neither the Holy Qur'an nor the Progeny because by forsaking the Purified Progeny, they forsook the Holy Qur'an, too, since the sacred tradition indicates that the Holy Qur'an and the Progeny shall never part from one another, as the Messenger of Allah clearly stated: "And the most Benevolent and Knowing has informed me that they (the Holy Qur'an and the Progeny) shall never part till they join me at the Pool."?![4]

How can we help wondering about people who claim to be the custodians of the Sunnah while their conduct, in fact, is contrary to what their own books classify as "authentic" Sunnah of the Prophet, of what he had done, ordered, or prohibited?[5]

---

[4] Imam Ahmad ibn Hanbal, *Musnad*, Vol. 5, p. 189, and also al-Hakim, *Mustadrak*, Vol. 3, p. 148. Al-Hakim comments thus: "This is an authentic tradition which both Shaykhs [al-Bukhari and Muslim] had verified and did not exclude (from their own books). Al-Dhahabi, too, has classified it as authentic in his book *Al-Talkhees*, admitting its authenticity, relying in doing so on both Shaykhs' endorsement."

[5] In his *Sahih*, al-Bukhari states that the Prophet prohibited congregational *taraweeh* prayers during the month of Ramadan, saying, "Offer prayers, O people, at your own homes, for the best prayers one can offer are the ones which he offers at home with the exception of obligatory prayers." But

But if we do believe in this tradition and in its authenticity, that is, the *hadith* saying, "I have left among you the Book of Allah and my Sunnah: so long as you uphold them (both), you shall never stray after me at all," as some Ahlul Sunnah like to word it nowadays, our amazement will be even greater, and the scandal will be even more obvious:

It is so due to the fact that their own dignitaries and imams are the ones who burnt the Sunnah which the Messenger of Allah had left behind for them, prohibiting everyone from copying it or transporting its texts, as we have already indicated above.

The said statement by Umar ibn al-Khattab is included in all *Sahih* books of "Ahlul Sunnah," including al-Bukhari and Muslim. [On his death bed] the Prophet said, "I have left among you the Book of Allah and my Sunnah," whereupon Umar said to him, "The Book of Allah suffices us, and we have no need for your Sunnah."

If Umar said so in the presence of the Prophet, Abu Bakr emphatically acted upon the view of his friend. And when he became caliph, Abu Bakr said, "Do not narrate any *hadith* of the Messenger of Allah, for whoever asks you, say to him, 'Between us and you is the Book of Allah, so act upon what it permits and abstain from what it prohibits.'"[6]

How can we help wondering about people who abandoned the Sunnah of their Prophet and left it behind their backs, substituting it with innovations for which Allah never sent any proof, then they call themselves and their followers "Ahlul Sunnah wal Jama`a"?!

Ahlul Sunnah ignored the Prophet's prohibition and followed the innovation started by Umar ibn al-Khattab.

[6] Al-Dhahabi, *Tadhkirat al-Huffaz*, Vol. 1, p. 3.

But our amazement disappears when we come to know that Abu Bakr, Umar and Uthman never heard such a label at all; Abu Bakr said once, "If you require me to implement the Sunnah of your Prophet, I cannot withstand it."[7]

How is it possible that Abu Bakr could not withstand the Sunnah of the Prophet?! Was the Prophet's Sunnah something impossible so Abu Bakr could not withstand it?! And how can Ahlul Sunnah claim that they uphold it if their first imam and the founder of their sect could not withstand it?!

Allah has said in its regard the following verses:

"You surely have in the Messenger of Allah a good example." (Holy Qur'an, 33:21)

"Allah never places a burden on a soul more than what it can bear." (Holy Qur'an, 65:7)

"He has not laid down upon you any hardship in religion." (Holy Qur'an, 22:78)

Did Abu Bakr and his friend Umar think that the Messenger of Allah invented a creed other than what Allah had revealed, so he ordered the Muslims to do what they could not, thus overburdening them?

Far from him is such an allegation, for he used to quite often say, "Disseminate glad tidings; make things easy, and do not make them hard. Allah has granted you an ease, so do not make things hard for yourselves." But Abu Bakr's admission that he could not tolerate the Prophet's Sunnah underlines our conclusion that he invented an innovation which he could "withstand" or "tolerate"

---

[7] Imam Ahmad ibn Hanbal, *Musnad*, Vol. 1, p. 4, and also on p. 126, Vol. 3, of *Kanz al-Ummal*.

according to his own wishes, one which agreed with the policies of the state he headed.

As for Mu'awiyah, he always opposed the Holy Qur'an and the Sunnah and challenged them. For example, while the Prophet said, "Ali is of me and I am of Ali; whoever curses Ali cruses me, and whoever curses me curses Allah,"[8] you find Mu'awiyah going to extremes in cursing and condemning Ali.

He was not satisfied with doing all of that, so he ordered all his governors and officials to curse and condemn him, and he dismissed from office then killed all those who refused. It was this Mu'awiyah who called himself and his followers "Ahlul Sunnah wal Jama'ah" in order to distinguish themselves from those who were referred to as the Shi'as, claiming thus to be the ones on the right track.

Some historians indicate that the year in which Mu'awiyah took control of the Islamic caliphate, after having concluded a peace treaty with Imam al-Hasan ibn Ali ibn Abu Talib, was called `Aam al-jama`ah, the year of the Jama`ah.

Amazement is dispelled when we understand that the word "Sunnah" according to the thinking of Mu'awiyah and his *jama`ah*, his group, was none other than the custom of cursing Ali ibn Abu Talib from the Muslims' pulpits during Fridays and Eid days. If such "Sunnah" was an invention of Mu'awiyah ibn Abu Sufyan, we plead to the most Glorified One to permit us to die following the *bid`at*, innovation, of Rafidism founded by Ali ibn Abu Talib and Ahlul Bayt!

Do not be surprised, dear reader, when you see how those who were expert in innovations and misguidnce call themselves "Ahlul

---

[8] Al-Hakim, *Mustadrak*, Vol. 3, p. 121; Ahmad ibn Hanbal, *Musnad*, Vol. 6, p. 323, Vol. 6; and al-Nasa'i, *Khasais*, p. 17.

Sunnah wal Jama'ah" while the Imams from Ahlul Bayt are charged with innovations.

Here is the great mentor Ibn Khaldun, one of the most famous scholars of "Ahlul Sunnah wal Jama'ah," insolently says, after having counted the sects of the majority, "And Ahlul Bayt became the exception to the rule through sects which they invented and *fiqh* which is totally their own, one which they built on their sect, a sect which criticizes a number of the *sahabah*."[9]

---

[9] This is stated on p. 494, in the part dealing with the science of fiqh and the injunctions upon which they are based, of Ibn Khaldun's *Muqaddimah* (Introduction).

OPPRESSIVE RULERS APPOINTED THE IMAMS OF AHLUL SUNNAH

What proves that the Imams of the four "Sunni" sects, too, acted in contradiction to the Book of Allah and the Sunnah of His Messenger who commanded them to follow the Purified Progeny, is that we could not find even one person among them who obeyed such a command, boarded their ship, and came to know who the Imam of his time was.

Abu Hanifah al-Nu`man, was a student of Imam al-Sadiq. He is famous for having said: *Lawla al sanatan, la halaka al-Nu`man*, that is, "Had it not been for those couple of years [during which he was a student of the Imam, as], al-Nu`man would have perished." Yet we find him inventing a sect based on analogy and the derivation of one's own opinion in opposition to the available clear *ahadith*.

Malik, who also learned from Imam al-Sadiq, is quoted saying, "No eyes have ever seen, nor ears have ever heard, nor anyone was ever impressed by anyone more acquainted with jurisprudence, or more learned, than Ja`far al-Sadiq."

Yet we find him, too, inventing an Islamic sect of his own, abandoning the Imam of his time for whom he testifies as being the most knowledgeable and the best informed of all people of his time with regard to jurisprudence. The fact is that the Abbasides who held the reins of authority propped him up and called him "Imam Dar al-Hijra," hence he became thereafter the man of influence and authority, the man whose word wielded a great deal of influence on people.

Al-Shafi`i, who is accused of being a follower of Ahlul Bayt, has said the following lines of poetry in their praise:

O Household of Allah's Messenger! Loving you is an obligation

Which Allah has enforced in His Honored Revelation;

Suffices you a great honor if one sends no prayer unto you all,

It will be as though he did not say his prayers at all.

And the following verses lauding them are also attributed to him:

When I saw people being carried away to the seas

Of misguidance and ignorance by their creeds, I boarded, in the Name of Allah, the Ark of Salvation:

The Household of the Prophet, the Seal of Revelation.

And I upheld Allah's Rope: them shall I obey and hope, That I obey the One Who commanded us to uphold His Rope.

He is also famous for having said these lines:

If one loving Muhammad's family is rebuked and called a Rafidi, Then O jinns and mankind: Testify That: Yes! A Rafidi am I!

If the jinns and mankind are to testify that he is Rafidi, then why did he follow the sects which were established to oppose Ahlul Bayt?! Rather, he himself, like the others, invented a sect carrying his own name, abandoning the Imams of Ahlul Bayt to whom he was a contemporary.

Ahmad ibn Hanbal made the name of Ali the fourth in the list of the "righteous caliphs," after being rejected as such. He wrote a book recounting Ali's merits. He became famous for having said, "Nobody among the *sahabah*, according to all authentic *musnads*, has as many virtues as Ali, may Allah be pleased with him..."

Yet he himself invented an Islamic sect called "al-Hanbali" despite the testimony of his contemporary scholars that he was not a *faqih* at all. Shaykh Abu Zuhra has said, "Many scholars of earlier times never counted Ahmad ibn Hanbal as a jurist; among them was Ibn Qutaybah, whose time was very close to that of Ahmad, and Ibn Jarir al-Tabari, and others."[1]

Then Ibn Taymiyyah came to lift the banner of the Hanbali sect. He incorporated into it some new theories which, among other things, prohibited the visiting of graves or the building of structures over them, or the seeking of nearness to Allah through the Prophet and his Ahlul Bayt; all of the above constituted, according to him, *shirk*, polytheism.

These are the four sects, and these are their imams and what they have said about the Purified Progeny of Ahlul Bayt.

So, they either say what they do not do, which is a big abomination very much hated by Allah, or they may not have invented these sects at all but, rather, their own followers among the henchmen of the Umayyads and Abbasides were the ones who founded them with the help of oppressive rulers then attributed them to these imams after the latter's death. This you will come to know, *InshaAllah*, in the next researches.

Are you not amazed about these imams who were contemporary to the Imams of guidance from Ahlul Bayt, then they turned away from the latter's Straight Path and were not guided by their guidance, nor were they enlightened by their light, nor did they prefer their *hadith* which quotes their grandfather the Messenger of Allah ? Rather, they preferred over them Ka`b al-Ahbar, a Jew, and Abu Hurayra the Dawsi about whom the Commander of the Faithful Imam Ali ibn Abu Talib has said, "The person who told the worst lies about the Messenger of Allah is Abu Hurayra al-Dawsi"?!

Hazrat Ayesha said the same about him. And they prefer over them Abdullah ibn Umar who was famous for his hatred of Imam

---

[1] This is recorded on p. 170 of Abu Zuhra's book Ahmad ibn Hanbal.

Ali, and who refused to swear the oath of allegiance to him, preferring to swear allegiance to the leader of misguidance al-Hajjaj ibn Yusuf al-Thaqafi instead. And they prefer over them Amr ibn al-As, Mu`awiyah's minister of deception and hypocrisy.

Do you not wonder how these imams granted themselves the authority to be the jurists of Allah's creed through their own views and personal opinions till they put an end to the Prophet's Sunnah through what they introduced of analogy and the belief in the sanctity of all the *sahabah*, closing the door of evidence and that of the public's secured interests, etc., up to the end of the list of their innovations for which Allah never sent down any proof?

Did Allah and His Messenger neglect the completing of the creed, permitting these men to complete it through their own *ijtihad* and permit and prohibit as they pleased?!

Do you not wonder about the Muslims who claim to uphold the "Sunnah" how they follow men who never knew the Prophet, nor did he know them?!

Do they have a proof from the Book of Allah, or from the Sunnah of His Messenger permitting them to follow and emulate those four Imams who founded those sects?!

I challenge the *thaqalayn*, the two species of mankind and the jinns, to bring about one single evidence for the above from the Book of Allah or from the Sunnah of His Messenger... No, by Allah! No! They will never be able to bring it about even if they assist one another.

No, by Allah! There is not a single proof in the Book of Allah, nor in the Sunnah of His Messenger, except to follow and emulate the Purified Imams from the Prophet's Progeny, peace of Allah and His blessings upon him and them. How to prove this can be done through numerous arguments, convincing proofs, and glorious facts.

So learn a lesson, O people who have vision! (Holy Qur'an, 59:2)

Surely it is not the eyes that are blind, but blind are the hearts that are in the breasts. (Holy Qur'an, 22:46)

THE SECRET WHY SUNNI SECTS ARE IN THE MAJORITY

One who researches history books and what is recorded by the predecessors will discover beyond any doubt that the reason why the four "Sunni" sects prevailed during those times is that it was due to the will and the management of the ruling authorities; it is for this reason that their followers are numerous, for people follow the creed of their rulers.

Such researchers will also find out that scores of sects came and disappeared because the rulers were not pleased with them, so they melted. Among them is the Awza`i sect, the sects founded by Hasan al-Basri, Abu Ayeenah and Ibn Abu Thuayb, Sufyan al-Thawri, Ibn Abu Dawood, Layth ibn Sa'd, and many others.

For example, Layth ibn Sa'd was a friend of Malik ibn Anas and was more knowledgeable and a better jurist than the latter according to the admission of Imam al-Shafi`i himself.[1] Yet his sect eroded, and his *fiqh* melted and went into oblivion because his contemporary government was not pleased with him. Ahmad ibn Hanbal has said, "Ibn Abu Thuayb is better than Malik ibn Anas except that Malik was more selective when choosing his friends."[2]

If we refer to history, we will find Malik, the one who established a sect bearing his name, sought to be close to the government and its rulers, making peace with them and following them. He, therefore, became the highly respected man and the famous scholar, and his sect was disseminated through the methods of both terrorizing and attracting people particularly in Andalusia where his student Yahya ibn Yahya went to lengths in befriending the ruler of Andalus. Because of that, he became one of the latter's

---

[1] Such admission is recorded on p. 524 of *al-Shafi`i's Manaqib*.
[2] *Tadhkirat al-Huffaz*, Vol. 1, p. 176.

favorite men. The said ruler rewarded him with the position of judge, since he never appointed anybody as a judge except one of his Maliki friends.

We also find out the fact that the reason why Abu Hanifah's sect was propagated after its founder's death because Abu Yusuf and al-Shaybani, who were followers of Abu Hanifah and among his most faithful students, were at the same time very close to Haroun al-Rasheed," the Abbaside caliph.

They played a major role in strengthening the latter's government and supporting and helping it, hence Haroun of the concubines and promiscuity did not permit anyone to be appointed as judge or *mufti* except with the consent of both of these men who never appointed any judge except if he was a follower of Abu Hanifah's sect.

Abu Hanifah, therefore, came to be regarded as the greatest scholar, and his sect as the greatest sect of *fiqh* implemented, despite the fact that his contemporary scholars went as far as calling him *kafir* and atheist. Among such scholars were both Imam Ahmad ibn Hanbal and Imam Abul-Hasan al-Ash`ari.

Likewise, the Shafi`i sect could not have spread nor gained any momentum had it not been for the support of Abbaside authorities during the time of al-Mu`tasim when Ibn Hanbal retracted his theory that the Holy Qur'an was created, so his star shone during the Nasibi caliph al-Mutawakkil. His sect gained strength and was disseminated when colonial authorities supported Shaykh Muhammad ibn Abd al-Wahhab during the past century, and when the latter cooperated with al-Saud who immediately lent him their support and assisted him and worked diligently to propagate his sect in Hijaz and the Arabian Peninsula.

The Hanbali sect, thus, became the sect attributed to three Imams the first of whom was Ahmad ibn Hanbal, who never claimed that he was a *faqih* but only a scholar of *hadith*, then to Ibn Taymiyyah whom they called "Shaykh al-Islam," mentor of Islam, and "Mujaddid al-Sunnah," the one who revived the Sunnah, and whom his contemporary scholars regarded as *kafir* because he decreed that all Muslims who sought nearness to Allah through the Prophet were polytheists.

Then came in the past century Muhammad ibn Abd al-Wahhab, henchman of British colonialism in the Middle East, who also tried to "revive" the Hanbali sect through verdicts which he borrowed from Ibn Taymiyyah. Ahmad ibn Hanbal became a thing of the past because now they call their sect Wahhabism.

There is no room to doubt the fact that the dissemination, fame and prominence of all these sects was through the support and with the blessing of various rulers. And there is also no room to doubt the fact that all those rulers, without any exception, were enemies of the Imams of Ahlul Bayt due to their continuous fear that those Imams threatened their very existence and the abolishment of their authority. They, therefore, were always trying to isolate them from the nation, belittling them and killing anyone who followed their creed.

It goes without saying that those same rulers were always appointing the scholars who were flattering them and who were issuing verdicts conducive to their government and authority, since people always need solutions for their legislative problems.

Since the rulers in all times did not know anything about the *Shari`a*, nor did they comprehend anything about *fiqh*, it was only natural that they appointed scholars to issue verdicts on their behalf and to mislead the public into thinking that politics and religion did not mix.

The ruler, therefore, was a man of politics, whereas the *faqih* was always a theologian as is the case with the president of any

Muslim republic: you always find him appointing the scholars who are close to him, calling them the "republic's *muftis*," or any such title, who are asked to look into issues related to religious verdicts, tenets, and rituals.

Yet in reality such a person does not issue any verdict or a ruling except according to the directives which he receives from the ruling authority and in agreement with the ruler or, at least, not in opposition to the government's policy or the execution of its programs.

This phenomenon came to exist since the time of the first three caliphs, namely Abu Bakr, Umar, and Uthman, for although they did not make a distinction between religion and politics, they granted themselves the right to be the legislators in order to legislate whatever served the interests of their caliphate and whatever secured its prestige and continuation.

Since those three caliphs used to meet with the Prophet and be in his company, they learned from him some traditions which were not in contradiction with their policies.

Mu`awiyah, for example, did not embrace Islam except in 9 A.H./630 A.D. according to the most famous and authentic narrative, so he did not accompany the Prophet except for a very short period of time and did not know anything worth mentioning about his Sunnah; therefore, he felt forced to appoint Abu Hurayra and Amr ibn al-As and some of the companions to issue verdicts according to his own liking.

The Umayyads and the Abbasides after him followed such "praiseworthy Sunnah," or what they labelled *al-bid`a al-hasana*, the good innovation. Each ruler, thus, seated the high judge beside him to appoint the judges whom he regarded as good for the state and who would strengthen and support its authority. You do not need to know, beyond that, except the nature of those judges who preferred to displease their God in order to please their masters and benefactors who had appointed them in their positions.

Having come to know all of that, you can understand the secret why the Infallible Imams from the Progeny of the Prophet were deliberately excluded from public life, and why not even one of them, across the centuries, was appointed as judge or *mufti*.

If we wish to document more facts relevant to the methods whereby the four "Sunni" sects were promoted by the rulers, we need to cite only one example by removing the curtains from the sect established by Imam Malik, a sect which is regarded as one of their greatest, most prestigious, and whose *fiqh* is the broadest. Malik gained fame particularly because of writing his book *Al-Mawatta'* which, according to "Ahlul Sunnah," is the most authentic book after the Book of Allah, and there are many scholars who regard it as superior to, and they prefer it over, al-Bukhari's *Sahih*.

Malik's fame was extra-ordinary, so much so that this query came to be a household word: "Can anyone dare to issue a verdict while Malik is in town?" We must also not forget that Malik had issued a verdict prohibiting the transaction of a sale through the use of force, and it was for this reason that Ja`far ibn Sulayman, Medina's governor, whipped him seventy lashes.

Malikis always use this incident to illustrate their man's opposition to the government, a conclusion which is quite erroneous, for those who narrated this incident are the same ones who narrated its sequel, and here are the details:

Ibn Qutaybah has said, "They have indicated that during Abu Ja`far al-Mansour's reign, Malik ibn Anas was whipped by [al-Mansour's governor over Medina] Ja`far ibn Sulayman. Al-Mansour was enraged when he came to know about it; he resented it and was very displeased with it, so he wrote an order expelling

Ja'far ibn Sulayman from his position as governor of Medina, ordering him to be brought to Baghdad on a bare hump.

Then he wrote another letter to Malik ibn Anas inviting him to come to meet him in Baghdad, but Malik refused and wrote Abu Ja'far al-Mansour back asking him to excuse him, providing him with some sort of excuse. Abu Ja'far al-Mansour wrote him again saying, "Meet me, then, during the next *hajj* season next year, for I will then be, *InshaAllah*, performing the rite."

So if the "commander of the faithful" Abu Ja'far al-Mansour, the Abbaside ruler, deposes his cousin Ja'far ibn Sulayman ibn al-Abbas from his post as governor of Medina because of beating Malik, this really makes one quite skeptical and forces him to contemplate.

The reason why Ja'far ibn Sulayman whipped Malik was only to support the caliphate and authority of his cousin the caliph; so, Abu Ja'far al-Mansour ought to have rewarded and promoted his governor rather than deposing and insulting him in such a manner. Instead, he deposed him and ordered him to meet him in the worst manner, chained and riding a bare hump. Then the caliph personally apologized to Malik in order to please him. This is truly strange.

This incident gives the impression that the governor of Medina Ja'far ibn Sulayman behaved like a fool who knew nothing about politics and their intricacies and schemes, and it does not give the impression at all that Malik was the caliph's reliable supporter and the bearer of his standard in both holy shrines; otherwise, he would not have deposed his cousin from the post of governor simply because he had whipped Malik who deserved to be whipped on account of issuing a verdict prohibiting a forced allegiance.

Such incidents happen to us and before our very eyes when some rulers resort to insulting someone or jailing him in order to enhance the prestige and security of the government. Then the same individual reveals his identity to be the relative of a cabinet minister, or one of the friends of the wife's president; the result: the governor is excused from his job and is ordered to take other responsibilities the nature of which is not known even to the governor himself!

This reminds me of an incident which took place during the French occupation of Tunisia. The shaykh of the Eisawi [sufi] *tareeqa* and his men were carrying their banners and raising their voices with their praise-offering chants at night. They passed by some streets before reaching the neighborhood where their shrine was located as was their custom. Upon passing by the residence of the French commander of the police force, they were met by the latter who went out of his residence and was steaming with anger.

He broke their banners and dispersed them because they did not honor the law of respecting one's neighbor and resorting to calm after 10:00 p.m. When the civil inspector, whom the Tunisians regarded as the equivalent of governor, came to know about this incident, he became very angry with the police officer whom he expelled from his job, giving him three days to leave the city of Qafsa.

Then he invited the shaykh of the Eisawi *tareeqa* to meet him, and he apologized to him on behalf of the French government and sought to please him by giving him generous amounts of money to buy new banners and furniture as a compensation for the broken items. When one of those who were close to him asked him why he had done that, he said, "It is much better for us to keep these savage people busy with carrying banners, senseless escapades, and with eating scorpions; otherwise, they would direct their attention to us and make a morsel out of us because we have usurped their rights."

Let us now go back to Imam Malik to hear him personally detailing the story of his meeting with the caliph Abu Ja`far al-Mansour.

MALIK MEETS ABU JA`FAR AL-MANSOUR

This narrative, provided by the great historian Ibn Qutaybah in his book *Tarikh al-Khulafa* (history of the caliphs), is a quotation of what Malik himself had said; so, we have to first and foremost point out to this fact and take it into consideration.

Malik has said: "When I arrived at Mina [during the next pilgrimage season], I came to the pavilions and sought permission [to meet al-Mansour], and permission was granted to me. The doorman came out to escort me after having obtained permission to let me in. I said to him, `Let me know when you reach the dome in which the commander of the faithful is.'

He kept passing by one dome after another. Each dome contained different men with swords unsheathed and knives raised. Then he said to me, `He is inside that dome,' leaving me after having said so. He kept watching me from a distance.

I walked till I reached the dome where he [al-Mansour] was, and I saw how he descended from his seat to the rug underneath it. He was wearing very simple clothes which did not suit people of his stature out of his own humbleness because of my visiting him, and nobody was in that dome except one guard standing with a raised unsheathed sword.

"When I came near him, he welcomed me and kept pointing to me to come closer and closer to him till my knees touched his. The first thing he said was, `By Allah Who is the One and only God, O father of Abdullah! What happened was something which I never ordered. I never knew about it before it actually happened, nor did I ever accept it after it had happened.'" Then Malik continued to say:

"So I praised Allah with regard to every condition and blessed the Messenger, then I told him that he was far from doing any such sort of thing or be pleased with it. Then he said to me, `O father of

Abdullah! The people of the two holy shrines will continue to be blessed so long as you are among them. And I think you are for them a security against Allah's torment and might. Allah did, indeed, shun through your own person a momentous calamity, for they are, as far as I know, the most swift people to dissenting and the weakest to bear the consequences; may Allah fight them whenever they plan a scheme. And I have already issued an order to bring the enemy of Allah[1] from Medina on a bare hump and I have ordered him to be humiliated and insulted to the extremes, and I shall most certainly afflict many times as much pain as he had inflicted upon you.' I said to him, `May Allah grant good health to the commander of the faithful and be generous to him! I have forgiven him due to his kinship to Messenger of Allah and to you.' Abu Ja`far said, `And may He forgive you too, and reward you.'"

Malik went on to say, "Then he discussed with me what happened to the predecessors and the scholars, and I found him to be the most knowledgeable person of them. Then he discussed knowledge and jurisprudence with me, and I found him the most knowledgeable of all people about what they agreed upon and the most informed of their disagreements. He had learned by heart many narrations and was fully comprehending all what he had heard. Then he said to me, `O father of Abdullah!

Organize your knowledge and write it down, and arrange what you write in book form, and avoid the extremism of Abdullah ibn Umar and the tolerance of Abdullah ibn Abbas and the oddities of Abdullah ibn Mas`ud, then seek common grounds, and record whatever the Imams and the *sahabah*, may Allah be pleased with them, had all agreed upon, so that we may oblige people, *InshaAllah*, to follow your knowledge, and we will disseminate

---

[1] He is referring to his cousin Ja`far ibn Sulayman ibn al-Abbas, then his governor over Medina.

your books in all lands and make sure that nobody disagrees with their contents nor judge except according to them.'

I said to him, `May Allah keep the *ameer* (ruler) on the path of righteousness, but the people of Iraq disagree with our knowledge, and they do not feel obligated to do what we do.' Abu Ja`far al-Mansour said, `The people of Iraq will be made to do it, and we will strike their heads with the sword and split their spines with our whips; so, hurry to do it, for Muhammad al-Mahdi, my son, will meet you next year, *InshaAllah*, and I hope he will find out that you have finished this task, *InshaAllah*.'"

Malik said after that, "While we were thus sitting, a small child came out from the back side of the dome underneath which we were, and when he saw him, he was frightened and went back. Abu Ja`far said to him, `Come, my loved one! This is the father of Abdullah, the *faqih* of the people of Hijaz!' Then he turned to me and said, `O Abu Abdullah! Do you know why the child was frightened and did not come here?' I said, `No.' He said, `By Allah, he was shocked to see how closely you have been sitting to me, for he has never seen anyone besides you doing so; this is why he retreated.'"

Malik went on to say, "Then he ordered for me a thousand gold dinars, a great outfit, and another thousand for my son. I sought his permission to depart, which he granted. I stood up, whereupon he bade me farewell and prayed for me, then I hurried out.

The eunuch caught up with me, bringing me the outfit which he put on my shoulder as it was their custom to give someone of great importance, a present so that he might be seen by people carrying it then handing it over to his servant. When the eunuch put that outfit on my shoulder, I leaned to avoid it, trying to disclaim it, whereupon Abu Ja`far ordered him to carry it to where my camel was tied."²

---

² Ibn Qutaybah, *Tarikh al-Khulafa*, Vol. 2, p. 150.

UNAVOIDABLE COMMENTARY SERVING THE RESEARCH

Anyone who examines this cordial meeting between Imam Malik and the oppressive caliph Abu Ja`far al-Mansour, and who studies their dialogue, will deduct the following conclusions:

FIRST: We notice that the Abbaside caliph deposed his governor over Medina, cousin and closest of kin, insulting him after having deposed him, then apologized to Imam Malik because of his governor's conduct, swearing by Allah that it was not ordered by him, nor did he know about it beforehand, nor was he pleased when he came to know about it.

All this underscores the harmony between both men and the status enjoyed by Imam Malik with Abu Ja`far al-Mansour to the extent that he met him alone wearing casual clothes and seated him in a way in which he never seated anyone else, so much so that even his son was frightened, and he retreated, upon seeing Malik's knees touching his father's.

SECOND: We can draw another conclusion from al-Mansour's statement to Malik: "The people of the two holy shrines will continue to be blessed so long as you are among them, and I think you are for them a security against Allah's torment and might, and Allah did, indeed, shun through your own person a momentous calamity" that might have befallen them had they contemplated staging a rebellion against the caliph and his oppressive authority.

Imam Malik had, in fact, calmed them, quelling their revolution, issuing a number of verdicts such as his saying that they were obligated to obey Allah, His Messenger, and the *wali al-amr*, the governor in this instance. Thus were people reluctant to rise against their caliph, and thus did Allah, through such a verdict, shun a genocide involving the caliph.[1] For this reason, al-Mansour said to Malik, "They are, as far as I know, the most swift people to dissenting and the weakest to bear the consequences; may Allah fight them whenever they plan a scheme."

THIRD: The caliph was recommending Malik to be the scholar looked up to in all Islamic lands then forcing his sect on people and obliging them to follow it through the carrot and the stick. A reference to his enticing methods was his statement, "... so that we may oblige people, *InshaAllah*, to follow your knowledge, and we will disseminate your books in all lands and make sure that nobody disagrees with their contents nor judge except according to them," and that they should send their envoys and messengers to him during the pilgrimage.

A clue referring to his methods of intimidating people to follow him is his statement: "The people of Iraq will be made to do it, and we will strike their heads with the sword and split their spines with our whips." This statement indicates the extent of persecution meted to the poor Shi'as then at the hands of oppressive rulers who were persecuting and killing them in order to force them to abandon their allegiance to the Imams from Ahlul Bayt and to follow Malik and his likes.

FOURTH: We notice that Imam Malik and Abu Ja`far al-Mansour were subscribing to the same tenets and biases towards certain *sahabah* rather than others, and to their allegiance to the

---

[1] There is no contradiction between his verdict prohibiting the securing of allegiance by force and his mandating obedience to the ruler, and they have, indeed, narrated many "traditions" supporting their viewpoint such as: "Whoever disobeys the ruler and dies disobeying him, his death will be the death of the days of jahiliyya." Another tradition they narrate says: "You are required to hear and obey even if the ruler takes your wealth and whips your back."

caliphs who had taken control of the caliphate by intimidation and persecution. Malik has said in this regard, "Then he discussed knowledge and jurisprudence with me, and I found him to be the most knowledgeable of all people about what is agreed upon and the most informed of their disagreements, etc."

There is no doubt that Abu Ja`far al-Mansour reciprocated the same views held by Malik whom he complimented in a statement he had previously made to him during a meeting between both of them which took place before this one; said he then, "By Allah! I do not find anyone more knowledgeable than the commander of the faithful or more acquainted with *fiqh*." By the "commander of the faithful" he meant, of course, himself.

From the above text we can understand that Imam Malik was a Nasibi: He never recognized the caliphate of the Commander of the Faithful Ali ibn Abu Talib at all. We have proven from the above that they all objected when Ahmad ibn Hanbal added the name of Ali to the list of the "righteous caliphs," making him the fourth. It is quite obvious that Malik died many years before the birth of Ahmad ibn Hanbal.

Add to the above the fact that Malik relied, while transmitting *hadith*, on Abdullah ibn Umar, the Nasibi who used to say that they never regarded anyone during the lifetime of the Prophet as being equal to Abu Bakr, then Umar, then, Uthman, and that the *sahabah* beyond that were all alike! Abdullah ibn Umar ranks as the most prominent among the narrators of *hadith* whom Malik quotes. Most traditions quoted in Malik's *Al-Mawatta'* are actually his. So is Malik's jurisprudence.

FIFTH: We notice that the politics which were based on oppression and injustice sought the support of the public through verdicts favorable to them written without any support from Qur'anic texts the texts of the Prophet's Sunnah. For example, al-Mansour, as indicated above, said to Malik, "Organize your knowledge and write it down, and arrange what you write in book form, and avoid the extremism of Abdullah ibn Umar and the tolerance of Abdullah ibn Abbas and the oddities of Abdullah ibn Mas`ud, and seek common grounds, and whatever the Imams and the *sahabah*, may Allah be pleased with them, had all agreed upon, so that we may oblige people, *InshaAllah*, to follow your knowledge, and we will disseminate your books..., etc."

This clearly shows that the sect followed by "Ahlul Sunnah wal Jama'ah" is but a mixture of "the extremism of Abdullah ibn Umar, the tolerance of Abdullah ibn Abbas, and the oddities of Abdullah ibn Mas`ud" in addition to whatever Malik recommended as "common grounds" among the "Imams," namely Abu Bakr, Umar, and Uthman, and what was agreed upon by the *sahabah* with whom caliph Abu Ja`far al-Mansour was pleased... It has none of the Sunnah of the Prophet which is derived from the traditions narrated by the Purified Imams of the Progeny of the Prophet some of whom were contemporaries to al-Mansour and Malik, and whom the said caliph isolated and murdered.

SIXTH: It is noticeable that the first book documenting the Sunnah as excerpted from selected traditions narrated by the Prophet's companions, and by those who learned from the latter, is *Al-Mawatta* by Imam Malik, and it was written according to the order issued by the caliph himself so that the latter might force people to accept it and to strike their heads with the swords if need be, according to al-Mansour.

Such traditions, in this case, were bound to be among the ones manufactured by the Umayyads and Abbasides to serve their interests and strengthen their influence and authority, and to distance people from Islamic facts conveyed by the Prophet of Mercy.

SEVENTH: We also notice that Imam Malik was apprehensive ONLY of the people of Iraq because they were avowed supporters of Ali ibn Abu Talib, people whose minds had absorbed his knowledge and *fiqh*, people who dedicated their religious following to the Purified Imams from his offspring, affording no face value whatsoever to Malik and his likes because they knew that these men were Nasibis who used to flatter the rulers and sell their religion for a dirham or a dinar.

This is why Malik said to the caliph, "... but the people of Iraq disagree with our knowledge and they do not feel obligated to do what we do," and al-Mansour, with his typical arrogance, responded by saying, "The people of Iraq will be made to do it, and we will strike their heads with the sword and split their spines with our whips."

This tells us how those sects, which the ruling authorities had invented and on which they placed the label of "Ahlul Sunnah wal Jama'ah," came to be. What is really strange is that you see Abu Hanifah in disagreement with Malik, and Malik in disagreement with Abu Hanifah, and both men in disagreement with both al-Shafi`i and al-Hanbali, while the latter is in disagreement with one another and with the other two!

There is hardly one single issue upon which all four men agree except very rarely, yet they all are regarded as "Ahlul Sunnah wal Jama'ah," followers of the Sunnah and the consensus! What consensus is it?! Is it Maliki consensus, or is it Hanafi, Shafi`i, or Hanbali?! It actually is neither this nor that; rather, it is the consensus of Mu`awiyah ibn Abu Sufyan, for they are the ones who agreed with the latter when he made the cursing of Ali ibn Abu Talib from the pulpits a "Sunnah" followed for more than eighty years...

And why do they accept their disagreements, while their *fatwa* views are so diverse with regard to one and the same issue, yet they call their disagreement "a mercy" so long as it was confined to the four sects, but when another *mujtahid* disagrees with them, they charge him with *kufr* and excommunicate him from Islam?!

Why do they not regard their disagreement with the Shi'as in the same light whereby they see the differences among themselves, had they only been fair and wise? But the Shi'as' crime cannot be forgiven because they prefer Ali ibn Abu Talib over all other *sahabah*, and this is the basis of the disagreement which "Ahlul Sunnah wal Jama'ah" cannot tolerate. It cannot be tolerated by those who agree on one single issue: the exclusion of Ali from the caliphate, and the hiding of his merits and the facts related thereto.

EIGHTH: We notice how the rulers who confiscated the Muslims' wealth by force and oppression distribute such wealth generously to evil scholars who seek to be close to them in order to win their support and to barter their conscience and creed for the life of this world. Malik has said, "Then he [al-Mansour] ordered a thousand dinars in gold to be given to me in addition to a great outfit and another thousand for my son, etc."

Such an admission by Malik is self-indicting, and there may be many similar incidents which are not discussed in public because Malik used to feel embarrassed of receiving gifts in public and hated to see people noticing him accepting them; this is clear from his statement: "When the eunuch put that outfit on my shoulder, I leaned to avoid it, trying to disclaim it;" so, when al-Mansour noticed that, he ordered the eunuch to carry it for Malik to where the latter's camel was tied so that people might not know about it.

THE ABBASIDE RULER TESTS THE SCHOLARS OF HIS TIME

The Abbaside caliph Abu Ja`far al-Mansour was one of the most shrewd men who knew how to control people's minds and buy their conscience. He tried his best to spread his influence and expand the area under his control by either enticing or terrorizing others (he followed the policy of "the carrot and the stick").

We have already come to know his cunning and conniving from the way he dealt with Malik after the latter had been whipped by the governor of Medina. This leads us to conclude that there was a very strong tie between Imam Malik and al-Mansour a long time before that incident took place.

Malik had, in fact, met al-Mansour fifteen years before the meeting to which we referred above. It took place when al-Mansour had just taken control of the reins of government.[1] Among what al-Mansour had said then to Malik was the following: "O Abu Abdullah! I have seen a vision." "May Allah grant success to the commander of the faithful to reach the right decision," Malik responded, adding, "and may He inspire him to utter guidance; so, what did the commander of the faithful see?"

---

[1] On p. 150, Vol. 2, of his book *Tarikh al-Khulafa*, Ibn Qutaybah indicates that their first meeting took place in 148 A.H./765A.D. and the second one took place during the season of the pilgrimage in 163 A.H./780 A.D. We say that Malik used to meet the caliph quite often, and that the reason why Ibn Qutaybah mentioned these meetings specifically is due to the fact that Malik had himself narrated their tales, and because such narrations contained very important issues. It is not rational to say that the caliph used to meet with his state's supreme judge only once every fifteen years.

Abu Ja`far al-Mansour said, "I saw that I should seat you in this house so you will be one of the custodians of the sacred House of Allah, and to oblige people to learn from you, and to get the residents of various countries send you their emissaries and messengers during the pilgrimage in order to guide them to what is right of their creed and to righteousness, *InshaAllah*, for knowledge is with the people of Medina, and you are the most learned among them..."[2]

Ibn Qutaybah says that when Abu Ja`far al-Mansour took hold of the reins of caliphate, he met with Malik ibn Anas, Ibn Abu Thuayb, and Ibn Sam`an, all in one meeting, then he asked them, "What sort of a man am I in your view? Am I a fair imam or an imam of oppression?" Malik said to him, "O commander of the faithful! I plead to you in the Name of Allah, the Most Exalted, and I seek intercession to you through Muhammad and his kinship to you, to excuse me from having to discuss it."

Al-Mansour said, "The commander of the faithful has excused you." Ibn Sam`an answered him by saying, "You, by Allah, are the best of men, O commander of the faithful! You perform the pilgrimage to the sacred House of Allah; you fight our foe, and you secure the safety of the highways; the weak feel secure through you against being devoured by the strong, and it is through you that the creed stands; so, you are surely the best of men and the most just of imams."

As for Abu Thuayb, he answered al-Mansour thus: "You, by Allah, in my view, are the very worst of all men; you took what belonged to Allah and His Messenger, and you confiscated the shares of those of kin, and of the orphans, and of the indigent; you annihilated the weak and exhausted the strong then took their wealth; so, what will be your excuse tomorrow when you stand

---

[2] *Ibid.*, Vol. 2, p. 142.

before Allah?" Abu Ja`far al-Mansour said to him, "Woe unto you! What do I hear you saying?! Have you lost your mind?! Look and tell me: Who do you see in front of you?" He said, "Yes, I see swords, but it is only death, and it is something which cannot be avoided; the sooner it comes the better."

After this conversation, al-Mansour dismissed Ibn Abu Thuayb and Ibn Sam`an, keeping Malik. Having granted him security, he said to him, "O Abu Abdullah! Go back to your country well-guided and guiding others. But if you prefer to stay with us, we will not prefer anyone over you, nor will we regard anyone as your peer."

Al-Mansour then sent each one of them a money sack containing five thousand dinars with one of his policemen. He instructed the policeman thus: "Give each one of these men one of these sacks. If Malik ibn Anas takes it, leave him alone, and if he does not, there is no harm on him if he refuses it. But if Abu Thuayb take it, cut his head off and bring it to me, but if he gives it back to you, leave him alone and do not harm him. If Ibn Sam`an refuses to take his, kill him and bring his head to me, but if he takes it, let that secure his safety."

Malik says, "The policeman took the sacks to all three of us. Ibn Sam`an accepted it, so he was safe.

Abu Thuayb refused to accept it, so he was safe. As for me, I was, by Allah, in need of it, so I took it."[3]

This incident demonstrates to us the fact that Malik knew very well how unjust and oppressive this caliph was. Yet, due to the friendly ties between him and al-Mansour, he begged him, invoking the name of Muhammad and his kinship to him, not to press him to

---

[3] Ibn Qutaybah, *Tarikh al-Khulafa*, Vol. 2, p. 144.

express his opinion. Hence, what pleased the Abbaside rulers, and what concerned them most during that age and time, was people glorifying and praising their kinship to the Prophet; this is why the caliph understood what Malik was driving at, which he appreciated, and this is why he excused him from voicing his opinion.

As for the second *faqih*, namely Ibn Sam`an, he complimented him for merits which he did not have out of fear of being killed, for the swordsman was standing there waiting for the caliph's signal. As for the third, that is, Ibn Abu Thuayb, he was brave; he did not fear anyone's reproach, and he was a sincere believer, a man of the truth who offered advice for the sake of pleasing Allah and His Messenger, and for the benefit of the general public; therefore, he confronted him with the facts and uncovered his falsehood and adulteration. And when he threatened to kill him, he fearlessly welcomed death.

Al-Mansour had instructed his policeman to cut off Abu Thuayb's head if the latter accepted his gift, and to do likewise to Ibn Sam`an if the latter refused to accept it.

Since Abu Ja`far al-Mansour was shrewd, you find him raising the status of Malik, forcing the public to embrace his sect, thus dealing the death blow to the sects established by Ibn Abu Thuayb despite the fact that the latter was more knowledgeable and much better than Malik as Imam Ahmad ibn Hanbal admitted.[4] Likewise, Layth ibn Sa'd was a better jurist than Malik as Imam al-Shafi`i had admitted.[5]

Needless to say, during that time, Imam Ja`far al-Sadiq was the best, the most knowledgeable, and the greatest jurist of all of

---

[4] *Tadhkirat al-Huffaz*, Vol. 1, p. 176.
[5] Such admission is recorded on p. 524 of al-Shafi`i's book *Al-Manaqib*.

these men as they themselves admitted.⁶ Did anyone in the nation reach his degree of knowledge or deeds, his merits or prestige, especially since his grandfather was Ali ibn Abu Talib who was the best, the most knowledgeable, and the greatest jurist among all people after the Messenger of Allah? But politics elevate the status of some people while lowering that of others, and wealth advances some people at others' expense.

What concerns us in this research is to prove through clear evidence and convincing arguments the fact that the four sects of "Ahlul Sunnah wal Jama'ah" are sects which were invented by the politics of their time, and the politicians who had invented them forced people to follow them by either terrorizing or enticing them, and by propagating for them; people simply follow the creed of their rulers.

Anyone who wishes to see more proofs and research them further ought to read the book titled *Al-Imam al-Sadiq wal Madhahib al-Arba`a* (Imam al-Sadiq and the four sects) by Shaykh Asad Haydar, may Allah have mercy on his soul. He will then get to know how much prestige and influence Imam Malik had gained: even Imam al-Shafi`i used to plead to the governor of Medina to beg Malik to permit him [al-Shafi`i] to meet with him. The governor said, "I prefer to walk bare-footed the whole distance from Medina to Mecca rather than stand at Malik's door because I feel no humiliation worse than having to stand at his door."

Here is Ahmad Ameen, the Sunni Egyptian scholar, stating the following in his book *Zahara al-Islam*:

---

⁶ You have already come across Malik's statement that, "No eyes had ever seen, nor ears have ever heard, nor anyone saw anyone a better jurist than Ja`far ibn Muhammad al-Sadiq.

The governments played a major role in supporting the sects of Ahlul Sunnah. When governments are strong, and when they support a particular sect, people will soon follow it, and it remains strong so long as the government remains strong.[7]

We say that the sect of Imam Ja`far al-Sadiq, which is the sect of Ahlul Bayt, if we were to call it a "sect" following in the Muslims' custom, otherwise it is nothing but authentic Islam brought about by the Messenger of Allah was not supported by any ruler nor recognized by any authority. On the contrary, rulers deliberately aimed at rendering it unsuccessful, trying by all means to put an end to it and turn people against it.

So if that "sect" nevertheless succeeded in penetrating the pitched darkness and maintained its supporters and followers across all those dark ages, it is only through the favor bestowed by Allah upon the Muslims: Allah's light can never be put out by any mouths, nor can the swords put an end to it, nor can it be rendered ineffective by false propaganda and purposeful rumors, and so that people will have no argument against Allah or be able to claim that they were unmindful.

Those who emulated the Imams of Guidance from the Purified Progeny were only a few; they were only a handful following the demise of the Prophet. Across history and as time passed by, they multiplied because the good tree is firmly rooted, and its branches are in the skies, timely bearing its fruit by the permission of its Lord, and what belongs to Allah continues and is never diminished...

Quraysh had wished to put an end to Muhammad at the dawn of his mission, and when they, by Allah's favor and by the favor of Abu Talib and Ali who were always ready to offer their lives to be

---

[7] *Zahara al-Islam*, Vol. 4, p. 96.

sacrificed for him, the culprits from Quraysh were unable to do so; therefore, they entertained themselves with the thought that the lineage of Muhammad would discontinue at the time of his death, and his issue will come to an end, so they grudgingly waited in anticipation.

But the Lord of the Worlds granted him al-Kawthar, and Muhammad became the grandfather of al-Hasan and al-Husayn, and he gave the glad tidings to the believers that they both were Imams whenever they stood up or sat down, and that all the Imams would be from the offspring of al-Husayn...

All this threatened Quraysh's interests and future. It was not to its liking at all. Quraysh, thus, broke out in rebellion immediately after the demise of Muhammad, trying to put an end to all his progeny. They surrounded Fatima's house with fire wood. Had Ali not sought peace with them, and had he not sacrificed his right to the caliphate and not stayed on peaceful terms with them, they would surely have finished him, and Islam would have become, starting from that very day, a thing of the past.

Quraysh became calm again when they felt that their grip over the reins of government was secure against anyone threatening their interests, especially if such a threat came from Muhammad's offspring. As soon as the caliphate was rendered to Ali, however, Quraysh once more lit the fires of war to crush him.

They did not calm down except after having put an end to him and brought caliphate back to the very worst among their clans, turning it a Kaiser-style monarchy wherein fathers would appoint their sons to succeed them. And when al-Husayn refused to swear the oath of allegiance to Yazid, Quraysh broke out thundering in revolt to deal the death blow to the Prophet's family and to anyone called an offspring of Muhammad ibn Abdullah, hence the massacre at Karbala...

In that massacre, they killed the offspring of the Prophet, including children and infants, and they wanted to uproot the tree of Prophethood in all its branches, but Allah, Glory and Exaltation are His, fulfilled His promise to Muhammad by saving Ali ibn al-Husayn [Imam Zain al-Abidin] and brought out of his loins the rest of the Imams. Thus, the east of the earth and the west is now full of his offspring, and such is al-Kawthar...

There is hardly any country, town, or place on earth without the presence of the offspring of the Messenger of Allah who enjoy people's respect and love. Nowadays, after the failure of all attempts, the population of the Shi'as who follow the Ja'fari *fiqh* alone outnumber 250 million world-wide.

They all emulate the Twelve Imams who descended from the Prophet's family, seeking nearness to Allah through loving and being loyal to them, hopeful of the intercession of their grandfather on the Day of Judgment. You cannot find such figure among the followers of any one particular sect if taken individually despite the rulers' power and finance.

And they plan, and Allah, too, plans, and surely Allah is the best of planners. (Holy Qur'an, 8:30)

Did Pharaoh not order every male born to the Israelites to be killed when the soothsayers told him that one of their newborns would threaten his kingdom with extinction? But "the best of planners" saved Moses from Pharaoh's mischief and looked after him till he grew up even in the lap of Pharaoh himself, thus bringing his kingdom to an end, annihilating his party, and the Command of Allah is always carried out.

Did not Mu`awiyah (the Pharaoh of his time) not curse Ali, killing him, his offspring, and supporters? Did he not prohibit anyone from mentioning any of his merits? Did he not try, through all his schemes, to put out the light of Allah and bring things to the way they used to be during the time of *jahiliyya*?

But "the best of planners" raised the name of Ali despite the nose of Mu`awiyah and his party, so Ali's grave became a shrine visited by numerous pilgrims, Sunnis and Shi'as; nay! Even Christians and Jews praise and laud Ali! Ali's became the second most frequently visited grave after that of the Messenger of Allah. Millions of Muslims circle it tearfully, seeking nearness to Allah. Above it is a gilt dome and lofty gilt minarets that steal everyone's sight.

As for Mu`awiyah, the emperor who ruled the land and filled it with corruption, nobody mentions him well. Do you see any shrine erected for him or any monument? Do you see any grave site for him visited by anyone other than a dark and neglected cemetery? Surely falsehood has a round, while the truth remains firmly seated; so, be admonished, O people of reason.

All Praise is due to Allah for having guided us. All praise is due to Allah Who clarified for us the fact that the Shi'as are the true followers of the Sunnah of His Messenger; they surely are the followers of the Prophet's Sunnah because they follow the example of Ahlul Bayt, the people of the house of Prophethood, and surely the people of the house know best what their house contains. They are, after all, the ones whom Allah chosen. He made them the inheritors of the knowledge of His Book.

He has also clarified for us the fact that "Ahlul Sunnah wal Jama'ah" followed the innovations of their rulers among their predecessors and the latter's posterity; moreover they truly cannot prove their claims at all.

HADITH AL-THAQALAYN ACCORDING TO SHI'AS

What points out to the fact that Shi'as are the followers of the authentic Prophetic Sunnah is *hadith al-thaqalayn* (tradition of the two weighty things) of the Messenger of Allah who is quoted saying:

I am leaving among you the Two Weighty Things: the Book of Allah and my `Itrat (Progeny), my Ahlul Bayt. So long as you (simultaneously) uphold both of them, you will never be misled after me; so, do not go ahead of them else you should perish, and do not lag behind them else you should perish; do not teach them, for they are more knowledgeable than you.[1]

According to some narrations, the Prophet added to the above saying, "The Most Benevolent, the all-Knowing, has informed me that they both shall never part till they meet me at the Pool (of al-Kawthar)."

This tradition of the Two Weighty Things in the wording indicated above is recorded by "Ahlul Sunnah wal Jama'ah" in more than twenty of their major *Sahih*[2] reference books and *Musnads*[3], and it is included by the Shi'as in all their books of *hadith*.

---

[1] This hadith is recorded in al-Tirmidhi's *Sahih*, in Muslim's *Sahih*, in al-Hakim's *Mustadrak al-Sahihayn*, in Ahmad's *Musnad*, in al-Nasa'i's *Khasais*, in Ibn Sa`d's *Tabaqat*, and by the books of al-Tabrani, al-Suyuti, Ibn Hajar, Ibn al-Athir, and many others [who all are Sunnis]. For the numbers of pages and volumes, refer to page 82 and the pages following it [of the original Arabic text] of the book titled *Al-Muraja`at* [by Sharaf al-Din Sadr ad-Din al-Musawi al-Amili].

[2] Compilations of traditions they regard as authentic.

[3] Books upon which religious rulings are based.

It is, as you can see, too clear to require any additional clarification in its implication that "Ahlul Sunnah wal Jama'ah" have, indeed, strayed because they did not uphold both of them simultaneously; they have strayed because they preferred their own views to those of Ahlul Bayt thinking that Abu Hanifah, Malik, al-Shafi`i, and Ibn Hanbal were more knowledgeable than the Pure Progeny, so they followed them and abandoned the Pure Progeny.

The claim expressed by some of them saying that they uphold the Holy Qur'an is groundless because the Holy Qur'an contains general issues and does not explain its injunctions in detail. It also accepts more than one interpretation. It needs someone to explain and interpret its verses as is the case with the Prophet's Sunnah which requires reliable narrators and knowledgeable interpreters.

There is no solution for this problem except to refer to Ahlul Bayt, I mean the Imams from the pure Progeny whom the Messenger of Allah named as his *wasis*, successors.

If we add other traditions to the tradition of the Two Weighty Things mentioned above which carry the same meaning and aim at the same goal, such as the following statement of the Prophet: "Ali is with the Qur'an, and the (knowledge of the) Qur'an is with Ali, and they shall never separate till they reach me at the Pool [of Kawthar],"[4] and also his statement, "Ali is with the truth and the truth is with Ali, and they shall never separate from one another till they reach me at the Pool [of al-Kawthar] on the Day of Judgment,"[5] we and any other researcher will then become certain that whoever abandons Ali abandons the true interpretation of the Book of Allah, the Most Exalted One, and whoever forsakes Ali

---

[4] Al-Hakim, *Mustadrak*, Vol. 3, p. 124, and it is also recorded by al-Dhahabi in his *Talkhis*.

[5] Al-Muttaqi al-Hindi, *Kanz al-Ummal*, Vol. 5, p. 30. Ibn Asakir, *Tarikh*, Vol. 3, p. 119, Vol. 3.

leaves the truth behind his back and follows falsehood, for there is nothing beyond the truth except falsehood.

We will also become certain that "Ahlul Sunnah wal Jama'ah" did, indeed, abandon the Holy Qur'an and the Prophet's Sunnah when they abandoned the truth, namely Ali ibn Abu Talib, peace be upon him. This also is a testimony to the accuracy of the Prophet's prophecy indicating that his nation will be divided into seventy-three parties (sects) all of whom will be wrong with the exception of one.

The saved party is the one that followed the truth and the guidance when it followed Imam Ali. It fought on his side and accepted the peace which only he concluded. It sought guidance from his knowledge then upheld the blessed Imams from his offspring.

They are the best of men. Their reward with their Lord is: gardens of eternity beneath which rivers flow, abiding therein forever; Allah is well pleased with them and they with Him; such is the reward of whoever fears his Lord. (Holy Qur'an, 98:7-8)

HADITH AL-THAQALAYN ACCORDING TO AHLUL SUNNAH

As we have indicated above, the tradition we quoted in the previous chapter is in the wording of the scholars of "Ahlul Sunnah wal Jama'ah" who admitted its authenticity in more than twenty of their famous classic reference books.

Since they have admitted the authenticity of this tradition, they, in fact, have testified against their own selves that they, by implication, are misguided because they did not uphold the Pure `Itrat*, embracing shaky sects for which Allah never revealed any proof, nor is there any reference to them anywhere in the Prophet's Sunnah.

What is strange in as far as the scholars of Ahlul Sunnah these days are concerned, after the extinction and annihilation of Banu Umayyah, when means of direct communications are abundant, when scientific research methods are available, why do they not repent and return to Allah when they can, so that they may be included among those to whom the Almighty refers when He says,

"And most surely I am most Forgiving to whoever repents and believes and does good then continues to follow the right guidance" (Holy Qur'an, 20:82)?

If people during past generations, during the time of caliphate, were forced by intimidation and oppression to follow their rulers, what is their excuse now especially since the ruler of any country is not concerned about anything related to the religion so long as his throne is secure and he gives "democracy" and "human rights," which include the freedom of thought and creed, his lip-service?

There are few among the scholars of Ahlul Sunnah who voice their objection to the said tradition of Two Weighty Things, wording it differently to read, "I have left among you the Book of Allah and my Sunnah."[1] The least we can say about them is that they are further from scholarly criteria and from the bases upon which research and knowledge stand, and they are distant from any ability to prove their claim by sound argument and evidence with the pure Progeny of Ahlul Bayt, peace be upon them, and that the residents of the house know best what their house contains.

---

[1] We have already stated, while discussing hadith, that the tradition worded "... the Book of Allah and my Sunnah" is transmitted without any bases, and it was not included in such wording by any of the *Sahih* books. Contrariwise, the same tradition worded "... the Book of Allah and my `Itrat" is an authentic tradition consecutively transmitted and which all authors of Sahih books, be they Sunnis or Shi`as, record.

IS IT "THE BOOK OF ALLAH AND MY PROGENY" OR "THE BOOK OF ALLAH AND MY SUNNAH"?

I have thoroughly dealt with this subject in my book *Ma`al Sadiqin* (*To be with the Truthful*). I said briefly that both traditions do not contradict one another because the authentic Sunnah is preserved.

Ali ibn Abu Talib is the gateway to the Prophet's Sunnah, and he is more worthy of being regarded as Islam's narrator of *hadith* than Abu Hurayra, Ka`b al-Ahbar[2], or Wahab ibn Munabbih.

Despite all of that, we have to provide more explanations and clarifications even if doing so will be at the cost of being repetitious, for there is always a benefit in repetition, perhaps some of them did not read it there, so they will be exposed to it here with additional explanations and clarifications.

The kind readers may find in this research what convinces them that the hadith reading "... the Book of Allah and my `Itrat (Progeny)" is the original one, and the caliphs deliberately altered its wording to read "... the Book of Allah and my Sunnah" so that they might thus be able to exclude Ahlul Bayt from life's stage.

We have to note here that the tradition reading "... the Book of Allah and my Sunnah" is not held as authentic even by "Ahlul Sunnah wal Jama'ah" because they themselves have narrated in their *Sahih* books that the Prophet prohibited them from writing his

---

[2] His full name is Abu Ishaq Ka`b ibn Mati` (d. 32 A.H./652 A.D.). He was a Jew from Yemen who pretended to have embraced Islam then went to Medina during the reign of Umar ibn al-Khattab. Then he went to Syria to be one of Mu`awiyah's advisers. He died in Hims. He is believed to have succeeded in injecting a great deal of Judaicas into the Islamic beliefs. Tr.

Sunnah down! So, if such a prohibition is proved to be true, how is it possible to imagine the Prophet saying, "I have left among you my Sunnah" while such Sunnah is neither recorded nor known to anyone?!

Moreover, were the tradition worded "... the Book of Allah and my Sunnah" authentic, how was Umar ibn al-Khattab justified in responding to the Messenger of Allah by saying, "The Book of Allah suffices us"?! Had the Messenger of Allah left a written Sunnah, how did Abu Bakr and Umar justify their burning of it and their prohibiting people from learning it?!

Were the tradition reading "... the Book of Allah and my Sunnah" authentic, why did Abu Bakr deliver a sermon following the demise of the Prophet in which he said, "Do not narrate anything about the Messenger of Allah; whoever asks you, say: `Between us and you is the Book of Allah, so follow what it permits and abstain from what it prohibits.'"?[3]

Had the tradition reading "... the Book of Allah and my Sunnah" been authentic, why did Abu Bakr violate it when he fought those who refused to pay *zakat* while the Messenger of Allah had said, "Whoever articulates: *La ilaha illa-Allah*, his life and wealth are to be protected, and his judgment will be on Allah"?!

Had the tradition worded "... the Book of Allah and my Sunnah" been authentic, how did Abu Bakr and Umar, and those who agreed with them from the *sahabah*, justify their violation of the sanctity of Fatima al-Zahra and their attack on her house and threat to burn it down and everyone inside it? Did they not hear the Prophet say about her, "Fatima is part of me; whoever angers her

---

[3] Al-Dhahabi, *Tadhkirat al-Huffaz*, Vol. 1, p. 3.

angers me, and whoever harms her harms me"? Yes, by Allah, they did hear and understand it... Did they not hear the verse saying,

"Say: I do not ask you for any reward for it except kindness to my kin" (Holy Qur'an, 42:23)

which was revealed in honor of Fatima's husband and sons? Did they regard kindness to Ahlul Bayt to be terrorizing them, threatening to burn them alive, and crushing Fatima's stomach till she miscarried?!

Had the tradition worded "... the Book of Allah and my Sunnah" been authentic, how did Mu`awiyah and the *sahabah* who swore the oath of allegiance to him and followed him permit themselves to curse Ali and condemn him from the pulpits during the entire Umayyad reign? Did they not hear Allah's commandment that they should bless him just as they bless the Prophet? Did they not hear the Prophet saying, "Whoever curses Ali curses me, and whoever curses me curses Allah"?[4]

Had the tradition reading "... the Book of Allah and my Sunnah" been authentic, why was such Sunnah unknown by most companions, so they were unfamiliar with it, hence they issued religious verdicts based on their own personal views, and so did the four Imams who resorted to analogy and *ijtihad*, to "consensus" and to closing the door of pretexts and those of public interests taken for granted, supporting their views by quoting certain companions, a number of rulers whom they liked, opting to choose the "lesser evil," etc.?!

---

[4] Al-Hakim, *Mustadrak*, Vol. 3, p. 121, quotes this tradition and says, "It is authentic according to the methods of verification followed by both Shaykhs [Bukhari and Muslim] who did not (!) record it." It is also recorded on p. 73 of al-Suyuti's book *Tarikh al-Khulafa*, on p. 24 of al-Nisai's *Khasais*, and on p. 82 of al-Khawarizmi's book *Al-Manaqib*.

Since the Messenger of Allah left "the Book of Allah and the Sunnah of His Prophet" in order to protect people against misguidance, there is no need for any of these things invented by "Ahlul Sunnah wal Jama'ah" especially since every innovation is misguidance, and every misguidance is in the fire of Hell, according to the sacred *hadith*.

Rational people and the people of knowledge blame the Prophet for neglecting his Sunnah and not ordering others to record and safeguard it against distortion, variation, invention and innovation, then saying to people, "I am leaving among you the Two Weighty Things, so long as you uphold them, you shall never stray after me: the Book of Allah and my Sunnah"!

But if these rational folks are told that he prohibited them from writing it down, it will be the greatest joke, for this is not the doing of the wise: How can he prohibit the Muslims from writing his Sunnah down then tell them that he is leaving his Sunnah among them?!

Add to the above the fact that the Glorious Book of Allah, when we add to it the Prophet's Sunnah which the Muslims wrote during many centuries, contains what abrogates and what is abrogated, and it has the specific and the general, and the fixed and what is similar to something else, for it is the sister of the Holy Qur'an.

But all the text of the Holy Qur'an is correct because Allah, Glory to Him, took upon Himself to protect it, and because it is recorded. As for the Sunnah, it contains more inaccuracies than accuracies. The Prophet's Sunnah is, first and foremost, in need of someone who is divinely protected against sinning to point out to its accuracies and to reveal all the changes made to it. Anyone who is not divinely protected against sinning can never do anything of this sort even if he were the scholar of scholars.

Both the Holy Qur'an and the Sunnah, moreover, need a very highly knowledgeable scholar who is deeply immersed in their injunctions and familiar with their secrets in order to show people, after the death of the Prophet, all the issues in which they differed and the ones with which they are familiar.

Have you not seen how Allah, the Most Praised One, pointed to the fact that the Holy Qur'an needs someone to explain it, saying,

"We have revealed the Reminder (Qur'an) so that you may clarify to men what has been revealed to them and so that perhaps they may reflect" (Holy Qur'an, 16:44)

Had the Prophet not been present among the people to explain the revelation to them, the Holy Qur'an would not have been revealed to them. They surely would not have come to know Allah's commandments even if the Holy Qur'an had been revealed in their language. This is simple common sense about which nobody contends, one which everyone knows.

Despite the revelation of the Holy Qur'an and its imposition of prayers, *zakat*, fast, and pilgrimage, the Muslims need the explanations of the Prophet especially since he was the one who showed them how to perform the prayers, how much *zakat* should be paid, what the injunctions related to the fast are, what rites the pilgrimage includes..., etc. Had it not been for him, people would never have come to know any of that.

If the Holy Qur'an, which contains no contradictions, and which no falsehood can approach from before it or from behind, needs someone to explain it, the Sunnah is in a greater need than the Holy Qur'an for someone to explain it due to the abundance of its contradictions which resulted from all the insinuations and lies that crept into it.

Such a need is quite natural, even a rational necessity that each Messenger should look after the Message with which he is sent, so he appoints someone to succeed him in doing so. Such an appointment of a successor and care-taker is done only through divine revelation so that the Message may not die when he dies; it is for this reason that each and every prophet had a successor.

It is to meet such a pressing need that the Messenger of Allah appointed his vizier and successor over his nation to be Ali ibn Abu Talib whom he raised since his childhood to be adorned with the conduct of prophethood. He taught him as he grew up the knowledge of the early generations and the last, acquainting him and only him with secrets which nobody else knows, guiding the nation to him time and over again, advising them in his regard repeatedly.

He, for example, told them once, "This is my Brother, Successor, and Caliph over you," and once, "I am the best of the prophets, while Ali is the best of the successors of the prophets and the best man whom I leave behind (after my demise)." He also said, "Ali is with the truth and the truth is with him," and "Ali is with the Qur'an and the [knowledge of the] Qur'an is with him," and "I fought for the sake of the revelation of the Qur'an while Ali will fight for [safeguarding] its interpretation, and he is the one who will explain to my nation whatever they differ about after me," and "Nobody pays my dues except Ali, and he is the *wali* of every believer after me," and "Ali to me is like Aaron was to Moses," and "Ali is of me and I am of him, and he is the gate of my knowledge."[5]

---

[5] All these traditions are regarded by "Ahlul Sunnah wal Jama'ah" as authentic, and they are recorded by many of their scholars who admit their authenticity. We have discussed them in our previous books. Anyone who

It has been scholarly and historically proven, as supported by the writings of biographers, that Ali was, indeed, the only authority upon whom the *sahabah*, be they the learned or the ignorant, depended. Suffices for that the admission of Ahlul Sunnah that Abdullah ibn Abbas, whom they call "the nation's scholar," is Ali's student who graduated from his school, and suffices for a proof the fact that all branches of knowledge with which Muslims are familiar were attributed to him, peace be upon him.[6]

Let us suppose that the tradition of "... the Book of Allah and my Sunnah" contradicted the one whose wording has "... the Book of Allah and my `Itrat*,*" the second should be preferred over the first so that a rational Muslim may refer to the pure Imams of Ahlul Bayt for explanations of the concepts embedded in the Holy Qur'an and Sunnah.

But if one accepts only the tradition containing the wording "... the Book of Allah and my Sunnah," he will be puzzled about both the Qur'an and the Sunnah and not find the reliable authority who can explain for him the injunctions which he could not understand, or the ones in which scholars differ a great deal, and about which the Imams of those sects said many different or contradictory statements.

There is no doubt that if one were to take what this scholar or that says, or were he to follow the views of this sect or that, he will be following and accepting without a proof the accuracy or the lack thereof of this jurist or that. To accept this sect and reject that is blind fanaticism, a baseless imitation. Allah, the most Exalted, has said the following in this regard,

---

wants to review their references ought to read *Al-Muraja`at* which is verified by Husayn al-Radi.

[6] Refer for more information to the Introduction to *Sharh Nahjul-Balaghah* by the Mu`tazilite scholar Ibn Abul-Hadid.

"And most of them follow only conjecture; surely conjecture will not avail anything against the truth; surely Allah is cognizant of what they do" (Holy Qur'an, 10:36).

Let me bring you one example so that the dear reader may get to know the authenticity of this tradition, and so that the truth may become distinct from falsehood:

If we take the Holy Qur'an and read the verse in it which refers to the *wudu* (ablution), we will read what Allah, the most Exalted, has said to be the following:

"... and rub (therewith) your heads and feet to the ankles" (Holy Qur'an, 5:6)

we will immediately understand that it implies that rubbing the feet is done in the same way the heads are rubbed. Yet if we look at what Muslims are actually doing, we will see them differing from one another: all "Ahlul Sunnah wal Jama'ah" *wash* them, whereas all Shi'as *rub* them! Thus we will be puzzled and become skeptical: which party is right?

If we refer to the scholars among "Ahlul Sunnah wal Jama'ah," and to the scientists of exegesis, we will find them differing from one another with regard to such ruling, each according to the traditions upon which he depends.

They say that there are two ways to read the original Arabic word, the object of rubbing or washing: one way suggests it should be pronounced *arjulakum*, and the other suggests its pronunciation should be *arjulikum*.

Then they argue saying that both methods are accurate, that whoever reads it *arjulakum* should wash his feet, and whoever reads it *arjulikum* should wipe them! A third scholar, one who is deeply acquainted with the Arabic language from Sunni scholars[7] says, "Both methods of reading this word obligate rubbing," adding that the Holy Qur'an indicates rubbing whereas the Sunnah has been to wash them!

As you can see, dear reader, the scholars of "Ahlul Sunnah wal Jama'ah" did not remove our confusion because of all the contradictions in their statements. Rather, they even increased our doubts when they said that the Sunnah has contradicted the Holy Qur'an, while the Prophet is cleared from being accused of doing anything contrary to the commandments stated in the Holy Qur'an; he could never have washed his feet when performing his ablution.

Had the Prophet washed his feet during his ablution, no highly respected *sahabi* would have ever contradicted him, knowing that the *sahabah* were men of knowledge and scholarship, and they were close to him and saw what he did. Among such *sahabah* was Ali ibn Abu Talib, Ibn Abbas, al-Hasan and al-Husayn, Huzayfah of Yemen, and Anas ibn Malik.

All the *sahabah* who read that word as *arjulikum*, who constitute most *qaris*, in addition to all Shi'as who emulate the Imams from the pure Progeny of the Prophet, have instituted that the feet must be rubbed, not washed, during the ablution.

So what is the solution?!

Have you not seen dear reader that any Muslim remains confused regarding his skepticism if he cannot refer to someone upon whom he can rely? He, otherwise, will not find what is right and how to distinguish what is the correct commandment of Allah and what is falsely attributed to Him.

---

[7] Al-Fakhr al-Razi states these views on p. 161, Vol. 11, of his book *Al-Tafsir al-Kabir*, the grand exegesis.

I have deliberately brought you, dear reader, this example from the Holy Qur'an so that you may get to know the extent of differences of views and the contradictions in which Muslim scholars from "Ahlul Sunnah wal Jama'ah" are wandering about regarding something which the Prophet used to do so many times each and every single day, and for twenty-three years...

This is something with which all people, the commoners and the elite, among the companions of the Prophet, should have been familiar. Yet we find the scholars of Ahlul Sunnah differing among themselves: some read one word [of the Holy Qur'an] this way, while others read it differently, deriving contradictory religious rulings, each party according to the way it reads it.

And such scholars have in their exegesis of the Book of Allah and the organization of its injunctions, according to the way they read it, numerous differences which are not foreign to the researchers. If their differences with regard to interpreting the Book of Allah are so obvious, more obvious are their differences with regard to the Prophet's Sunnah..., so what then is the solution?

If you say that we have to refer to someone who can be relied upon to explain and clarify the accurate injunctions derived from the Holy Qur'an and Sunnah, we will then demand that you name such a wise speaker, for the Holy Qur'an and Sunnah do not [by themselves] protect anyone from straying; they both are silent; they do not speak, and they permit many interpretations, as we have stated above with regard to the verse relevant to the ablution. We have already agreed dear reader that we must follow the scholars who are knowledgeable of the facts relevant to the Holy Qur'an and Sunnah, and the disagreement between us remains in getting to know who such scholars are.

If you say that they are the nation's scholars headed by the respected *sahabah*, we have already come to know about their differences regarding the verse relevant to the ablution, and about many other issues, and we have also come to know that they fought one another and called one another *kafir*; therefore, we cannot depend on all of them; rather, only the righteous among them should be relied upon, and the problem still lingers.

And if you say that we should refer to the Imams of the four [Sunni] sects, you have also come to know that they have differed among themselves in most issues, so much so that some of them regarded the articulation of the *bismillah* as abominable, whereas others have decided that without it, the prayers are void. You have also come to know how these sects came about, that they were manufactured by the oppressive rulers, and that they are far from the time of the Message and did not know the *sahabah*, let alone the Prophet, in person.

We have at hand only one single solution which is: to refer to the Imams of the pure `Itrat, the Progeny of the Prophet, of Ahlul Bayt from whom Allah removed all abomination and whom He purified with a perfect purification, the doers of good, the scholars whom nobody could surpass in their knowledge or asceticism, in safeguarding the creed and piety. They, and only they, are the ones protected by Allah against lying or erring as the Holy Qur'an testifies[8] and according to the testimony of the great Prophet.[9]

---

[8] One such testimony is in verse 33 of Surat al-Ahzab (Chapter 33) which reads, *"Surely Allah wills to remove from you, O Ahlul Bayt, all abomination, and to purify you with a perfect purification."*

[9] Among such testimonies is his statement, peace and blessings be upon him and his progeny, *"Uphold the Book of Allah and my `Itrat (Progeny); so long as you uphold them both (simultaneously), you shall never stray after me."* Just as the Book of Allah is protected by Allah from any error, so is the case with the pure Progeny. Anyone who is not infallible cannot be relied upon to guide others. One who himself is liable to err is in need of guidance.

Allah has permitted them to inherit the knowledge of His Book after having chosen them for this task, and the Messenger of Allah taught them all what people need, recommending them to the nation, saying, "The similitude of my Ahlul Bayt among you is like the ark of Noah: whoever boards it is saved, and whoever lags behind it is drowned." Ibn Hajar, one of the scholars of "Ahlul Sunnah wal Jama'ah," has said the following while explaining this tradition and admitting its authenticity:

The reason why he compared them to the ark is that whoever loves and venerates them as means to thank the One Who bestows His blessings upon them, following the guidance of their scholars, will be saved from the darkness of transgression, whereas whoever lags behind them will be drowned in the sea of ingratitude to Allah's blessings and will perish in the paths of oppression.[10]

Add to the above the fact that you cannot find even one scholar in the past or present Islamic nation, since the time of the *sahabah* and till today, who claimed that he was more knowledgeable or better than the Imams of the Prophet's pure Progeny, nor can you find anyone at all in this nation who claimed that he taught any of the Imams from Ahlul Bayt or guided them in anything at all. If you, dear reader, wish to review more proofs and explanations thereto, you ought to read *Al-Muraja`at* and *Al-Ghadeer*.[11]

---

[10] This is stated on p. 151 of *Al-Sawa`iq al-Muhriqa* by the Shafi`i scholar Ibn Hajar.

[11] To the best of my knowledge, no English translation of the 11 Volume encyclopedia titled *Al-Ghadeer fil Kitab wal Sunnah wal Adab* by Abd al-Husayn Ahmad al-Amini al-Najafi is available yet. Its fourth edition was published in 1397 A.H./1977 A.D. by Dar al-Kitab al-Arabi of Beirut, Lebanon. This book needs a book all by itself to describe its literary value, the knowledge it contains, and the data with which it is filled. Tr.

Yet what I have offered you ought to be sufficient if you are fair, especially since the tradition that starts with "I have left among you the Two Weighty Things..., etc." is the truth which reason and feeling endorse and which is supported by both the Sunnah and the Holy Qur'an.

Thus does it become clear to us once again, through clear proofs which cannot be refuted, that Imamite Shi'as are the followers of the true Prophetic Sunnah, whereas "Ahlul Sunnah wal Jama'ah" have obeyed their rulers and dignitaries who misled them and left them groping in the dark.

All Praise is due to Allah, the Lord of the Worlds, for having guided those whom He has chosen from His servants.

SHI`A SOURCES OF LEGISLATION

Anyone who traces the *fiqh* of Imamite Shi'as will find the latter referring in all juristic injunctions with the exception of those relevant to our modern time[1] to the Prophet through the avenue of the Twelve Imams from his Ahlul Bayt, peace be upon them. They have two, and only two, such sources, namely: the Book of Allah and the Sunnah.

By the first I mean the Holy Qur'an, and by the Sunnah I mean the Sunnah of the Prophet, blessings of Allah and peace be upon him for having brought it to his nation and the world. This is what the Shi'as have always been saying, and they are the statements of all the Imams from Ahlul Bayt who never claimed, not even once, that they acted according to their own personal views.

Take, for example, the first Imam Ali ibn Abu Talib: When they selected him to be the caliph, they preconditioned his government to be based on the "Sunnah" of both Shaykhs, namely Abu Bakr and Umar, yet he insisted on saying, "I do not rule except in accordance with the Book of Allah and the Sunnah of His Messenger."[2]

---

[1] We mean by these the ijtihad of the scholars with reference to issues regarding which there is no text and which took place following the occultation of the Twelfth Imam.

[2] According to some narratives, he said, "And besides these (two), I shall follow my own ijtihad," a false addition and a lie invented by those who believe in and who follow ijtihad. Imam Ali never, not even for one day, did he claim that he followed his own view. Rather, he always derived the injunctions from the Book of Allah and the Sunnah of His Messenger, or he would say, *"We have al-saheefa al-jami`a: in it there is everything people need, including the penalty for slightly scratching one's cheek."* This Saheefa was dictated by the Messenger of Allah and written in Ali's hand-writing, and

In our forthcoming researches, we will explain how he, peace be upon him, always followed the Sunnah of the Prophet to the letter, not going beyond it at all, trying by all means and might to bring people back to it, so much so that this caused the anger of some caliphs and the aversion of the populace from him due to his strictness in following Allah's Commandments and his upholding the Sunnah of the Prophet.

Imam al-Baqir, too, used to always say, "Had we followed our own views in your regard, we would have become misled just as those before us have, but we tell you about our Lord's clear argument which He had explained to His Prophet who, in turn, explained it to us." On another occasion, he said to one of his companions, "O Jabir! Had we been following our own view and desire in dealing with you, we would have perished; rather, we tell you according to *ahadith* from the Messenger of Allah which we treasure just as these folks treasure their gold and silver."

Imam Ja`far al-Sadiq has said, "By Allah! We do not say what we say according to our own desires, nor do we pass our own judgment. We do not say anything except what our Lord has said; so, whenever I provide you with any answer, it is from the Messenger of Allah; we never express any of our own views."

People of knowledge and scholarship know such facts about the Imams from Ahlul Bayt; they never recorded one single statement made by any of them claiming to follow his own view, or resorting to analogy, or to preference..., or to anything besides the Holy Qur'an and the Sunnah.

Even if we refer to the great religious authority the martyred Ayatullah Muhammad Baqir al-Sadr, may Allah be pleased with

---

we have already discussed it in the chapter headed "Ahlul Sunnah and the Obliteration of the Sunnah" in this book.

him, we will find him indicating in his book of instructions (*risala*) to his followers titled *Al-Fatawa al-Wadiha* (the clear religious verdicts) the following:

We find it essentially important to briefly point out to the major references upon which we relied in order to derive these clear verdicts which, as we indicated when we started this discussion, are: the Glorious Book of Allah and the sacred Sunnah as transmitted by reliable transmitters who fear Allah when transmitting anything regardless of their sect.[3]

As for analogy, or preference, or the like, we see no legislative basis for depending on them. As for what is called the rational evidence about which *mujtahids* and scholars of *hadith* differed, whether or not it should be acted upon, although we believe that it can be acted upon, we never found even one legislative injunction whose proof depends on the rational evidence applied in such sense.

Instead, anything rationally proven is also fixed at the same time by the Book of Allah or by the Sunnah. As for what is called consensus, it is not a [third] source besides the Book of Allah and the Sunnah; rather, it is not relied upon only because it can sometimes be used as a means to prove certain points. Hence, the only two sources are: the Book of Allah and the Sunnah, and we supplicate to Allah to enable us to uphold them, for "Whoever upholds them upholds the secure niche which is never loosened, and Allah is all-Hearing, all-Knowing."[4]

Yes, we find this to be the dominant phenomenon prevailing upon the Shi'as in the past and the present, and they do not depend on any source other than the Book of Allah and the Sunnah, and we

---

[3] This is stated on p. 98 of *Al-Fatawa al-Wadiha* by Martyr al-Sadr.
[4] *Ibid.*

do not find even one of them issuing a verdict based on analogy or preference. The incident involving Imam al-Sadiq and Abu Hanifah is well known.

It demonstrates how the Imam prohibited Abu Hanifah from applying analogy in deriving verdicts. Said he, "Do not use analogy with regard to the religion of Allah, for if you apply analogy to the *Shari`a*, it will be obliterated. The first person who applied analogy was Iblis when he said, `I am better than him: You created me of fire while creating him of mud.'"

These are the legislative sources of the Shi'as since the time of Ali ibn Abu Talib and till our time; so, what are the legislative sources of "Ahlul Sunnah wal Jama'ah"?

THE SOURCES OF SHARI`A ACCORDING TO "AHLUL SUNNAH WAL JAMA'AH"

If we trace the sources of the legislative system (*Shari`a*) of "Ahlul Sunnah wal Jama'ah," we will find them to be beyond the limits of the Book of Allah and the Sunnah which Allah and His Messenger had outlined. These sources, according to them, in addition to the Book of Allah and the Sunnah, are: the "Sunnah" of the "righteous caliphs," the "Sunnah" of the *sahabah*, the "Sunnah" of the *tabi`in* (the scholars who learned from the *sahabah*), the "Sunnah" of the rulers which they call *sawafi al-umara* (the "Sunnah" of the elite rulers), then comes *qiyas*, analogy, then *istihsan* (highly recommending something), then *ijma`* (consensus), and finally *sadd bab al-tharai`*, closing the door of pretexts.

As you can see, they are ten all in all according to them, all playing havoc with Allah's creed. And so that we may not say anything without a proof, or speak arbitrarily, or so that some people may not accuse us of exaggerating, we have to provide proofs from their own statements and books so that the kind reader will clearly see everything.

We do not argue with "Ahlul Sunnah wal Jama'ah" about the first two references, namely the Book of Allah and the Sunnah, for this is something which accepts no argument; rather, it is what has to be followed as dictated by narration, reason, and consensus, and it conforms with these verses:

"Whatever the Messenger gives you, take it, and whatever he prohibit you from, abstain therefrom" (Holy Qur'an, 59:7),

"Obey Allah and obey the Messenger" (Holy Qur'an, 5:92),

"When Allah and His Messenger decree..." (Holy Qur'an, 33:36),

and many other such clear verses. They all mandate that rulings should conform ONLY to the Book of Allah and the Sunnah of His Messenger. But we argue with them about the other sources which they added.

1. THE "SUNNAH" OF THE "RIGHTEOUS CALIPHS"

They have sought (in order to justify this addition) the argument one *hadith* contains; it says, "Uphold my Sunnah and the Sunnah of the guided and wise caliphs; uphold it and stubbornly cling thereto."[1]

In my book *Ma`al Sadiqin* (*To be with the Truthful*), I proved that these guided caliphs referred to in this tradition are the Imams of Ahlul Bayt, and I would like to add the following for the benefit of those who did not have a chance to read that book:

Al-Bukhari and Muslim, as well as all scholars who came after them, have recorded saying that the Messenger of Allah confined his successors to twelve, saying, "The caliphs after me shall be twelve: all of them are to be from Quraysh." This tradition proves that they are meant to be the Imams from Ahlul Bayt, peace be upon them, not the "caliphs," i.e. rulers, who usurped the caliphate.

One may say, "Whether those implied is meant (by this tradition) are the twelve Imams from Ahlul Bayt, as the Shi'as claim, or the four righteous caliphs as Ahlul Sunnah claim, the sources of the legislative system remain three: the Qur'an, the [Prophet's] Sunnah, and the caliphs' Sunnah." This statement is accurate only according to "Ahlul Sunnah;" it is inaccurate according to the views of the Shi'as because the Imams from Ahlul Bayt, as we have already stated, never derived any ruling according to their own views or opinions; rather, everything they said was the Sunnah of their grandfather the Messenger of Allah from whom they learned it and kept it in order to refer to it whenever they needed.

---

[1] This tradition is recorded by al-Tirmidhi, Ibn Majah, al-Bayhaqi, and Ahmad ibn Hanbal.

As for "Ahlul Sunnah wal Jama'ah," their books are full of rulings based on the "Sunnah" of Abu Bakr and Umar which they treated as a source of their legislative system, even when in contradiction with the Book of Allah and the Sunnah of His Prophet.

What increases our conviction that Abu Bakr and Umar were not implied in this *hadith* is the fact that Ali refused to rule according to their "Sunnah" when such ruling was presented to him by the *sahabah* as a prerequisite. Had the Messenger of Allah meant by these guided caliphs Abu Bakr and Umar, it would not have been appropriate for Ali to reject their "Sunnah;" therefore, this proves that this *hadith* excludes Abu Bakr and Umar from such guided or "righteous" caliphs.

But "Ahlul Sunnah wal Jama'ah" have always considered by the "righteous caliphs" to be Abu Bakr, Umar, and Uthman, and nobody else, because Ali was not counted by them among such caliphs. His name was added to the list at a later time as we have pointed out, and also because he used to be cursed from the pulpits; so, how could they follow his Sunnah?!

If we read what is narrated by Jalalud-Din al-Suyuti in his book *Tarikh al-Khulafa*, we will see all this to be the truth. Quoting the caliph's chamberlain, al-Suyuti says, "I saw Umar ibn Abd al-Aziz once delivering a sermon in which he said, `What the Messenger of Allah and both his companions [Abu Bakr and Umar] brought is the religion which we follow and to which we refer, and we defer anything besides that."[2]

The truth of the matter is that most companions as well as Umayyad and Abbaside rulers were of the view that what Abu

---

[2] Al-Suyuti, *Tarikh al-Khulafa*, p. 160.

Bakr, Umar, and Uthman had regulated was a creed from which they could derive their beliefs and to which they would always refer. Since all these three caliphs deliberately obstructed the Sunnah of the Messenger of Allah, as we have come to know from the previous chapters, what remain of the Sunnah are injunctions they have regulated in addition to whatever the said rulers decreed.

2. The "Sunnah" of the Sahabah *En Masse*

We find quite a few proofs and testimonials regarding "Ahlul Sunnah wal Jama'ah" following the "Sunnah" of the general masses of the *sahabah* without any exception.

They derive their argument from a false tradition with which we dealt in detail in our book *Ma`a al-Sadiqin*. That "tradition" states: "My *sahabah* are like the stars: whoever you follow, you shall be guided." This "tradition" is used by Ibn al-Qayyim al-Jawziyyah to prove that it is alright to accept the view of any companion of the Prophet.[1] This fact is also admitted by Shaykh Abu Zuhrah who says, "We have found all of them (meaning Sunni jurists) to be of the view that a companion's verdict is always accepted." He adds the following in another place:

Deriving arguments from what the companions had said, or from the verdicts which they had themselves issued, is the general trend of the mass of jurists, but the Shi'as[2] hold a contrary view. Ibn Abu al-Qayyim al-Jawziyyah, however, has supported the view of the general public by citing about forty-six texts, all being strong arguments...

We say to Shaykh Abu Zuhrah: How can these texts which contradict the Book of Allah and the Sunnah of His Messenger be labelled as "strong"?! In fact, all the texts produced by Ibn al-Qayyim are as weak as spider's cobweb, and you yourself, Shaykh, undermined them when you said:

---

[1] *A'lam al-muqi'in*, vol. iv. p. 122

[2] This is another proof provided by Shaykh Abu Zuhrah testifying to the fact which we have already stated: Shi`as do not accept to add to the Shari`a to include anything besides what the Glorious Book of Allah and the Prophet's Sunnah contain.

But we found al-Shawkani saying, "In truth, what a companion says cannot be used as a proof because Allah, Glorified and Exalted is He, did not send this nation anyone besides Prophet Muhammad, and we have only one single Prophet, and the companions and all those who came after them are equally obligated to follow his *Shari`a* in as far as the Book of Allah and the Sunnah are concerned. Anyone who argues that a religious ruling can be derived from any source other than these two, is, in fact, making a claim regarding the religion of Allah which he cannot prove, establishing a "Shari`a" which Allah never enjoined.[3]

So salutations to al-Shawkani who said the truth and was not influenced by the sect. His statement, then, is in full agreement with the stand taken by the Imams of guidance from the pure Progeny of the Prophet. May Allah be pleased with him, and may He please him if his actions agreed with his statements.

---

[3] This is stated on p. 102 of Shaykh Abu Zuhrah's book.

3. THE "SUNNAH" OF THE TABI`IN OR "ULEMA AL-ATHAR"

Likewise, we find "Ahlul Sunnah wal Jama'ah" deriving their arguments from the views expressed by the *tabi`in* whom they call "ulama al-athar," scholars who followed in the footsteps of the *sahabah*, such as al-Awza`i, Sufyan al-Thawri, Hasan al-Basri, Ibn Ayeenah, and many others. And they all agree about deriving rulings from and following the *ijtihad* of the Imams of the four sects despite the latter being among those who followed the *tabi`in*.

This is so despite the fact that the companions themselves admit having committed quite a few errors, and that they do not do according to what they know. For example, here is Abu Bakr giving the following answer upon being asked a question, "I shall give you my answer; if I am right, it is by the Grace of Allah, but if I err, it is either my fault or that of Satan." Umar once said to his fellows, "I may enjoin you to do something which may not be good for you, and I may prohibit you from doing the things that may be good for you."[1]

If such is the extent of their knowledge, and since they follow only conjecture while

"... surely conjecture will not avail anything against the truth; surely Allah is cognizant of what they do" (Holy Qur'an, 10:36),

how can any Muslim who knows what Islam is all about consider their actions and statements a "Sunnah" to be followed and a source of *Shari`a*? After having quoted their own statements, let me ask you the following: Does the "tradition" saying "My

---

[1] *Tarikh Baghdad*, Vol. 14, p. 81. We say to these folks: If such is the extent of your knowledge, then why did you put yourselves ahead of the person who has with him the knowledge of the early generations and that of the last ones, depriving the nation of his guidance and light and leaving it groping in dissension, ignorance, and misguidance?!

sahabah are like the stars: whoever you follow, you shall be guided" still hold any water?!

If such is the case of the *sahabah* who had attended meetings where the Prophet was present, and who learned from him, make such statements, what is the *status quo* of those who came after them, who learned from them, and who actively participated in the dissension?

If the Imams who invented the four sects express their own personal views with regard to Allah's creed, declaring and admitting that there is always a possibility of error in what they rule, while one of them says, "This is what I think to be correct, yet someone else's view may actually be correct," why did they require the Muslims to emulate them?!

4. THE "SUNNAH" OF THE RULERS

This is referred to by "Ahlul Sunnah wal Jama'ah" as "*sawafi al-umaraa*," the "Sunnah" of the elite among the rulers. They rely in their argument on the Qur'anic verse saying,

"Obey Allah and obey the Messenger and those in authority from you" (Holy Qur'an, 4:59).[1]

"Those in authority," according to them, are the rulers even if they rule by sheer brutal force, even if they are oppressors. They think that their rulers were brought to authority by Allah in order to fare with the lives of His servants as they pleased; so, obedience to them is obligatory, and so is following their "Sunnah."

Ibn Hazm[2] al-Zahiri responded to "Ahlul Sunnah wal Jama'ah" with a strong rebuttal in which he said,

"Based on what you say, rulers have the right to discard any parts of the *Shari`a* that Allah and His Messenger enjoined, and they also have the right to add to it, for there is no difference between adding or deleting therefrom. All this is apostasy committed by anyone who permits it without any contention."[3] Al-Dhahabi responded to Ibn Hazm by saying, "This is a faulty statement and a terrible mistake, for the nation, with the exception of Dawood ibn Ali and those who followed him, is of the consensus that the rulers have the right to resort to their own views, and to the principle of *ijtihad* only in the absence of a revealed text.

---

[1] In our book *Ma`a al-Sadiqin*, we proved, through convincing arguments, that "those in authority from among you" are the Imams of guidance from among the pure Progeny and not meant to be the rulers who usurp power by force. It is impossible that Allah, Glory to Him, orders us to obey the oppressors, the promiscuous, or the apostates.

[2] Ibn Hazm's *Mulakhkhas ibtal al-qiyas*, p.37

They say that they are not permitted to express their views or to resort to *ijtihad*, when they are aware of the existence of a revealed text. This shows that they have the right to add to the *Shari`a* an addition which the *Shari`a* itself commends while they are not permitted to discard whatever they desire of its injunctions."

We say to al-Dhahabi: How can you talk about the nation's "consensus" while excluding Dawood ibn Ali and whoever follows him? And why don't you identify those who follow him? And why did you not also exclude the Shi'as and the Imams from Ahlul Bayt? Do you regard the latter as being outside the folds of the Islamic nation?! Or is your habit of flattering the rulers lets you permit them to add to the *Shari`a* so that they may add more to the amounts of money they pay you, and to enhance your fame?!

And did the rulers who ruled the Muslims in the name of Islam know the Qur'anic texts and the Prophet's *ahadith* well enough so that they may not go beyond them? If both caliphs, namely Abu Bakr and Umar, deliberately contradicted the Qur'anic texts and the *hadith*, as proven above, how can anyone who succeeded them obligate himself to follow such texts which were altered, adulterated, bypassed, and regarded as a thing of the past?

When the jurists from "Ahlul Sunnah wal Jama'ah" issue verdicts permitting the rulers to express whatever views they like about Allah's creed, it is not strange to find al-Dhahabi following their example. In *Tabaqat al-Fuqaha*, Sa`id ibn Jubayr is quoted saying, "I asked Abdullah ibn Umar about supplicating loudly; he said, `Do you want to say that Ibn Umar says that Ibn Umar says such-and-such [i.e. that he quotes himself]?!' I said, `Yes, and we accept what you say and will be satisfied with it.' Ibn Umar then said, `This is what the rulers say [that it is alright to raise the voice while supplicating]; rather, Allah and His Messenger and those who quote them say so.'"

Sa`id ibn Jubayr has said, "Raja ibn Haywah used to be regarded as the most knowledgeable *faqih* in Syria, but if you provoke him, you will find him Syrian in his views quoting Abd al-Malik ibn Marwan saying such-and-such."[4]

Also in Ibn Sa'd's *Tabaqat*, al-Musayyab ibn Rafi` is quoted saying, "Whenever something related to jurisdiction, which was not supported either by the Book of Allah or the Sunnah, is mentioned, it will be labelled *sawafi al-umara* (what elite rulers have determined), so it will be discussed by the scholars, and whatever they agree about by way of consensus is regarded as accurate."[5] All we can say is to quote the following verse:

"Had the truth followed their own desires, surely the heavens and the earth and all those therein would have perished. Nay! We have brought them the Reminder (Qur'an), but from their Reminder do they turn aside" **(Holy Qur'an, 23:71)**

---

[4] *Tabaqat al-Fuqaha*, in the biography of Sa`id ibn Jubayr.
[5] See Ibn Sa`d, *Tabaqat*, Vol. 6, p. 179.

5. THE REST OF SOURCES OF LEGISLATION ACCORDING TO AHLUL SUNNAH

Among these we would like to mention *qiyas* (analogy), *istihsan* (deeming something as good or appealing), *istishab* (emulating or legislating something said or done by a *sahabi*), and the closing of the door of pretexts; as for *ijma`* (consensus), it is very famous among them and very well known.

Abu Hanifah in particular gained a reputation for following analogy and rejecting *ahadith*. Malik gained a reputation for referring to what the people of Medina did, and for closing the door of pretexts. Imam al-Shafi`i gained a reputation for referring to the verdicts issued by the companions whom he categorizes into different levels and degrees, putting on top of their list the ten *sahabis* who were given (by the Prophet) the glad tidings of going to Paradise, followed by the early immigrants (*Muhajirun*), then by the supporters (*Ansar*), then by those who accepted Islam after the conquest of Mecca, namely the free men among them.[1] Imam Ahmad ibn Hanbal gained a reputation for rejecting *ijtihad* and distancing himself from issuing verdicts (*fatwas*) and accepting any companion whosoever he might have been.

Al-Khateeb al-Baghdadi has narrated about him saying that a man once asked him about something whether it is permitted or prohibited. Ahmad said to him, "Ask, may Allah grant you good health, someone else."

The man said, "But I wish to know your own view, O Father of Abdullah!" Ahmad said, "Ask, may Allah grant you good health, someone else. Ask Abu Thawr."[2] Al-Maroozi quoted him saying, "As for *hadith*, we have relieved ourselves from its headache. As

---

[1] Imam al-Shafi`i, *Al-Manaqib*, Vol. 1, p. 443.

[2] *Tarikh Baghdad*, Vol. 2, p. 66.x

for queries, I have made up my mind not to answer anyone who asks me about anything."[3]

There is no doubt that Ahmad ibn Hanbal is the one who inspired the idea that all *sahabah*, barring none, are just; hence, his sect greatly influenced "Ahlul Sunnah wal Jama'ah." Al-Khateeb, for example, has mentioned in Vol. 2 of his book *Tarikh Baghdad*, relying on the authority of Muhammad ibn Abd al-Rahman, the money changer, saying, "I said to Ahmad ibn Hanbal, `If the companions of the Messenger of Allah disputed among themselves about a particular issue, should we look into what each one of them says so that we may know which view is right and follow it?' He said to me, `No companion of the Prophet should be preferred over another.' I said, `Then what is the solution?' He said, `You may follow whoever among them you like.'"

We say: Is it permissible to follow someone who cannot distinguish truth from falsehood? It is very strange to see Ahmad, who avoids issuing verdicts, issuing a verdict permitting the following of whoever is a companion you like and without even looking into their statements to know the truth!

Having thus briefly surveyed the sources of Islamic legislative system (*Shari`a*) according to both the Shi'as and "Ahlul Sunnah wal Jama'ah," it becomes quite clear for us without any confusion that the Shi'as are the ones who truly uphold the Sunnah of the Prophet and who do not accept any alternative for it, so much so that the Prophet's Sunnah became their motto according to the testimony of their opponents. As for "Ahlul Sunnah wal Jama'ah," they follow the "Sunnah" of any companion or *tabi`i* (a follower of a companion who was contemporary to the Prophet) and any ruler. Their books and statements testify against them, and they suffice for a testimony, and we will, *InshaAllah*, discuss in a following

---

[3] This is recorded on p. 57 of *Manaqib Imam Ahmad ibn Hanbal*.

chapter their deeds so that you may come to know that such deeds have nothing to do with the Sunnah of the Prophet.

I would like to leave the reader to himself to deduct the conclusion as to who the followers of the Sunnah really are, and who the innovators are.

A COMMENT NECESSARY TO COMPLETE THE RESEARCH

We ought to point out here to the fact that the Shi'as have always insisted that the sources of the *Shari`a* must be: the Book of Allah and the Sunnah of His Prophet, adding nothing to them due to their conviction that there are sufficient texts with their Imams relevant to all problems for which people seek solutions.

One may find it strange, maybe even highly unlikely, that the Imams from Ahlul Bayt have texts that satisfy all the needs of people across all centuries and till the Hour. In order to make this fact clear to the reader, we have to point out to the following:

If a Muslim is convinced that Allah, Glory to Him, sent Muhammad a legislative system (*Shari`a*) which complements all previous systems and overwhelms them in order to complete the human march on this earth so that it may be prepared for the eternal life hereafter,

"It is He Who sent His Messenger with the guidance and the religion of the truth in order to make it prevail over all other religions." (Holy Qur'an, 9:33)

... and if a Muslim is convinced that Allah, Glory to Him, wanted mankind to submit to His commandments regarding everything humans say or do, and to let Him fare with them as He pleases,

"Surely the (true) religion with Allah is Islam." (Holy Qur'an, 3:19)

"Whoever prefers any religion besides Islam, it will not be accepted from him." (Holy Qur'an, 3:85)

... and if the case is as such, then Allah's commandments are bound to be complete and inclusive, covering all what man needs in his arduous journey to overcome all obstacles and stand firmly in the face of challenges till he reaches the anticipated goal. To express this fact, He, Glory and Exaltation to Him, has said,

"We have not neglected anything in the Book" (Holy Qur'an, 6:38).

Based on this verse, there is nothing excluded from the Book of Allah, the most Exalted One, yet man, due to his limited mentality, cannot realize all the things which Allah, Glory and Exaltation to Him, has stated because of a great wisdom which only people of knowledge realize. For example, the most Glorified and Exalted One says,

"There is not a single thing which does not glorify Him with His praise, but you do not understand [the method of] their glorification" (Holy Qur'an, 17:44).

The phrase "There is not a single thing" does not exclude anything at all and is indicative of the fact that mankind, animals, and even inanimate objects celebrate the praise of Allah. Man may comprehend how animals and living beings, including plants, celebrate the praise of their Maker, but his mind may not be able to comprehend how rocks, for example, can also do so, yet the Almighty has already said,

"Surely We made the mountains sing the glory (of Allah) in unison with him in the evening and at sunrise" (Holy Qur'an, 38:18).

If we accept all the above and believe in it, we will have to accept and believe that the Book of Allah contains all injunctions which people need till the Day of Judgment, but we simply do not realize them except when we refer to the one to whom that Book was revealed and who comprehended all the meanings it contains, namely the Messenger of Allah. The most Exalted One has said,

"We have revealed the Book to you clearly explaining everything and guidance, mercy, and glad tidings for those who submit" (Holy Qur'an, 16:89).

If we believe that Allah, Glory to Him, has clarified everything for His Messenger so that he may explain to people what revelation has been sent to them, we will have to believe that the Messenger of Allah has clarified everything, leaving nothing needed by people till the Day of Judgment without giving a ruling in its regard.

If such a clarification has not reached us, or if we do not now know it, then this is only the outcome of our own shortcoming, negligence and ignorance, or it may be the outcome of the deficiency of the means linking us to it, or it may have resulted from the ignorance of the companions and their lack of awareness of what he had clarified.

But Allah, Glory and Exaltation are His, is too wise to ignore the fact that all these are possibilities, or even realities, so He does not let His *Shari`a* suffer loss; therefore, He chose from His servants certain Imams whom He permitted to inherit the knowledge of His Book and the ability to explain it to others so that people may not have an argument against Allah; He has said,

"Then We gave the Book for an inheritance to those whom We chose from Our servants" (Holy Qur'an, 35:32).

The Messenger of Allah has, indeed, explained to people everything they need and selected Ali to be his successor whom he taught everything people will need after his demise till the Hour due to the merits which Ali enjoyed over all other companions: very sharp intelligence, keen understanding, excellent memory, clear retention of what he hears. The Prophet, therefore, taught him everything he knew and guided the nation to him, telling it that Ali is the gate from which his knowledge can be reached.

If someone were to say that the Messenger of Allah was sent by Allah for all mankind, so he had no right to choose one particular person to teach while depriving all the rest, we would say that the Messenger of Allah had nothing to do with that; rather, he was a servant of Allah who received and carried out his Lord's inspiration. Allah is the One Who ordered him to do so.

Islam is the religion of unity and is based on unitarianism regarding everything; so, people have to be united and gathered under one leadership. This is a matter of simple common sense regulated by the Book of Allah and necessitated by reason and sentiment. Allah Almighty has said,

"Had there been many gods in them, they would surely have become in a state of disarray" *(Holy Qur'an, 21:22),*

and also

"Never was with Him any (other) god: in that case, each god would certainly have taken away what he created, and some of them would certainly have overpowered others" *(Holy Qur'an, 23:91).*

Likewise, had Allah sent two messengers spontaneously, people would have been divided into two nations. Two parties, one opposing the other, would have resulted. The Almighty has said,

"And there is no nation except that a warner has gone among them" *(Holy Qur'an, 35:24).*

This is why every prophet left behind him a successor among his people and nation to protect them against dissension.

This, by my life, is quite natural; all people know it, be they scholars or illiterate, believers or unbelievers. Have you not seen how each tribe, party, or state has to have only one single president to preside over it and lead it, and two presidents cannot be followed simultaneously?

Because of all the above, Allah, Glory to Him, selected from the angels carriers of His Message, and likewise from the people, granting them the honor of bearing the responsibility of leading His servants to Him, making them Imams guiding others according to His commandments. Allah has said,

"Surely Allah chose Adam and Noah and the descendants of Abraham and the Descendants of Imran above the nations" *(Holy Qur'an, 3:33).*

The Imams whom Allah selected to conclude His Messages with that of Muhammad are the Imams of guidance from the Prophet's Progeny, and they have all descended from Abraham, one progeny descending from another, and they are the ones to whom he referred when he said, "The caliphs after me are twelve: all of them are from Quraysh."[1]

For every age and time there is an imam, so "Whoever dies without knowing who the Imam of his time is dies the death of *jahiliyya*," as another tradition says. When Allah, Glory and Praise are due to Him, chooses an Imam, He purifies him and protects him against sinning or erring and teaches him; He surely does not bestow wisdom except upon those who deserve it and are worthy of it.

If we go back to the basis of the subject-matter, which is the Imam knowing all what people need of the injunctions of the *Shari`a* from the texts available in the Book of Allah and the Sunnah, and which are suitable for mankind's progress till the time of the Hour, we will not find anyone in the Islamic nation claiming to be as such other than the Imams of Ahlul Bayt who declared the

---

[1] Al-Bukhari, *Sahih*, Vol. 8, p. 127. Muslim, *Sahih*, Vol. 6, p. 3. According to some narrations of the same tradition, they are to be the descendants of Hashim rather than Quraysh, but they are still descendants of Abraham as everyone knows.

same quite often, saying that with them is the *saheefa jami`a* which was dictated by the Messenger of Allah and written down in the handwriting of Ali ibn Abu Talib, and that it contains everything people need till the Day of Judgment, including the penalty for slightly scratching one's cheek. We have already referred to this *saheefa jami`a* which used to be carried by Ali with him and to which al-Bukhari and Muslim have referred, each in his own *Sahih* book, and not even one Muslim can say that this is not true.

Based upon the above, the Shi'as who restricted their loyalty to the Imams of Ahlul Bayt have always issued their juristic rulings according to the texts of the Holy Qur'an and the Sunnah without resorting to any other source, at least during the Twelve Imams' three generations.

As for "Ahlul Sunnah wal Jama'ah," these were forced to resort to *ijtihad* and *qiyas* and other things because of the loss of *hadith* and because of their Imams' ignorance thereof since the days of the first period of caliphate.

If their caliphs deliberately burned the Prophet's *ahadith* and prohibited their circulation and dissemination, and if their most prominent one says, "The Book of Allah suffices us," thus discarding the Prophet's Sunnah, it is quite natural that they lack the texts which explain the injunctions embedded in the Holy Qur'an.

We all know that apparent Qur'anic injunctions are very few in number. They, generally speaking, need the explanations provided for them by the Prophet. This is why we read the following verse in the Holy Qur'an:

"And We have revealed to you the Reminder so that you may clarify for men what has been revealed to them" (Holy Qur'an, 16:44).

Because the pillars of "Ahlul Sunnah wal Jama'ah" burnt the Sunnah which explained the Holy Qur'an, thus losing the texts that explained the Holy Qur'an or even the Sunnah itself, they had no choice, since the case is as such, except to resort to their own personal views, to analogy, and to consulting their scholars to select what the latter liked, and what served their own temporal interests. It is quite natural, then, that they have always needed all of that in the absence of such texts; they resort to all such means only due to their dire need.

TAQLID AND MARAJI' ACCORDING TO SHI'AS

Every Muslim adult, as long as he is not a *mujtahid*, that is, one capable of deriving religious rulings from the Book of Allah and the Sunnah, is obligated to follow a religious authority who combines in him the requirements of knowledge, justice, piety, asceticism and the fear of Allah in accordance with the verse saying,

"So ask the followers of the Reminder if you do not know" (Holy Qur'an, 16:43).

If we research this subject, we will find out that Imamite Shi'as have kept up with the sequence of events, with no interruption in their chain of *maraji`* (religious authorities), since the demise of the Prophet and till our time.

Shi'as continue to follow the Twelve Imams from Ahlul Bayt, peace be upon them. The actual presence of these Imams continued for more than three centuries uninterruptedly without anyone of them contradicting the other in anything he said.

This is due to the fact that the texts related to the *Shari`a* are always derived from the Book of Allah and the Sunnah. These have always been their reference. They followed neither analogy nor their own views. Had they done so, the disagreement among them would have become obvious to everyone as is the case with the followers of "Ahlul Sunnah wal Jama`ah."

We conclude from the above that any sect of "Ahlul Sunnah wal Jama'ah," be it Hanafi, Maliki, Shafi`i, or Hanbali, is based on the views of one man who was distant from the time when the Message was revealed; he had no direct link with the Prophet at all.

As for the sect of Imamite Shi'as, it is consecutive from the Twelve Imams who descended from the Prophet: the son quotes his father, and so on. One of them, namely Imam Ja`far al-Sadiq, says,

"The *hadith* I narrate is that of my father and grandfather, and the hadith of my grandfather is the hadith of the Commander of the Faithful Ali ibn Abu Talib who quotes the Messenger of Allah, and the hadith of the Messenger of Messenger of Allah is that of Gabriel, peace be upon him, which is the speech of the Almighty."

"Had it not been from anyone other than Allah, they would have found in it a great deal of discrepancy." (Holy Qur'an, 4:82)

Then came the post-occultation period of the Infallible Imam. This period has referred people to follow the learned *faqih* among them who combines in him all the conditions listed above.

Then the chain of *mujtahid faqihs* started since then, and it has continued till our present time uninterruptedly. During each period, one or more *marji`* rises to distinction among the nation whom the Shi'as follow in their actions.

This is done in accordance with the scholarly books of instruction (*risalas*) which each *marji`* derives from the Book of Allah and the Sunnah without expressing any personal views except in reference to issues related to modern times. Such views are relevant to modern scientific and technological progress such as heart or organ transplantation operations, artificial insemination, banking transactions, etc.

One particular *mujtahid* may be distinguished with prominence over all the rest through the degree of his knowledge. Shi'as refer to such a *mujtahid* as *al-marji` al-a`la*, the supreme religious authority, or the head of the sect or of *al-hawza al-`ilmiyya*, the university-type circle of top scholars. This wins him the regard and respect of all other authorities.

Across the centuries, Shi'as follow their contemporary *faqih* who studies whatever problems other people go through and is concerned about whatever concerns them, so they ask him and he provides them with the answers.

Thus have the Shi'as in all ages maintained the two basic sources of Islamic *Shari`a*: the Book of Allah and the Sunnah, in addition to the texts transmitted by the Twelve Imams from the pure Progeny of the Prophet.

Hence, their scholars feel no need at all to resort to analogy, or to express a personal viewpoint, because Shi'as have taken pains to record and safeguard the Prophet's Sunnah since the time of Ali ibn Abu Talib and will continue to do so till the Day of Judgment. The Imams from his offspring have been inheriting the same: son from father, and so on, treasuring such texts as people treasure their gold and silver.

We have already quoted the statement of the Martyr Ayatullah Muhammad Baqir al-Sadr which he records in his own *risala* indicating that he does not rely except on the Holy Qur'an and Sunnah. Mentioning Martyr al-Sadr is only an example; all Shi`a authorities without any exception do the same.

This brief research about the issue of religious following with regard to the *Shari`a* and religious authorities makes it clear for us that Imamite Shi'as are the ones who follow the Holy Qur'an and the Prophet's Sunnah as transmitted directly by Ali, the gate of the Prophet's knowledge, the divinely guided scholar and the nation's adviser after the Prophet and who, according to the Holy Qur'an, was created of the Prophet's soul.[1]

---

[1] This is a reference to the verse saying, *"Say: Come let us call our sons and your sons, and our women and your women, and our near people and your near people, then let us be earnest in prayer and pray to Allah to curse the liars"* (Holy Qur'an, 3:61), whereupon he invited Ali ibn Abu Talib, as Muslim records in his Sahih in a chapter dedicated to the virtues of Ali, peace be upon him.

So whoever comes to the city and enters through its gate will reach the pure fountainhead; he will take his fill and be fully refreshed. He will also have upheld the niche which shall never be untied because the Almighty says,

"Enter the houses through their doors" (Holy Qur'an, 2:189).

Whoever enters the houses anywhere other than through their doors will be called a burglar and will not be able to enter, nor will he come to know the Sunnah of the Prophet, and Allah will surely apprehend and penalize him for having thus transgressed.

TAQLID AND ISLAMIC AUTHORITIES ACCORDING TO AHLUL SUNNAH WAL JAMA'AH

If we research the topic of *taqlid* (religious following) and *marji'iyya* (high religious authority) according to "Ahlul Sunnah wal Jama'ah," we will be quite confused while trying to find any link between them and the Messenger of Allah. We all know that "Ahlul Sunnah wal Jama'ah" refer in their religious following to the four Imams, namely Abu Hanifah, Malik, al-Shafi'i, and Ibn Hanbal, and all these men never knew the Messenger of Allah, nor were they among his companions.

After the demise of the Prophet, Shi'as made *taqlid* to Ali ibn Abu Talib, peace be upon him, who never parted with the Prophet as long as he lived. Then, after Ali's martyrdom, they followed the Two Masters of the Youths of Paradise: Imam al-Hasan and Imam al-Husayn, grandsons of the Prophet. Then they followed Imam Ali ibn al-Husayn Zaynul-Abidin then his son Imam al-Baqir then his grandson Imam al-Sadiq, peace be upon all of them.

During that time, "Ahlul Sunnah wal Jama'ah" did not have any cohesive ideological existence. History does not tell us which Imam they followed, if any, and to whom they referred with regard to the injunctions of the *Shari'a* from the time of the Prophet's death and till the appearance of their four sects.

It was only after that time did the four sects start appearing on the stage one after another separated by variable periods of time depending on the desires of the Abbaside rulers as we have already indicated.

Then a bloc appeared combining all four sects under a shiny banner which stole people's minds called "Ahlul Sunnah wal Jama'ah." All those who were antagonistic to Ali and the pure Progeny of the Prophet, and who supported the first three caliphs and all Umayyad and Abbaside rulers, rallied around that banner. People embraced those sects willingly or unwillingly because the rulers went to lengths in promoting them through either enticing or terrorizing others to follow them, and people usually follow the creed of their rulers.

Then we find "Ahlul Sunnah wal Jama'ah," after the death of all their four Imams, closing the door of *ijtihad* in the face of their own scholars, prohibiting them from doing anything other than following those Imams who had already died...

Those rulers and sovereigns who closed the doors of *ijtihad* and did not permit their scholars to critique or examine religious matters may have done so fearing the surge of an intellectual freedom which could have caused them problems and dissension threatening their interests and very existence.

"Ahlul Sunnah wal Jama'ah," hence, became restricted to following a dead man whom they never saw nor knew so that they might have felt comfortable with his justice, piety and the extent of his knowledge. Rather, they simply had to think well of their predecessors as each party went to lengths listing the imaginary merits of their particular Imam. Most of those "merits" proved to be visions which were no more than dreams, notions, or scruples; each party was happy with what it had.

Had educated contemporary followers of "Ahlul Sunnah wal Jama'ah" looked into the merits narrated by their predecessors, and the contradictions recorded in their regard, which went as far as causing some of them to fight the others, or to call them apostates..., they would have entertained different thoughts about those Imams, and they would have been guided.

How can any wise Muslim, in this time and age, follow a man who did not know anything about modern issues, nor can he provide him with the solutions to some of his problems? Surely

Malik and Abu Hanifah and others will dissociate themselves from "Ahlul Sunnah wal Jama'ah" on the Day of Judgment and say, "Lord! Do not punish us on account of these folks whom we never knew and who never knew us, and to whom we never, not even for one day, told that they had to follow us."

I do not know what the answer of "Ahlul Sunnah wal Jama'ah" will be when the Lord of the Worlds asks them about the Two Weighty Things. He will then bring the Messenger of Allah to testify against them, and they will most surely be unable to disprove his testimony even if they argue that they just obeyed their masters and dignitaries.

If He asks them, "Did you find in My Book, or in the Sunnah of My Messenger, any covenant, or agreement, or argument mandating you to follow these four sects?" What will their answer be? The answer to this question is too well known, and it does not require much knowledge: Neither the Book of Allah nor the Sunnah of His Messenger contains anything like that; rather, the Book of Allah and the Sunnah of His Messenger contain a clear order to uphold the pure Progeny and not to lag behind them.

And they may say,

"Lord! We have seen and heard, so send us back so we may do good; surely we (now) are certain" (Holy Qur'an, 32:12),

and the answer will surely be, "No! It is only a statement which you say."

And the Prophet will say: "Lord! My nation deserted this Qur'an, for I enjoined them to follow my Progeny after me and conveyed to them what You ordered me to convey, that is, to be kind to my kin, but they violated my covenant and severed their ties with my offspring; they even slaughtered my children and permitted my sanctity to be violated; so, O Lord! Do not grant them my intercession."

"And the day when the unjust one shall bite his hands saying: O Would that I had taken a way with the Messenger! O woe unto me! Would that I had not taken so-and-so for a friend! Certainly he led me astray from the Reminder after it had come to me, and Satan ever fails to aid man. And the Messenger cried out: Lord! Surely my people have treated this Qur'an as a forsaken thing. And thus have We made for every prophet an enemy from the sinners, and sufficient is your Lord to guide and help." (Holy Qur'an, 25:27-31)

THE RIGHTEOUS CALIPHS ACCORDING TO THE SHI'AS

These are the Twelve Imams from the pure progeny of the Prophet arranged chronologically as follows:

- The first is the Commander of the Faithful and the Imam of the pious, the leader of the elite, the master of Muslims and the religion's drone, Allah's victorious lion, Ali ibn Abu Talib, peace be upon him, the gate of knowledge who challenged the minds, dazzled the hearts, and enlightened the intellect, the man without whom the Messenger of Allah could not have been able to set the foundations of the creed.
- Second is Imam Abu Muhammad al-Hasan ibn Ali, peace be upon him, Master of the Youths of Paradise, the fragrant flower of the Prophet in this nation, the ascetic worshipper of Allah, the faithful adviser.
- Third is Imam Abu Abdullah al-Husayn ibn Ali, peace be upon him, the Master of the Youths of Paradise and the fragrant flower of the Prophet in this nation, the master of martyrs and the one who was slaughtered on Karbala and who sacrificed his all seeking to reform the nation of his grandfather.
- Fourth is Imam Ali ibn al-Husayn Zaynul-Abidin, peace be upon him, the master of all those who prostrated to their Lord.
- Fifth is Imam Muhammad ibn Ali al-Baqir, peace be upon him, who penetrated the knowledge of the early generations and the last.
- Sixth is Imam Ja`far ibn Muhammad al-Sadiq, peace be upon him, the like of whom no eyes had ever seen nor anyone had ever heard nor any mind had ever realized with regard to the knowledge of *fiqh*; none was more learned, or better in deeds, than him.

- Seventh is Imam Musa ibn Ja`far al-Kazim, peace be upon him, the descendant of the prophet, the treasure of knowledge.
- Eighth is Imam Ali ibn Musa al-Rida, peace be upon him, who was granted wisdom even as a child.
- Ninth is Imam Muhammad ibn Ali al-Jawad, peace be upon him, the Imam of generosity and giving, the Imam of excellent conduct.
- Tenth is Imam Ali ibn Muhammad al-Hadi, peace be upon him, the one who received Allah's favors, who was the lighthouse of guidance.
- Eleventh is Imam al-Hasan ibn Ali al-Askari, peace be upon him, the Imam of asceticism and piety.
- Twelfth is Imam Muhammad ibn al-Hasan al-Mahdi, peace be upon him, who will fill the world with justice and equity after being filled with inequity and oppression, and the son of Maryam, peace be upon him, will pray behind him, and Allah will complete through him His Light, and through him will the believers be very pleased.

These are the Imams of the Shi'as, all twelve of them; so, if one says "Imamite Shi'as" or "Ithna-Asheri Shi'as" or "Ja'fari Shi'as," it is all the same, and they will be the ones identified as such. None among all Islamic groups accepted their Imamate besides the Shi'as.

If we study the Qur'anic verses revealed in their honor and which explain their merits, lofty status, goodness of substance, purity of the soul, and true greatness, we will come across verses such as the one enjoining us to be good to the Prophet's kin, or the one referring to Allah purifying them, or the verse of *Mubahala* (a challenge to make *ibtihal* – supplication invoking the curse of Allah on the liars), or the verse identifying them as the ones obedient to their Lord, or the verse of blessing and praising them..., etc.

If we study the sacred *hadith*, we will find it enumerating their merits and elevating their status above all the rest among the nation, pointing out to their superiority of knowledge and infallibility. If we do all of that, we will most surely surrender to their Imamate and regard them as the nation's security against misguidance and its only means to guidance.

We will also find it quite clear that the Shi'as are the winners because they upheld the strong rope of Allah which is: loyalty to these Imams and upheld the niche which cannot be untied, which is loving them. They will have then boarded the ark of salvation. They achieved security against drowning, and safety from perdition.

It is for these reasons that we decide, being fully convinced and aware, that Imamite Shi'as are the true followers of the Sunnah of Muhammad.

"Certainly you were heedless of it, but now We have removed your veil, so your sight today is sharp indeed." (Holy Qur'an, 50:22)

Surely Allah, the Great, has said the truth.

THE RIGHTEOUS CALIPHS ACCORDING TO AHLUL SUNNAH WAL JAMA'AH

These, according to them, are the four caliphs who ascended the seat of caliphate following the demise of the Messenger of Allah. "Ahlul Sunnah wal Jama'ah" advocate these caliphs' superiority over all other people with the exception of the Prophet in the same chronological order of their caliphate. This is what we hear even these days.

We have, however, come to know from previous researches that Imam Ali ibn Abu Talib, peace be upon him, was not counted among them as one of the caliphs, much less a righteous one; rather, Imam Ahmad ibn Hanbal added his name at a much later time to the list. Prior to that, he used to be cursed from the pulpits in all Muslim lands and throughout the Umayyad empire.

In order to shed more light on this subject, and so that the reader may feel comfortable about the truth regarding this regretful fact, his attention is invited to the following:

We have already said that Abdullah ibn Umar is regarded by "Ahlul Sunnah wal Jama'ah" as one of the most prominent *faqihs*, and Malik makes him his major authority upon whom he depends in his book *Al-Muwatta'*. He is also relied upon by both al-Bukhari and Muslim in the *Sahih* written by each of them. All other transmitters of *hadith*, without any exception, rely on him.

This man was famous for his open hatred of the Commander of the Faithful Ali ibn Abu Talib. History tells us that he refused to swear the oath of allegiance to Ali, yet he rushed to swear his oath of allegiance to the cursed al-Hajjaj, the enemy of Allah and His Messenger.[1]

Abdullah ibn Umar revealed what he was hiding in his chest and disclosed his best kept secret when he said that he could not count even one single favor or merit or good quality of Ali that warranted placing him in the fourth place after Uthman ibn Affan.

We have already come to know that he favored only Abu Bakr and Umar; as for Ali, peace be upon him, he, in his assessment, was among the commoners, if not the very least important among them. Let me provide you with another fact which narrators of *hadith* and historians have recorded, and which openly expresses the hateful and antagonistic nature of Ibn Umar towards Ali and all Imams from the pure Progeny of the Prophet:

Abdullah ibn Umar has said the following while trying to explain the tradition of the Prophet in which he said, "The caliphs after me shall be twelve; all of them are from Quraysh":

---

[1] Al-Hajjaj ibn Yusuf al-Thaqafi is the one who is very well known for his promiscuity, apostasy, crimes, and total lack of respect for the faith. Al-Hakim has recorded on p. 556, Vol. 3, of his *Al-Mustadrak*, and Ibn Asakir has also recorded on p. 69, Vol. 4, of his book, the fact that al-Hajjaj used to say, "Ibn Mas'ud claims that he recited a Qur'an revealed from Allah, and Allah is nothing more than a filth of the Arabs." He also used to say, "Fear Allah as much as you want, for doing so is completely futile, and listen to and obey the commander of the faithful Abd al-Malik ibn Marwan for you will then be generously rewarded." Also Ibn Aqeel records on p. 81 of his book *Al-Nasaih al-Kafiya* saying that al-Hajjaj delivered a speech once in Kufa and referred to those who were visiting the grave site of the Prophet at Medina thus: "May they perish! They go around sticks and decaying cadaver; why don't they go round the mansion of the commander of the faithful Abd al-Malik? Don't they know that someone's successor is better than his messenger?"

This nation shall have twelve caliphs who are: Abu Bakr al-Siddiq, Umar al-Farooq, Uthman Dhul Noorain, Mu'awiyah and his son as the kings of the holy lands (Mecca and Medina), al-Saffah, Salam, Mansour, Jabir, al-Mahdi, al-Ameen, Ameer al-Asab, who all are from Banu Ka'b ibn Luayy, and they are righteous and peerless.[2]

So read this statement, dear reader, again and wonder about such *faqih* who is so highly respected by

"Ahlul Sunnah wal Jama'ah" and notice how he distorts the facts and turns them upside down, making Mu'awiyah and his son Yazid as well as al-Saffah [a title meaning: the blood-shedder] the best of Allah's servants, further stating that they are peerless!

Surely grudge and ignorance have blinded his eye sight just as envy and animosity have blinded his mind[3] to the extent that he cannot see any merit or favor for the Commander of the Faithful Ali over whom he prefers Mu'awiyah, the morally depraved man, and his atheist, criminal, and blood-thirsty son Yazid.

Abdullah ibn Umar is the son of his father. Whatever comes from its source surprises nobody, and every pot drips of its contents. His father used all possible means to exclude Ali, peace be upon him, from the caliphate, and to make him look insignificant in the eyes of the public.

---

[2] This is stated on p. 140 of al-Suyuti's book *Tarikh al-Khulafa*, p. 140. *Kanz al-Ummal*, Vol. 6, p. 67, and also in the history books of Ibn Asakir and al-Dhahabi.

[3] Read it and do not forget the statement of the Prophet which al-Bukhari and Muslim recorded and which says: "Loving Ali ibn Abu Talib is a sign of *iman* (faith, conviction), and hating him is a sign of hypocrisy," and the hypocrites during the time of the Prophet used to be identified by their hatred towards Ali.

And here we see his [Umar ibn al-Khattab's] spiteful and hateful son, despite Ali's ascension to the caliphate after Uthman's murder and after having received the oath of allegiance from the Muhajirun and Ansar, refusing to swear the oath of allegiance to Ali and trying his best to put his light out and stir people against him in order to cause his downfall. He, therefore, kept making statements and fooling people into thinking that Ali, peace be upon him, had no merits, and that he was like any other ordinary man.

Abdullah ibn Umar served the Umayyad dynasty and crowned both Mu`awiyah and his son Yazid with the crown of caliphate, telling lies and fabrications about the Prophet, recognizing the caliphate of al-Saffah and al-Mansour and all promiscuous rulers of Banu Umayyah, preferring them over the master of the Muslims and the *wali* of the believers according to the text of the Holy Qur'an and the Sunnah. Yet he did not recognize Ali's caliphate even when it actually took place! How strange!

THE PROPHET REJECTS THE LEGISLATION OF AHLUL SUNNAH WAL JAMA'AH

We have already come to know that the Shi'as, following in the footsteps of the Imams among Ahlul Bayt, peace be upon them, never followed their own views nor analogy, nor did they prohibit anyone from doing so.

This is due to the fact that the Prophet's statements had the final word and the conclusive verdict in as far as they are concerned; they have inherited such written statements sons from fathers, and we have already referred to *al-saheefa al-jami`a*, the length of which is seventy yards, and which contains all what Muslims need till the Hour.

We have also come to know that "Ahlul Sunnah wal Jama'ah" felt forced to follow their own views as well as the principle of *qiyas* (analogy) due to the absence of the Prophet's texts with them and their need for the same simply because their prominent men and masters rejected them, burned them, and prohibited anyone from recording them.

The supporters of *ijtihad* resorted to the suggestion that they needed to coin *hadith* in the wording of the Messenger of Allah in order to support their sect and make wrong look right. They, hence, claimed that the Messenger of Allah dispatched Ma`az ibn Jabal to Yemen and asked him, "What if you do not find it [i.e. the answer to a problem] in the Book of Allah?"

He said, "Then I will judge according to the Sunnah of the Messenger of Allah." He then asked him, "What if you do not find it in the Sunnah of His Messenger?" Ma`az ibn Jabal, they claim, said, "If I do not find it, I will then follow my own *ijtihad*." The Prophet, the story goes on, then said, "All Praise is due to Allah

Who has enabled the messenger of the Messenger of Allah to please Allah and His Messenger."

This "tradition" is false, and it can never be attributed to the Messenger of Allah, for how can the Prophet say to Ma`az, "What if you do not find it in the Book of Allah and the Sunnah of His Messenger?" while Allah Himself says the following to His Messenger,

"And We revealed unto you the Book explaining everything" (Holy Qur'an, 16:89),

and also,

"We have not neglected anything in the Book" (Holy Qur'an, 6:38), and also,

"Whatever the Messenger gives you, accept it, and from whatever he forbids you, stay away therefrom" (Holy Qur'an, 59:7)?

A NECESSARY POST SCRIPT

When we discuss "Ahlul Sunnah wal Jama'ah" in the coming chapters, we mean by them our contemporaries. We have indicated in several previous chapters that these are innocent people who do not have a hand in what their predecessors had committed, or any sin or transgression. We have already indicated that they are the victims of plots and the misrepresentation of history which the Umayyads and Abbasides and their henchmen had coined in order to obliterate the Prophet's Sunnah and bring things to the way they used to be during the pre-Islamic period.

We used to be among them,[1] following in their footsteps, being guided by them, then Allah blessed us and guided us to the Ark of Salvation. We plead to Him, the most Glorified, to likewise guide all the Muslim nation so that nothing remains except the truth.

One may ask the following: "Thus criticizing and undermining the integrity of the *sahabah* hurts the feelings of the majority of Muslims who believe that they were all just and equitable; they regard them the best of all people after the Prophet." We say: Muslims are required to believe in Allah and His Messenger and to carry out their Will and abide by the limits which they outlined. The salvation of the Muslims, including the *sahabah*, depends on it, for the destiny of whoever strays from this line will be hell even if he were an uncle or a son of the Prophet.

Our criticism of some companions is dictated by the historical events with which they interacted, by the dissension among them, and by their causing the nation to be divided upon itself, thus afflicting it with the greatest of calamities.

---

[1] The author used to follow the Hanbali sect before embracing the Shi`a creed. Tr.

ENMITY OF AHLUL SUNNAH TOWARDS AHLUL BAYT REVEALS THEIR IDENTITY

Any researcher stands dumbfounded when he collides with the reality about "Ahlul Sunnah wal Jama'ah" and comes to know that they were the enemies of the pure Progeny of the Prophet, following those who fought Ahlul Bayt and cursed them and spared no means to murder them and obliterate their legacy.

This is why you find "Ahlul Sunnah wal Jama'ah" placing the label of "reliable" on all traditionists if they are Kharijites or Nasibi followers of Uthman. They charge and accuse all the traditionists who are loyal to Ahlul Bayt of being "weak."

You do not find such matters recorded openly in their books. But when they try to challenge the authenticity of accurate traditions recounting the merits of Ali ibn Abu Talib, they label them as "weak," saying, "Among the chain of its narrators is so-and-so who is a Rafidi."[1] And they label as *sahih*, authentic, false traditions which were fabricated in order to raise the status of and glorify the other caliphs even if their narrators were Nasibis. Being a Nasibi, according to them, is indicative of one's zeal about the Sunnah.

Ibn Hajar, for example, says the following about Abdullah ibn Idris al-Azdi, a very well known Nasibi, "He was a man who followed the Sunnah and Jama`ah, a zealot with regard to the Sunnah, and a follower of Uthman."[2] About Abdullah ibn Awn al-Basri he says, "He is held as reliable, and he is a man of piety and zeal about the Sunnah and toughness against the people of

---

[1] What they mean by "Rafidi" [literally: rejectionist] is someone who follows Ali and rejects the caliphate of those who preceded him in ruling over the Muslims.

[2] Ibn Hajar, *Tahdhib al-Tahdhib*, Vol. 5, p. 145 and Vol. 1, p. 82.

innovations. Ibn Sa'd has said that Abdullah ibn Awn al-Basri was a follower of Uthman."[3]

And about Ibrahim ibn Ya`qub al-Jawzjani, who was famous for hating Ali, peace be upon him, he says that his sect was Hareezi, i.e. a follower of Hareez ibn Uthman of Damascus, the sect known as Nasibism.[4] Ibn Hayyan describes Ibrahim as being zealous about the Sunnah, a man who memorized *hadith*.

It is noteworthy that this same Nasibi whom they praise by saying that he is zealous about the Sunnah and that he memorized *hadith* used to take the opportunity of other traditionists gathering at his door [asking permission to enter] to send one of his slave-girls with a hen in her hand to tour the town then to go back to her master, Ibrahim ibn Ya`qub al-Jawzjani, to tell him that she could not find anyone to slaughter it for her; he would then cry out: "*Subhan-Allah!* There is none to slaughter a hen whereas Ali in broad day light slaughters twenty thousand Muslims!"

Through such cunning and conniving, the Nasibis, enemies of Ahlul Bayt, try to dissuade people from following the truth and mislead them through such false accusations in order to fill the Muslims' hearts, especially those of traditionists [such as the ones who used to meet al-Jawzjani to learn *hadith* from him] with hatred and animosity towards Ali ibn Abu Talib, peace be upon him, and thus permit cursing, taunting, and condemning him.

---

[3] It is well known that the followers of Uthman are the Nasibis who accused Ali of being kafir, apostate, and they accused him of killing Uthman ibn Affan. They are headed by Mu`awiyah ibn Abu Sufyan, Uthman's cousin; so, he is their chief and leader.

[4] The Nasibis are Ali's enemies and the enemies of his Ahlul Bayt from among the Kharijites, the Qasitis, and the renegades who antagonized him and fought him. After his martyrdom, they took to cursing and condemning him.

You can find such phenomenon even in our time. Despite the claim of contemporary "Ahlul Sunnah wal Jama'ah" that they love Ahlul Bayt and seek Allah's Pleasure with our master Ali, *karrama-Allahu wajhahu* (Allah glorified his countenance), as they say, if you narrate one *hadith* containing one of the virtues of Ali, peace be upon him, they ridicule you, charge you with Shi`ism, with being an innovator, and with being "extremist."

When you, however, discuss the caliphs Abu Bakr and Umar, and other *sahabah* they feel very comfortable talking to you.

This is exactly the doctrine of their "good predecessors." Historians have transmitted saying that Imam Ahmad ibn Hanbal used to label as "weak" any traditionist who belittled Abu Bakr, Umar, or Uthman, while holding in high esteem Ibrahim al-Jawzjani, the afore-mentioned Nasibi, praising him a great deal. Imam Ahmad ibn Hanbal corresponded with him, recited his books from the pulpit, and used his works in support of his arguments.

If this is the case with regard to Ahmad ibn Hanbal who forced his contemporaries to recognize the caliphate of Ali, whom he ranked as their fourth, do not ask me about the others who did not admit even one single merit for Ali, or about those who cursed and condemned him from the pulpits during Fridays and Eids.

Al-Daraqutni, for example, says, "Ibn Qutaybah, spokesman of Ahlul Sunnah, inclines to ascribing human characteristics (to Allah) and deviates from the line of the Prophet's `Itrat."[5] This proves that most "Ahlul Sunnah wal Jama'ah" deviated from the path of the Progeny of the Messenger of Allah.

Al-Mutawakkil, whom traditionists called *muhyi al-Sunnah*, the person who revived the Sunnah, and whom Ahmad ibn Hanbal used to respect and hold in high regards and whose orders he

---

[5] Al-Dhahabi, *Lisan al-Mizan*, Vol. 3, p. 357.

endorsed in appointing judges, was one of the most notorious Nasibis who were antagonistic towards Ali and his Ahlul Bayt, so much so that his grudge prompted him to desecrate the graves of both Ali and his son Husayn, peace be upon them. He used to forbid anyone from visiting their sites and would kill anyone named "Ali."

In his dissertation, al-Khawarizmi quotes him saying that he used to generously reward with money only those who cursed the descendants of Abu Talib, peace be upon them, and support the sect of Nasibism.[6]

Needless to say, Nasibism is one of the sects of "Ahlul Sunnah wal Jama'a;" therefore, the promoter of Nasibism, namely al-Mutawakkil, is the same one labelled as *muhyi al-Sunnah*, the person who revived the Sunnah; so, consider.

Ibn Kathir, in his *Al-Bidaya wal Nihaya*, tells us that when "Ahlul Sunnah wal Jama'ah" heard al-A`mash narrating the tradition of the roasted bird, which contains a praise of Ali ibn Abu Talib (peace be upon him), they took him out of the mosque then washed the place where he used to sit.[7]

They also opposed the burial of Imam Muhammad ibn Jarir al-Tabari, author of *Al-Tafsir al-Kabir* (the great exegesis) and the great historian, for no reason other than his admission of the authenticity of *hadith* al-Ghadeer in which the Prophet is quoted saying, "Whoever regards me as his/her *mawla* (master), this Ali is (henceforth) his/her master." He collected its sources from various avenues. Those sources were quite numerous, so they came to be referred to as *mutawatir*, consecutively reported.

---

[6] Refer to p. 135 of al-Khawarizmi's *Rasaail* (Letters).

[7] [As an act of purification from *najasa*, uncleanness or filth.] This incident is narrated on p. 147, Vol. 11, of Ibn Kathir's book *Al Bidaya wal Nihaya*.

Ibn Kathir has said, "I have seen one of his books wherein he compiled the traditions relevant to the Ghadeer incident, and it was in two huge volumes, in addition to another book in which he compiles the incidents relevant to the tradition of the roasted bird."[8]

Ibn Hajar, too, has discussed him in his book *Lisan al-Mizan*, saying, "He is the great Imam and the highly respected interpreter of the Qur'an; he is trustworthy, truthful, and there is a good deal of Shi`ism in him and support (for Ahlul Bayt, as) which is not detrimental (to his reliability)."[9]

When Imam al-Nasa'i, the great traditionist and one of the authors of *Al-Sihah al-Sittah* (the six books of traditions which the Sunnis regard as *sahih*, authentic), wrote a book dealing with the merits of the Commander of the Faithful Ali, he was asked about Mu`awiyah's "merits," whereupon he answered: "I do not know of any except that the Messenger of Allah said to him once: `May Allah never satisfy your stomach.'" He was, therefore, beaten on his genitals till he lost consciousness. His body was carried to some place to die of such beating.

Ibn Kathir tells us the following in his *Tarikh* where he describes the violent confrontations that took place in Baghdad in 363 A.H./954 A.D. between the Shi'as and "Ahlul Sunnah wal Jama'ah" on the anniversary of Ashura:

A group from Ahlul Sunnah seated a woman on an animal to play the role of Ayesha and brought some of their men to play Talhah and al-Zubayr. They expressed their objective thus: "We want to fight the followers of Ali." A large number of people were

---

[8] *Ibid.*

[9] This is mentioned when Ibn Hajar, author of *Lisan al-Mizan*, discusses the biography of Ibn Jarir al-Tabari.

killed.[10] This is what goes on nowadays, too: "Ahlul Sunnah wal Jama'ah" attack Shi'as on Ashura in order to prohibit them from participating in the commemorative procession, killing many innocent Muslims.

After having conducted such an expose, it becomes clear to us that the Nasibis who antagonized Ali, peace be upon him, and who fought Ahlul Bayt, peace be upon them, are the ones who labelled themselves "Ahlul Sunnah," and we have already come to know what "Sunnah" they mean and to what "consensus" they refer.

It is self-evident that whoever antagonizes the Progeny of the Messenger of Allah is an enemy of their grandfather the Prophet, and whoever antagonizes the Messenger of Allah is an enemy of Allah.

It is likewise self-evident that anyone who is an opponent of Allah, His Messenger and Ahlul Bayt cannot be among the true servants of the Merciful One, nor can he be among the followers of the Sunnah except when such a "Sunnah" is meant to be the "sunnah" of the devil. As for the Sunnah of the Merciful One, it is loving Allah and His Messenger and Ahlul Bayt, following them and following in their footsteps.

The most Exalted One has said,

"Say: I do not ask you for any reward for it except to love my near relatives" (Holy Qur'an, 42:23).

So how can one compare Mu`awiyah with Ali, or the "imams" of misguidance with the Imams of guidance?

"This is a clear statement for people, and guidance, and admonition, to those who fear their Lord." (Holy Qur'an, 3:138)

---

[10] Ibn Kathir, *Al-Bidaya wal Nihaya fil Fitan wal Malahim*, Vol. 11, p. 275.

HOW AHLUL SUNNAH WAL JAMA'AH DISTORT THE BLESSING OF MUHAMMAD AND HIS PROGENY

Carefully discern this chapter, may Allah look after you, for you will come to know what "Ahlul Sunnah wal Jama'ah" conceal, and to what extent they have gone in hating the Progeny of the Prophet, leaving no virtue of Ahlul Bayt without distorting it.

Among such distortions is the sending of blessings unto Muhammad and his Progeny as ordained in the Holy Qur'an. Al-Bukhari and Muslim, as well as all Sunni scholars who came after them, indicate that the *sahabah* once came to meet with the Prophet when the following verse was revealed:

"Surely Allah and His angels bless the Prophet; O you who believe! Invoke (Divine) blessings unto him and salute him with a becoming salutation." (Holy Qur'an, 33:56)

They said, "O Messenger of Allah! We know how to salute you, but we do not know who to bless you!"

The Prophet said, "You should say: `O Allah! Bless Muhammad and the Progeny of Muhammad (Aali Muhammad) just as You blessed Ibrahim and the progeny of Ibrahim, surely You are often Praised, Glorified.'"[1]

Other traditionists have added to the above saying that the Prophet said (furthermore) to them: "Do not bless me with a curtailed blessing." They asked him, "And what is a curtailed blessing, O Messenger of Allah?" He said, "It is your saying: `O Allah! Bless Muhammad,' then you stop. Allah is Perfect and

---

[1] Al-Bukhari, *Sahih*, Vol. 4, p. 118.

accepts nothing less than perfection." This is why Imam al-Shafi`i was prompted to openly advocate that if anyone does not bless Ahlul Bayt, his prayers are not accepted by Allah.

Relying on the authority of Ibn Mas`ud al-Ansari, al-Daraqutni indicates the following in his *Musnad*:

The Messenger of Allah has said: "Whoever prays without blessing me and my Ahlul Bayt, his prayers will never be accepted."[2]

In his book *Al-Sawa`iq al-Muhriqa*, Ibn Hajar says, "Al-Daylami has quoted the Prophet saying that everyone's supplication is withheld till he invokes Allah's blessings unto Muhammad and the Progeny of Muhammad."[3] Likewise, al-Tabrani in his *Al-Awsat* has quoted Ali, peace be upon him, saying that everyone's supplication is withheld till he invokes divine blessings unto Muhammad and his Progeny.[4]

Thus do we come to know how the *Sahih* books of "Ahlul Sunnah wal Jama'ah" describe the correct way of invoking Allah's blessings unto Muhammad and his Progeny, that Allah does not accept the prayers of anyone unless he blesses Muhammad and his Progeny, and that the supplication of every Muslim is withheld till he invokes Allah's blessings unto Muhammad and his Progeny. It is, by my life, a great virtue and a sublime feat whereby Ahlul Bayt are favored over all other humans; through them does a Muslim seek nearness to his Lord.

---

[2] This is recorded on p. 136 of al-Daraqutni's *Sunan*.

[3] This is recorded on p. 88 of Ibn Hajar al-`Asqalani's book *Al-Sawa`iq al-Muhriqa*.

[4] Fayd al-Qadeer, Vol. 5, p. 19. *Kanz al-Ummal*, Vol. 6, p. 173.

But "Ahlul Sunnah wal Jama'ah" were angered by leaving this feat of Ahlul Bayt alone. They realized the dire consequences of doing so. No matter how many false "merits" and alleged "feats" can one attribute to Abu Bakr, Umar, Uthman, and all the *sahabah*, such "merits" and "feats" can never reach the lofty status of Ahlul Bayt, nor can they reach its zenith simply because the prayers of all those who thus attribute and allege can never be accepted by Allah so long as they do not seek nearness to Him by invoking His blessings unto Ali ibn Abu Talib next to Muhammad, since he is the master of the `Itrat*, as everyone knows.

It is for this reason that they resorted to its adulteration by adding something from their own selves which the Messenger of Allah never mandated in the hope of enhancing the status of their masters among the *sahabah*, deliberately curtailing this invocation from the very first century. Notice how whenever they wrote a book, they left it without stating the complete blessing unto Muhammad and his Progeny, and whenever they mention "Muhammad", or "the Prophet", or "the Messenger of Allah", they say: *Salla Allahu alaihi was sallam* (Allah blessed and saluted him), removing any reference to the Progeny of Muhammad. And if you converse with one of them and ask him to bless Muhammad, he will answer you by saying: *Salla Allahu alaihi wa sallam*, without referring to his Progeny. Some of them go as far as circumventing it even more, saying only: *Salli wa sallim* (bless and salute).

But if you ask any Shi`a, be he from Arabia or Persia, etc., to bless Muhammad, he would say: *Allahomma Salli ala Muhammadin wa Aali Muhammad* (O Allah! I invoke You to bless Muhammad and the Progeny of Muhammad).

The books written by "Ahlul Sunnah wal Jama'ah" quote the Messenger of Allah mandating to "Say: *Allahomma Salli ala Muhammadin wa Aali Muhammad*," applying the present and future tense in the form of a supplication, an invocation, directed to the most Glorified One. Despite all of that, they are satisfied with the phrase "Salla Allahu Alaihi wa sallam," applying the past tense and in the narrative mode without making any reference to the Prophet's Progeny.

Indeed, the leader of "Ahlul Sunnah wal Jama'ah," namely Mu`awiyah ibn Abu Sufyan, tried to remove any reference whatsoever to Muhammad in the *azan*.[5] No wonder, then, to find those who follow and emulate him deliberately circumventing and distorting sending blessings unto him. Had they been able to eliminate it altogether, they would have done just that, but there is no way they could or can ever do so. No way!

You may nowadays hear those who ascend the pulpits, especially Wahhabi pulpits, offering nothing but the adulterated invocation of Allah's blessings unto him and his progeny. They may either use the curtailed supplication or, if they feel obligated to complete it, they will then add to it the phrase: "... and unto all his *sahabah*," or they may say, "... and unto his good and pure *sahabah*," thus changing the Qur'anic verse referring to the purification of Ahlul Bayt to make it sound as though it was revealed in honor not of Ahlul Bayt but of the *sahabah*. They do so in order to mislead the general public into thinking that the *sahabah* enjoy the same merits enjoyed by Ahlul Bayt.

They have, in fact, learned the art of adulterating and distorting from their very first *faqih* and "great leader" Abdullah ibn Umar of whose hatred towards Ahlul Bayt we are already fully aware. In his *Al-Mawatta*, Malik indicates that Abdullah ibn Umar

---

[5] For documentation of this claim, refer to p. 46 of my book *Ask Those Who Know*.

used to stand at the grave of the Prophet, blessing him, Abu Bakr, and Umar.[6]

If you, dear researcher, contemplate on the *status quo*, you will find such an addition, that is, the blessing of the *sahabah* in addition to blessing the Prophet and his Progeny, has no basis neither in the Holy Qur'an nor in the Prophet's Sunnah.

Rather, both the Holy Qur'an and the Sunnah have enjoined blessing Muhammad and his Progeny, and the command is directed to the *sahabah* before anyone else. You do not see such an addition except with "Ahlul Sunnah wal Jama`ah." How many are the innovations in the creed which they have invented, calling them "Sunnah," aiming thereby to cover someone's merit or to hide a fact?

"They wish to put out the Light of Allah with their mouths, while Allah insists upon completing His Light though the unbelievers are averse thereto." (Holy Qur'an, 61:8)

---

[6] Explanation to Malik, *Al-Muwatta'*, Vol. 6, p. 180, the chapter titled "Tanweer al-Hawalik" (enlightening the dark areas).

ALLEGATIONS REFUTED BY FACTS

In this chapter, we would like to make clear for every wise person who is free from bias, who abandons fanaticism, and who removes the curtain from both his vision and insight in order to pursue the right guidance and the truth. We would like to tell him that all pillars of "Ahlul Sunnah wal Jama'ah," as well as their Imams, have acted against the clear Sunnah of the Prophet, leaving it behind their backs, deliberately and willingly forsaking it.

No Muslim should be deceived by what he hears here or there of false praise based on neither a clear evidence nor a good argument. While unveiling these facts, we do not charge them with anything, nor do we add anything to what they themselves have stated in their Sahih, Musnad, and Tarikh books.

We have already indicated some of these facts in our previous books, and we graciously passed by them, yet there is no harm in mentioning them here in detail so that the sun of guidance may shine, the clouds of misguidance may be dispelled, and the light may replace the darkness.

In the following chapter, we will discuss the Imams and the pillars relied upon by "Ahlul Sunnah wal Jama'ah," the ones whom the latter regard as the zenith of scholarship and jurisprudence. They prefer them over the pure Imams from the offspring of the Prophet, deliberately ignoring a number of certain *sahabah* who were known to the elite, as well as to the commoners, be they scholars or illiterate-as being immoral, remote from the spirit and ethics of Islam.

Among the latter are: Mu'awiyah and his son Yazid[1], Ibn al-As, Ibn Marwan, Ibn Shu'bah, and their likes. Despite all of this,

---

[1] Ibn Sa'd, *Al-Tabaqat al-Kubra*, Vol. 5, p. 47, where Abdullah, who was bathed by the angels, is quoted saying, "By Allah! We did not disobey

we do not waste our time by writing about these men to unveil their faults; some unbiased men among the historians and thinkers have already spared us this task.

Instead, we will discuss in this research those Imams who gained fame as being righteous, fair, ascetic, and God-fearing; in short, those regarded by "Ahlul Sunnah wal Jama'ah" as the pillars, so that we may closely become familiar with their distortion of the Sunnah of the Prophet.

They invented in this nation innovations which caused dissension and misguidance, thus causing the collapse of the lofty structure erected by the Messenger of Allah who spent his entire life struggling to safeguard and firm its foundations.

I have chosen twelve of the pillars of "Ahlul Sunnah wal Jama'ah" who played a very significant role in influencing the events, in changing the characteristics of the creed, and in dividing and fragmenting the nation.

Yazid till we feared lest we should be hurled with stones from the skies, (for he is) a man who sleeps with his mothers, daughters, and sisters, who drinks wine and forsakes the prayers. By Allah! Had I had none to assist me, I would have done my best to fight him, seeking nearness to Allah." Yes; such is Yazid, the man well known for his wines and sins, the man who killed the fragrant flower of the Messenger of Allah as he was accompanied by all the Prophet's Progeny, permitting his soldiers to violate the sanctity of the Medina of the Prophet. Despite all of this, you can still find an "Islamic" state writing a book titled Facts about Ameer al-Momineen Yazid ibn Mu`awiyah!

IMAMS AND PILLARS OF AHLUL SUNNAH WAL JAMA'AH

These are:

1. Abu Bakr ibn Abu Quhafa, the first caliph
2. Umar ibn al-Khattab, the second caliph
3. Uthman ibn Affan, the third caliph
4. Talhah ibn Ubaydullah
5. al-Zubayr ibn al-Awwam
6. Sa'd ibn Abu Waqqas
7. Abdul-Rahman ibn Awf
8. Ayesha daughter of Abu Bakr, Mother of the Faithful
9. Khalid ibn al-Waleed
10. Abu Hurayra al-Dawsi
11. Abdullah ibn Umar
12. Abdullah ibn al-Zubayr

These are twelve personalities whom I have selected from many pillars of "Ahlul Sunnah wal Jama'ah" due to the fact that they are quite often referred to and praised, or to the abundance of their narrations and the proliferation of their knowledge, as they claim.

We will briefly discuss each one of them and highlight how they violated the Prophet's Sunnah either deliberately or due to ignorance, so that it will become evident to the researcher that "Ahlul Sunnah wal Jama'ah" claim what is not theirs, following their own inclinations, alleging that they are right whereas all others are wrong.

1. ABU BAKR "AL-SIDDIQ" IBN ABU QUHAFA

In some of our previously published researches, we proved how he collected five hundred *ahadith* of the

Prophet, burnt them, then delivered a sermon in which he said, "Do not quote any *hadith* of the Messenger of Allah; whoever asks you, say: `Between us and you is the Book of Allah; so, act upon what it permits and stay away from what it prohibits.'" We also indicated that he violated the Sunnah of the Prophet in recording the Book, supporting Umar in his statement in which he said, "The Messenger of Allah is hallucinating, and the Book of Allah suffices us."

He also discarded all the *ahadith* mandating the caliphate of Ali, thus usurping the caliphate for himself.

And he abandoned the Sunnah of the Prophet with regard to the appointment of Usamah as his [military] leader, refusing to participate in his campaign.

And he abandoned the Sunnah of the Prophet by hurting the feelings of the Prophet's daughter Fatima al-Zahra, earning her anger.

And he abandoned the Sunnah of the Prophet by fighting and killing the Muslims who refused to pay him their *zakat*.

And he abandoned the Sunnah of the Prophet by using burning to death as a form of cold blooded execution even though the Prophet prohibited such an action.

And he abandoned the Sunnah of the Prophet when he stopped giving money to those whose hearts could have been won and inclined to Islam, following Umar's view in their regard.

And he abandoned the Sunnah of the Prophet when he appointed Umar as the caliph over the Muslims without even consulting with them.

Yes; all these and other actions are violations of the Sunnah of the Prophet recorded by the authors of the Sahih books of "Ahlul Sunnah wal Jama'ah" and by their historians. They are violations filling their biography books.

So, if the Prophet's Sunnah is what the scholars have defined as "every statement or action of or endorsement by the Messenger of Allah," Abu Bakr has violated the Sunnah through his statements, actions, or decisions.

Among the Prophet's statements which he violated is this one: "Fatima is part of me; whoever angers her angers me." Fatima died angry with Abu Bakr according to al-Bukhari. Another is the Prophet's statement saying: "The curse of Allah be upon anyone who lags behind Usamah's army." He said so when they challenged his appointment of Usamah over them and refused to go to war with him and under his military command. Abu Bakr, despite such admonition, lagged behind Usamah's army under the pretext of taking care of the issue of caliphate.

Among his actions in violation of the Sunnah is what the Messenger of Allah used to do with those whose hearts could be won towards Islam; he was very kind to them and even gave them a portion of the *zakat* as commanded by Allah, the Most Exalted One. But Abu Bakr deprived them of that right which the Holy Qur'an had already mandated, and which was carried out by the Prophet, only to please Umar ibn al-Khattab who said to them, "We have no need for you."

Among the decisions whereby he violated the Sunnah was a decree made by the Prophet to write his *ahadith* down and to disseminate them among the public: Abu Bakr burnt them instead and prohibited everyone from disseminating or quoting them.

Add to all the above the fact that he was ignorant about many Qur'anic injunctions. He was, for instance, asked once about the rule with regard to one who dies leaving some wealth but neither a will nor dependents. He answered by saying, "I shall state my own view in its regard; if it is correct, it is by the Grace of Allah; but if it is wrong, it is my own error and that of Satan."[1]

How can you help being amazed about the caliph of the Muslims who is asked about an injunction which Allah explains in His Book and which the Messenger of Allah has clarified in his Sunnah, so he sets aside both the Book and the Sunnah to state his own personal view, then he admits that Satan may over-power his mind?!

All this comes in the light of the fact that Muslim scholars had already decided that anyone who expresses his own view with regard to the Book of Allah commits apostasy. We have also come to know that the Prophet never stated his own personal view, nor did he ever employ *qiyas*. Add to all this the fact that Abu Bakr used to say, "Do not force me to act upon the Sunnah of your Prophet, for I cannot bear it." If Abu Bakr could not bear the Sunnah of the Prophet, how can his followers and supporters claim to be the followers of the same Sunnah?

---

[1] This statement is quoted in Ibn Kathir's *Tafsir* and in that of al-Khazin, in addition to *Al-Tafsir al-Kabir* of al-Fakhr al-Razi, who all explain the verse in Surat al-Nisaa (Women) saying "They ask you for a decision; say: Allah decides for you with regard to the kalala, etc."

He may be unable to tolerate it because it reminds him of his own deviation therefrom and his distance from the Messenger; otherwise, how can you interpret the verses saying,

"He (Allah) has not laid upon you any hardship in the religion" (Holy Qur'an, 22:78),

"Allah desires ease for you, and He does not desire for you any hardship" (Holy Qur'an, 2:185), *"Allah does not overburden any soul with more than what it can bear"* (Holy Qur'an, 2:286), and

"Whatever the Messenger brings you, accept it, and keep back from whatever he forbids you" (Holy Qur'an, 59:7)?

Abu Bakr's statement that he cannot bear the Prophet's Sunnah is his response to the above verses. If Abu Bakr, the first caliph after the Prophet, was unable to bear his Sunnah, during that time and age, how can Muslims of our time be asked to uphold Allah's injunctions as embedded in His Book and act upon the Sunnah of His Messenger?! But we have found Abu Bakr violating the Prophet's Sunnah even in easy matters which can be undertaken by poor and ignorant people:

Abu Bakr abandoned the offering of sacrifices which the Messenger of Allah used to do and stress, and all Muslims came to know that to offer such sacrifices was a highly recommended and emphasized Sunnah; so, how could the caliph of Muslims abandon them?!

In his chapter on the mother, al-Shafi`i, as well as others, have said:

Abu Bakr and Umar, may Allah be pleased with them, never offered sacrifices because they hated others to follow their example and consider doing so as being obligatory.

This is an erroneous and a groundless justification; all the *sahabah* had by then come to know that offering sacrifices was a

Sunnah, a commendable act, not an obligation. Even if we suppose that people thought that they were obligatory, what harm could have resulted especially after having seen how Umar invented the *Taraweeh* prayers which were neither a Sunnah nor an obligation; rather, the Prophet had prohibited them, yet most "Ahlul Sunnah wal Jama'ah" nowadays think that they are obligatory?

By abandoning the Prophet's Sunnah with regard to offering sacrifices, Abu Bakr and Umar may have desired to mislead the people into thinking that not all what the Messenger of Allah had done was obligatory, and that it could be abandoned and ignored. This may explain their statement: "The Book of Allah suffices us," and so will the statement made by Abu Bakr wherein he said, "Do not quote any of the Prophet's *ahadith* and say: `Between us and you is the Book of Allah; so, act upon what it permits and stay away from what it prohibits.'" Thereupon, had someone argued with Abu Bakr about the Prophet's Sunnah relevant, for example, to offering sacrifices, Abu Bakr would probably have answered him by saying, "Do not talk to me about anything relevant to the Prophet, and show me where the Book of Allah refers to offering sacrifices."

Thus can a researcher understand why the Prophet's Sunnah remained unknown to them, forsaken, and why they altered the injunctions of Allah and His Messenger to fit their own views and *qiyas* and whatever they liked of matters agreeing with their own inclinations.

The examples which we have put forth here are only a drop in the bucket compared to what Abu Bakr had done to the revered Sunnah of the Prophet and to the insults, burning, negligence with which he meted it. If we wished, we could write a separate book discussing them.

How can any Muslim feel comfortable about a person the extent of whose knowledge is this much, whose relationship to the revered Sunnah of the Prophet is like that, and how can his followers call themselves Ahlul Sunnah?! Followers of the Sunnah do not forsake the Sunnah, nor do they burn it. Nay! Ahlul Sunnah are those who follow and revere it.

"Say: If you love Allah, follow me so that Allah may love you and forgive your sins, and Allah is oft-Forgiving, Merciful. Say: *Obey Allah and the Messenger, but if they turn away, Allah does not love those who disbelieve."* (Holy Qur'an, 3:31-32)

2. UMAR IBN AL-KHATTAB "AL-FAROOQ"

We have come to know from our previously published researches that he was the hero of the opposition to the honored Sunnah of the Prophet and the one who defied the Prophet's last order, saying: "The Messenger of Allah is hallucinating, and the Book of Allah suffices us." According to the statements of the Messenger who never uttered anything out of his own inclination, Umar is behind the misguidance of those who strayed in this nation.[1]

We also came to know that he insulted, hurt the feelings of and terrorized Fatima al-Zahra, frightening her and her children when he assaulted her house and threatened to burn it.

We also came to know that he collected the books recording the Prophet's Sunnah then burnt them, forbidding people from quoting the Prophet.

Umar violated the Prophet's Sunnah as long as he lived, even when the Prophet was still alive, and he violated the Sunnah of the Prophet who required him to be among those recruited for Usamah's army. But he did not go with Usamah on the pretext of assisting Abu Bakr with the matters relevant to the caliphate.

And he violated the Qur'an and the Sunnah when he stopped the distribution of the share of *zakat* due to those whose hearts could be won for Islam.

---

[1] What proves this is the statement of the Messenger: "Let me write you a book beyond which you will never stray." Ibn Abbas has said, "Had he written it, no couple in this nation would have disputed with one another." Since it was Umar who prohibited the Messenger of Allah from writing it, accusing him of hallucinating so that he would not insist on its writing, we can conclude that he is the one responsible for the misguidance of the misguided and the one who deprived the Islamic nation of guidance.

And he violated the Qur'an and the Sunnah with regard to *mut`at al-hajj* and also to *mut`at al-nisaa*.

And he violated the Qur'an and the Sunnah which required the pronouncement of the divorce statement thrice, making such a requirement only once.

And he violated the Qur'an and the Sunnah with regard to the obligation of *tayammum*, invalidating the prayers in the absence of water.

And he violated the Qur'an and the Sunnah which prohibited people from spying on one another, inventing espionage.

And he violated the Qur'an and the Sunnah when he eliminated a part of the *azan* and substituted it with something from his own.

And he violated the Qur'an and the Sunnah when he failed to penalize Khalid ibn al-Waleed whom he used to threaten of penalizing.

And he violated the Qur'an and the Sunnah which prohibit the *nafl* prayers being prayed in congregation, inventing the Taraweeh.

And he violated the Qur'an and the Sunnah with regard to the distribution of public money, inventing discrimination and creating class distinction in Islam.

And he violated the Qur'an and the Sunnah when he set up *majlis al-shura*, entrusting Ibn Awf to be in charge of it.

Is not all of this indicative of Banu Umayyah's ridicule and mockery of Islam and Muslims when they attribute such "merits" to a man who was very well known of being rough and heavy handed and continuously opposing the Prophet?[2] It is as though those Umayyads were saying to the Muslims, "Muhammad's time and whatever it contained has passed away, while our own time has come to issue whatever religious rules we like and prefer. Now you have become our slaves even against your wish and against the will of the Prophet in whom you believe."

Is this not a sort of reaction and an attempt to seek revenge so that Quraysh's leadership would be rendered back to Banu Umayyah who fought Islam and the Prophet of Islam?

If Umar ibn al-Khattab tried very hard to obliterate the Prophet's *ahadith*, ridiculing them and acting to their contrary them even during the lifetime of the Prophet himself, it is no wonder that Quraysh handed the reins of its leadership to him, making him its supreme leader. This is so due to the fact that after the dawn of Islam, Umar became its articulate spokesman and the hero of its opposition. After the demise of the Prophet, he became the symbol of its wielding might and great hope in realizing its dreams and ambitions to ascend to authority.

It is not a mere coincident to find Umar ibn al-Khattab acting in contradiction to the Prophet's Sunnah and trying to relocate Ibrahim's standing place at the House of Allah and place it where it used to be during the days of ignorance (*Jahiliyya*). Ibn Sa'd has said the following in his *Tabaqat* just as other historians have:

When the Prophet conquered Mecca, he attached Ibrahim's standing place (*maqam*) to the House just as it used to be during the time of Ibrahim and Isma`eel, peace be upon them, because the

---

[2] Muslim, *Sahih*, Vol. 4, p. 59, commenting by saying that Ibn Abbas and Ibn al-Zubayr disputed with one another with regard to both types of mut`a. Jabir ibn Abdullah al-Ansari said, "We used to do both when we were in the company of the Messenger of Allah, then Umar prohibited us, so we stopped."

Arabs during the period of Jahiliyya had separated it and relocated it where it is now. During the lifetime of the Prophet and that of Abu Bakr, it used to be attached to the House.[3]

Can you, by your Lord, find a justification for Umar ibn al-Khattab deliberately killing a Sunnah of the Prophet who did what both Ibrahim and Isma`eel had done. He revived the traditions of *jahiliyya* by rebuilding the *maqam* as it used to be during that time?

How could Quraysh not have preferred him over others and narrate in his praise what goes beyond one's imagination, so much so that even his friend Abu Bakr, who had preceded him in being the caliph, never acquired such a praise? According to al-Bukhari, "Abu Bakr's temper was tainted with some weakness, but Umar took it (caliphate) from him, and no genius could have ever committed such a calumny." This is only a small portion of the innovations which he introduced in Islam. They all contradict the Book of Allah and the Sunnah of His Messenger. If we wish to compile all the innovations and injunctions wherein he followed his own personal views and which he forced people to adopt, a separate book will be needed, but we only desired here to be brief.

One may say, "How could Umar ibn al-Khattab have contradicted the Book of Allah and the Sunnah of His Prophet while Allah, the Exalted One, says, `It does not behove any believing man or woman to make any choice in their matter once Allah and His Apostle have decided it, and whoever disobeys Allah and His Messenger surely strays off a manifest straying?"* (Holy Qur'an, 33:36)

Actually, this question is often repeated by most people nowadays as though they are in disbelief, not accepting the fact that Umar ibn al-Khattab did any such things.

---

[3] Ibn Sa`d, *Tabaqat*, Vol. 3, p. 204. Al-Suyuti, *Tarikh*, where the caliphate of Umar ibn al-Khattab is discussed.

To these folks we would like to say: "This is confirmed by his own friends and followers from `Ahlul Sunnah wal Jama`a' who unknowingly prefer him over the Prophet." If what is said about him (above) is falsehood, then their Sahih books would be rendered unworthy of any consideration, and they will have no argument beyond that to support their own beliefs! Yet most historical events were recorded during the government of "Ahlul Sunnah wal Jama'ah" whose love, respect, and regard for the son of al-Khattab can never be doubted.

But if they are authentic, which is the unavoidable truth, then the Muslims nowadays are bound to rethink their stands and reconsider all their beliefs if they truly are followers of the Sunnah and the consensus.

You can find most researchers these days, having been too dumbfounded to refute these narratives and historical events which are recorded by all scholars and traditionists, being unable to disprove them. You can find them interpreting and seeking weak pretexts which cannot be based on any scholarly argument. Some of them took to enumerating his (Umar's) innovations, turning them into merits to his credit for which he should be thanked! It is as though Allah and His Messenger did not know what the best interest of the Muslims is, so they overlooked such innovations we seek Allah's forgiveness so Umar discovered them and enacted the rules for them following the demise of the Messenger of Allah!

Since Umar is the leader and Imam of "Ahlul Sunnah wal Jama'ah," then I clear myself before Allah from such Sunnah and Jama`a, pleading to Him, the Most Glorified One, to take my soul away at the moment of death as a follower of the Sunnah of the last of His Prophets and the master of all Messengers, our master Muhammad, and a follower of the path of his good Progeny, the purified ones.

3. UTHMAN IBN AFFAN "DHUL-NOORAYN"

He is the third caliph who reached caliphate through the schemes of Umar ibn al-Khattab and Abdul Rahman ibn Awf who made him swear to rule the Muslims according to the Book of Allah and the Sunnah of both caliphs (who had preceded him). I personally doubt his having acted upon the second condition, that is, to follow (by implication) the Sunnah of the Messenger of Allah.

It is so because Abdul-Rahman ibn Awf knew, more than anyone else, that both caliphs, Abu Bakr and Umar, did not rule according to the Sunnah of the Prophet, that they, instead, ruled according to their own *ijtihad* and personal views, and that the Prophet's Sunnah would have been rendered completely non-existent during the reign of both Shaykhs had not Imam Ali stood to revive it whenever the circumstances permitted him to do so.

Most likely, he preconditioned the Commander of the Faithful Ali ibn Abu Talib to rule among them according to the Book of Allah and the Sunnah of both Shaykhs, but Ali refused this condition saying, "I do not rule except according to the Book of Allah and the Sunnah of His Messenger." Ali, therefore, lost his chance then to become the caliph because he wanted to revive the Sunnah of the Prophet, whereas Uthman won it because he agreed to continue the march in the footsteps of Abu Bakr and Umar who had stated more than once that, "We have no need for the Prophet's Sunnah; rather, the Qur'an suffices us; so, let them act according to what it permits and stay away from what it prohibits."

What increases our conviction with regard to this assumption is that Uthman ibn Affan understood this condition as implying following his own views in as far as the [Islamic] injunctions are concerned, as did both of his friends; such is the "Sunnah" enacted by both Shaykhs following the demise of the Prophet.

This is why we find out that Uthman gave way to his own views and followed *ijtihad* more than his predecessors had ever done, so much so that the *sahabah* resented it and went to Abdul-Rahman ibn Awf to blame him saying, "This is the doing of your own self!" When opposition to and resentment towards Uthman intensified, the latter stood to deliver a sermon to the *sahabah* in which he said, "Why did you not express your resentment to Umar ibn al-Khattab who (too) followed his own views? Was it so because he used to scare you with his cane?!" Ibn Qutaybah narrates the following:

Uthman stood on the pulpit to deliver a sermon when people expressed their resentment to him. He said: "By Allah, O fellow Muhajirs and Ansars! You have found fault with many things I have done and condemned many others though you had endorsed similar actions done by the son of al-Khattab, but he shut your mouths and subdued you, and none of you dared to look him in the eyes nor point a finger at him. By Allah! My kinsfolk number more than those of the son of al-Khattab, and they are more ready to come to my aid."[1]

I personally think that the *sahabah* who belonged to the Muhajirun and Ansar did not oppose Uthman's *ijtihad*, for they had by then become used to it and even blessed it from day one, but they resented his deposing them from their government posts to replace them with the promiscuous ones from his cousins and relatives who had only recently been fighting Islam and Muslims.

The Muhajirs and the Ansars did not voice their objection to Abu Bakr or to Umar simply because they did share authority with both of them. Both caliphs gave the Ansars and the Muhajirun the posts which paid very well and which made them powerful.

---

[1] Ibn Qutaybah, *Tarikh al-Khulafa*, Vol. 8, p. 31.

As for Uthman, he deposed most of them and doled out huge sums of money to Banu Umayyah without a measure. It was then that they denounced him, cast doubts about his authority, till in the end they killed him. This is the truth which the Messenger of Allah had predicted when he said to them, "I do not fear lest you should commit *shirk* after me, but I do fear lest you should fiercely compete with one another (to obtain wealth and political power)."

Imam Ali had said, "It is as though they had never heard the verse of the Most Exalted One saying, `Such is the last abode: We assign it for those who have no desire to exalt themselves on earth, nor to cause mischief, and the good end is for the righteous."* (Holy Qur'an, 28:83)

Yes, by Allah, they had heard and comprehended that verse, but the life of this world appeared very sweet in their eyes, and they liked its glitter.

This is the truth. If we presume that they condemned his distortion of the Sunnah of the Prophet, this cannot be proven. Since they had not condemned the same when done by Abu Bakr and Umar, how can they condemn his (Uthman's) doing it? The assumption is that Uthman ibn Affan had indeed a larger number of relatives and supporters than Abu Bakr and Umar, as he himself had stated, because he was the chief of Banu Umayyah, and Banu Umayyah were closer in kinship to the Prophet than Taym or Adiyy, the tribes to which Abu Bakr and Umar belonged respectively, more powerful, more influential, more prestigious, and more distinguished in descent.

Because the *sahabah* did not denounce what Abu Bakr and Umar did, rather they emulated these men's Sunnah and knowingly abandoned the Sunnah of the Prophet, they could not have denounced something which Uthman did and which they had already endorsed when done by someone else.

The proof testifying to this fact is that they were present on many occasions during which Uthman altered the Sunnah of the Prophet such as performing the complete prayers when he was travelling, his prohibition of *talbiya*, his leaving out the *takbir* from the prayers, his prohibition of *mut`at al-hajj*..., etc., without anyone expressing his objection other than Ali ibn Abu Talib, as we will come to clarify by the will of Allah.

The *sahabah* knew the Prophet's Sunnah very well, yet they deliberately contradicted it for the sake of pleasing caliph Uthman.

In his book *Al-Sunan al-Kubra*, al-Bayhaqi quotes Abd al-Rahman ibn Yazid saying, "We were in the company of Abdullah ibn Mas`ud once when he entered Mina's mosque. `How many *rak`ats* did the commander of the faithful (meaning Uthman) pray?' asked he. He was told that he had prayed four *rak`ats*.

We, therefore, asked him, `Did you not narrate one *hadith* to us telling us that the Prophet had prayed only two *rak`ats*, and so did Abu Bakr?' He answered by saying, `Yes, I did. And I can now repeat the same, but Uthman is now the Imam, and I shall not dissent from anything he does, since dissension is evil.'"[2]

So read such a statement and wonder about this *sahabi*, Abdullah ibn Mas`ud, who was one of the most distinguished *sahabah*, labelling dissenting with Uthman as evil while contradicting the Messenger of Allah as goodness all of it! Can anyone say beyond this that they resented his forsaking the Prophet's Sunnah?!

Sufyan ibn Ayeenah has quoted Ja`far ibn Muhammad saying:

---

[2] Al-Bayhaqi, *Al-Sunan al-Kubra*, Vol. 3, p. 144.

While staying at Mina, Uthman fell sick, whereupon Ali came. Ali was asked by people to lead the prayers. Ali, therefore, said, "If you wish, but I shall perform the prayers according to the way the Messenger of Allah used to pray, I mean two *rak`ats*." They said: "No, we insist on four *rak`ats* prayers performed by commander of the faithful Uthman." Ali refused to lead their prayers.³

So read and wonder about these companions, who were thousands in number, and who were at Mina during the *hajj* season, how they openly refused to follow the Sunnah of the Messenger of Allah and did not accept anything other than the *bid`at* invented by Uthman!

If Abdullah ibn Mas`ud regarded dissenting from Uthman as evil, so he performed four *rak`ats* despite the fact that he narrated about the Prophet praying only two, he might have done so out of his fear of those who were counted in the thousands, and who accepted nothing other than what Uthman used to do, discarding the Prophet's Sunnah.

Do not forget, having come to know this much, to salute and greet the Prophet and the Commander of the Faithful Ali ibn Abu Talib who refused to lead their prayers in any way other than that performed by the Messenger of Allah, desiring to revive the Sunnah which those folks had violated, fearing nobody's blame, showing no apprehension of their multitudes or schemes.

It is noteworthy in this regard to point out to the fact that Abdullah ibn Umar had said, "Prayers of a traveler are in two *rak`ats*; whoever violates the Sunnah commits *kufr* (apostasy)."⁴ Thus, Abdullah ibn Umar [implicitly] labels as *kafir* caliph Uthman

---

³ Ibn Hazm, *Al-Muhalla*, Vol. 4, p. 270.

⁴ This is stated on p. 140, Vol. 3, and also by al-Tabrani in his book *Al-Mu`jam al-Kabir*, and on p. 310, Vol. 2, of *Ahkamal-Qur'an* of al-Jassas.

ibn Affan and all the *sahabah* who followed his *bid`at* by performing a complete prayer while travelling. Despite all of this, we shall return to this *faqih*, namely Abdullah ibn Umar [ibn al-Khattab] in order to judge him according to what he himself had judged others.

Al-Bukhari has stated the following in his *Sahih*:

I heard Uthman and Ali, may Allah be pleased with both of them, when they were in the area between Mecca and Medina, while Uthman was banning the mut`a and the combination of both *hajj* and `*umra*.

When Ali saw that, he [contradicted him and] said, after shouting "Allahu Akbar," *Labbayka `umratan wa hajjan ma`a!* ("At your service, O Lord, do I perform both the `*umra* and the *hajj together*"). Uthman, therefore, said, "You see me forbidding people from doing something, yet you do it yourself?!" Ali said, "Never shall I abandon the Sunnah of the Messenger of Allah because of what someone else says."[5]

Can you help being amazed at seeing the caliph of the Muslims openly violating the Sunnah and going beyond that to forbid people from following it, yet none opposes him except Ali ibn Abu Talib who would never abandon the Sunnah of the Messenger of Allah even if he were to pay for his life for it?

Tell me, by your Lord, do you find among the companions of Muhammad anyone other than the father of al-Husayn truly acting upon the Prophet's Sunnah?

Despite the ruler's might and toughness, and despite the support meted to him by the *sahabah*, Ali never abandoned the

---

[5] Al-Bukhari, *Sahih*, Vol. 2, p. 151, in a chapter dealing with mut`a and with combining both `umra and hajj.

Sunnah, and here are their books and Sahihs testifying to the truth of our conclusion that he, greeting from Allah be upon him, tried his best to revive the Prophet's Sunnah and bring people back to it, but "No value is there for the view of anyone who is not obeyed," as he himself had said. In that time and age, none was there to obey him and follow his instructions except the Shi'as who accepted him as their leader, who followed in his footsteps, and who referred to him in every regard.

Thus does it becomes very clear to us that the *sahabah* did not find anything wrong with Uthman altering the Prophet's Sunnah. We have come to know from reviewing their Sahih books how they contradict the Sunnah of the Prophet, but they do not contradict Uthman in his innovation.

They, nevertheless, revolted against him out of their pursuit of the good things in this insignificant life, running after wealth, power, and authority. They are the ones who were unrelenting in their fight against Ali because he did not give them government posts but demanded their returning the money which they had wrongfully amassed to *bayt al-mal* of the Muslims so that the indigent might benefit from it.

May Allah support you, O father of al-Hasan ! O you who safeguarded the Book of your Lord and the Sunnah of your cousin the Messenger of Allah and were an Imam for the righteous, the supporter of the downtrodden! Your Shi'as are the ones who shall attain victory, for they upheld the Book of Allah and the Sunnah of His Messenger by rallying around you and referring to you.

Can you believe, dear reader and discreet researcher, after all the researches which you have come across, that the followers of Uthman ibn Affan can be regarded as the followers of the Sunnah while the followers of Ali are the "rejectionists" and the inventors of *bid`ats*?! So pass your judgment in the light of what Allah has shown you if you are fair.

"Surely Allah commands you to return the trusts to their rightful owners, and that when you judge among the people, you should judge justly; surely Allah admonishes you with what is excellent; surely Allah is hears and sees." (Holy Qur'an, 4:58)

4. TALHAH IBN UBAYDULLAH

He is one of the most prominent and renowned companions of the Prophet and one of the six persons recommended by Umar ibn al-Khattab to be caliphs. About him, Umar had said that "He is a believer when pleased, an apostate when angry; one day he acts as a human being, another as a devil," and he is one of the ten men who received the glad tidings of going to Paradise as "Ahlul Sunnah wal Jama'ah" claim.

When we research the books of history trying to define his personality, it becomes obvious to us that he was one of those who loved this world, who were deceived and dragged by it, who sold their creed for its sake, thus losing their souls; their trade was in vain, and on the Day of Judgment, they will be among those who will deeply regret.

He is Talhah who, whenever he used to say, "Once the Messenger of Allah dies, I shall marry Ayesha, for she is my cousin," he hurt the feelings of the Messenger of Allah. When the Messenger of Allah heard this statement, he felt deeply hurt. And when the verse referring to the veil and to the Prophet's women being required to be veiled from the public, Talhah said, "Is Muhammad prohibiting us from seeing our cousins and preferring to marry them himself? Should anything happen to him, I shall most certainly marry his wives after that."[1] When the feelings of the Messenger of Allah were hurt, this verse was revealed:

"It does not behove you to hurt [the feelings of] the Messenger of Allah, nor should you marry his wives after him at all; this surely is grievous in the sight of Allah." (Holy Qur'an, 33:53)

---

[1] This statement is recorded in the tafsir books written by Ibn Kathir, al-Qurtubi, al-Alusi, and many others who all quote it while explaining the sacred verse saying, "It did not befit you to harm [the feelings of] the Messenger of Allah, nor should you marry his wives after him."

This is the same Talhah who came to see Abu Bakr before the latter's demise and after his putting his promise of caliphate to Umar ibn al-Khattab in writing and said to him, "What will you say to your Lord after having installed over us a ruler who is rough and heavy handed?" Abu Bakr then taunted him with profane language.[2]

Yet we find him taking to silence and endorsing the new caliph, even becoming one of his supporters, working hard to amass wealth and buy slaves especially after having coveted the post of caliph following his being recommended by Umar to be the caliph after him.

Talhah is the same man who betrayed Imam Ali and joined the ranks of Uthman ibn Affan due to his prior knowledge that were the caliphate to be vested upon Ali, he would have no reason after that to be hopeful of attaining it himself. In this regard, Ali said, "So one of their men listened to his grudge, while another supported his son-in-law, despite weakness in this and in that..." Shaykh Muhammad Abdoh says the following in his Sharh:

Talhah was inclined towards Uthman due to the kinship between them according to what is recorded by the biographers. His mere inclination towards Uthman rather than Ali may be rendered to his being a man of Taym, for both Banu Hashim and Banu Taym had objected to the appointment of Abu Bakr to the caliphate.[3]

Undoubtedly, Talhah is one of those who attended the swearing of allegiance to Ali at Ghadeer Khumm and who had

---

[2] This is what Ibn Qutaybah records in his book *Al-Imama wal Siyasa* while discussing Abu Bakr's death and his appointment of Umar as the next caliph.

[3] Ibn Abul-Hadid, *Sharh Nahjul-Balagha*, Vol. 1, p. 88, commenting on the Shaqshaqia sermon.

heard the Prophet saying, "To whomsoever I have been the master, this Ali is his master." And there is no doubt that he heard the Messenger of Allah saying, "Ali is with the truth and the truth is with Ali." He was present on Khaybar day when he gave the standard to Ali saying that Ali loved Allah and His Messenger and they both loved him. He also knew that Ali was to the Prophet like Aaron to Moses. And he knew more and more...

But deeply rooted grudge and spite had filled his heart, so much so that he could see nothing except fanaticism to his tribe and bias to his cousin Ayesha daughter of Abu Bakr whom he aspired to marry after the demise of the Prophet, but the Qur'an made it impossible.

Yes, Talhah joined Uthman and swore to be loyal to him because Uthman used to give him many grants and gifts. When Uthman ascended the seat of caliphate, he showered Talhah without a measure with the wealth which belonged to the Muslims.[4] His wealth, therefore, and his cattle and slaves increased till his income from his property in Iraq alone reached one thousand dinars a day.

In his *Tabaqat*, Ibn Sa'd says, "At the time of his death, Talhah had left thirty million dirhams. The cash was two hundred thousand dinars, two million and two hundred thousand dirhams, and the rest was in the form of hamlets and real estate."[5] This is why Talhah was turned into an oppressor. He became arrogant and

---

[4] In *Al-Fitnat al-Kubra*, al-Tabari, Ibn Abul-Hadid, and Taha Husayn all say that Talhah had borrowed fifty thousand dinars from Uthman once. One day, he said to him, "Preparations have been made to pay you your money back; so, send someone to receive it." Uthman then said to him, "I have granted it to you, O father of Muhammad, in order to assist you in your manly support [of my government]." It is also said that Uthman had also given Talhah once as much as two hundred thousand dinars.

[5] Ibn Sa'd, *Tabaqat*, Vol. 3, p. 858.

started instigating people against his close friend Uthman in order to depose him and take his place.

Mother of the faithful Ayesha may have tempted him with the promise of caliphate because she, too, tried her best to undermine Uthman, and she had no doubt that caliphate would be the lot of her cousin Talhah.

When the news of Uthman's murder reached her, and when she was told that people had sworn the oath of allegiance to Talhah, she was very delighted and said, "Away with Na`thal[6] and may he be crushed! Congratulations to you, man of the finger, father of lion cubs! Congratulations to you, cousin! Allah bless your father! By Allah, they have found Talhah worthy of it!"

Yes, such was the way how Talhah rewarded Uthman, the man who made him wealthy. He betrayed him because of his own desire to succeed him as the caliph. He instigated people to revolt against him and was the most zealous in encouraging them to kill him, so much so that he even prohibited drinking water from reaching Uthman when the latter's house was under siege.

Ibn Abul-Hadid quotes Uthman saying the following when his house was besieged: "Woe unto me from the son of the woman of Hadramaut (meaning Talhah)! I gave him such-and-such in pure gold, and now he is seeking to shed my blood, encouraging others to kill me! O Allah! Do not permit him to enjoy it (caliphate), and let him face the evil ends of his mischief!"

Yes; such is Talhah who [first] sided with Uthman and selected him for the caliphate in order to distance Ali from it, and because Uthman had given him gold and silver, he now is instigating people against him, ordering them to kill him, prohibiting drinking water from reaching his house! And when they

---

[6] A bad name she coined for Uthman.

250

brought Uthman's corpse to be buried, he forbade them from burying it at the Muslims' cemetery, so Uthman had to be buried at Hish Kawkab where the Jews used to bury their dead![7]

Yet after all of that, we see Talhah as the very first person to swear the oath of allegiance to Imam Ali following Uthman's assassination, then he reneged from his oath and joined his cousin Ayesha at Mecca and suddenly started seeking revenge for Uthman! Praise be to Allah! Is there any calumny greater than this?!

Some historians justify this conduct by saying that Ali had refused to appoint him as the governor of Kufa and surrounding areas, so he reneged from his oath of allegiance to him and went out to fight the same Imam to whom he only yesterday had sworn to follow! Such is the nature of those who sink in their love for this world up to their summit, those who sell their hereafter and whose concern is nothing more than authority, power, and wealth.

Taha Husayn writes the following:

Talhah, then, used to represent a special type of opposition: He accepted whatever was secured for him of wealth and prestige, but when he coveted more, he joined the opposition till he caused many people to perish before he, too, finally perished.[8]

Such is Talhah who only yesterday swore the oath of allegiance to Imam Ali: He comes out only a few days later dragging the wife of the Messenger of Allah Ayesha to Basra, killing innocent people, plundering their wealth, and terrorizing them in order to force them to disobey Ali. Then he shamelessly

---

[7] These facts are recorded by: al-Tabari in his *Tarikh*, and by both al-Mada'ini and al-Waqidi while discussing Uthman's assassination.

[8] Taha Husayn, *Al-Fitna al-Kubra*, Vol. 1, p. 150.

stood to fight the Imam of his time to whom he had willingly and out of his own choice promised to obey and support.

Despite all of that, Imam Ali sought him shortly before the battle started, found him in the midst of the ranks of dissidents, and asked him, "Did you not swear the oath of allegiance to me? What caused you to dissent, O Talhah?" He said, "Seeking revenge for Uthman's murder." Ali said, "May Allah kill the foremost person responsible for Uthman's murder."

According to Ibn Asakir's narration, Imam Ali asked Talhah, "I ask you in the Name of Allah, O Talhah, did you hear the Messenger of Allah saying, `To whomsoever I have been the master, this Ali is his master; O Allah! Befriend whoever befriends him and be the enemy of whoever antagonizes him!'?" Talhah said, "Yes." Ali then asked him, "Why do you then fight me?" His answer was, "To seek revenge for Uthman's murder." Ali's answer was, "May Allah kill the foremost person responsible for Uthman's murder."

Allah did, indeed, favorably respond to Ali's supplication: Talhah was killed on that same day at the hands of Marwan ibn al-Hakam whom Talhah had brought there to fight Ali!

He is the Talhah of dissension, falsehood, and the turning of facts upside down without any regard for the call of conscience or for a sworn oath or for a promise made. Nor did he hear the call for justice. Imam Ali reminded him of his oath, thus driving his argument against him home, but he persisted, became puffed up with pride, and went to extremes in his misguidance, straying from the right path and causing others to stray with him.

Because of him, a great multitude of innocent people were killed, people who did not have anything to do with Uthman's assassination, nor did they even know him as long as they lived, nor did they even leave Basra...

Ibn Abul-Hadid has transmitted saying that when Talhah reached Basra, Abdullah ibn al-Hakeem al-Tameemi came to him to ask him about letters which he had received from him. He asked him, "*Ya Abu Muhammad!* (O father of Muhammad)! Are these the letters which you had sent us?" He answered in the affirmative. "But you had written us only yesterday,"

Abdullah went on, "urging us to depose Uthman and kill him; now you have killed him, you come to us seeking revenge for him! By my life! This is not what you have in mind; you only seek this world. Wait for a moment! If this is your view, why did you agree when Ali invited you to swear the oath of allegiance to him, so you willingly and obediently swore the oath of allegiance to him, then you reneged from your oath of allegiance, then you came to us to get us to join you in your dissension?!"[9] Yes; this is the naked truth about Talhah ibn Ubaydullah as narrated by the authors of the books of Sunnah and by the historians belonging to "Ahlul Sunnah wal Jama'ah." Yet they say that he is one of the ten men who received the glad tidings of going to Paradise...!

"Does every man among them covet to enter Paradise?" (Holy Qur'an, 70:38)

"Or shall We make those who belief and do good deeds like those who cause corruption in the land, or shall We make the righteous like the debauchees?" (Holy Qur'an, 38:28)

"Is one who believes like one who disbelieves? Surely they are not equal." (Holy Qur'an, 32:18)

"As for those who believe and do good deeds, for them are the gardens of refuge as their homes because of what they did. As for those who disbelieved, their abode is the fire: whenever they want

---

[9] The [Egyptian] Mu'tazilite scholar Ibn Abul-Hadid, *Sharh Nahjul-Balagha*, Vol. 2, p. 500.

to get out of it, they are returned into it, and it is said to them: Taste the torture of the fire in which you disbelieved." (Holy Qur'an, Surat al-Sajda, verses 19-20)

5. AL-ZUBAYR IBN AL-AWWAM

He, too, is among the most distinguished *sahabah* and one of the foremost in migrating to Medina. He enjoyed kinship with the Messenger of Allah: Safiyya daughter of Abd al-Muttalib, the Prophet's aunt, was his mother. He was also husband of Asmaa daughter of Abu Bakr and sister of Ayesha. He is also one of the six men recommended by Umar ibn al-Khattab to become caliphs.[1]

He is also one of those who received "the glad tidings of going to Paradise," according to "Ahlul Sunnah wal Jama`ah." No wonder, then, when we find him always in the company of his like Talhah: whenever Talhah's name is mentioned, it is always followed by al-Zubayr's and vice versa.

He is also one of those who competed with others for the riches of this world, filling their stomachs therewith. According to al-Tabari, his heritage amounted to fifty thousand dinars, one thousand horses, one thousand slaves, and many hamlets in Basra, Kufa, Egypt, and elsewhere.

In this regard, Taha Husayn says, "People vary with regard to the distribution of al-Zubayr's legacy.

---

[1] Umar ibn al-Khattab had invented that idea in order to pave the way for opposition to and competition with Ali simply because the *sahabah* knew fully well that caliphate rightfully belonged to Ali and was usurped by Quraysh. When Fatima al-Zahra argued with them in this regard, they said to her, "Had your husband and cousin was the foremost in approaching us (seeking to be the caliph), we would not have regarded anyone as his peer." But Umar ibn al-Khattab did not feel comfortable with the idea that the caliphate would go back after his death to its rightful owner, so he thus created an opposition party against him. Hence, each one of those men coveted caliphate for himself, and they all aspired to become chiefs, trading their creed for their world; their trade was never profitable

Those who mention the least say that his heirs divided thirty-five million [dinars] among them, whereas those who provide the maximum figure say that they divided fifty-two million. Moderates say that they divided forty million among them.

This should not surprise us. Al-Zubayr used to own real estate in Basra and Kufa, eleven houses in Medina, and property and real estate elsewhere.[2] Yet al-Bukhari narrates saying that al-Zubayr had left fifty million two hundred dinars.[3]

We do not intend by stating this expose to audit the *sahabah* with regard to their earnings of goods, or to the wealth they amassed, which may all be *halal*, but when we see how both Talhah and al-Zubayr expressed so much interest in worldly gains and come to know that they reneged from their oath of allegiance to the Commander of the Faithful Ali ibn Abu Talib simply because he decided to retrieve the money which Uthman had given away in order to return it to the Muslims' *bayt al-mal*, it is then that we entertain doubts about these men. Add to the above the fact that upon becoming caliph, Imam Ali immediately took to bringing people back to the Sunnah of the Prophet which he started by the distribution of the wealth in *bayt al-mal*, giving each and every Muslim three dinars, be he an Arab or a non-Arab, and this is exactly what the Prophet used to do as long as he lived. Thus, Ali put an end to the *bid`at* invented by Umar ibn al-Khattab who favored the Arabs over the non-Arabs, giving each Arab twice the share he gave the non-Arab.

Ali's efforts to bring people back to the Sunnah of the Prophet was sufficient reason for the *sahabah* to revolt against him since

---

[2] Taha Husayn, *Al-Fitna al-Kubra*, Vol. 1, p. 147.

[3] Al-Bukhari, *Sahih,* Vol. 4, p. 53, in a chapter dealing with the blessing in the wealth of a living or dead participant in a *ghazwa* (battle in which Prophet Muhammad (s) also participated).

they liked what Umar had invented. This is something which we overlooked while analyzing Quraysh who loved and sanctified Umar. He had favored Quraysh over all other Muslims, thus encouraging nationalistic Arab fanaticism, Qurayshi tribalism, and bourgeois class distinction.

How could Ali come a quarter of a century after the demise of the Prophet to bring Quraysh back to the way they used to be during the time of the Prophet who gave everyone the same, giving Bilal the Ethiopian as much as he gave his uncle al-Abbas? Quraysh, indeed, had resented the Messenger of Allah establishing such equality, and by sifting the biography of the Prophet, we can find how Qurayshites used to oppose him most of the time only for this reason.

It is also for this reason that Talhah and al-Zubayr were angry with the Commander of the Faithful Ali who gave all of them equally, and who deprived them of ruling the Muslims then decided to hold them accountable for the wealth which they had amassed in order to return stolen money to the indigent.

What is important, however, is that we should bear in mind that when he lost all hope of Ali appointing him as the governor of Basra and preferring him over others and fearing lest the new caliph should hold him accountable for amassing his legendary wealth, al-Zubayr came accompanied by his friend Talhah to seek Ali's permission to perform the `umra. It is then that Ali realized these men's hidden evil intentions. He then said about them, "By Allah! They do not seek to perform the `umra! Rather, they seek to carry out their treacherous scheme!"

Al-Zubayr joined his sister-in-law Ayesha daughter of Abu Bakr, took her and Talhah out heading in the direction of Basra. When the dogs at Hawab barked at her, Ayesha wanted to go back; therefore, they brought her fifty persons who were introduced to her as men of truth and integrity to swear falsely in order the mother of the faithful might continue disobeying her Lord and husband and keep marching to Basra.

They knew, the shrewd men that they were, that her influence over people was greater than theirs. For quarter of a century, they publicized for her and misled people into thinking that was the one whom the Messenger of Allah loved most, describing her as the "humayraa"[4] daughter of al-Siddiq who had half the creed with her.

What is really odd with regard to al-Zubayr is that he, too, had sought revenge for Uthman, as he claimed, whereas the righteous among the *sahabah* accused him of being the very same person who worked hard to kill Uthman. For example, Imam Ali said the following to him when he met him on the battle-field: "Are you holding me responsible for Uthman's blood and seeking revenge against me while you yourself had killed him?"[5]

In his *Mustadrak*, al-Hakim writes the following: "Talhah and al-Zubayr came to Basra where people asked them: `What brought you here?' `Seeking revenge for Uthman's murder,' they answered. Al-Husayn said, `Glory to Allah! Do you think that people are brainless so they will not say that nobody killed Uthman other than you yourselves?!'"

Al-Zubayr, like his friend Talhah, had done likewise: he betrayed Uthman and instigated people to kill him, then he willingly swore the oath of allegiance to Imam Ali, then he violated his oath and came to Basra seeking revenge for Uthman! Having entered Basra, he took part in many crimes, killing seventy of the city's guards and stealing everything its *bayt al-mal* had contained. Historians say that they signed a truce with Uthman ibn Haneef, Basra's governor, pledging to treat him respectfully till Ali's arrival.

---

[4] The meaning of this title is: one whose complexion is slightly reddish. Tr.
[5] Al-Tabari, *Tarikh*, Vol. 5, p. 204. Ibn al-Athir, *Al-Kamil*, Vol. 3, p. 102.

Then they violated their truce agreement and pledge and attacked Uthman ibn Haneef as he was leading the evening prayers. They tied a number of people then killed them, and they even attempted to kill Uthman ibn Haneef whom Ali had appointed as the governor of Basra, but they were afraid his brother Sahl ibn Haneef, governor of Medina, might hear about it and seek to avenge his murder from their own people; so, they beat him severely, shaved his beard and moustaches, then attacked *bayt almal*, killing forty of its guards. They jailed Uthman and subjected him to severe torture.

Commenting on this treachery, Taha Husayn writes the following about Talhah and al-Zubayr:

'These folks were not satisfied with violating their oath of allegiance to Ali but added to it their violation of the truce which they had signed with Uthman ibn Haneef, killing a number of the people of Basra who voiced their denunciation of such violation of the truce, the jailing of the *amir*, the robbing of all what *bayt al-mal* had contained, and the killing of a number of its guards.[6]

When Ali reached Basra, he did not fight the rebels; rather, he invited them to accept the arbitration of the Book of Allah, which they refused. They went as far as killing those who had carried the Holy Qur'an to them. Despite all of this, the Imam called him, too, and did as he had done with Talhah, saying:

O Zubayr! Do you remember when you, while in the company of the Messenger of Allah, passed by Banu Ghanam and smiled in the face of the Prophet immediately after he had looked at me, smiled, then said, "The son of Abu Talib never abandons his vanity," whereupon the Messenger of Allah said to you, "Hold your

---

[6] Taha Husayn, *Al-Fitna al-Kubra*, Vol. 2, p. 37.

tongue; there is no vanity in him, and you will fight him while you yourself will be the unjust one"?[7]

Ibn Abul-Hadid quotes in his book a sermon delivered by the Commander of the Faithful Ali ibn Abu Talib in which the Imam says:

Lord! Al-Zubayr had severed my ties of kinship, reneged from his oath of allegiance to me, and supported my foe against me! O Lord! I implore You to spare me his evil with whatever means You will.[8]

In *Nahjul-Balagha* of Imam Ali, the Imam writes the following about Talhah and al-Zubayr:

Lord! They both boycotted and were unjust to me, then they reneged from their oath of obedience to me and instigated people against me; so, I implore You to untie what they had tied, to foil the scheme which they plotted, and to make them see the evil of what they aspired to do and for which they strove hard! I sought their repentance before the battle, and I solicited their patience before the clamor, but they despised Your bounty and rejected my offer to spare their lives.[9]

In a letter he sent them before the fighting had begun, he said, "Go, O *shaykhs*, back to your senses, for now the greatest of your affair is shame, before shame is combined with the fire of hell, and peace be with you."[10]

---

[7] This statement is stated by al-Tabari in the discussion of the Battle of the Camel, in al-Mas'udi's *Tarikh*, in A'tham's *Tarikh*, and by others.

[8] Ibn Abul-Hadid, *Sharh Nahjul-Balagha*, Vol. 1, p. 101.

[9] Ibn Abul-Hadid, *Sharh Nahjul-Balagha*, p. 306, quoting Muhammad Abduh.

[10] *Ibid.*, p. 626.

This is the painful truth, and this is how al-Zubayr was finished. No matter how hard some historians try to convince us that he (al-Zubayr) had, indeed, recalled to memory the *hadith* of the Prophet of which Ali reminded him, so he repented and retired from fighting and went to the lions' ravine where he was killed by Ibn Jarmooz..., all this does not hold water when compared with the prophecy of the Messenger of Allah who had predicted that, "You will fight him (Ali) while you yourself will be the unjust one."

Some historians say that he wanted to retire when Imam Ali reminded him of the said *hadith*, but his son Abdullah taunted him of being a coward, so he was overwhelmed with zeal and returned to fight till he was killed.

This is closer to the truth and to the sacred tradition containing some knowledge of the unknown provided by one who never speaks out of his own inclination.

Had he truly regretted, repented, and renounced his error and injustice, why did he not act upon the statement of the Messenger of Allah saying: "To whomsoever I have been the master, this Ali is his master; O Allah! Befriend whoever befriends him and be the enemy of whoever antagonizes him; support whoever supports him, and betray whoever betrays him"?

Why did he not support, accept the authority of, and seek to please, Ali? Suppose he cannot do any of that, why did he not address the people whom he had brought for the battle to tell them that he saw the light of the truth and recalled to memory what he had forgotten and ask them to stop the war in order to safeguard the lives of innocent Muslims?

But none of this ever took place. We, hence, get to know that the myth of his repentance and retirement is the brainchild of the imagination of fabricators who were dazzled by Ali's light and al-Zubayr falsehood. Since his friend Talhah was killed by Marwan ibn al-Hakam, they selected Ibn Jarmooz to assassinate al-Zubayr in order to be able to provide their own interpretation of the fate of Talhah and al-Zubayr so that they may not deprive them of entering Paradise, especially since Paradise is one of their possessions: they permit into it whoever they like and prohibit whoever they wish.

Suffices us to prove the fallacy of their tale what is stated in Imam Ali's letter where he invited them to renounce the war: "Now the greatest of your affair is shame..., before shame is combined with the fire of hell."

Nobody narrates saying that they responded to his invitation, or submitted to his order, or even answered his letter. Add to this the fact that before the war had started, the Imam invited them to accept the arbitration of the Book of Allah, as we indicated above, but they refused and even killed the young messenger who had carried the Qur'an to them. It was then that Ali made fighting them permissible.

You may read some ludicrous accounts of historians which tell you that some of them are not familiar with the truth, nor do they comprehend it. One account says that when al-Zubayr came to know that Ammar ibn Yasir came in the company of Ali ibn Abu Talib, he said, "Oh! May my nose be cut off! May my spine be split!"

Then he snatched a weapon which shook in his hand. Having seen all of this, one of his companions said, "May my mother lose me! Is this the same al-Zubayr with whom I wanted to die or live?! By the One Who holds my life, whatever afflicted this man must be something which he had seen or heard from the Messenger of Allah!"[11]

---

[11] Al-Tabari, *Tarikh*, Vol. 5, p. 205.

By fabricating such stories, they intend to claim that al-Zubayr remembered the Prophet's *hadith* saying, "Ammar shall be killed by the oppressive gang," so he became afraid, and he was shaken for fear of being among such gangsters!

Those who despise our power of reason wish to ridicule us, but we have sound minds, praise to Allah, and what they tell us is unacceptable. How can al-Zubayr become afraid and shake upon remembering the tradition saying, "Ammar shall be killed by the oppressive gang," and not fear nor shake on account of numerous statements made by the Prophet in praise of Ali ibn Abu Talib ? Was Ammar according to al-Zubayr better and greater than Ali?! Did not al-Zubayr hear these traditions:

-- "O Ali! Nobody loves you except a true believer, and nobody hates you except a hypocrite."

-- "Ali is with the truth, and the truth is with Ali, revolving with him wherever he revolves."

-- "To whomsoever I have been the master, this Ali is his master; O Allah! Befriend whoever befriends him, and be the enemy of whoever antagonizes him! Support whoever supports him, and betray whoever betrays him."

-- "O Ali! I fight whoever fights you and am peaceful unto whoever seeks peace with you."

-- "I shall give the standard tomorrow to a man who loves Allah and His Messenger and who is loved by Allah and His Messenger."

-- "I fight them with regard to the revelation of the Qur'an, whereas you (Ali) will fight them with regard to its interpretation."

-- "O Ali! I promise you that you will fight the renegades, the unjust, and the apostates."

... in addition to many, many such traditions? The last of such traditions is a statement made by the Prophet to al-Zubayr himself: "You will fight him (Ali) while you yourself will be the unjust one." Where does al-Zubayr stand with regard to these facts which are known to people, those directly concerned as well as the outsiders, the son of the Prophet's aunt, and the son of Ali's aunt, that he is?!

Blockheads which could not confront historical events and the facts they contain in vain try, with all their might and means, to find some feeble pretexts in order to mislead the people and deceive them into believing that Talhah and al-Zubayr are among the residents of Paradise.

"Such are their hopes. Say: Bring your proof, if you are truthful." (Holy Qur'an, 2:111)

"Those who disbelieve in Our Signs, haughtily rejecting them, the gates of the heaves shall not be opened for them, nor shall they enter Paradise till the camel passes through the needle's hole, and thus do We reward the criminals." (Holy Qur'an, 7:40)

6. SA'D IBN ABU WAQQAS

He, too, is one of the most distinguished companions of the Prophet and among the foremost to embrace Islam. He was one of the earliest to migrate with the Prophet to Medina. He was among those who participated in the Battle of Badr. He was one of the six men recommended by Umar ibn al-Khattab to be caliphs, and one of the ten men who, as "Ahlul Sunnah wal Jama'ah" claim, received the glad tidings of going to Paradise.

He is also the hero of the Battle of al-Qadisiyya which took place during the caliphate of Umar ibn al-Khattab. It is said that some *sahabah* cast doubts about and questioned his descent, thus hurting his feelings, yet they narrate saying that the Prophet confirmed his descent, tracing it to Banu Zuhra.

In his book *Al-Imama wal-Siyasa*, Ibn Qutaybah transmits saying that following the demise of the Prophet, Banu Zuhra gathered to meet with Sa'd ibn Abu Waqqas and Abdul-Rahman ibn Awf at the sacred mosque (Masjid al-Nabi). When Abu Bakr and Abu Ubaydah came to them, Umar said to them, "Why do I see you thus forming circles? Stand up and swear the oath of allegiance to Abu Bakr, for I and the Ansar have already done so." Sa'd and Abdul-Rahman ibn Awf, as well as all those who were then present with them from Banu Zuhra, stood and swore.[1]

It is narrated that Umar ibn al-Khattab deposed him from his post as governor, but he recommended the caliph who would succeed him to reinstall him, since he had not deposed him due to any treachery. Uthman ibn Affan, therefore, carried out Umar's recommendation and appointed him as governor of Kufa.

It is noteworthy that Sa'd ibn Abu Waqqas did not leave a huge wealth behind him compared to his friends. His legacy, as

---

[1] Ibn Qutaybah, *Tarikh al-Khulafa*, Vol. 1, p. 18.

narrators tell us, amounted to three hundred thousand dinars. Also, he neither participated nor encouraged the assassination of Uthman as did Talhah and al-Zubayr. Ibn Qutaybah, in his history book (quoted above), narrates saying that Amr ibn al-As wrote Sa'd ibn Abu Waqqas asking him about who had killed Uthman. In his answer, Sa'd wrote saying,

'You asked me about who killed Uthman. I am telling you that he was killed by a sword unsheathed by Ayesha, polished by Talhah, and poisoned by Abu Talib's son.' Al-Zubayr remained silent and made a hand signal, whereas we did nothing. Had we willed, we would have defended him, but Uthman made many changes, and he himself changed, doing good and bad things. If what we did was good, then that was good indeed, but if what we did was wrong, we seek Allah's forgiveness.

I also am telling you that al-Zubayr is subdued by the overwhelming number of his kinsfolk, and by his sin. Had Talhah wished to rend his stomach, due to his love for authority, he would have rent it.'[2]

But what is strange in as far as Sa'd ibn Abu Waqqas is concerned is that he did not swear the oath of allegiance to the Commander of the Faithful Ali, nor did he support him while he knew the Imam fully well and realized his merits. He himself narrated several of Ali's merits which both Imam al-Nasa'i and Imam Muslim record in their respective *Sahih* books. Here are a couple of examples:

Sa'd has said, "I heard the Messenger of Allah stating three of Ali's merits; had I had one of them, it would have been better for me than red camels. I heard him saying, `He (Ali) to me is like

---

[2] Ibn Qutaybah, *Tarikh al-Khulafa*, Vol. 1, p. 48.

Aaron to Moses except there will be no prophet after me.' And I heard him saying, 'I shall give the standard tomorrow to a man who loves Allah and His Messenger and who is loved by Allah and His Messenger.'

And I heard him saying, 'O people! Who is your master?' They thrice said that Allah and His Messenger were their master, whereupon he took Ali's hand, made him stand up, then said, 'Whoever has accepted Allah and His Messenger as his master, this Ali is his master; O Allah! Befriend whoever befriends him, and be the enemy of whoever antagonizes him.'"[3]

In Muslim's *Sahih*, Sa'd ibn Abu Waqqas is quoted as having said, "I heard the Messenger of Allah saying to Ali, 'Are you not pleased to be to me what Aaron used to be to Moses, except there will be no prophet after me?'

During the Battle of Khaybar, I heard him saying, 'I shall give the standard tomorrow to a man who loves Allah and His Messenger and who is loved by Allah and His Messenger,' so we were very anxious and hopeful about it. He said, 'Bring Ali here.' And when the verse saying

"... say: Come: let us call our sons and your sons, and our women and your women, and our near people and your near people, then let us be earnest in prayer and pray for the curse of Allah on the liars" (Holy Qur'an, 3:61),

the Messenger of Allah brought Ali, Fatima, Hasan and Husayn and said, 'O Allah! These are my Ahlul Bayt'."[4]

How could Sa'd ibn Abu Waqqas know all these facts yet refuse to swear the oath of allegiance to Ali ? How could Sa'd hear

---

[3] This is indicated on p. 18 and p. 35 of Imam al-Nasa'i's *Khasa'is*.

[4] Muslim, *Sahih,* Vol. 7, p. 119, where the virtues of Ali ibn Abu Talib are discussed.

the Messenger of Allah saying, "Whoever has accepted Allah and His Messenger to be his master, this Ali is his master; O Allah! Befriend whoever befriends him, and be the enemy of whoever antagonizes him," which he himself narrates, then refuse to accept his mastership or to support him?

How could Sa'd have been ignorant of the *hadith* of the Messenger of Allah in which he said, "One who dies without having sworn the oath of allegiance dies the death of *jahiliyya*," a tradition which was narrated by Abdullah ibn Umar, so Sa'd would die the death of *jahiliyya* on account of his reluctance to swear the oath of allegiance to the Commander of the Faithful, the master of all *wasis*, the leader of the peerless men of virtue?

Historians indicate that Sa'd came to Imam Ali to apologize and said, "O Commander of the Faithful! There is no doubt in my mind that you are the most worthy among people of the caliphate, and that you are the custodian of the creed as well as of worldly affairs, but some people will dispute with you in this regard; so, if you desire my oath of allegiance, give me a sword whose tongue tells me to take this and leave that."

Ali said to him, "Have you seen anyone who has contradicted the Qur'an in word or in deed [because of swearing the oath of allegiance to me]? The Muhajirun and the Ansar have sworn the oath of allegiance to me on the condition that I deal with them according to the Book of Allah and the Sunnah of His Prophet; so, if you yourself wish, you may swear; otherwise, you may stay at home, for I am not going to force you to do it."[5]

Is not such a stand by Sa'd ibn Abu Waqqas odd?! While he testifies that no doubts entertain him about Ali, that he is the most worthy person of being the caliph, that he is the custodian over

---

[5] Al-A'tham, *Tarikh*, p. 163.

religious as well secular affairs, yet despite all of that he demands a sword with a tongue as a condition for swearing the oath of allegiance so that he would thus be able to distinguish truth from falsehood?! Is this not a contradiction rejected by rational people?

Is this not demanding the impossible, a demand put forth by a haughty person who had already come to know the truth from the bearer of the message embedded in traditions five of which he himself used to narrate?!

Was not Sa'd present when Abu Bakr, Umar, and Uthman received the oath of allegiance, an occasion from which anyone who lagged behind was killed for fear of dissension?

Yet Sa'd did swear the oath of allegiance to Uthman, unconditionally giving his support to him. He also heard Abdul-Rahman ibn Awf threatening Ali with a sword which he raised over his head, saying, "So do not harm your own self, for it will then be the sword and nothing else." He was also present when Ali refused to swear the oath of allegiance to Abu Bakr, invoking a threat against him by Umar ibn al-Khattab who then said to him, "Swear...; otherwise, by Allah Who is the One and Only God, we shall strike your neck with the sword."[6]

Did anything embolden those who did not swear the oath of allegiance to Ali, and who dared to behave arrogantly towards the successor of the Prophet such as Umar, Usamah ibn Zayd, and Muhammad ibn Maslamah, other than the reluctance of Sa'd ibn Abu Waqqas to swear it?

You can easily notice how the five men who were appointed by Umar ibn al-Khattab to compete with Ali in becoming caliphs played the exact role outlined for them by Umar ibn al-Khattab, namely prohibiting Ali from becoming caliph. Abd al-Rahman, for

---

[6] Ibn Qutaybah, *Al-Imama wal Siyasa*, Vol. 1, p. 20.

example, chose his son-in-law Uthman and threatened to kill Ali if he refused to swear the oath of allegiance to him. This is all due to the fact that Umar gave Abd al-Rahman the upper hand over the rest.

After the death of Abdul-Rahman ibn Awf and the assassination of Uthman ibn Affan, the only remaining contenders for Ali's caliphate were three: Talhah, al-Zubayr, and Sa'd. When these men saw that al-Muhajirun and the Ansar rushed to Imam Ali and swore the oath of allegiance to him and did not pay attention to anyone among them, they then entertained evil thoughts against him and sought to kill him. Talhah and al-Zubayr fought him, whereas Sa'd betrayed him.

Do not forget that Uthman ibn Affan did not die before creating a new contender for Ali who was more dangerous than all of them, more cunning and more shrewd, one whose party was larger in number and better in equipment: Uthman paved the way for him to take control over the caliphate by adding to his authority, which lasted for twenty years, the most important states from which two-thirds the entire revenue for the Islamic government came; this contender was Mu`awiyah who had no creed, nor ethics, nor concern except reaching the caliphate at any price, and by any means whatsoever.

Despite all of this, Commander of the Faithful Ali did not force people to swear the oath of allegiance to him as was done by the caliphs who preceded him. Rather, he upheld, peace of Allah be upon him, the injunctions of the Qur'an and the Sunnah, neither altering nor substituting anything for them in the least.

Have you noticed how he said to Sa'd, "The Muhajirun and the Ansar have sworn the oath of allegiance to me on the condition that I deal with them in accordance to the Book of Allah and the Sunnah of His Prophet; so, if you yourself wish, you may swear;

otherwise, you may stay at home, for I am not going to force you to do it"?

Congratulations to you, O son of Abu Talib, O you who revived the Qur'an and the Sunnah after being laid to rest by others before you! Here is the Book of Allah calling:

"Those who swear the allegiance to you swear it to Allah; the hand of Allah is above theirs; so whoever reneges (from his faith), he reneges to the detriment of his own soul, and whoever fulfills the promise which he made to Allah, He shall grant him a great reward." (Holy Qur'an, 48:10)

"...will you then force people to believe?" (Holy Qur'an, 10:99)

There is no compulsion in the religion, nor is there any Islamic provision for forcing anyone to swear the oath of allegiance to anyone, nor did Allah ever order His Prophet to fight people to force them to swear the oath of allegiance to him.

Such is the Sunnah of the Prophet and his honorable conduct: It tells us that he never forced anyone to pay him homage. But the caliphs and the *sahabah* were the ones who established such an innovation, threatening people to kill them if they refused to swear the oath of allegiance to them.

Fatima herself was threatened to be burned if those at her house, who did not swear the oath of allegiance [to Abu Bakr], refused to come out to swear it. Ali himself, the man whom the Messenger of Allah appointed as the caliph, was threatened to be killed. They swore by Allah to kill him if he refused to swear the oath of allegiance to Abu Bakr. If such is the case, do not ask about the condition of the other *sahabah* who were deemed weak in their eyes such as Ammar, Salman, Bilal, and others.

What is important is that Sa'd ibn Abu Waqqas refused to swear the oath of allegiance to, or to curse, him when Mu`awiyah ordered him, according to Muslim's *Sahih*. But this is not enough, nor does it secure Paradise for him, since the sect of the Mu`tazilites which he founded under the banner of "I am neither with you nor against you" is neither accepted in, nor endorsed by, Islam.

This is so due to the fact that Islam says that there is nothing beyond the truth except falsehood. It is so because the Book of Allah and the Sunnah of His Messenger outlined the characteristics of dissension, forewarned of it, and put limits for it so that those who perish do so according to a clear proof, and those saved are saved according to a clear proof.

The Messenger of Allah had clarified everything when he said with reference to Ali, "O Allah! Befriend whoever befriends him, and be the enemy of whoever antagonizes him! Support whoever supports him, and betray whoever betrays him! And make right revolve with him wherever he revolves!"

Imam Ali had clarified the motives which prohibited Sa'd from siding with him when he said in his *shaqshaqi* sermon, "... so a man among them listened to his hidden grudge."

Commenting on the above statement, Shaykh Muhammad Abdoh says,

'Sa'd ibn Abu Waqqas used to conceal something against Ali, may Allah glorify his countenance, something which originated from his uncles on the mother's side: his mother is Hamna daughter of Sufyan ibn Umayyah ibn Abd Shams, and Ali's killing of their most courageous men is a well-known fact.'[7]

Deeply rooted grudge and envy blinded Sa'd, so much so that he could not see Ali's virtues as he could those of Ali's opponents. It is stated that when Uthman installed him governor of Kufa, he

---

[7] Egyptian scholar Muhammad Abdoh, *Sharh Nahjul Balagha*, Vol. 1, p. 88.

delivered a sermon in which he said, "Obey the best of all people: Uthman, the commander of the faithful."

Sa'd ibn Abu Waqqas was inclined towards Uthman during the latter's lifetime and even after his assassination. Thus do we understand the reason why he accused Ali of participating in the assassination of Uthman when he wrote Amr ibn al-As saying, "Uthman was killed by a sword unsheathed by Ayesha, poisoned by the son of Abu Talib..., etc." It is a false accusation to whose falsehood history testifies. In fact, nobody offered more counsel nor more solace to Uthman during his calamity than Ali, if only his views were heeded.

What we deduct from Sa'd's languid stands is exactly what the Imam had described: he was a spiteful person. Despite his knowledge of Ali's right, grudge and spite stood between him and the truth, so much so that he remained puzzled, confused, torn by a conscience that rebuked him and stirred in him the torch of conviction and a sick mentality crippled by the customs of the days of ignorance. Sa'd listened to the voice of his grudge, and his evil self-subdued his conscience, dragging it down, holding him from supporting the right course.

What proves the above is the testimony given by many historians who recorded his puzzling stands. Ibn Kathir, for example, says the following in his book of history,

'Sa'd came once to visit Mu`awiyah ibn Abu Sufyan. Mu`awiyah asked him, "Why didn't you fight Ali?" Sa'd said, "A dark storm passed by me, so I alighted from my camel till it was over. Having come to know the way, I carried on." Mu`awiyah said, "The Book of Allah does not tell you to alight; rather, Allah has said, *`If two groups from the believers fight one another, you should make peace between them, but if one of them oppresses the other, you should fight the one that oppresses till it returns to obeying the commands of Allah'* (Surat al-Hujurat, 9).

By Allah! You did not side with the oppressive party against the oppressed one, nor were you with the just one against the unjust." Sa'd said, "I would not fight a man to whom the Messenger of Allah said, 'You are to me like Aaron to Moses, except there will be no prophet after me.'" Mu'awiyah asked him,

"Who else besides you heard it?" He said, "So-and-so..., and Umme Salamah, too," whereupon Mu'awiyah stood up, went to Umme Salamah and asked her about it. She repeated the same *hadith* quoted by Sa'd. Mu'awiyah then said, "Had I heard this *hadith* before today, I would have become a servant of Ali till the death of either one of us.'"[8]

Al-Mas'udi has transmitted in his *Tarikh* a conversation like this one between Mu'awiyah and Sa'd ibn Abu Waqqas, adding that Mu'awiyah said to Sa'd after what happened following the status *hadith*, "Now I regard none as more mean than you; why did you not support him? Why did you hesitate to swear the oath of allegiance to him? Had I heard the Prophet say the like of what I heard you quoting him, I would have spent the rest of my life as a servant of Ali."[9]

What Sa'd ibn Abu Waqqas narrated to Mu'awiyah with regard to Ali's virtues is one of hundreds of such *ahadith* which carry the same theme and aim at the same goal: Ali ibn Abu Talib is the only individual who represented the Islamic message after the demise of the Messenger of Allah, and none can do so besides him. Since the matter is as such, all righteous Muslims ought to serve him as long as they live.

---

[8] Ibn Kathir, *Tarikh*, Vol. 8, p. 77.

[9] This is quoted in al-Mas'udi's book of history known as *Muruj al-Dhahab* when the author discusses the biography of Sa'd ibn Abu Waqqas.

Mu'awiyah's statement in which he said that had he heard that tradition, he would have served Ali as long as he lived is a privilege of which every believing man and woman prides himself/herself. But Mu'awiyah did not say so except out of his desire to ridicule and slight Sa'd ibn Abu Waqqas in order to charge him with meanness and to insult him simply because he had refused to curse Ali and condemn him, thus going against Mu'awiyah's wish; otherwise, Mu'awiyah knows more than one status *hadith* in praise of Ali ibn Abu Talib. He also knows that he was the most meritorious person after the Messenger, and this is exactly what he admitted in a letter he sent to Muhammad ibn Abu Bakr which we will mention later, *InshaAllah*.

Did that stop Mu'awiyah from cursing and condemning the Commander of the Faithful after having come to know that *hadith* from Sa'd ibn Abu Waqqas and verified its authenticity with Umme Salamah whom he asked about it?

No, indeed; rather, he went to extremes in his misguidance and was overcome with insistence on being wrong to the extent that he started cursing Ali and all his Ahlul Bayt and forced people to do likewise till the youngsters grew up doing the same, and the youth grew old doing likewise, for eighty years or more.

"But whoever disputes with you in this matter after what has come to you of the knowledge, say: Come: let us call our sons and your sons, and our women and your women, and our near people and your near people, then let us be earnest in prayer and pray for the curse of Allah on the liars." (Holy Qur'an, 3:61)

7. ABDUL-RAHMAN IBN AWF

His name during the period of *jahiliyya* used to be Abd Amr, so the Prophet renamed him "Abd al-Rahman." He belonged to Banu Zuhra, and he was a cousin of Sa'd ibn Abu Waqqas.

He was one of the most prominent *sahabah* and among the first to migrate with the Prophet to Medina. He was in the company of the Prophet during all his battles. He was one of the six persons recommended by Umar ibn al-Khattab to be caliphs; rather, the latter gave him the upper hand over the rest, saying, "If you dispute among yourselves, be in the party where Abdul-Rahman ibn Awf is." He, as "Ahlul Sunnah wal Jama'ah" believe, is also one of those who received the glad tiding of going to Paradise.

Abdul-Rahman ibn Awf, as is well known, is one of the leading businessmen of Quraysh, a man who left behind him a huge wealth which, according to historians, included one thousand camels, one hundred horses, ten thousand she-camels, and arable lands growing twenty different types of crops. The inheritance of each one of his four wives amounted to eighty-four thousand dinars.[1]

Abdul-Rahman ibn Awf was the brother-in-law of Uthman ibn Affan: he married Umme Kulthoom daughter of Uqbah ibn Abu Mu'eet, Uthman's half-sister (his sister from the mother's side).

We have come to know from reviewing history books that he played a significant role in keeping Ali away from the post of caliph when he introduced his condition of following in the footsteps of caliphs Abu Bakr and Umar, knowing beforehand that Ali would never accept such a condition simply because the

---

[1] This is tallied by al-Tabari, al-Mas'udi, Ibn Sa'd, Taha Husayn, and others.

"Sunnah" of both of these men contradicted the Book of Allah and the pristine Sunnah of the Prophet.

This alone suffices us as a proof testifying to the fanaticism of Abdul-Rahman ibn Awf in upholding the *bid'ats* of the days of ignorance, to his being distant from Muhammad's Sunnah, and to his practically participating in a great plot to eradicate the Progeny of the Prophet in order to keep the caliphate as Quraysh's sole property to fare with as it pleased.

In his "Book of *Ahkam*" in his *Sahih*, al-Bukhari has a chapter dealing with how an Imam receives people's oath of allegiance. In it, he quotes al-Masoor saying,

Abd al-Rahman knocked at my house door in the heart of the night and kept knocking till I woke up. He said to me, "I see you are sleeping! By Allah! My eyes have not enjoyed much sleep tonight; so, go and invite al-Zubayr and Sa'd [ibn Abu Waqqas] to come here." So I brought them in, whereupon he consulted with them for a while then called me to come close to him and told me to invite Ali whom I accordingly invited to meet with us. He remained talking to him till most of the night had passed.

Then Ali stood up to leave, feeling hopeful, and Abd al-Rahman used to always be apprehensive of Ali. Then he told me to invite Uthman [ibn Affan] whom I accordingly invited. He kept consulting with him till the call to prayers forced them to part from one another to perform the *fajr* prayers. When people prayed the *fajr* prayers, and as these same men assembled near the pulpit, he sent for those of the Muhajirun and Ansar who were then in town.

Then he sent for the military commanders who were present that year with Umar. Once they all assembled, Abd al-Rahman pronounced the *shahada* then said, "O Ali! I have looked in the people's matter and I found them equaling none with Uthman; so, do not bring about your own harm." Then he addressed Uthman thus, "I swear the oath of allegiance to you according to the Sunnah of Allah and of His Messenger and of both caliphs after him." Abd al-Rahman swore the oath of allegiance to him, then the Muhajirun and the Ansar did so followed by military commanders and the rest of Muslims.[2]

The researcher can easily understand from this narration recorded by al-Bukhari the fact that the plot was planned during the night, and he can appreciate the shrewdness of Abdul-Rahman ibn Awf, and the fact that Umar did not hand pick him at random.

Reflect on the statement of the narrator, al-Masoor, saying, "... told me to invite Ali whom I accordingly invited to meet with us. He remained talking to him till most of the night had passed. Then Ali stood up to leave, feeling hopeful," that is, Ali felt optimistic about becoming the next caliph.

This proves to us that Abdul-Rahman ibn Awf is the one who made Ali hopeful with regard to becoming caliph so that he might not boycott this fake *shura* and be the cause of the nation falling again in dissension as happened at the *Saqifa* following the inauguration of Abu Bakr as the caliph. What confirms the accuracy of this probability is the narrator's statement: "... and Abd al-Rahman used to always be apprehensive of Ali."

Accordingly, Abd al-Rahman played the role of an evasive and cunning person who gave Ali assurances of being the next caliph, and even congratulated him on it, but when the morning approached, and the commanders of the army, as well as tribal chiefs and leaders of Quraysh assembled, it was then that Abd al-Rahman reversed his tactic and surprised Ali by telling him that people did not regard anyone as equal to Uthman, and that he had either to accept his scheme or allow himself to perish; that is, that

---

[2] Al-Bukhari, *Sahih*, Vol. 8, p. 123.

he would be killed if he refused to swear the oath of allegiance to the man of their choice, namely Uthman ibn Affan.

The researcher clearly understands from reading the last paragraph of the narration how al-Masoor said, "Once they all assembled, Abd al-Rahman pronounced the *shahada* then said, "O Ali! I have looked in the people's matter and found them equaling none with Uthman; so, do not harm your own self."

Why, then, did Abd al-Rahman direct his statement only at Ali from all those present then and there? Why did he not say something like, "O Ali, Talhah, al-Zubayr..., etc."? This is why we concluded that the plot was hatched during the night, and that the folks had from the beginning decided to select Uthman and exclude Ali.

We have to underscore the fact that they all used to be apprehensive of Ali if he became caliph lest he should revert to justice and equity and revive the Sunnah of the Prophet and put to rest the *bid'at* of the son of al-Khattab with regard to favoring one person over another. This is particularly so in the light of the fact that Umar ibn al-Khattab had pointed out before his death to the same, warning them against Ali's danger, saying, "If they hand it [caliphate] over to the bald-headed man [meaning Ali, peace be upon him], he will surely force them to follow the tracks," meaning the Prophet's Sunnah which neither Umar nor the general body of Quraysh liked. Had they liked the Sunnah of the Prophet, they would have selected Ali instead, and he would certainly have forced them to follow the right tracks. He would have brought things back to the way they used to be [during the Prophet's time], for he is the one charged with it; he is the custodian of the Sunnah...

As we indicated above while discussing Talhah, al-Zubayr, and Sa'd, they planted the thorn spikes and harvested loss and remorse.

Let us, therefore, take a close look at Abd al-Rahman and at the outcome of his scheming. Historians say that Abd al-Rahman suffered from his intense regret upon seeing how Uthman contradicted the path followed by both his predecessors, giving the high official posts of governors to his own relatives to whom he doled out huge sums of money.

He, therefore, went once to meet with Uthman; he said to him, "I preferred you over all others[3] on the condition that you lead us on the path of Abu Bakr and Umar, but you have acted contrarily to them and sought to please your own relatives, granting them authority over the fate of the Muslims."

Uthman said, "Umar used to severe his ties with his kinfolks, while I maintain them." Abd al-Rahman said, "I have vowed to Allah never to talk to you again," and he, indeed, never did till he died angry with Uthman. While he was ill prior to his death, he was visited by Uthman. He turned his face away from Uthman to face the wall, insisting on saying nothing to him.[4]

Thus did Allah, Glory to Him, respond favorably to Imam Ali's supplication with regard to Abd al-Rahman just as He had responded to his supplication with regard to Talhah and al-Zubayr who were both by then killed.

The Mu`tazilite author Ibn Abul-Hadid says in his book *Sharh Nahjul-Balagha* that Ali was very angry on account of that "shura," and he knew what Abdul-Rahman ibn Awf had schemed, so he said to him:

---

[3] His using the first person singular "I" indicates the forcing of his own personal view over all others, and that he did not consult the masses of the populace as others claim.

[4] This tale is stated in several references; among them are: p. 166, Vol. 1, of Abul Fida's *Tarikh*, p. 57, Vol. 5, of al-Baladhuri's book *Ansab al-Ashraf*, and p. 261, Vol. 2, of *Al-Iqd al-Fareed* by the Maliki author Ibn Abd Rabbih.

By Allah! You have not done it except because you expect of him to do for you what each one of you expects his friend to do for him! May Allah bring between you both Mansham's[5] perfume.[6]

What the Imam meant to say is that Abd al-Rahman hoped that Uthman would nominate him as his successor in the post of caliph just as Abu Bakr had done to Umar. Ali had also said to him, "Milk some milk in which there is a portion for you, and tie his knot today so that tomorrow he may return the favor to you."

As for Mansham's perfume which Ali, peace be upon him, invokes here, it is a saying common among people who would say, "This is more ominous than Mansham's perfume," a reference to discord and infighting.

Allah did, indeed, favorably respond to the Imam's supplication. Hardly a few years passed before He afflicted them with enmity. Abd al-Rahman became an opponent of his son-in-law; he did not speak to him till death. Nobody at all was permitted to perform the funeral prayers for him...

This brief research clearly demonstrates to us the fact that Abdul-Rahman ibn Awf is one of the heads of Quraysh who obliterated the Prophet's Sunnah and substituted it with the *bid`as* of both caliphs. It also becomes clear to us that Imam Ali is the only person who sacrificed his post of caliph, as well as everything related thereto, in order to safeguard Muhammad's Sunnah which his Brother and cousin Muhammad ibn Abdullah, peace and

---

[5] According to p. 577, Vol. 12, of Ibn Manzur's lexicon *Lisan al-Arab* Mansham was a woman from Hamadan who used to sell perfume. Whenever the Arabs bought perfume from her, a war among them would intensify; so, she became proverbial in ill luck. Tr.

[6] Ibn Abul-Hadid, *Sharh Nahjul-Balagha*, Vol. 1, p. 63.

blessings of Allah be upon him and his good and pure Progeny, had introduced.

You have, dear reader, no doubt come to know "Ahlul Sunnah wal Jama'ah" as they really are. You have personally come to know who the adherents to the Sunnah are. A believer is noble and is never bitten twice from the same hole.

8. AYESHA DAUGHTER OF ABU BAKR "MOTHER OF THE FAITHFUL"

She is wife of the Prophet and the mother of the faithful. The Prophet married her in the second or third year after the Hijra and, according to the most famous accounts, she was eighteen years old when the Prophet died.

Allah prohibited the believers to marry the Prophet's wives after his demise; He says, *"It does not behove you to hurt [the feelings of] the Messenger of Allah, nor should you marry his wives after him at all; this surely is grievous in the sight of Allah."* (Holy Qur'an, 33:53), and also,

"The Prophet has a greater authority over the faithful than they have over their own selves, and his wives are (like) their mothers" (Holy Qur'an, 33:6).

We have already pointed out to the fact that the Prophet was annoyed when he heard that Talhah had said, "When Muhammad dies, I shall marry my cousin Ayesha." Allah, Glory to Him, wanted to tell the faithful that they were prohibited from marrying the Prophet's wives just as they are prohibited from marrying their own mothers. Ayesha did not bear any children.

She was one of the greatest personalities known to Muslims, for she played a major role in bringing certain people closer to the post of caliph while distancing others therefrom. She endorsed some people while ignoring others. She participated in the wars, leading the battles and the men in war, sending letters to the heads of tribes, ordering them to do or not to do, appointing or deposing military leaders. She led the Battle of the Camel, and both Talhah and al-Zubayr served under her military command.

We do not wish to go into detail in narrating the role she had played during her lifetime, for we have discussed her extensively in our book *Ask Those Who Know*; so, researchers may review it if they want to know the same. What concerns us in this research, however, is her own *ijtihad*, her altering the Sunnah of the Prophet.

A few examples have to be highlighted so that we may understand from discussing those "great" personalities of whom the people of "Ahlul Sunnah wal Jama'ah" are proud and whom they regard as their role models, preferring them over the pure Imams from the Progeny of the Prophet.

This, in fact, is nothing but a tribal fanaticism which effaced the Prophet's Sunnah, buried its saline features, and put its light out. Had it not been for Ali and the Imams from his offspring, we would not have found today anything left of the Sunnah of the Prophet.

We have also come to know that Ayesha did not act upon the Sunnah of the Messenger of Allah, nor did she have the least regard for it. Although she had heard numerous *ahadith* in praise of Ali, she denied them and acted to their contrary.

She defied the command of Allah, as well as the order of His Messenger which he had directed personally to her, so she came out to lead the infamous Battle of the Camel wherein sanctities were violated and innocent people were killed. She betrayed her written pledge to Uthman ibn Haneef, and when they brought her his men tied up, she ordered them to be beheaded.[1]

Leave aside the fires of war and dissension which the mother of the faithful ignited, causing the land and those on it to be burned thereby, and let us discuss her own interpretations, and the following of her own views, in as far as Allah's creed is concerned. If the view of the *sahabi* is taken for granted and his statement is held as an argument, what would you say about one from whom half the creed is supposedly derived?!

---

[1] Al-Bukhari, *Sahih*, Vol. 8, p. 91, and also in "The Book of Iman" in Muslim's *Sahih*.

Al-Bukhari in his *Sahih*, in a chapter on praying *qasr* prayers, al-Zuhri quotes Urwah quoting Ayesha, may Allah be pleased with her, saying, "The first obligatory of the prayers are two *rak`ats*, so the traveler's prayers were thus fixed, then the prayers of one who is not on a journey were to be prayed in full." Al-Zuhri said, "I asked Urwah, "Why is Ayesha then saying her prayers [while travelling] in full?" He said, "She is following the same interpretation as that made by Uthman."[2]

Are you not surprised how the mother of the faithful and wife of the Prophet abandoned the Sunnah of the Messenger of Allah, which she herself had narrated and to whose authenticity she testified, just to follow the *bid`at* of Uthman ibn Affan, whom she was encouraging people to kill, claiming that he altered the Sunnah of the Prophet and who wore it out before his own shirt was worn out?!

Yes, this is exactly what happened during Uthman's caliphate, but she changed her mind again during the reign of Mu`awiyah ibn Abu Sufyan. She urged people to kill Uthman, but once she came to know that they did kill him, and that they swore the oath of allegiance to Ali, she changed her mind and came out demanding revenge for him!

We deduct from the narrative stated above is that she prayed, while travelling, the full number of *rak`ats*, four in number, instead of two. She did so during the reign of Mu`awiyah who took pains to revive all the innovations of his cousin and benefactor Uthman ibn Affan.

People follow the creed of their rulers. Ayesha was among those who reconciled with Mu`awiyah after their hostility; he is the

---

[2] Al-Bukhari's *Sahih*, Vol. 2, p. 36.

one who had killed her brother Muhammad ibn Abu Bakr and mutilated his corpse in the worst manner. Despite all of that, mutual worldly interests bring enemies together and create brotherhood among antagonists; so, Mu`awiyah sought to please her, and she sought to please him, and he started sending her presents and huge sums of money.

Historians say that when Mu`awiyah reached Medina, he went to visit Ayesha. Having sat down, she said to him, "O Mu`awiyah! Do you feel secure against my hiding someone to kill you in revenge for your killing my brother Muhammad ibn Abu Bakr?" Mu`awiyah said, "Rather, I have entered a house of security." "Did you fear Allah," she continued, "when you killed Hujr b. `Adi and his followers?" He said, "Rather, those who testified against them killed them."[3]

They also narrate saying that Mu`awiyah used to send her gifts, clothes, and other encased items, and that he sent her once one hundred thousand dinars in one lump sum.[4] He also sent her once when she was in Mecca a necklace worth one hundred thousand dinars and paid all her debts which amounted to eighteen thousand dinars in addition to whatever she used to give to others.[5]

In my book titled *Ask Those Who Know*, I indicated that in one single day, she set free forty-one slaves as atonement for breaking her oath.[6]

---

[3] This is stated by Ibn Kathir in his *Tarikh* and by Ibn Abd al-Birr in his *Al-Isti`ab* where he discusses the biography of Hujr b. `Adi.

[4] This is what both Ibn Kathir states on p. 136, Vol. 7, of his *Tarikh* and al-Hakim on p. 13, Vol. 4, of his *Al-Mustadrak*.

[5] Ibn Kathir, *Tarikh*, Vol. 7, p. 137.

[6] Al-Bukhari, *Sahih*, Vol. 7, p. 90, in a volume dealing with etiquette in a chapter discussing the Hijra.

Rulers and governors belonging to Banu Umayyah used also to seek her pleasure and send her presents and money.⁷

Remember that Abu Bakr is the one who shared the authority with Mu`awiyah whom he appointed as *wali* of Syria after the death of his brother, and Mu`awiyah used to always appreciate Abu Bakr's favors on him; without Abu Bakr, Mu`awiyah would never have even dreamed of becoming caliph.

Mu`awiyah, moreover, used to meet with the group when they were plotting their great plot to obliterate the Sunnah and annihilate the Progeny of the Prophet. There was no enmity between Mu`awiyah and Ayesha. Even her asking him, "Do you feel secure against my hiding someone to kill you in revenge for your killing my brother Muhammad ibn Abu Bakr?" was no more than teasing him; she never loved the son of the woman from the tribe of Khath`am, namely Muhammad ibn Abu Bakr, who fought her after having sided with Ali and who regarded killing her as *halal*.

She also shares Mu`awiyah's hatred towards "Abu Turab" to the extreme limit and with more animosity than anyone can imagine. In all of this, I do not know which one of them earned higher marks: Was it not he who fought, cursed, and condemned him [Imam Ali] and put out his light for good?

Or was it she who worked hard to exclude him from the caliphate, fought him and tried her best to obliterate his name from existence and went out riding a mule urging Banu Umayyah to fight him, seeking their assistance against Banu Hashim saying, "Do not permit anyone I do not like to enter my house"? She even tried to wage another war, so much so that some of her relatives asked her, "Is not sufficient [shame] for us what you did on the `Day of the

---

⁷ Imam Ahmad ibn Hanbal, *Musnad*, Vol. 6, p. 77.

red Camel' so that people may have another 'Day of the Gray Mule'?!"

She undoubtedly was contemporary to an extended period of Banu Umayyah's reign and had heard them cursing Ali and Ahlul Bayt from the pulpits without expressing her resentment of it, nor did she prohibit it; she may even have indirectly encouraged it.

Imam Ahmad ibn Hanbal, for example, writes the following in his *Musnad*:

A man came to Ayesha and spoke ill of both of Ali ibn Abu Talib and Ammar ibn Yasir. Ayesha said, "As for Ammar, I have heard the Prophet saying that whenever he [Ammar] had to opt between one of two matters, he always opted for the most rational one."[8]

We are not surprised, then, to see Ayesha laying the Sunnah of the Prophet to rest while reviving

Uthman's *bid'at* with regard to praying the full number of *rak`ats* while on a journey in order to please Mu`awiyah and other Umayyad rulers who followed her wherever she went, glorifying her and deriving their creed from her.

It becomes clear to us that "Ahlul Sunnah wal Jama'ah" worship Allah in the light of texts which Allah never revealed, without thoroughly examining or verifying them. Had they verified such *bida'ts* (innovations in religion), they would surely have found them repugnant, and they would have willingly abandoned them. This is what I personally experienced with some open-minded Sunni scholars. When they came across the tradition relevant to grown-ups suckling, they were very surprised and dumbfounded, and they assured me that they had never heard it before.

---

[8] Ahmad ibn Hanbal, *Musnad*, Vol. 6, p. 113.

This is a common phenomenon among "Ahlul Sunnah wal Jama`ah." A great number of *ahadith* which the Shi'as cite to argue with them are recorded in Sunni *Sahihs* while the Sunnis are unaware of them and regard anyone who narrates them as an apostate.

"Allah sets forth an example to those who disbelieve: the wife of Noah and the wife of Lot; they were under two of Our righteous servants, but they betrayed them, so they (their husbands) could not protect them against Allah in the least, and it was said to them: Enter both into the fire with those who enter". (Holy Qur'an, 66:10)

9. KHALID IBN AL-WALEED

Khalid ibn al-Waleed ibn al-Mugheerah belonged to Banu Makhzum, and he is given by "Ahlul Sunnah wal Jama'ah" the title of "The Sword of Allah."

His father was one of the wealthiest men whose wealth was immeasurable. Abbas Mahmud al-Aqqad says, "He was the wealthiest man alive according to their commonly known wealth criteria: gold, silver, orchards, vineyards, merchandise, real estate, servants, concubines, slaves, etc. This is why he was called the peerless."[1] His father is none other than al-Waleed ibn al-Mugheerah who was forewarned of being burned in the fire of hell and of a very mean resort by the Holy Qur'an in the following verses:

"Leave Me and him whom I created alone and gave him vast riches, and sons dwelling in his presence, and I adjusted his affairs for him most appropriately, yet he desires that I should add even more! By no means! Surely he opposes Our Signs. I will make a distressing punishment overtake him. Surely he reflected and guessed, but may he be cursed how he guessed! Again may he be cursed how he guessed; then he looked, then he frowned and scowled, then he turned back and was big with pride, then he said: This is naught but an enchantment narrated (by others); this is naught but the word of a mortal. I will cast him into hell. And what will make you realize what hell is? It leaves naught nor does it spare aught. It scorches the mortal. Over it are nineteen." (Holy Qur'an, 74:11-30)

It is said that al-Waleed came to see the Prophet once to lure him with wealth so that he might abandon the religion he was preaching, whereupon Allah revealed these verses in that regard:

---

[1] Abbas Mahmud al-Aqqad, *Abqariyyat Khalid*, p. 24.

"And do not yield to any mean one who swears, defames, going about with slander, forbidding goodness, out-stepping the limits, sinful, ignoble, (and) besides all that, base-born, (only) because he possesses wealth and sons. When Our Signs are recited to him, he says: Tales of those of yore. We shall brand him on the nose..." (Holy Qur'an, 68: 10-16)

Al-Waleed thought that he deserved to be prophet more than Muhammad; he used to say, "Should the Qur'an and Prophethood be revealed unto Muhammad the indigent while I, the master of and the greatest among Quraysh, be left out?"

On such a doctrine did Khalid ibn al-Waleed grow up bearing animosity towards Islam and the Prophet of Islam who ridiculed his father's dreams and undermined his power base. Khalid, therefore, participated in all the wars waged against the Messenger of Allah.

Khalid undoubtedly used to share his father's belief that the latter was more worthy of Prophethood than Muhammad, the indigent orphan. Since Khalid, like his father, was one of the most prominent figures in Quraysh, if not the very most prominent one, he felt he should have had the lion's share of the Qur'an and prophethood had they only been his father's lot, and he would have inherited prophethood and authority just as Solomon had inherited David. It is to refer to such belief that Allah, Glory to Him, says,

"When the truth came to them, they said: This is sorcery, and in it are we disbelievers. And they said: Why was this Qur'an not revealed to a man of importance in both towns?" (Holy Qur'an, 43:30-31)

No wonder, then, to see how he tried all he could to put an end to Muhammad and his mission. We find him raising a huge army financed from his wealth during the Battle of Uhud, lying in ambush for the Prophet in an attempt to put an end to him. During the year of the Hudaybiyyah treaty, he also tried to assassinate the

Prophet, but Allah, Glory to Him, foiled all his schemes, rendering them a failure, while supporting His Prophet on all occasions.

When Khalid came to know, as did other prominent members of Quraysh, that the Messenger of Allah was invincible, seeing how people were accepting the religion of Allah in large numbers, it was then that he surrendered to reality while suppressing his sighs. His acceptance of Islam, therefore, came as late as the eighth year after the Hijra, only four months before the conquest of Mecca.

Khalid inaugurated his acceptance of Islam by behaving contrarily to the orders issued by the Messenger of Allah not to kill anyone. Khalid entered Mecca on the conquest day after having killed more than thirty men who belonged mostly to Quraysh although the Prophet had clearly instructed them not to kill anyone.

No matter how many excuses some people may find for Khalid by saying, for example, that he was banned from entering Mecca, and that they faced him with their weapons, he was not justified in killing anyone after having been prohibited by the Prophet from doing so; he could have gone to another gate to enter the city without a fight as others did, or to send a message to the Prophet seeking his advice with regard to those who were prohibiting him from entering. But none of that happened. Rather, Khalid followed his own opinion, challenging what he had clearly heard from the Messenger of Allah.

Since we are talking about those who follow their own opinions at the expense of contradicting the available text, something which gained many supporters and enthusiasts, or say it acquired a school of its own from which many great *sahabah* and legislators graduated, a school which was later called the school of the caliphs, we cannot avoid pointing out here to the fact that *ijtihad* in such sense is nothing other than disobedience to Allah and His Messenger.

We have become accustomed to seeing references made to *ijtihad* versus the available texts, so much so that it appears as though it is perfectly legitimate. In fact, we have to say that Khalid disobeyed the Prophet's order instead of saying that he followed his own view in the face of an existing text. This is what the Qur'an teaches us to do; Allah says,

"Adam disobeyed his Lord, so his life became evil to him...." (Holy Qur'an, 20:121).

This is so because Allah had prohibited him from eating of the forbidden tree. Since Adam did eat of it, we must not say: "Adam followed his own *ijtihad* as opposed to the available text."

Each and every Muslim has to keep himself at his limit rather than transgress and voice his own view in an issue regarding which an order permitting or prohibiting it had already been issued by Allah or His Messenger, for that will be obvious apostasy. Allah said to the angels, "Prostrate to Adam." This is an order.

"So they prostrated" (Holy Qur'an, 20:116);

this is a positive response, an act of submission, an expression of obedience. The exception was Iblis: he followed his own view, so he said, "I am better than him; why, then, should I prostrate to him?" Here we encounter a rebellion, a mutiny, regardless of who is better than who: Adam or Iblis. This is why the most Glorified One says,

"It does not behove any believing man or woman to make any choice in their matter once Allah and His Apostle have decided it, and whoever disobeys Allah and His Messenger surely strays off a manifest straying" (Holy Qur'an, 33:36).

It is to this fact that Imam Ja'far al-Sadiq referred when he said once to Abu Hanifah, "Do not apply qiyas (analogy), for if it is applied to the Shari`a, it will be obliterated, and the first person to apply qiyas was Iblis when he said, *'I am better than him; You created me of fire while creating him of dust'"* (*Holy Qur'an, 7:12 and 38:76*).

His statement that "... if it is applied to the Shari`a, it will be obliterated" is the best expression of the invalidity of *qiyas*. If people follow their own diverse views in the face of available texts, there will be no Shari`a at all.

"Had the truth followed their own (low) desires, the heavens and the earth and all those therein would then have perished" (*Holy Qur'an, 23:71*).

Having made this brief expose of the principle of *ijtihad*, let us see how Khalid ibn al-Waleed disobeyed the order issued by the Messenger of Allah on another occasion when he was sent by the Prophet to Banu Juthaymah to invite them to Islam. The Prophet did not order Khalid to fight anyone.

Yet Khalid went there and afflicted them with treachery even after their declaration of acceptance of Islam, killing some of them in cold blood, so much so that Abdul-Rahman ibn Awf, who was an eye witness to that incident, said that Khalid had killed them only out of his desire to seek revenge for both of his uncles whom Banu Juthaymah had killed.[2]

---

[2] On p. 61, Vol. 2, of his *Tarikh*, al-Ya`qubi says that Abd al-Rahman said, "By Allah! It is Khalid who killed these people though they are Muslims." Khalid responded by saying, "Rather, I have killed them to avenge your father Awf ibn Abd Awf." Abd al-Rahman then said to him, "No, you did not avenge my father, but you avenged your uncle al-Faqih ibn al-Mugheerah." See, may Allah protect you, how Khalid did not deny that he killed those people although they were Muslims but rather admitted that he killed them seeking revenge for Awf, Abd al-Rahman's father. Does this, according to Allah's creed, permit him to massacre a group of people for the murder of one single man? Is it permissible to kill several Muslims for the killing of one kafir?

When the Messenger of Allah heard about that shameful treachery, he thrice dissociated himself before Allah from what Khalid ibn al-Waleed had done. Then he sent them Ali ibn Abu Talib bearing a great deal of wealth to them to pay their blood money, the blood spilled by Khalid.

No matter how many excuses "Ahlul Sunnah wal Jama'ah" may find for Khalid ibn al-Waleed, the pages of history are full of the tragedies which he inflicted and of his violating the Book of Allah and the Sunnah of His Messenger.

Suffices the researcher to read his biography and what he did in the Yamama during the time of Abu Bakr, how he betrayed Malik ibn Nuwayrah and executed his men in cold blood although they were Muslims then married Malik's wife and cohabited with her on the same night of her husband's murder, discarding Islam's Shari`a and the Arabs' principles of valor.

Even Umar ibn al-Khattab, despite his being laxing in enforcing Islam's injunctions, exposed him and called him the enemy of Allah, promising to stone him to death.

Researchers are obligated to review history with keen eyes and from the stand of constructive criticism which leads them to the truth without any abstraction or bias. Nor should they be overtaken by sectarian fanaticism so they evaluate the individuals basing their evaluation on fabricated *ahadith* of the Prophet. "Ahlul Sunnah wal Jama'ah," who, in fact, are Banu Umayyah, wipe out all historical events with one single tradition which they themselves fabricate in order to thus stop the researchers short of reaching the truth.

How easy it is for one of them to say, "The Messenger of Allah said to Khalid ibn al-Waleed, `Welcome, O Sword of Allah!'" so this false tradition takes control of the hearts of innocent Muslims who think well of others and who do not know what others hide and what schemes the Umayyads plot. Based on this fabricated tradition, they, therefore, interpret everything said about Khalid of facts and find excuses for him. This is called the psychological effect on people, and it is the acute ailment obstructing one from reaching the truth, turning the facts upside down.

Let me give you an example:

Abu Talib, uncle of the Prophet is said to have died as an apostate, and that the Prophet said about him,

"Abu Talib is inside a lake of fire from which his brains boil." Because of this fabricated "tradition," "Ahlul Sunnah wal Jama'ah" believe that Abu Talib is an apostate, and that he is in the fire. They, therefore, do not accept any rational analysis which leads them to the truth. Through this "tradition," the biography of Abu Talib, his struggle in defense of Islam because of which his own people became antagonistic towards him, and he towards them, so much so that he accepted to endure the boycott at Mecca's ravine for three years for the sake of his nephew, a boycott during which he had to eat leaves to survive, and his heroic stands as well as doctrinal poetry in defense of the Prophet's call..., all this is undermined.

Because of it, they ignore all what the Prophet had done in praise of his uncle, how he washed his corpse and shrouded it in his own shirt and personally laid it to rest in his grave, naming the year when he lost him as `aam al-huzn, the year of grief, saying, "By Allah! Quraysh was unable to harm me except after the death of Abu Talib. Allah sent me the *wahi* saying: `Get out of it [Mecca], for your supporter has died,'" whereupon he migrated from Mecca instantly.

Take another example:

Sufyan ibn Harb, Mu`awiyah's father, is said to have accepted Islam after the conquest of Mecca, and that the Prophet said about him, "Whoever entered Abu Sufyan's house will be safe." Based on this tradition which contains no virtue whatsoever nor any merit for him, "Ahlul Sunnah wal Jama'ah" believe that Abu Sufyan became Muslim, that his acceptance of Islam was very good, and that he is in Paradise because Islam cancels his past deeds.

They do not accept, beyond this, the rational analysis which enables them to reach the truth. And it is through this "hadith" that all what Abu Sufyan had done towards the Messenger and his Message is forgiven, and forgotten are all the wars which he had led and financed in order to put an end to Muhammad. And his animosity and grudge towards the Prophet is forgotten.

When they came to him and said, "Accept Islam or else we should strike your neck with the sword," he said, "I testify that there is no god but Allah." They said to him, "Testify that Muhammad is the Messenger of Allah." He responded by saying, "As for this one, I have within myself something against it."

Whenever he met the Prophet after having accepted Islam, he would silently say to himself, "By what did this person overcome me?" It is then that the Prophet would audibly respond to him by saying, "Through Allah have I overcome you, O father of Sufyan!"

These are only two examples I have brought from our Islamic history so that the researchers may clearly observe some people's psychological effect on others, and how such an effect veils them from the truth. Thus do we come to understand that "Ahlul Sunnah wal Jama'ah" surrounded the *sahabah* with a halo of false traditions which provided them with immunity and sanctity in the hearts of simple-minded people who can no longer accept any criticism or blame.

If a Muslim is convinced that these men had been given by the Messenger of Allah the glad tidings of going to Paradise, he will never accept any criticism of them, and everything they did will then be underestimated; he will find excuses and interpretations for them provided the door is closed in his face from the very beginning.

This is why they attached for each of their chief men a title which they claimed to have been given by the Messenger of Allah: This person is "al-Siddiq," whereas this one is "al-Farooq;" this was the beloved one of the Messenger of Allah, and those are his *huris*, while this particular woman is his beloved wife. This man is the "nation's trust," while that is the "narrator of Islam."

This one is the *"wahi's* recorder," whereas this man is the one with the two sandals; this is the cupper of the Prophet, while that is "The Sword of Allah," and this is this, and that is that... All these titles, in fact, neither fatten nor satisfy when it comes to the balance of truth with Allah;

"... names which you yourselves, and your fathers, named; Allah has not sent down any authority for them" (Holy Qur'an, 12:40).

What counts with Allah is one's own good needs.

History is the best witness of deeds through which we evaluate anyone; we do not hold in high esteem anyone about whom falsehood is uttered. This, in fact, is exactly what Imam Ali has said: "If you get to know the truth, you will get to know who follows it." Since we have studied history and come to know what Khalid ibn al-Waleed had done and come to distinguish the truth from falsehood, we cannot call him "The Sword of Allah."

We have also the right to ask when the Messenger of Allah ever named him so. Did he name him Allah's sword when he killed the people of Mecca on the conquest day, having come to know that he had prohibited him from fighting anyone?

Or was it when he sent him with the army commanded by Zayd ibn al-Haritha and dispatched to Mu'tah, saying, "If Zayd is killed, then Ja`far ibn Abu Talib (should take the command), and if Ja`far is killed, then Abdullah ibn Ruwahah [should lead]," without nominating him except in the fourth position to lead the army, yet after all these three men were killed, Khalid fled from the battle field accompanied by the remnant of that army...? Or did he give him that title when he accompanied him to attack Hunayn in twelve thousand warriors. There, too, he fled, leaving behind him on the battle grounds the Messenger of Allah who had no more than twelve men who stood steadfastly with him?

Since Allah says,

"And whoever turns his back to them that day, neither maneuvering nor supporting one company, he will then incur the wrath of Allah, and his abode will be hell, and what an evil abode it is" (Holy Qur'an, 8:16), how could he permit himself to flee? It truly is amazing!

I personally think that Khalid, in the first place, never knew this title as long as the Prophet lived, nor did the Messenger of Allah ever call him so. Rather, Abu Bakr was the one who bestowed this badge of courage on him when he sent him to silence those who revolted against him and opposed his caliphate, so he did to them what he did, so much so that Umar ibn al-Khattab (because of what Khalid had done) said to Abu Bakr, "Khalid's sword is quite excessive," and he surely knew him best. It was then that Abu Bakr responded to Umar by saying, "Khalid is one of the swords of Allah which He unsheathed against His foes," which is a totally erroneous way of looking at things, hence the title.

In his book *Al-Riyad al-Nadira*, al-Tabari indicates that Banu Saleem had reneged, whereupon Abu Bakr sent them Khalid ibn al-Waleed who gathered some of their men inside animal sheds then set them to fire. When Umar ibn al-Khattab came to know about this incident, he went to see Abu Bakr and said, "Why do you let a man employ the same method of torture employed by Allah, the

Most Exalted One, the Great?" Abu Bakr answered him by saying, "By Allah! I shall not shame a sword which Allah unsheathed against His foes till He Himself shames it," then he ordered him to leave, whereupon he instantly went out to see Musaylamah.³

This is how "Ahlul Sunnah wal Jama'ah" came to call Khalid "The Sword of Allah" even though he had disobeyed the order of the Messenger of Allah and burnt people with the fire, thus totally discarding the Sunnah.

In his *Sahih*, al-Bukhari indicates that the Messenger of Allah had said, "Nobody employs the fire for torture except Allah," and also, "None torments with the fire except the fire's God."⁴ And we have already indicated how Abu Bakr used to say before his death, "I wish I never burnt al-Salami!"

We say: We wish there had been someone to ask Umar ibn al-Khattab, "Since you already knew that none torments with the fire except Allah, why did you swear after the death of the Prophet to burn the house of Fatima al-Zahra and everyone inside it if they refused to swear the oath of allegiance [to Abu Bakr]? Had Ali not surrendered and ordered everyone to go out to swear it, you would certainly have carried your threat out."

Sometimes I doubt whether Umar opposed Abu Bakr and whether the latter did not heed his opposition, for this would be quite unusual. We have already seen how Abu Bakr did not stand in the face of Umar, nor did he maintain his stand in the face of his opposition. More than once did he say to him, "I had already told you that you are stronger than me in handling this matter, but you subdued me."

---

³ Al-Tabari, *Al-Riyad al-Nadira*, Vol. 1, p. 100.
⁴ Al-Bukhari, *Sahih*, Vol. 4, p. 325.

On another occasion, when he complained to him about those whose hearts could be won towards Islam and what Umar did to the covenant which he had written for them, how he spitted on it and tore it to pieces, he was asked, "Are you the caliph or is it Umar?" He answered by saying, "He, Allah willing, is."

For this reason, I say that the one who opposed Khalid's ugly deeds may have been none other than Ali ibn Abu Talib, but the early historians and narrators used to quite often avoid mentioning his name, so they substituted it with that of Umar as testified by several narrations traced back to "Zaynab's father"[5] or to "a man," meaning thereby Ali but not openly revealing his name.

Actually, this is not a mere probability, or we may accept what is stated by some historians who write saying that Umar ibn al-Khattab used to hate Khalid and could not stand looking at him in the face because he was jealous of him: Khalid had won people's hearts because of his victories. It is also said that Khalid had wrestled with Umar during the days of *jahiliyya*, winning the match and breaking Umar's leg.

What is important is that once he became caliph, Umar deposed Khalid but did not carry out his threat of stoning him as he had threatened. The result: Khalid and Umar ibn al-Khattab vied with one another in their toughness and arrogance; each one of them was stone-hearted, and each deliberately violated the Prophet's Sunnah and disobeyed the Prophet during his life and after his death.

Moreover, both hated the Prophet's *wasi* and tried very hard to distance him from public life. Khalid plotted with both Umar and Abu Bakr to assassinate Ali shortly after the death of the Prophet8

---

[5] Zaynab was one of Imam Ali's daughters.

⁶but Allah, Glorified and Exalted is He, saved him from their mischief so that he might carry out something which He had decreed.

Once again it becomes clear to us, having briefly studied the personality of Khalid ibn al-Waleed whose praise is sung by "Ahlul Sunnah wal Jama'ah," that the latter are quite distant from the Prophet's Sunnah, and that they emulate those who acted to its contrary and abandoned it behind their backs and had no respect at all for it nor for the Book of Allah.

---

⁶ For more details of this plot, refer to al-Tabarsi's book *Al-Ihtijaj*.

10. ABU HURAYRA AL-DAWSI

One of the *sahabah* of the latter period of Islam's dawn and, according to the sequence employed by Ibn Sa'd in his *Tabaqat*, Abu Hurayra ranks in the ninth or tenth class.

He came to the Messenger of Allah near the end of the seventh Hijri year. Hence, historians say that he accompanied the Prophet no more than three years[1] according to the best estimates, while other historians say it was no more than two years if we take into consideration the fact that the Prophet sent him to accompany Ibn al-Hadrami to Bahrain, then the Messenger of Allah died while he was still in Bahrain.

Abu Hurayra was not known for his *jihad* or valor, nor was he among those who were regarded as brilliant thinkers, nor among the jurists who knew the Qur'an by heart, nor did he even know how to read and write. He came to the Messenger of Allah in order to satisfy his hunger as he himself said, and as the Prophet came to understand from him, so he lodged him among the people of the Saffa to whom the Prophet used to send some food.

Yet he became famous for the abundance of *ahadith* which he used to narrate about the Messenger of Allah. The number of these *ahadith* reached almost six thousand. This fact attracted the attention of verifiers of hadith especially since he had not remained in the company of the Prophet for any length of time and to the fact that he narrated traditions regarding battles which he had never attended.

Some verifiers of hadith gathered all what was narrated by the "righteous caliphs" as well as by the ten men given the glad tidings

---

[1] Al-Bukhari, *Sahih*, Vol. 4, p. 175, where the author quotes Abu Hurayra talking about himself in a chapter dealing with the characteristics of Prophethood.

of going to Paradise in addition to what the mothers of the faithful and the purified Ahlul Bayt, and they did not total one tenth of what Abu Hurayra had narrated all alone. This came despite the fact that among the latter was Ali ibn Abu Talib who remained in the company of the Prophet for thirty years.

Then fingers were pointed to Abu Hurayra charging him with telling lies and with fabricating *and forging hadith*. Some went as far as labelling him as the first narrator in the history of Islam thus charged. Yet "Ahlul Sunnah wal Jama'ah" bestow upon him the title of "Islam's narrator," surrounding him with a great deal of respect, totally relying on him.

Some of them may even regard him as being more knowledgeable than Ali due to one particular tradition which he narrates about himself and in which he says, "I said, `O Messenger of Allah! I hear a great deal of your *hadith* which I have been forgetting!' He said, `Stretch your mantle,' so I stretched it, whereupon he made a handful then said, `Close upon it,' whereupon I closed upon it and never forgot of it a thing ever since."[2]

Abu Hurayra kept narrating so many *ahadith* that Umar ibn al-Khattab beat him with his cane and said to him, "You have quoted too many *ahadith*, and it seems that you have been telling lies about the Messenger of Allah." This was due to one particular narration which he reported in which he quoted the Prophet saying that Allah had created the heavens, the earth, and all creation in seven days.

When Umar heard about it, he called him in and asked him to repeat that *hadith*. Having heard him repeating it, Umar struck him and said to him, "How so when Allah Himself says it was done in six days, while you yourself now say it was done in seven?" Abu

---

[2] Al-Bukhari, *Sahih*, Vol. 1, p. 38, in a chapter on acquiring knowledge, and also on p. 2, Vol. 3, of the same reference.

Hurayra said, "Maybe I heard it from Ka`b al-Ahbar..." Umar said, "Since you cannot distinguish between the Prophet's *ahadith* and what Ka`b al-Ahbar says, you must not narrate anything at all."[3]

It is also narrated that Imam Ali ibn Abu Talib has said, "Among all the living, the person who has told the most lies about the Messenger of Allah is Abu Hurayra al-Dawsi."[4] Mother of the faithful Ayesha, too, testified to his being a liar several times in reference to many *ahadith* which he used to attribute to the Messenger of Allah.

For example, she resented something which he had once said so she asked him, "When did you hear the Messenger of Allah say so?" He said to her, "The mirror, the kohl, and the dyestuff have all diverted you from the *hadith* of the Messenger of Allah," but when she insisted that he was lying and scandalized him, Marwan ibn al-Hakam interfered and took upon himself to verify the authenticity of the *hadith* in question.

It was then that Abu Hurayra admitted, "I did not hear it from the Messenger of Allah; rather, I heard it from al-Fadl ibn al-Abbas."[5] It is because of this particular narration that Ibn Qutaybah charged him with lying saying, "Abu Hurayra claimed that al-Fadl ibn al-Abbas, who had by then died, testified to the authenticity of that tradition which he attributed to him in order to mislead people into thinking that he had heard it from him."[6]

---

[3] Refer to the book titled *Abu Hurayra* by the Egyptian author Mahmud Abu Rayyah.

[4] Ibn Abul-Hadid, *Sharh Nahjul-Balagha*, Vol. 4, p. 28.

[5] Al-Bukhari, *Sahih*, Vol. 2, p. 232, in a chapter dealing with a fasting person who wakes up finding himself in the state of *janaba* (major pollution). Malik, *Muwatta'*, Vol. 1, p. 272.

[6] This is stated in al-Dhahabi's book *Siyar A`lam al-Nubala*.

In his book *Ta'weel al-Ahadith*, Ibn Qutaybah says, "Abu Hurayra used to say: 'The Messenger of Allah said such-and-such, but I heard it from someone else." In his book *A`lam al-Nubala*, al-Dhahabi says that Yazid ibn Ibrahim once cited Shu`bah ibn al-Hajjaj saying that Abu Hurayra used to commit forgery.

In his book [Siyar] *A`lam al-Nubala*, Ibn Kathir [Ed. this should be al-Dhahabi] indicates that Yazid ibn Ibrahim heard Ibn al-Hajjaj saying that Abu Hurayra used to forge hadith.

In his book *Al-Bidaya wal Nihaya*, Ibn Kathir states that Yazid ibn Haroun heard Shu`bah ibn al-Hajjaj accusing him of the same, that his, that he forges hadith, and that he used to narrate what he used to hear from Ka`b al-Ahbar as well as from the Messenger of Allah without distinguishing one from the other.

Ja`far al-Iskafi has said, "Abu Hurayra is doubted by our mentors; his narrations are not acceptable."[7]

During his lifetime, Abu Hurayra was famous among the *sahabah* of lying and forgery and of narrating too many fabricated *ahadith* to the extent that some of the *sahabah* used to deride him and ask him to fabricate *ahadith* agreeable with their own taste.

For example, a man belonging to Quraysh put on once a new *jubbah* (a long outer garment) and started showing off. He passed by Abu Hurayra and [sarcastically] said to him, "O Abu Hurayra! You narrate quite a few traditions about the Messenger of Allah; so, did you hear him say anything about my *jubbah*?!"

Abu Hurayra said, "I have heard the father of al-Qasim saying, `A man before your time was showing off his outfit when Allah caused the earth to cave in over him; so he has been rattling in it

---

[7] Ibn Abul-Hadid, *Sharh Nahjul-Balagha*, Vol. 4, p. 68.

and will continue to do so till the Hour.' By Allah! I do not know whether he was one of your people or not."[8]

How can people help doubting Abu Hurayra's traditions since they are so self-contradictory? He narrates one "hadith" then he narrates its antithesis, and if he is opposed or his previously narrated traditions are used against him, he becomes angry or starts babbling in the Ethiopian language.[9]

How could they help accusing him of telling lies and of forgery after he himself had admitted that he got traditions out of his own pouch then attributed them to the Prophet?

Al-Bukhari, in his *Sahih*, states the following:

Abu Hurayra said once, "The Prophet said, 'The best charity is willingly given; the higher hand is better than the lower one, and start with your own dependents. A woman says: 'Either feed me or divorce me.' A slave says, 'Feed me and use me.' A son says, 'Feed me for the woman who will forsake me.'" He was asked, "O Abu Hurayra! Did you really hear the Messenger of Allah say so?" He said, "No, this one is from Abu Hurayra's pouch."[10]

Notice how he starts this "tradition" by saying, "The Prophet said," then when they refuse to believe what he tells them, he admits by saying, "... this one is from Abu Hurayra's pouch"! So congratulations for Abu Hurayra for possessing this pouch which is full of lies and myths, and for which Mu`awiyah and Banu Umayyah provided a great deal of publicity, and because of which he acquired position, authority, wealth, and mansions. Mu`awiyah made him the governor of Medina and built him the Aqeeq mansion

---

[8] Ibn Kathir, *Al-Bidaya wal Nihaya*, Vol. 8, p. 108.

[9] Al-Bukhari, *Sahih*, Vol. 7, p. 31.

[10] Al-Bukhari, *Sahih*, Vol. 6, p. 190, in a chapter dealing with spending on the wife and children.

then married him off to a woman of honorable descent for whom he used to work as a servant...

Since Abu Hurayra was the close vizier of Mu`awiyah, it is not due to his own merits, honor, or knowledge; rather, it is because Abu Hurayra used to provide him with whatever traditions he needed to circulate. If some *sahabah* used to hesitate in cursing "Abu Turab," finding doing that as embarrassing, Abu Hurayra cursed Ali in his own house and as his Shi'as heard:

Ibn Abul-Hadid says,

When Abu Hurayra came to Iraq in the company of Mu`awiyah in the Year of the Jama`a, he came to Kufa's mosque. Having seen the huge number of those who welcomed him, he knelt down then beat his bald head and said, "O people of Iraq! Do you claim that I tell lies about the Messenger of Allah and thus burn myself in the fire?! By Allah! I heard the Messenger of Allah saying, `Each prophet has a sanctuary, and my sanctuary is in Medina from here to [the mountain of] Thawr; so, anyone who makes it unclean will be cursed by Allah, the angels, and all people, and I bear witness that Ali had done so." When Mu`awiyah came to hear this statement, he gave him a present, showered him with his generosity, and made him the governor of Medina.[11]

Suffices us to prove the above the fact that he was created governor of Medina by none other than Mu`awiyah. There is no doubt that verifiers and researchers who are free from prejudice will doubt anyone who befriended the enemy of Allah and His Messenger and who was antagonistic towards the friend of Allah and His Messenger...

There is no doubt that Abu Hurayra did not reach that lofty position of authority, namely the governor of Medina, the then

---

[11] Ibn Abul-Hadid, *Sharh Nahjul-Balagha*, Vol. 4, p. 67.

capital of the Islamic domains, except by virtue of the services which he had rendered to Mu`awiyah and other authoritative Umayyads. Praise to the One Who changes the conditions!

Abu Hurayra had come to Medina with nothing to cover his private parts other than a tiny striped piece of cloth, begging passers-by to feed him. Then he suddenly became ruler of the sacred precincts of Medina, residing in the Aqeeq mansion, enjoying wealth, servants and slaves, and nobody could say a word without his permission. All of this was from the blessings of his pouch!

Do not forget, nor should you be amazed, that nowadays we see the same plays being repeatedly enacted, and history certainly repeats itself. How many ignorant indigent persons sought nearness to a ruler and joined his party till they became feared masters who do and undo, issuing orders as they please, having a direct access to wealth without being accounted for it, riding in automobiles without being watched, eating foods not sold on the market...?

One such person may not even know how to speak his own language, nor does he know a meaning for life except satisfying his stomach and sexual appetite. The whole matter is simply his having a pouch like the one Abu Hurayra used to have with some exception, of course, yet the aim is one and the same: pleasing the ruler and publicizing for him in order to strengthen his authority, firm his throne, and finish his foes.

Abu Hurayra loved the Umayyads and they loved him since the days of Uthman ibn Affan, their leader. His view with regard to Uthman was contrary to that of all the *sahabah* who belonged to the Muhajirun and the Ansar; he regarded all the *sahabah* who participated in or encouraged the killing of Uthman as apostates.

Undoubtedly, Abu Hurayra used to accuse Ali ibn Abu Talib of killing Uthman. We can derive this conclusion from the statement he made at Kufa's mosque and his saying that Ali made Medina unclean and that he, therefore, was cursed by the Prophet, the angels, and everyone else. For this reason, Ibn Sa'd indicates in his *Tabaqat* that when Abu Hurayra died in 59 A.H./679 A.D., Uthman's descendants carried his coffin and brought it to the Baqee` to bury it as an expression of their appreciation of his having had high regards for Uthman.[12]

Surely Allah has his own wisdom in faring with His creation. Uthman ibn Affan, the master of Quraysh and their greatest, was killed although he was the Muslims' caliph bearing the title of "Dhul-Noorayn" and of whom, according to their claim, the angels feel shy. His corpse did not receive the ceremonial burial bath nor was it shrouded; moreover, it was not buried for full three days after which it was buried at the Jewish cemetery.

Yet Abu Hurayra died after having enjoyed pomp and power. He was an indigent man whose lineage and tribal origins were not known to anybody. He had no kinship to Quraysh. Despite all of this, the caliph's sons, who were in charge of running the affairs during Mu`awiyah's reign, took to bearing his corpse and to bury it at the Baqee` where the Messenger of Allah was buried...! But let us go back to Abu Hurayra to examine his attitude towards the Prophet's Sunnah.

In his *Sahih*, al-Bukhari quotes Abu Hurayra saying, "I learned the fill of two receptacles [of *ahadith*] from the Messenger of Allah: I have disseminated only one of them; as for the other, if I disseminate it, this throat will be slit."[13]

Since we indicated in our previous researches that Abu Bakr and Umar had burnt the recorded Prophet's Sunnah and prohibited

---

[12] Ibn Sa`d, *Tabaqat*, Vol. 2, p. 63.

[13] Al-Bukhari, *Sahih*, Vol. 1, p. 38, in a chapter dealing with learning.

traditionists from conveying it to others, here is Abu Hurayra revealing what erstwhile is hidden, testifying to our own conclusion, admitting that the only traditions he quoted were the ones that pleased the ruling authorities.

Building upon this premise, Abu Hurayra used to have two pouches, or two receptacles, as he called them. He used to disseminate the contents of one of them, the one which we have discussed here that contains whatever the rulers desired.

As for the other, which Abu Hurayra kept to himself and whose *ahadith* he did not narrate for fear his throat would be slit, it is the one containing the authentic traditions of the Prophet. Had Abu Hurayra been a reliable authority, he would have never hidden true *ahadith* while disseminating illusions and lies only to support the oppressor, knowing that Allah curses whoever hides the clear evidence.

Al-Bukhari quotes him saying once,

"People say that Abu Hurayra narrates too many ahadith. Had it not been for two [particular] verses in the Book of Allah, I would not have narrated a single hadith: *'Those who conceal what We have revealed of clear proofs and the guidance, after Our having clarified [everything] for people in the Book, these it is whom Allah shall curse, and those who curse shall curse them, too"* (Holy Qur'an, 2:159).

Our brethren from the Muhajirun used to be busy consigning transactions at the market-place, while our brethren from the Ansar used to be busy doing business with their own money, while Abu Hurayra kept in the shadow of the Prophet in order to satisfy his hunger, attending what they did not attend, learning what they did not learn."[14]

---

[14] *Ibid.*, Vol. 1, p. 37.

How can Abu Hurayra say that had it not been for a couple of verses in the Book of Allah, he would not have narrated a single hadith, then he says, "I learned two receptacles [of *ahadith*] from the Messenger of Allah: I have disseminated one of them; as for the other, if I disseminate it, this throat will be slit"?! Is this not his admission of having concealed the truth despite both verses in the Book of Allah?!

Had the Prophet not said to his companions, "Go back to your people and teach them"?[15] Had he not also said, "One who conveys is more aware than one who hears"? Al-Bukhari states that the Prophet urged the deputation of Abd Qays to learn belief and scholarship "... then convey what you learn to those whom you have left behind."[16]

Can we help wondering why should the throat of a *sahabi* be slit if he quotes the Prophet ?! There must be a secret here which the caliphs do not wish others to know. We actually pointed out to this very secret in our past researches embedded in our book *Ask Those Who Know*. Here, we would like to briefly say that "the people of the remembrance" was [a phrase in] a Qur'anic verse revealed to refer to Ali's successorship of the Prophet.

Abu Hurayra is not to blame; he knew his own worth and testified against his own soul that Allah cursed him, and so did those who curse, for having hidden the Prophet's hadith. But the blame is on "Ahlul Sunnah wal Jama'ah" who call Abu Hurayra the narrator of the Sunnah while he himself testifies that he hid it then testifies that he fabricated it and told lies in its regard, then he further goes on to testify that it became confused for him, so he could not tell which one was the statement of the Prophet and which one was made by others. All of these *ahadith* and correct

---

[15] Al-Bukhari, *Sahih*, Vol. 1, p. 30.
[16] *Ibid.*

admissions are recorded in al-Bukhari's *Sahih* and in other authentic books of hadith of "Ahlul Sunnah wal Jama'ah".

How can "Ahlul Sunnah wal Jama'ah" feel comfortable about a man whose justice was doubted by the Commander of the Faithful Ali ibn Abu Talib who charged him with lying, saying that among the living, nobody told more lies about the Prophet than Abu Hurayra. Umar ibn al-Khattab, too, charged him of the same, beat him and threatened to expel him.

Ayesha doubted his integrity and many times called him a liar, and many other *sahabah* cast doubts about his accuracy and rejected his contradictory *ahadith*, so he would once admit his error and would sometimes prattle in Ethiopian.[17] A large number of Muslim scholars refuted his traditions and charged him with lying, fabricating, and throwing himself at Mu`awiyah's dinner tables, at his coffers of gold and silver.

Is it right, then, for Abu Hurayra to become "Islam's narrator" from whom the religion's injunctions are learned?

Judaica and Jewish doctrines have filled the books of hadith. Ka`b al-Ahbar, a Jew, may have succeeded in getting such doctrines and beliefs included into the books of hadith, hence we find traditions likening or personifying Allah, as well as the theory of incarnation, in addition to many abominable statements about the prophets and messengers of Allah: all of these are cited through Abu Hurayra.

So, are "Ahlul Sunnah wal Jama'ah" now going to repent and go back to their senses in order to know who they should learn the true Sunnah from? If they ask us, we would say, "Come to the Gate of Knowledge and the Imams from his offspring, for they are the

---

[17] Abu Hurayra was bi-lingual. He spoke Arabic (his mother tongue) and Amharic, an Ethiopian Semitic language. Tr.

custodians of the Sunnah, the security of the nation, the ark of salvation, the Imams of guidance, the lanterns that shatter the dark, the mighty niche, and the strong Rope of Allah."

11. ABDULLAH IBN UMAR

He is one of the famous *sahabah* who played a major role in shaping the events that took place during the reign of the third caliph as well as that of Banu Umayyah. Suffices him the fact that his father was Umar ibn al-Khattab to be glorified and loved by "Ahlul Sunnah wal Jama'ah" who consider him as one of the greatest *faqihs* and of all those who learned the "Prophet's *ahadith*."

Even Imam Malik relies on him in deducting most of his *ahkam*, filling his book *Al-Muwatta'* with his traditions. And if we turn the pages of the books of "Ahlul Sunnah wal Jama'ah," we will find them referring to him quite often, full of his praise.

Yet if we read the same that with researchers' discerning eyes, it will become clear to us that he was far from being just or truthful; rather, he was distant from the Prophet's Sunnah, from *fiqh,* and from the *Shari`a*.

Our first observation will be his extreme enmity and hatred towards the master of the Prophet's Progeny, Commander of the Faithful Ali ibn Abu Talib: he went as far as instigating others against him and regarded as a commoner.

We have already indicated that he circulated many false *ahadith* the gist of which is that the *sahabah* during the lifetime of the Prophet used to compare each one of them with the other in the presence of the Prophet heard, saying that the best of people was Abu Bakr then Umar then Uthman, then people after the latter were all alike, and that the Prophet used to hear all of this comparison without denying it. This is a blatant lie derided by any rational person.

We researched the life of Abdullah ibn Umar during the Prophet's lifetime, and we found out that he was too young to reach adolescence. He had no influence whatsoever among those who had a say, nor was his view taken into consideration. The Messenger of

Allah died when Abdullah ibn Umar was, according to the best estimates, nineteen years old; so, how could he have said that they (the *sahabah*) used to compare each one of them with the other?

This could only be children gossiping among themselves, the children of Abu Bakr, Uthman, in addition to his own brothers. Nevertheless, it cannot be right to say that the Prophet was listening to such comparison without voicing his objection to it. This proves that this "tradition" is false and is indicative of ill intentions.

Add to the above the fact that the Prophet never permitted Abdullah ibn Umar to accompany him during his battles with the exception of the Battle of the Trench (*khandaq*) and the other campaigns that followed it, when Abdullah was fifteen years old.[1]

There is no doubt that he was present at the Battle of Khaybar which took place in 7 A.H./628 A.D. and saw with his own eyes how both Abu Bakr and his father fled from the battle field. He undoubtedly heard the Messenger of Allah saying, "I shall give the flag of army tomorrow to a man who loves Allah and His Messenger and who is loved by Allah and His Messenger, a brave one who attacks and never flees, a man the conviction of whose heart Allah has ascertained." When it was morning, he gave it to the one who terminated the pleasure of those who indulged therein, who dispersed the groups, who dispelled the clouds of calamities, who was adorned with graces, the ever-victorious Lion of Allah Ali ibn Abu Talib.[2]

---

[1] Al-Bukhari, *Sahih*, Vol. 3, p. 158, in a chapter dealing with children reaching the age of adolescence. It is also mentioned in a chapter on adolescence in the Book of Government of Muslim's *Sahih*.

[2] The tradition of the standard is mentioned by al-Bukhari, Muslim, al-Tirmidhi, al-Nasa'i, Imam Ahmad ibn Hanbal, Abu Dawud, and all other traditionists.

The tradition of the standard referred to above clearly highlights Ali's merits and superiority over all other *sahabah*. It demonstrates his status with Allah and His Messenger and his having won the love of Allah and His Messenger. Because of his hatred towards Ali, Abdullah ibn Umar regarded Ali as one of the commoners!

We have already indicated that "Ahlul Sunnah wal Jama'ah" acted upon this tradition which their master Abdullah ibn Umar inspired to them, so they did not rank Ali ibn Abu Talib among the righteous caliphs. No, they did not do that, nor did they even recognize his caliphate except during the time of Ahmad ibn Hanbal as we proved above.

They were exposed when traditions and traditionists became quite numerous, and when fingers were pointed at them accusing them of being Nasibis and of hating the Ahlul Bayt of the Prophet, and when all Muslims came to know that hating Ali was one of the most obvious signs of hypocrisy. It was then that they felt compelled to recognize Ali's caliphate. It was only then that they added his name to the list of the "righteous caliphs." It was only then that they pretended, being pretentious and perfidious, to love Ahlul Bayt.

We wish there had been someone to ask Ibn Umar the following question: "Why did all, or most of, Muslims after the demise of the Prophet dispute about who deserved most to be the caliph and narrowed their dispute to only Ali and Abu Bakr, and why neither your father [Umar ibn al-Khattab] nor Uthman ibn Affan had any popularity at that time?"

Was there anyone to ask the son of Umar ibn al-Khattab, "If the Prophet agreed with your view that nobody was the peer of Abu Bakr then Umar then Uthman, then why did he two days before his death choose a young man who grew no beard nor a moustache to be their leader, ordering them to march under his order and command? Was he then hallucinating, as your father described him of doing?"

We wish someone had asked Abdullah ibn Umar this question: "Why did the Muhajirun and the Ansars, having witnessed Abu Bakr swearing his oath of loyalty to Fatima al-Zahra, say to her: `By Allah! Had your husband and cousin come to us before Abu Bakr, we would not have equated him with any man at all,' which is an admission from the most prominent of the *sahabah* that they did not equate Ali with anyone else, had they not already sworn their oath of allegiance to him, an oath which they later called a mistake?" What is the value of the view of Abdullah ibn Umar, the conceited teenager who did not know how to divorce his wife, compared to that of such prominent *sahabah*?

Finally, was there anyone to ask Abdullah ibn Umar, "Why did not the *sahabah* choose Ali ibn Abu Talib to be their caliph after Umar's murder and prefer him over Uthman, had it not been for his own refusal of the condition put forth by Abd ul-Rahman ibn Awf that he had to rule them according to the "Sunnah" of both shaykhs?"[3]

But Abdullah ibn Umar was influenced by his father. He lived during the caliphate of Abu Bakr, Umar, and Uthman, and he noticed how Ali ibn Abu Talib was kept at bay, having no place among the ruling group nor any government post, with the people turning away from him after the death of his cousin and wife, the Leader of all Women, having had no material gains to attract people thereby.

Undoubtedly, Abdullah ibn Umar was the closest person to his father. He used to listen to his views, and he knew his friends and

---

[3] Al-Tabari, *Tarikh,* Vol. 5, p. 40. Al-Suyuti, *Tarikh al-Khulafa,* p. 104. Ibn Qutaybah, *Tarikh.* Ahmad, *Musnad,* Vol. 1, p.75.

foes; hence, he grew up nurtured in hatred, grudge and animosity towards Ali in particular and Ahlul Bayt in general. Once he saw Ali receiving the oath of allegiance from the Muhajirun and Ansar following Uthman's murder, and he could not tolerate it.

He, then, revealed his hidden animosity and refused to swear the oath of allegiance to the Imam of the righteous and the *wali* of the faithful. He could no longer tolerate living in Medina, so he left it for Mecca pretending to perform the `umra.

Then we see Abdullah ibn Umar doing all he could do to discourage people and dissuade them from supporting the truth or fighting the oppressive group the fighting of which was ordered by Allah Himself till it reverted to His command. He, therefore, was among the earliest to betray the Imam of his time whom he was required to obey.

Once Imam Ali was killed, and Mu`awiyah attained victory over Imam al-Hasan ibn Ali, thus usurping the caliphate from him, Mu`awiyah delivered a speech to people in which he said, "I did not fight you so that you may pray or fast or perform the pilgrimage; rather, I fought you in order to take charge of you, and Allah has given me just that."

We then see Abdullah ibn Umar racing to swear the oath of allegiance to Mu`awiyah under the pretext that people were united in accepting his leadership after their disunity! I think it was he who named that year "Am al-jama`ah," year of the group, for he and his group of Banu Umayyah became "Ahlul Sunnah wal Jama'ah" and will remain so till the time of the Hour.

Was there anyone to ask Abdullah ibn Umar and those who held his views from "Ahlul Sunnah wal Jama`a": "Had there ever been any consensus in history such as the one attained for the Commander of the Faithful Ali ibn Abu Talib?" Abu Bakr's caliphate was "a mistake whose evil Allah shunned,"[4] and it was boycotted by a large number of the *sahabah*.

Umar's caliphate was by recommendation; rather, it was a promise granted by Abu Bakr, and the *sahabah* had neither view, nor say, nor anything else to do with it. And Uthman's caliphate was achieved through a committee of three persons selected by Umar; rather, it was due to Abdul-Rahman ibn Awf forcing his own view over the rest.

As for Ali's caliphate, it was done through the voluntary and peaceful oath of allegiance of the Muhajirun and the Ansar; he wrote all Islamic domains asking those in charge of them to grant him their oath of allegiance, which they all did with the exception of Mu`awiyah in Syria.[5]

What Ibn Umar and "Ahlul Sunnah wal Jama'ah" were supposed to do was to kill Mu`awiyah ibn Abu Sufyan for declaring his mutiny and demanding the caliphate for himself according to the narrations which they themselves have recorded in their Sahih books. One of these traditions states that the Messenger of Allah said, "If two caliphs receive oaths of allegiance, one after the other, you should kill the second."[6]

He has also said, as recorded in Muslim's *Sahih* and in other books of *hadith*, "Whoever swears the oath of allegiance to an Imam, shakes his hand, and grants him his heart, let him grant him

---

[4] This statement was made by Umar ibn al-Khattab at the Prophet's Mosque in Medina shortly before his death. Tr.

[5] Ibn Hajar, *Fath al-Bari*, Vol. 7, p. 586.

[6] Muslim, *Sahih*, Vol. 6, p. 23. Al-Hakim, *Mustadrak*, Vol. 2, p. 156. Al-Bayhaqi, *Sunan*, Vol. 8, p. 144.

his all, but if another person comes to dispute with him, you should kill the latter."⁷

But Abdullah ibn Umar did exactly the opposite: Instead of acting upon the Prophet's tradition, submit to his orders, fight and kill Mu`awiyah for having contested the caliph of the Muslims and lit the fire of dissension, he, we find out, refused to swear the oath of allegiance despite the Muslims' consensus in its regard. Instead, he swore it to Mu`awiyah who declared his mutiny, who disputed with the Imam and killed a number of innocent people, causing dissension the aftermath of which lingers till our time.

For this reason, I think that Abdullah ibn Umar was Mu`awiyah's accomplice in all the crimes and sins the latter had committed because he erected his authority and assisted him in forcing people to accept it, and in his confiscation of the caliphate which Allah and His Messenger decreed to be out of the reach of the promiscuous and the sons of the promiscuous according to the sacred hadith.

Abdullah ibn Umar was not satisfied with doing all of that, so he rushed to swear the oath of allegiance to Yazid ibn Mu`awiyah, the Yazid of wines, corruption, and apostasy, the promiscuous son of the promiscuous father, the cursed one and the son of the accursed.

Since Umar ibn al-Khattab, according to Ibn Sa'd who discusses him in his *Tabaqat*, used to say, "Caliphate is not suitable for a promiscuous person, nor for the son of a promiscuous person, nor for those who accept Islam after being vanquished,"⁸ then how

---

⁷ This is recorded in Muslim's *Sahih*, in al-Bayhaqi's *Sunan*, and in Ibn Majah's *Sunan*.

⁸ Ibn Sa`d, *Tabaqat*, Vol. 3, p. 248.

did Abdullah contradict his own father with regard to this principle which he himself had recorded?

If Abdullah ibn Umar thus contradicted the Book of Allah and the Sunnah of His Messenger with regard to the issue of caliphate, we will not then be surprised to find him doing the opposite of what his father had stated.

We would like to ask Abdullah ibn Umar this question: "What consensus was there with regard to swearing the oath of allegiance to Yazid ibn Mu`awiyah from whom the righteous in the nation and the remnants of the Muhajirun and Ansar, including the master of the youths of Paradise Imam al-Husayn ibn Ali, Abdullah ibn al-Zubayr, Abdullah ibn Abbas, and all those who kept them company and shared their views, dissociated themselves?"

What is well known is the fact that he himself used to be among those who in the beginning denounced Yazid receiving the oath of allegiance, but Mu`awiyah knew how to win him over: He sent him one hundred thousand dirhams which he accepted as a gift. When it was mentioned to him that the sender was soliciting his oath of allegiance to his son Yazid, he said, "Is this what he wanted? My creed, then, must be quite cheap..."[9]

Yes, Abdullah ibn Umar sold his creed very cheaply as he himself admitted. He ran away from having to swear it to the Imam of the righteous but rushed to swear it to the leader of oppressors Mu`awiyah, then to the leader of the fornicators Yazid, thus bearing on his shoulders the burdens of the crimes committed by Mu`awiyah's oppressive government.

He, no doubt, carried the burdens of Yazid's crimes on his head for violating the sanctity of the

---

[9] Al-Baladhuri, *Ansab al-Ashraf*, Vol. 5, p. 31. Ibn Abd al-Birr, *Al-Isti`ab*, Vol. 2, p. 396. *Usd al-Ghabah*, Vol. 3, p. 289.

Messenger of Allah and for killing the fragrant flower, the master of the youths of Paradise and of the Progeny of the Prophet, together with the righteous among the sons of the nation whom he killed in Karbala in the Battle of the Harrah[10].

Abdullah ibn Umar was not satisfied with this much of the oath of allegiance to Yazid, so he pressured people to follow in his footsteps, terrorizing anyone who contemplated doing otherwise.

Al-Bukhari in his *Sahih* and other compilers of *hadith* state that Abdullah ibn Umar gathered his offspring, servants, and slaves when the people of Medina rejected Yazid ibn Mu`awiyah and said to them, "We swore the oath of allegiance to this man acting upon swearing it to Allah and His Messenger[11], and I have heard the Messenger of Allah saying, `One who betrays will have a standard erected for him on the Day of Judgment, and it will be said to him:

This is the betrayal of so-and-so,' and the worst type of betrayal, after associating someone with Allah, is one who swears the oath of allegiance to Allah and His Messenger then betrays it,[12]

---

[10] For details of this horrific historic event, pls see: https://www.al-islam.org/battle-of-harrah-muhammad-ali-chenarani

[11] Did Allah and His Messenger enjoin swearing the oath of allegiance to adulterers and criminals? Or did He enjoin swearing it to the righteous when He said, "Surely Allah is your Wali and His Messenger and those who believe who uphold the prayers and who pay the zakat even as they prostrate"?

[12] How we wish Ibn Umar had said the same to Talhah and al-Zubayr who reneged from their oath of allegiance to Ali and fought him, and how we wish "Ahlul Sunnah wal Jama`ah" acted according to this tradition in classifying men! If violating the oath of allegiance is one of the greatest sins which follow apostasy, what is the fate of Talhah and al-Zubayr who did not only violate their oath of allegiance but also violated people's honor, killed innocent people and confiscated their wealth, and betrayed the promise?

and none of you should unseat Yazid, nor should anyone among you see such unseating as honorable, else something tragic should happen between me and him."[13]

Yazid's oppression received a boost when Abdullah ibn Umar supported him and urged people to swear the oath of fealty to him, so he raised an army under the command of Uqbah, one of the leading adulterers of his time, ordering him to assault Medina, the city of the Prophet, permitting him to do whatever he wished in it. Uqbah, therefore, killed ten thousand *sahabis* and took their wives as captives then confiscated their property.

He also killed seven hundred *huffaz* of the Holy Qur'an according to al-Baladhuri, permitting his army to rape many free Muslim women to the extent that the latter gave birth to an estimated one thousand illegitimate babies. Then he forced them to swear that they were all slaves of his master Yazid...

Was not Abdullah ibn Umar his accomplice in all of that, since he supported and empowered him? I leave the researchers to derive their own conclusion.

Abdullah ibn Umar was not satisfied with all of that; rather, he went beyond it to swear the oath of allegiance to Marwan ibn al-Hakam, the bedeviled accursed one, the promiscuous adulterer, who fought Ali openly and killed Talhah and did so many horrible things such as burning the House of Allah and shelling it with catapults, demolishing one of its corners and killing in that incident Abdullah ibn al-Zubayr, in addition to other shameful actions.

Then Ibn Umar reaches in swearing his oath of allegiance new heights when he swore it to al-Hajjaj ibn Yusuf al-Thaqafi, the greatest apostate who used to make fun of the Holy Qur'an and

---

[13] Al-Bukhari, *Sahih*, Vol. 1, p. 166. Ahmad, *Musnad*, Vol. 2, p. 96. Al-Bayhaqi, *Sunan*, Vol. 8, p. 159.88.

label it as Arab martial poetry, preferring his master Abdul-Malik ibn Marwan over the Messenger of Allah. This al-Hajjaj is the same one who was known by the elite as well as the commoners as having belittled all Islamic tenets.

In his *Tarikh*, the *hafiz* Ibn Asakir indicates that two men disputed with one another about al-Hajjaj. One of them said that he was a *kafir*, an apostate, whereas the other said that he was a *daall mu'min*, a believer who went astray. When they persisted, they asked al-Sha`bi about his view. Al-Sha`bi said, "He is a mu'min [believer] in as far as oppression and tyranny are concerned, a *kafir* [disbeliever] in Allah, the Great."[14]

This criminal al-Hajjaj is the one who violated everything which Allah decreed not to be violated. Historians record that he was excessive in killing, torturing and mutilating the corpses of the righteous of the nation, especially Shi`a followers of Muhammad's, for these suffered at his hands more than at the hands of anyone else.

In his *Tarikh*, Ibn Qutaybah says that in one single day, al-Hajjaj killed more than seventy thousand men to the extent that the blood flow reached the mosque's door as well as the highways.[15] And in his *Sahih*, al-Tirmidhi, having counted those executed by al-Hajjaj, says, "After his [al-Hajjaj's] death, eighty thousand prisoners were found in his jail, including thirty thousand women."[16]

Al-Hajjaj used to compare himself to the Lord of Might and Honor: whenever he passed by the jail and heard the prisoners

---

[14] Ibn Asakir, *Tarikh*, Vol. 4, p. 81.
[15] Ibn Qutaybah. *Tarikh al-Khulafa*, Vol. 2, p. 26.
[16] Al-Tirmidhi, *Sahih*, Vol. 9, p. 64.

crying of pain and pleading for mercy, he used to say to them [what the Almighty says in the Holy Qur'an]:

"Remain in abjection therein, and do not speak to me" (Holy Qur'an, 23:108).

Such is al-Hajjaj who was prophesied by the Messenger of Allah before his demise; he said, "There is in [the tribe of] Thaqeef a liar and an annihilator." What is strange is that the narrator of this tradition is none other Abdullah ibn Umar himself![17]

Yes, Abdullah ibn Umar was reluctant to swear the oath of allegiance to the best of mankind after the Prophet and did not support him, nor did he even pray behind him; therefore, Allah, Glory to Him, humiliated him. He went to al-Hajjaj once and said, "I have heard the Messenger of Allah saying, `Whoever dies owing an oath of allegiance will die the death of *jahiliyya*.'"

Al-Hajjaj the accursed, thereupon, despised him and pointed his foot at him saying, "My hand is busy right now; so, swear your oath of allegiance to this." He used to pray behind al-Hajjaj, the apostate, and behind his *wali* Najdah ibn Amir, head of the Kharijites.[18]

There is no doubt that Abdullah ibn Umar preferred to pray behind these men only because they were famous for cursing and denouncing Ali after the prayers. Ibn Umar used to gratify his hidden grudge and animosity whenever he heard such cursing, feeling very contented at heart and very satisfied therewith.

For this reason, we find the sect of "Ahlul Sunnah wal Jama'ah" enjoining prayers behind the righteous as well as the

---

[17] Al-Tirmidhi, *Sahih*, Vol. 9, p. 64. Imam Ahmad ibn Hanbal, *Musnad*, Vol. 2, p. 91.

[18] Ibn Sa`d, *Al-Tabaqat al-Kubra*, Vol. 4, p. 110. Ibn Hazm, *Al-Muhalla*, Vol. 4, p. 213.

promiscuous based on what their master and the *faqih* of their sect Abdullah ibn Umar doing likewise and praying behind the apostate al-Hajjaj and the Kharijite Najdah ibn Amir.

As for the Prophet's statements such as these: "The one who should be the Imam of people is their best in reciting the Book of Allah. If they all recite it equally well, he should be the most knowledgeable of the Sunnah.

If they all know the Sunnah equally well, he should be their foremost in having participated in the Hijra. If they had all participated in the Hijra at the same time, he should be the foremost in having accepted Islam...," they surely are discarded...

None of these four merits, namely reciting the Holy Qur'an, safeguarding the Sunnah, early participation in the Hijra, and early acceptance of Islam, applies to those to whom Ibn Umar swore his oath of allegiance and behind whom he prayed: neither in Mu`awiyah, nor in Yazid, nor in Marwan, nor in al-Hajjaj, nor in Najdah, the Kharijite...

This, of course, is only one of the Sunnah injunctions which Abdullah ibn Umar violated. He discarded them altogether and acted exactly to their contrary. He abandoned the master of the Prophet's purified Progeny, namely Ali, in whom all these and many more merits were combined. Rather, he turned his back to him and went to join the corrupt ones, the Kharijites, the apostates, the enemies of Allah and His Messenger, praying behind them!

How many are the violations of the *faqih* of "Ahlul Sunnah wal Jama'ah" Abdullah ibn Umar, violations of both the Book of Allah and the Sunnah of His Messenger?! If we wish, we can gather them in a separate book, but the following examples, which are quoted from their own books and Sahihs, should suffice to back our argument:

VIOLATIONS OF ABDULLAH IBN UMAR OF THE BOOK AND THE SUNNAH

Allah, the Most Exalted One, has said in His Glorious Book,

"Fight the one [party] that acts wrongfully till it returns to obeying Allah's Command" (Holy Qur'an, 49:9).

The Messenger of Allah has said, "O Ali! You shall fight after me the renegades, those who equal others with Allah, and the heretics."

Abdullah ibn Umar violated this text of the Holy Qur'an as well as the above quoted tradition, and he violated the consensus (*ijma`*) of the nation, of the Muhajirs and the Ansar who fought beside the Commander of the Faithful, following his own view and saying, "I shall not fight in the dissension, and I shall pray behind whoever wins."[1] Ibn Hajar has indicated that Abdullah ibn Umar was of the view that one should avoid fighting during a dissension even if one of the two parties is right and the other is wrong.[2]

Truly strange, by Allah, is the case of Abdullah ibn Umar who sees one party being right and the other being wrong yet refraining from supporting the right one or from curbing the wrong party till it returns to obedience to Allah! He performed his prayers behind whoever won, albeit if the winner was a wrong doer!

This is exactly what happened to Ibn Umar, for Mu`awiyah won and subdued the nation, forcing his authority on it. Ibn Umar then came and swore the oath of allegiance to Mu`awiyah and prayed behind him despite all the crimes and sins which he had committed and which are beyond one's imagination and with which Ibn Umar was fully familiar.

---

[1] Ibn Sa`d, *Al-Tabaqat al-Kubra*, Vol. 4, p. 110.

[2] Ibn Hajar states this fact on p. 39 of his book *Al-Fath al-Bari*

The wrong doers from the leaders of oppression, due to their numerical superiority, won victory over the leaders of the truth who were the Imams of Ahlul Bayt. So the latter were excluded from authority, whereas the promiscuous, the adulterers, the straying criminals, came to rule the nation with force and oppression.

Ibn Umar abandoned the truth, all of it, so history does not record any friend for him nor any affinity towards Ahlul Bayt five of whose Imams were his contemporaries. He did not pray behind a single one of them. He did not quote one of their *ahadith*, and he did not recognize a single virtue or merit of any of them.

We have come to know, while discussing the Twelve Imams in this book, what his view with regard to the ones whom he labelled as the twelve caliphs was. He regarded as authentic the caliphate of Abu Bakr, Umar, Uthman, Yazid, al-Saffah, Salam, al-Mansour, Jabir, al-Mahdi, al-Amin, and their team head [Mu`awiyah], saying, "All these twelve are descendants of Banu Ka`b ibn Luayy, and they are all unmatched in righteousness."[3]

Do you see among these men any of the Imams of guidance from the Prophet's Progeny who were described by the Messenger of Allah as the ark of salvation and the peers of the Qur'an?!

For this reason, you cannot trace any presence for them among "Ahlul Sunnah wal Jama'ah," nor is there even one Imam from Ahlul Bayt on the list of imams and caliphs they emulate. Such is the case of Abdullah ibn Umar in his violation of the Book of Allah and the Sunnah of His Messenger. As for his own ignorance of the same, you may say whatever you wish.

---

[3] Al-Suyuti quotes this statement in his book *Kanz al-Ummal*, and it is quoted in the history books of both Ibn Asakir and al-Dhahabi. To know the other references with the number of their pages and volumes, refer to the chapter in this book dealing with the twelve successors according to the Sunnis.

Among the indications of such ignorance is his being unaware of the fact that the Prophet permitted women to wear sandals when wearing the *ihram* garb; Ibn Umar issued *fatawa* prohibiting it.[4]

Another is the leasing of his farms during the lifetime of the Messenger of Allah as well as during the reign of Abu Bakr, Umar, Uthman, and Mu`awiyah to the extent that one of the *sahabah* talked to him near the end of Mu`awiyah's reign and told him that the Messenger of Allah had prohibited it.[5]

Yes; such is the *faqih* of "Ahlul Sunnah wal Jama`a;" he did not know that it was *haram* to lease farms, and there is no doubt that he used to issue his verdicts permitting it during that entire period which lasted from the time of the Prophet to the end of Mu`awiyah's reign, a period of about fifty years...

Yet another example is Ayesha denouncing his verdict that a deceased person is tormented because of the weeping of the living over him, and also with regard to morning *azan*, and his saying that the month is twenty-nine days. She opposed him in several other issues as well.

Other examples are recorded by both shaykhs, namely al-Bukhari and Muslim, in the *Sahih* of each one of them: Abdullah ibn Umar was told that Abu Hurayra used to say, "I heard the Messenger of Allah saying, `Whoever walks behind a coffin will receive one karat of rewards.'" Ibn Umar responded by [sarcastically] saying, "Abu Hurayra has surely been generous with such karats!" Ayesha, however, testified to the authenticity of Abu Hurayra's tradition saying, "I heard the Messenger of Allah saying

---

[4] Abu Dawud, *Sunan*, Vol. 1, p. 289. Al-Bayhaqi, *Sunan*, Vol. 5, p. 25. Imam Ahmad ibn Hanbal, *Musnad*, Vol. 2, p. 29.

[5] Al-Bukhari, *Sahih*. Muslim, *Sahih*, Vol. 5, p. 21.

so." It was then that Ibn Umar said, "We surely have missed quite a few karats!"⁶

Suffices us in this regard the testimony of Umar ibn al-Khattab with regard to his son Abdullah: On his death bed, Umar was asked by a flatterer, "Why don't you recommend Abdullah ibn Umar to be the next caliph?" Umar said, "Shall I recommend a man who does not know even how to divorce his wife [according to the Shari`a]?!"

Such is Abdullah son of Umar ibn al-Khattab, and nobody knew him better than his father.

As for the false traditions whereby he served his master Mu`awiyah, these are quite numerous indeed. We would like to mention a few of them by way of sampling:

He said, "The Messenger of Allah said, `A man from the people of Paradise will soon come to you,' whereupon Mu`awiyah came. Then he said, `Tomorrow, a man from the people of Paradise will come to you;' Mu`awiyah came. Then he repeated the same about the next day, whereupon Mu`awiyah came."

Another is his saying, "When the Ayat al-Kursi was revealed, the Messenger of Allah told Mu`awiyah to write it down. `What shall I get if I do so?' asked Mu`awiyah. He said, `Whenever anyone recites it, you will receive the reward of its recitation.'"

Another is his saying, "Mu`awiyah will surely be resurrected on the Resurrection Day outfitted with a robe of the light of *iman*."

I do not know why "Ahlul Sunnah wal Jama'ah" did not add Mu`wiyah's name to the list of the ten men who received the glad

---

⁶ This is recorded by al-Bukhari in his *Sahih* in a chapter dealing with the virtues of walking behind borne coffins in his Kitab al-Janaaiz (Book of Borne Coffins).

tidings of going to Paradise since their master Ibn Umar emphasized thrice, in three consecutive days, that Mu`awiyah was to go to Paradise. Since people on the Resurrection Day will be raised bare-footed, naked, Mu`awiyah will be their very best because he will be outfitted with a robe made of the light of *iman*! So read such statements and wonder!

Such is Abdullah ibn Umar; such is the extent of his knowledge; such is his *fiqh* and violation of the Book of Allah and the Sunnah of the Prophet; such is his enmity towards the Commander of the Faithful and the pure Imams from the Progeny of the Prophet, and such is his loyalty and flattery of the enemies of Allah and His Messenger, the enemies of humanity.

12. ABDULLAH IBN AL-ZUBAYR

His father, al-Zubayr ibn al-Awwam, was killed during the Battle of the Camel, a battle labelled in the Prophet's Sunnah as the "War of the Perfidious." His mother was Asmaa daughter of Abu Bakr ibn Abu Quhafa. His aunt was mother of the faithful Ayesha daughter of Abu Bakr and wife of the Prophet. He was one of the main opponents of Imam Ali and of those who hated him most.

He may have prided himself in the caliphate of his grandfather Abu Bakr and in his aunt Ayesha, so he inherited from both of them such hatred which lasted all his life. Imam Ali, peace be upon him, used to say to al-Zubayr, "We used to consider you as one of the offspring of Abd al-Muttalib till your evil son created dissension between us and you."

It is well known in history that he was during the Battle of the Camel one of the most prominent elements and immediate commanders, so much so that Ayesha introduced him to lead people in the prayers after having dismissed both Talhah and al-Zubayr for disputing with one another, each desiring to lead it.

It is also said that he is the one who brought his aunt Ayesha fifty men to falsely swear that the place where she had arrived was not called Hawab. This is why she consented to continue her march towards the Battle of the Camel.

Abdullah is the one who reproached his father for deciding to retire from the battle after having been reminded by Imam Ali, peace be upon him, of one particular *hadith* of the Prophet wherein he informed al-Zubayr that he, being oppressive, would fight Ali. He kept reproaching his father to the extent that the latter said to him, "What is wrong with you?! May Allah shame you for being such an ominous son!" It is said that he continued to reproach and excite his father till he succeeded in getting him to attack Ali's army; he was killed and his father's calling him an ominous son proved to be quite right.

This is the tale which we have chosen for you due to its accuracy, and due to its being descriptive of al-Zubayr's spiteful psychology as well as that of his ominous son Abdullah. Al-Zubayr could not have so easily pulled himself away from that battle, leaving behind Talhah and his men in addition to slaves and servants whom he had brought all the way from Basra.

He could not have left the mother of the faithful Ayesha, sister of his wife, in such peril. If we accept that he abandoned them, they would not have let him get away with it that easily especially his son Abdullah the forcefulness of whose determination we have already come to know.

Historians indicate that Abdullah ibn al-Zubayr used to curse and condemn Ali. Once he said about him: "The mean villain is approaching you." He once delivered a speech to the people of Basra urging them to fight Ali in which he said, "O people! Ali killed the rightful caliph Uthman oppressively, then he raised armies to take control over you and to take your city; so, be men who demand revenge for your slain caliph, protect your women, and defend your daughters, kinfolks, and tribes. Surely Ali does not consider in this issue anyone's view other than that of his own and, by Allah, if he achieves victory over you, he will annihilate your creed and world."[1]

His hatred and animosity reached the limit where he abandoned invoking Allah's blessings unto His Prophet; so, no blame should be put on him, nor should his lies to people surprise us, nor his thus charging Imam Ali, peace be upon him, whom he

---

[1] Ibn Abul-Hadid, *Sharh Nahjul-Balagha*, Vol. 1, p. 358. Al-Mas'udi, *Tarikh*, Vol. 5, p. 163.

accused of everything abominable such as the accusations in his speech cited above when he addressed the people of Basra and said to them, "... by Allah, if he achieves victory over you, he will annihilate your creed and world." It is nothing but blatant falsehood and a great defamation coming from Abdullah ibn al-Zubayr to whose heart the truth could not find a way.

What testifies to the above is the fact that when Ali ibn Abu Talib won victory over the people of Basra and arrested most of them, and among those arrested was Abdullah ibn al-Zubayr himself, he forgave all of them and set them free and was generous to Ayesha, protecting her honor and sending her back to her home to Medina. He also prohibited his men from taking any booty or taking women or children captive or killing the wounded, so much so that such prohibition cost him the mutiny of some of his forces and doubts were cast at his judgment.

Ali, peace be upon him, was the embodiment of the Sunnah of the Prophet and the most knowledgeable of the Book of Allah, the Book which none then knew it better than him. Hypocrites and infiltrators in his army instigated rebellion against him; they said, "How could he permit us to fight them yet prohibit us from taking their women captive?"

Such talk duped a large number of his fighting men, but he, peace of Allah be upon him, argued with them through the Book of Allah saying, "Place your bets on who among you will take your mother Ayesha as his captive!" It was then that they realized that he was right; so, they said to him, "We seek Allah's forgiveness [against doing so]; you are right while we are wrong."

What Abdullah ibn al-Zubayr had said about the Imam was a lie and obvious defamation: his hatred towards Ali, peace be upon him, blinded both his eyes and mind, bringing him out of conviction. Ibn al-Zubayr never repented after that incident, nor did he learn any lesson, nor did he derive any wisdom from that war to the benefit of his soul...

No, indeed; rather, he rewarded a good deed with a bad one, and his grudge and hatred against the descendants of Hashim in general and the master of the Purified Progeny in particular increased, and he did all he could to put out their light and to put an end to them.

Historians narrate saying that he, following the assassination of Imam Ali, started seeking to be the caliph of the faithful, and some people rallied behind him, so he grew stronger. He managed to have Muhammad ibn al-Hanafiyya, son of Imam Ali (peace be upon him), jailed together with al-Hasan ibn Ali and seventeen other men belonging to Banu Hashim.

Then he wanted to burn them alive, so he gathered in front of the jail a great deal of fire wood then set it on fire. Had it not been for the arrival of al-Mukhtar's army at the right moment and its putting the fire out, the son of al-Zubayr would have achieved his evil objective.[2]

Marwan ibn al-Hakam then sent him an army led by al-Hajjaj who surrounded his house, killed him, then hanged his corpse at the mosque. Thus ended the life of Abdullah ibn al-Zubayr just as the life of his father had ended before. Each one of them loved this life and did his best to attain power and authority and to receive people's oath of allegiance, fighting others for its sake, killing many in the process till he himself was killed falling short of achieving his objective.

Abdullah ibn al-Zubayr had views with regard to *fiqh* which reflected a negative reaction to the *fiqh* of Ahlul Bayt whom he

---

[2] Al-Mas'udi, *Tarikh*, Vol. 5, p. 185. Ibn Abul-Hadid, *Sharh Nahjul-Balagha*, Vol. 4, p. 487.

hated. One of his most famous views was his saying that the *mut`a* marriage was Islamically unlawful. He once said to Abdullah ibn Abbas [the greatest traditionist], "O you blind man! If you do it, I shall most certainly stone you." Ibn Abbas responded to him by saying, "My eye-sight is blind, it is true, but you are blind in your own insight; so, if you wish to know how *halal* the *mut`a* is, go and ask your mother about it!"³

We do not wish to go into details in tackling this subject which has been discussed a great deal, but we simply wanted to expose Ibn al-Zubayr's opposition to Ahlul Bayt in every aspect, including *fiqh* matters where his foot was not firmly rooted.

All these twelve men have gone, in their good and in their evil, leaving the afflicted nation sailing in a sea of blood, drowning in the ocean of misguidance, with most of its members not distinguishing between truth and falsehood. This, in fact, is what Talhah, al-Zubayr, and even Sa'd ibn Abu Waqqas had admitted.

The only person who was on clear guidance from his Lord, who never doubted the truth even for twinkling of an eye, was Ali ibn Abu Talib, Allah's peace be upon him, with whom truth revolved wherever he revolved, accompanying him wherever he went. So congratulations to whoever follows and emulates him. In fact, the Messenger of Allah himself said, "You, O Ali, and your followers [Shi'as] are surely victorious on the Day of Judgment."⁴

---

³ In his old age, Ibn Abbas grew blind. As for telling Abdullah ibn al-Zubayr to go and ask his mother, it is due to the fact that his father, Ibn al-Zubayr, had a mut`a marriage with Asmaa, and Abdullah himself was the product of that mut`a marriage. It is said that Abdullah did, indeed, go to his mother whom he asked about it. She told him, "Did I not prohibit you from meeting Ibn Abbas who best knows the Arabs' defects?"

⁴ Jalal al-Din al-Suyuti quotes this hadith in his exegesis of the Holy Qur'an titled *Al-Durr al-Manthur* as he explains the meaning of Surat al-Bayyinah.

"Is He then Who guides to what is right more worthy of being followed, or he who does not guide unless he himself is guided? What is the matter with you? How do you judge?" (Holy Qur'an, 10:35)

Surely Allah, the Great, has said the truth.

ACCORDING TO SHI'AS, THE PROPHET'S SUNNAH DOES NOT CONTRADICT THE QUR'AN

Having researched the faith of both parties, i.e. that of the Shi'as as well as that of "Ahlul Sunnah wal Jama'ah," we found out that the Shi'as derive all their juristic injunctions only from the Holy Qur'an and the Prophet's Sunnah.

Then they put the Holy Qur'an first and the Prophet's Sunnah second. We mean, by saying so, that they submit the Sunnah to scrutiny, comparing it with the Book of Allah, the Exalted One. They accept it when it agrees with Allah's Book and they act accordingly while rejecting and disregarding it when it contradicts it.

In doing so, Shi'as refer to what the Imams from Ahlul Bayt, peace be upon them, have sanctioned for them. These Imams do so in accordance with the *hadith* they narrate from their grandfather the Messenger of Allah wherein he says, "If someone quotes one of my *ahadith* to you, compare it with the Book of Allah. If it agrees with Allah's Book, act according to it, and if it disagrees with Allah's Book, discard it."[1]

Imam Ja`far al-Sadiq, peace be upon him, has quite often said, "Any *hadith* which does not agree with the Qur'an is nothing but a trifling." *Usul al-Kafi* indicates that the Prophet delivered a sermon once at Mina wherein he said, "O people! Anything you hear about me which agrees with the Book of Allah is something which I said, and whatever you hear about me that contradicts the Book of Allah is something which I never said."

---

[1] The exact words of the Prophet were: "... slam it on the wall," an expression the Arabs use meaning "discard" or "ignore" it. Tr.

Upon such foundation have the Shi'as set up the foundations of their jurisprudence and creed. No matter how accurate the *isnad* of one *hadith* may be, they still weigh it thus, comparing it with the Book which no falsehood can approach from before it or from behind it. And Imamite Shi'as are the only ones among the followers of Islamic sects who insist on such a prerequisite especially in a field wherein narrations and stories contradict one another.

In his book *Tasheeh al-I'tiqad*, Shaykh al-Mufeed says, "The Book of Allah, the most Exalted One, is given preference over *ahadith* and narrations. It is the final judge in as far as the authenticity of narrations, or the lack thereof, is concerned.

Only its decision is correct." According to this condition, that is, comparing the *hadith* with the Book of Allah, the most Exalted One, Shi'as differ from "Ahlul Sunnah wal Jama'ah" with regard to many *fiqh* related injunctions as well as many beliefs.

Any researcher will find out that the *ahkam* and beliefs of the Shi'as are in total agreement with the Book of Allah, unlike the case with "Ahlul Sunnah wal Jama`ah." One who thoroughly researches this issue will find the beliefs and injunctions upheld by the latter clearly contradict the Holy Qur'an. You will come to know the truth in this regard, and we will shortly provide you with some of our own proofs, *InshaAllah*.

The researcher, therefore, will also come to understand that the Shi'as do not label any of their books of *hadith* as "*Sahih*" or grant it the sanctity they grant the Holy Qur'an as is the case with "Ahlul Sunnah wal Jama'ah" who brand as "*Sahih*" all the *ahadith* narrated by al-Bukhari and Muslim although they have among them hundreds of *ahadith* which contradict the Book of Allah.

Suffices you to know that the book titled *Al-Kafi*, though written by a great author, namely Muhammad ibn Ya`qoob al-

Kulayni, who delved in depth in the science of *hadith*, Shi`a `ulama never claim that all what is compiled in it is "*Sahih*," authentic. Rather, some of their scholars have discredited and labelled as "unauthentic" half of its contents.

Even the author of *Al-Kafi* himself does not claim that all the *ahadith* he compiled in his book are authentic. All this may be the outcome of the policy of the caliphs with regard to each of these two groups. "Ahlul Sunnah wal Jama'ah," on one hand, followed in the footsteps of religious leaders who were ignorant of the Sunnah and of the injunctions of the Holy Qur'an, or they knew them but preferred to follow their own *ijtihad*, thus contradicting the existing texts for various reasons some of which we have already explained above. Shi'as, on the other hand, emulated the purified Progeny of the Prophet who were the peers of the Holy Qur'an and the ones who explained it. Shi'as do not contradict these Imams, nor do they differ among themselves in this regard.

"Can they [at all] be (like) those who accept a Clear (Sign) from their Lord, and who are taught by a witness from Himself, as did the Book of Moses before it, [who was] a guide and a mercy?" (Holy Qur'an, 11:17)

Surely Allah has said the truth.

THE SUNNAH AND THE QUR'AN ACCORDING TO AHLUL SUNNAH WAL JAMA'AH

Having come to know that Imamite Shi'as give preference to the Qur'an over the Sunnah, making it the final judge and the dominating authority, "Ahlul Sunnah wal Jama'ah" are exactly the opposite: they advance the Sunnah over the Qur'an, making it the final judge, the ultimate authority. We come to this conclusion when we observe how they call themselves "Ahlul Sunnah," followers of the Sunnah, due to the line of thinking which they adopted; otherwise, why did they not say that they were the followers of the Qur'an and the Sunnah especially since they narrate in their books saying that the Prophet had said, "I have left among you the Book of Allah and my Sunnah"?

Because the Sunnis neglected the Qur'an and gave it the back seat, upholding the alleged Sunnah and giving it the front seat, we understand the main reason why they now say that the Sunnah over-rules the Qur'an, which is quite odd.

I think they found themselves forced to do so when they discovered that they were doing things which contradicted the Qur'an, things which they made up after the rulers they obeyed forced them to act upon them. In order to justify doing those things, they fabricated *ahadith* which they falsely attributed to the Prophet. And since those *ahadith* contradict the injunctions of the Qur'an, they claim that the Sunnah over-rules the Qur'an, and that it abrogates the Qur'an.

Let me give you a clear example of what every Muslim individual does many times daily: the ablution (*wudu*) that precedes the prayers:

The Holy Qur'an states the following:

"*O you who believe! When you stand for the prayers, wash your faces and hands to the elbows and wipe your heads and feet to the ankles*" (Holy Qur'an, 5:6).

No matter how much is said, and regardless of where the accent marks are placed when one recites [the original Arabic text of] this verse, al-Fakhr al-Razi, who is one of the most famous scholars of Arabic among "Ahlul Sunnah wal Jama'ah," has said that the feet have to be rubbed (or wiped).[1] Ibn Hazm has also said, "Whether the accent mark is placed underneath or above the *laam*, it is at any rate an injunction joining the heads in the same action (as that done to the feet), and no other possibility is valid."[2]

Yet although he admits that the Qur'an mandates the rubbing of the feet in either case, al-Fakhr al-Razi is found fanatically supporting his Sunni sect and saying, "... but the Sunnah came to mandate the washing of the feet, thus abrogating the Qur'an."[3]

Such an example of the alleged Sunnah which over-rules or abrogates the Qur'an has many similar examples to be found with "Ahlul Sunnah wal Jama`ah." Quite a few fabricated *ahadith* idle Allah's commandments based on the [false] claim that the Messenger of Allah was the one who abrogated it.

If we examine the verse referring to the ablution in Surat al-Maaida and take into consideration the consensus of Muslims that this Sura was the very last one revealed of the Holy Qur'an, it is said that it was revealed only two months before the demise of the Prophet, how and when did the Prophet abrogate the injunction in it referring to ablution?!

---

[1] He says so in his book *Al-Tafsir al-Kabir* (the grand exegesis), Vol. 11, p. 161.

[2] Ibn Hazm, *Al-Muhalla*, Vol. 3, p. 54.

[3] Al-Fakhr al-Razi, *Al-Tafsir al-Kabir*, Vol. 11, p. 161.

The Prophet had already spent twenty-three years performing his ablution, rubbing (not washing) his feet, doing so many times each day; is it reasonable to accept that only two months before his death, and after his having received the verse saying, "... and wipe your heads and feet," he deliberately washed his feet contrarily to the commandment revealed in Allah's Book?! This is unbelievable...

How can people believe that such a Prophet invited them to uphold the Book of Allah and to act according to it, telling them, "This Book guides to what is best," actually does the opposite of what the Qur'an enjoins?! Would his opponents, the polytheists and the hypocrites, then say to him, "Since you yourself do the opposite of what the Qur'an enjoins, how can you order us to follow it?!"

The Prophet would then find himself in an embarrassing situation, not knowing how to refute their argument; so, we do not believe such a claim, a claim which reason and tradition reject and is rejected by anyone who knows the Book of Allah and the Sunnah of His Messenger.

But "Ahlul Sunnah wal Jama'ah" who, as we have come to know in past researches, are in fact Umayyad rulers and those who followed in their footsteps, deliberately fabricated many *ahadith* which they attributed to the Prophet in order to thus justify the views and the *ijtihad* of the imams of misguidance, and to bestow upon the latter religious sanctity.

They did so in order to justify the *ijtihad* of such persons *versus* the available texts, claiming that the Prophet himself had adopted *ijtihad* (and followed his own personal views) contrarily to the Qur'anic texts, thus abrogating whatever he desired of such texts. Those who harbored *bid'ats* would thus derive their legitimacy in contradicting the Qur'anic texts. They claim that they only follow the Prophet, something which is quite untrue; it is simply a lie.

In a previous research, we provided strong proofs and arguments that the Messenger of Allah never, not even for one day, followed his own view, nor did he ever adopt the principle of *qiyas*; rather, he always waited for revelation. This is proven by the verse *saying,*

"... so that you may judge between people according to what Allah has taught you" (Holy Qur'an, 4:105)".[4]

After all, is he not the one who cited His Lord saying,

"And when Our clear Signs are recited to them, those who do not wish for the meeting with Us say: Bring us a Qur'an other than this one, or change it. Say: It is not for me to change it of my own accord; I only follow what is revealed to me. I fear lest I should disobey my Lord the torment of a great Day" (Holy Qur'an, 10:15"

Did his Lord not threaten him in the strongest terms against his trying to attribute one single word to Allah? He, the Sublime, the most Exalted One, said,

"And had he fabricated against Us any statement, We would certainly have seized him by the right hand, then We would certainly have cut off his aorta, and none of you could then have withheld Us from him" (Holy Qur'an, 69:44-47).

Such is the Holy Qur'an, and such is the Prophet whose conduct was the embodiment of the injunctions of the Holy Qur'an. But "Ahlul Sunnah wal Jama'ah,"[5] because of the intensity of their animosity towards Ali ibn Abu Talib and Ahlul Bayt (peace be upon them), deliberately contradicted the latter in everything, so much so that their motto was to oppose Ali and his Shi'as in every

---

[4] Al-Bukhari, *Sahih*, Vol. 8, p. 148.

[5] We mean those early ones who made a covenant with Ali and his offspring after him and who founded the sect of "Ahlul Sunnah wal Jama'ah."

aspect, even if that meant contradicting a Sunnah which they themselves regard as authentic.[6]

Since Imam Ali was famous for reciting the *bismillah* audibly even while reciting the inaudible prayers in order to revive the Prophet's Sunnah, a number of the *sahabah* expressed their view that it is *makrooh* to recite it in the prayers. So is the case with regard to holding the hands versus placing them on the sides, the supplication during the *qunoot*, in addition to other issues relevant to the daily prayers.

Anas ibn Malik, therefore, used to weep and complain thus: "By Allah! I hardly find anything being done anymore which the Messenger of Allah used to do." He was asked, "What about the prayers?" He said, "You have altered it, too."[7]

What is strange is that "Ahlul Sunnah wal Jama'ah" remain silent about such differences: Their four sects differ with one another, yet they do not find anything wrong with it, saying that their differences are a mercy.

Yet they scandalize the Shi'as whenever the latter differ from them about any issue; it is then that mercy turns into a calamity. They do not endorse except the views of their Imams although the latter are no match to the Imams from the purified Progeny of the Prophet in their knowledge, deeds, merits, or dignity.

Just as we have indicated with regard to washing the feet [versus wiping them], and despite the fact that their books testify that rubbing is what the Holy Qur'an enjoins, and that it is also the

---

[6] We have discussed this issue in detail and quoted their own statements which they have published in their books as well as the statements of their imams in a book we called *Ma`a al-Sadiqin (To be with the Truthful)*; so, it must be referred to it.

[7] Al-Bukhari, *Sahih*, Vol. 1, p. 74.

Sunnah of the Prophet,[8] they resent the Shi'as doing any of that, accusing them of interpreting the Qur'an and contradicting the creed.

The second example which has also to be mentioned is the *mut`a* marriage to which the Holy Qur'an refers and which was sanctioned by the Prophet's Sunnah. In order to justify Umar's following his own *ijtihad* in this regard and his prohibition of it, they invented a false tradition which they attributed to the Prophet. They aimed by it to scandalize the Shi'as for permitting such marriage relying on the *hadith* narrated by Imam Ali ibn Abu Talib, peace be upon him.

Add to this the fact that their *Sahih* books testify that the *sahabah* practiced it during the life of the Messenger of Allah and during the reign of Abu Bakr and a portion of the reign of Umar before the latter outlawed it. They also testify that the *sahabah* differed among themselves about it: some permitting it while others prohibiting it.

Arguments in this subject are quite numerous. They prove that the Sunnis abrogate the Qur'anic text through their use of false traditions. We have stated a couple such examples, and our objective is to remove the curtain from the sect followed by "Ahlul Sunnah wal Jama'ah" and acquaint the reader with the fact that the Sunnis prefer *hadith* over the Holy Qur'an and openly say that the Sunnah over-rides the Qur'an.

The jurist Imam Abdullah ibn Muslim ibn Qutaybah, traditionist and jurist of "Ahlul Sunnah wal Jama'ah," who died in

---

[8] Ibn Sa`d, *Al-Tabaqat al-Kubra*, Vol. 6, p. 191.

276 A.H./889 A.D., openly says, "The Sunnah overrides the Book (Qur'an); the Book does not override the Sunnah."[9]

The author of the book titled *Maqalat al-Islamiyyin* cites Imam al-Ash`ari, the chief Imam of "Ahlul Sunnah wal Jama'ah" with regard to the *usul* saying, "The Sunnah abrogates the Qur'an and cancels its injunctions, whereas the Qur'an neither abrogates nor cancels the Sunnah."[10]

Ibn Abd al-Birr also says that Imam al-Awza`i, one of the major Imams of "Ahlul Sunnah wal Jama'ah," has said, "The Qur'an is more in need of the Sunnah than the Sunnah of the Qur'an."[11]

Since statements like these testify to their creed, it is quite natural that these folks contradict what is said by Ahlul Bayt in as far as comparing the *hadith* with the Book of Allah and weighing it accordingly. The Qur'an is the one that determines the Sunnah. It is also natural that they reject these traditions and refuse to accept them, even though they were narrated by the Imams from Ahlul Bayt, simply because they undermine their sect entirely.

Al-Bayhaqi, in his book *Dala'il al-Nubuwwah*, transmits saying that the tradition wherein the Prophet says, "If you come across one *hadith* reported about me, compare it with the Book of Allah," says, "This tradition is false and inaccurate, and it is self-contradictory, for there is no evidence in the Qur'an suggesting making a comparison between the *hadith* and the Qur'an."

Ibn Abd al-Birr quotes Abd al-Rahman ibn Mahdi saying that the tradition in which the Prophet is quoted saying, "Whenever I

---

[9] Al-Darimi, *Sunan*, Vol. 1, p. 145. Ibn Qutaybah, p. 199, in the section dealing with interpreting disputed traditions.

[10] *Maqalat al-Islamiyyyin*, Vol. 2, p. 251.

[11] *Jami` Bayan al-`Ilm*, Vol. 2, p. 234.

am quoted to you, compare it with the Book of Allah; if it agrees with the Book of Allah, then I have said it, but if it contradicts the Book of Allah, then I never said it," cannot be accepted by people of knowledge as having been authentic, especially since traditions to its contrary have been authenticated. He concludes by saying that atheists and Kharijites were the ones who fabricated it.[12]

Notice such blind fanaticism which leaves no room for scientifically verifying something and the yielding to the finding: they label the narrators of this tradition, who are the Imams of guidance from the purified Progeny of the Prophet, as atheists and Kharijites, accusing them of fabricating *hadith*!

Can we ask them, "What is the goal of atheists and Kharijites behind fabricating this tradition which makes the Book of Allah, the one which falsehood can never approach from the front or the back, the reference for everything?!

Any fair-minded wise person would even sympathize with these so-called "atheists" and "Kharijites" who thus glorify the Book of Allah and give it the highest status to derive legislation therefrom rather than with such "Ahlul Sunnah wal Jama'ah" who put an end to the Book of Allah through the medium of false traditions and abrogate its injunctions through alleged innovations.

"A grievous word, indeed, comes out of their mouths; surely what they utter is a lie." (Holy Qur'an, 18:5)

Those whom they label as "atheists" and "Kharijites" are none other than the Imams of the Prophet's family, the Imams of guidance, the lanterns that shatter the dark, the ones who were described by their grandfather the Messenger of Allah as the security of the nation against dissension: if one tribe differs from them, it will become the party of Satan.

---

[12] *Jami` Bayan al-`Ilm*, Vol. 2, p. 233.

Their only "sin" is that they upheld the Sunnah of their grandfather and rejected anything besides it of innovations introduced by Abu Bakr, Umar, Uthman, Mu`awiyah, Yazid, Marwan, and Banu Umayyah. Since the ruling authority was in the hands of the afore-mentioned individuals, it is only natural that they condemned their opponents, labelling them as "Kharijites" and "atheists," fighting and denouncing them. Were not Ali and Ahlul Bayt cursed from their pulpits for eighty years? Did they not poison Imam al-Hasan ? Did they not kill Imam al-Husayn and his offspring?

Let us not go back to discuss the tragedy of Ahlul Bayt, injustice to whom is still ongoing, and let us go back to those who call themselves "Ahlul Sunnah wal Jama'ah" and who reject the *hadith* enjoining comparing the Sunnah with the Qur'an.

Why did they not label Abu Bakr "al-Siddiq" a Kharijites since it was he who burnt the *hadith* then delivered a sermon in which he said, "You quote *ahadith* about the Messenger of Allah regarding which you differ with one another, and people after you will be more intense in their differences; so, do not quote anything about the Messenger of Allah. If anyone asks you, say: `Between us and you is the Book of Allah; so, follow what it permits and refrain from what it prohibits."[13]

Did Abu Bakr not put the Sunnah ahead of the Qur'an? He even regarded it as the sole reference, rejecting the Sunnah altogether, claiming his reason for doing so was people differing among themselves about it.

Why did they not call Umar ibn al-Khattab a Kharijite since he was the one who rejected the Sunnah from day one saying, "The Book of Allah suffices us"? He, too, burnt all what the *sahabah* had

---

[13] Al-Dhahabi, *Tadhkirat al-Huffaz*, Vol. 1, p. 3.

collected of the *ahadith* and *sunan* during his reign[14], going beyond that to forbidding the *sahabah* from publicly narrating *hadith*.[15]

Why did they not call the mother of the faithful Ayesha, from whom they derive half of their creed, a Kharijite since she was the one who was famous for comparing the *hadith* with the Holy Qur'an? Whenever she heard one *hadith* with which she was not familiar, she would compare it with the Book of Allah and reject it if it contradicted the Qur'an.

She, for example, objected when Umar ibn al-Khattab quoted one *hadith* saying, "A dead person is tormented in his grave on account of his family weeping over him." She said to him, "Suffices you to refer to the Qur'an where it says: `No sin-bearing soul shall ever bear the sin of another.'"[16]

She also rejected one *hadith* narrated by Abdullah ibn Umar saying that the Prophet came once to a cemetery where some atheists were buried after having been killed at the Battle of Badr and communicated with them then turned to his companions and said, "They most surely hear what I say." Ayesha denied the dead could hear. She said, "Rather, the Messenger of Allah said, `They now know that what I used to tell them is the truth,'" then she cited the following verse to testify to the falsehood of that tradition:

---

[14] Ibn Kathir, *Kanz al-Ummal*, Vol. 5, p. 237. Al-Dhahabi, *Tadhkirat al-Huffaz*, Vol. 1, p. 5.

[15] Al-Dhahabi, *Tadhkirat al-Huffaz*, Vol. 1, p. 5.

[16] This is quoted in al-Bukhari's *Sahih* in 'The Book of Coffins' in a chapter dealing with the Prophet's hadith: "A dead person is tormented even by a little of the weeping of his family over him." It is also recorded in Muslim's *Sahih* in 'The Book of Coffins' in a chapter dealing with a dead person tormented by his family grieving over him.

"And surely you cannot make those in the graves hear you" (Holy Qur'an, 35:22).[17]

She rejected many other *ahadith*. In each time, she would compare each *hadith* with the Book of Allah. Once someone told her that Muhammad had seen his Lord, so she said to him, "My hair stands on account of what you have just said... Where do you stand with regard to three things about which anyone who narrates a tradition lies: whoever tells you that Muhammad saw his Lord is a liar," then she cited the verse saying,

"No vision can ever conceive him while He conceives all vision, and He knows the subtleties, the Aware" (Holy Qur'an, 6:103), and also the verse saying, *"And it is not for any mortal to speak to Allah except by revelation or from behind a barrier"* (Holy Qur'an, 42:51).

"And whoever tells you," she went on, "that he knows what tomorrow holds for him is a liar." Then she cited the verse saying,

"No soul knows what it shall earn tomorrow" (Holy Qur'an, 31:34).

"And whoever tells you," she continued, "that he kept any revelation for himself (without revealing it to others) is a liar," then she cited the verse saying,

"O Messenger! Convey what has been revealed to you from your Lord" (Holy Qur'an, 5:67).

Likewise, Abu Hurayra, the narrator of Ahlul Sunnah, used to quite often narrate one *hadith*, then he would say: "Recite whatever you please of what the Exalted One says," then he compares his *hadith* with the text of the Book of Allah so that the listeners might believe him.

---

[17] This is recorded in both al-Bukhari's and Muslim's *Sahih* books in The Book of Coffins written by each in the chapter referred to above.

So why don't "Ahlul Sunnah wal Jama'ah" call all these persons "Kharijites" or "atheists" since they all compare the *ahadith* they hear with Allah's Book and falsify whatever contradicts the Qur'an?! Surely they would not dare to do that.

But if the matter involves the Imams from Ahlul Bayt, they will not hesitate to curse them and attribute shortcomings to them without these Imams having committed any sin other than comparing the *hadith* with the Book of Allah in order to expose those who fabricate and forge, those who wish to render Allah's commandments idle through the medium of false *ahadith*.

They do so because they fully realize that had their *ahadith* been compared with Allah's Book, nine out of ten of them will be found contradicting the Book of Allah, and the remaining tenth, which agrees with the Book of Allah because it actually is the speech of the Prophet, they interpret it in a way which the Messenger never intended it.

Examples include the *hadith* saying, "The caliphs after me are twelve; all of them are from Quraysh," and the one saying, "Uphold the Sunnah of the righteous caliphs after me," and the one saying, "The differences among my nation are a mercy," besides many traditions whereby the Prophet meant to refer to the Imams from his purified Progeny. But they claimed they referred to their own usurping caliphs, and to some turn-coat *sahabah*.

Even the titles which they attach to the *sahabah*, such as their calling Abu Bakr "al-Siddiq," Umar "al-Farooq," Uthman "Dhul-Noorayn," and Khalid "Sayf-Allah," all these titles were given by the Prophet to

Ali; for example, he has said, "The *siddiqs* are three: (1) Habib al-Najjar, the believer referred to in Surat Yasin, (2) Ezekiel, the believer who belonged to the family of Pharaoh, and (3) Ali ibn Abu Talib who is their best."[18]

Ali himself used to say, "I am the greatest *siddiq*; none says so besides me except a liar." And he also is the greatest *farooq* through whom Allah distinguished the truth from falsehood.[19] Did not the Messenger of Allah say that loving Ali is a sign of conviction, while hating him is a sign of hypocrisy that the truth revolves around him wherever he went?

As for the title of "Dhul-Noorayn,"[20] Ali, peace be upon him, is the father of al-Hasan and al-Husayn, peace be upon them, masters of the youths of Paradise, two lights that descended from the loins of Prophethood. As for "Sayf-Allah," Ali is the one who was described by Gabriel, peace be upon him, during the Battle of Uhud thus: "There is no youth like Ali, and there is no sword like Dhul-Fiqar."

And Ali in truth is the sword of Allah whom He sent upon the polytheists to kill their heroes, arrest their brave warriors, and crush

---

[18] This tradition is quoted on p. 223, Vol. 2, of al-Haskani's book *Shawahid al-Tanzil*, Vol. 2, p. 223. on p. 417 of *Ghayatal-Maram*, p. 417. *Al-Riyad al-Nadira*, Vol. 2, p. 202.

[19] This is indicated in al-Tabari's *Tarikh* in a chapter dealing with Ali's conviction. Ibn Majah, *Sunan*, Vol. 6, p. 44. Al-Nasa'i, *Khasa'is*. Al-Hakim, *Mustadrak*, Vol. 3, p. 112.

[20] "Ahlul Sunnah wal Jama'ah" call Uthman "Dhul-Noorayn," justifying it by saying that he had married Ruqayya and Umme Kulthoom who, according to them, were the Prophet's daughters. This is not true. The truth is that they were his step-daughters. Even if you suppose [erroneously] that they were his daughters, how can they be described as "Noorayn," two lights, since the Prophet never narrated any of their merits? Why not attach this title to Fatima whom he described as the Leader and the light of all the women of the world? Why did they not call Ali "Dhul-Noor" based on such a premise?

their noses till they submitted to the truth against their wish. He is the sword of Allah who never ran away from any battle, nor did he ever dread any duel. He is the one who opened the fort of Khaybar, a task that frustrated the most distinguished *sahabah* who had to flee away in defeat.

The caliphate, since its inception, was based on isolating Ali and stripping him of all distinctions and merits. When Mu`awiyah ascended the seat of government, he went far in cursing and belittling Ali, elevating the status of his opponents, attributing to them each and every merit of Ali, including his titles, out of his perfidy and calumny. And who could at that time oppose Mu`awiyah or call him a liar especially since they agreed with him on cursing and condemning Ali, dissociating themselves from Ali?

Mu`awiyah's followers from "Ahlul Sunnah wal Jama'ah" turned all facts upside down, so much so that right appeared to them as wrong and *vice versa*, to the extent that Ali and his Shi'as came to be labelled as Kharijites, and Rafizis the cursing and the killing of whom was permissible, while the enemies of Allah, of His Messenger, and of his Ahlul Bayt came to be identified as the ones who adhere to the Sunnah..., so read and wonder, and if you have any doubts in this regard, research and investigate.

"The similitude of the two parties is like the blind and the deaf, the seeing and the hearing: are they alike? Will you not mind?" (Holy Qur'an, 11:24) Surely Allah says the truth.

PROPHET'S AHADITH REPORTED BY AHLUL SUNNAH CONTRADICT ONE ANOTHER

A researcher may come across numerous traditions attributed to the Prophet which are in fact nothing but *bid'ats* invented by a number of companions after his demise. These were forced on people till the latter thought that they were, indeed, what the Prophet had indeed said and done. For this reason, most of these *bid`ats* contradict one another, and they differ from the Qur'anic text; therefore, Sunni scholars felt obligated to interpret them and to say that the Prophet did this once, and once he did something else, and so on.

For example, they say that he once offered his prayers reciting the *bismillah* audibly and prayed another time without reciting the *bismillah*, that he once wiped his feet while performing the ablution but washed them at another time, that he once put his right hand over his left one and once he put them both on his side... Some Sunnis went as far as saying that he did so deliberately in order to lighten the burden from his nation so that every Muslim could choose whatever mode of action suited him.

This is nothing but falsehood rejected by Islam which was built on the principle of Tawhid, on unity of worship even in appearance: Islam did not permit anyone who is to wear the *ihram* garb during the pilgrimage to put on whatever he liked, be it in shape or in color. Nor did Islam permit one who follows an Imam (during the prayers) to differ from him in his movements, be they standing, bowing, prostrating, or sitting.

It is also falsehood because the purified Imams from Ahlul Bayt reject such narrations and refuse to accept them when they permit people to differ with one another with regard to the rituals' form or context.

359

If we go back to discuss the contradictions in the *ahadith* narrated by "Ahlul Sunnah wal Jama'ah," we will find them quite numerous, beyond counting, and we will try to compile them in a special book *InshaAllah*.

As has been our habit, we would like to briefly mention some examples so that it may become clearer for the researcher the bases upon which "Ahlul Sunnah wal Jama'ah" established their sect and creed.

In Muslim's *Sahih*, as in *Sharh al-Muwatta'* by Jalal ad-Din al-Suyuti, Anas ibn Malik is quoted saying, "I prayed once behind the Messenger of Allah, Abu Bakr, Umar, and Uthman, and I never heard any of them reciting *Bismillahir-Rahmanir-Rahim*." In another narration, it is said that the Messenger of Allah was not of the habit to audibly recite *Bismillahir-Rahmanir-Rahim*. While at this time, this tradition is narrated by Anas ibn Qatadah, Thabit al-Banani and others. Each of these men traces the chain of its narrators back to the Prophet. But all these traditions contain quite a few variations in their wording. Some of them say that they did not recite *Bismilaahir-Rahmanir-Rahim*, while others say they did not audibly recite it, while still others say that they were, indeed, reciting *Bismillahir-Rahmanir-Rahim* audibly.

Still others say that they never left out the recitation of *Bismillahir-Rahmanir-Rahim*. Some of them say that they started their recitation with: *Alhamdu Lillahi Rabbil Alamin*. Then the compiler adds saying, "This is confusion with which no argument can stand on any ground with any *faqih*."[1]

---

[1] This is the commentary of the author of *Tanweer al-Hawalik: Sharh ala Muwatta' Malik*. We say: All Praise is due to Allah when "a witness from her family testified" with regard to the confusion of and contradiction among their traditions. Just as he has said, the argument of none of their faqihs can be accepted. Rather, the argument stands with the purified

We wish to know the real reason behind such contradictions and confusion as admitted by the narrator himself, namely Anas ibn Malik, who used to be constantly in the company of the Prophet. He was the Prophet's *hajib*. He narrates once saying that the Messenger of Allah and the three caliphs used not to recite the *bismillah*, yet he is quoted saying that they never left it out!

This is the painful and regrettable truth with regard to what most *sahabah* did while transmitting and narrating *hadith*: they followed the dictates of the political interests, seeking to please those who were in authority.

There is no doubt that he narrated saying that they never recited the *bismillah*; that was during the reign of Banu Umayyah who tried hard to alter the Sunnah of the Prophet. Ali ibn Abu Talib, though, persisted in upholding it. He tried very hard to keep it alive.

Their policy was based on contradicting Ali in everything, doing the opposite what he used to do, so much so that he, peace be upon him, came to be famous for going to extremes in reciting the *bismillah* even as he performed the inaudible prayers. This is not what we or other Shi'as claim; we have not relied in anything we have written except on the books and the statements of "Ahlul Sunnah wal Jama'ah."

Imam al-Nishapouri, in his book *Tafsir Ghara'ib al-Qur'an*, after having mentioned Anas ibn Malik's contradictory narrations, says, "... and they contain another charge: that Ali (may Allah be pleased with him) used to go to extremes to audibly recite the *bismillah*. When Banu Umayyah came to power, they went to extremes to prohibit such an audible recitation in an attempt to put

---

Imams of Guidance who never differed from one another with regard to anything.

an end to Ali ibn Abu Talib's influence. It is possible he (Anas ibn Malik) feared them, hence the contradiction in his statements."[2]

Shaykh Abu Zuhra, too, made a statement almost similar to this one; he said, "The Umayyad regime must be responsible for the disappearance of a great deal of the influence of Ali (peace be upon him) on jurisdiction and on the issuing of verdicts simply because it is not rational to find them cursing Ali from the pulpits while leaving the scholars discussing his knowledge and transmitting his verdicts and whatever he told people, especially with regard to anything related to the foundations of the Islamic government."[3] So all Praise is due to Allah Who permitted the truth to be articulated by some of their own scholars who admitted that Ali used to go to extremes to audibly recite the *bismillah*.

We can draw the conclusion that what caused him, peace be upon him, to go to extremes in reciting the *bismillah* audibly was the fact that the rulers who preceded him had left it out either deliberately or inadvertently, and people followed suit, so it became an established custom, one, no doubt, which rendered the prayers invalid once the *bismillah* was deliberately left out; otherwise, Imam Ali (peace be upon him) would not have gone to extremes to articulate it even in his inaudible prayers.

We also sense from reviewing Anas ibn Malik's traditions his attempts to be close to and to please Banu Umayyah who, in turn, praised him and showered him with wealth and even built him luxurious mansions simply because he, too, was an opponent of Ali (peace be upon him). He publicly demonstrated his hatred towards the Commander of the Faithful (peace be upon him) when he

---

[2] Al-Nishapouri, *Tafsir Ghara'ib al-Qur'an*, Vol. 1, p. 77, in a footnote commenting about al-Tabari's Tafsir.

[3] Shaykh Abu Zuhra makes this statement on p. 161 of his book *Al-Imam al-Sadiq*.

narrated the story of the roasted bird in which the Prophet is quoted supplicating thus: "O Allah! Bring me the one whom You love most to share this bird with," whereupon Ali came asking permission to enter, but thrice Anas refused to let him in. When the Prophet came to know in the fourth attempt, he asked Anas, "What caused you to do what you have done?" Anas said, "I was hoping it would be one of the Ansars instead."[4]

Suffices this *sahabi* to hear the Prophet invoking his Lord to bring him the one whom He loves most, so Allah responds to his invocation when Ali (peace be upon him) comes to him. But the hatred borne by Anas towards him forces him to lie and to send Ali back claiming the Prophet had no need for him. And he repeated his lie three consecutive times only because he did not accept Ali (peace be upon him) as the one whom Allah loves most next only to His Messenger.

But Ali forced the door open the fourth time and entered, whereupon the Prophet asked him, "O Ali!

What kept you away from us?" "I came to see you," Ali answered, "but Anas sent me back thrice." The Prophet asked Anas, "What made you do that, O Anas?" He said, "O Messenger of Allah! I heard your supplication, and I wished it would be a man from my own people."

History tells us beyond this incident that Anas remained hating Imam Ali as long as he lived, and that he was the one whose

---

[4] This story is narrated by al-Hakim in his *Mustadrak* where he comments by saying, "This tradition is authentic according to both shaykhs [al-Bukhari and Muslim]." Al-Tirmidhi cites it on p. 299, Vol. 2, of his *Sahih*. Al-Tabari quotes it on p. 160, Vol. 2, of his book *Al-Riyad al-Nadira*. It is also narrated on p. 171, Vol. 3, of *Tarikh Baghdad*. It is cited on p. 406, Vol. 6, of *Kanz al-Ummal*. It is quoted by al-Nasa'i on p. 5 of his book *Al-Khasa'is*, and it is stated on p. 30, Vol. 4, of Ibn al-Athir's book *Usd al-Ghaba*.

testimony was sought by Ali on "the Day of the Rahba" to testify to his having heard the Ghadeer *hadith*, but he concealed his testimony.

It was then that the Imam (peace be upon him) invoked Allah to curse him: the man hardly left the place before being afflicted with leprosy. So how could Anas not be an opponent of Ali (peace be upon him) since he hated him so much and sought nearness to his enemies by dissociating himself from him?

It is for all these reasons that his narration with regard to the *bismillah* came wreaking with his own loyalty to Mu`awiyah ibn Abu Sufyan; he says, "I prayed behind the Prophet, Abu Bakr, Umar, and Uthman...," meaning that he never accepted to pray behind Ali. This is exactly what Mu`awiyah and his Umayyad followers liked to hear; their objective was to elevate the name of these three caliphs and obliterate that of Ali (peace be upon him) and not even mention him in any *hadith*.

Since it has been proven through the avenue of the purified Progeny and their followers that Ali (peace be upon him) used to audibly recite the *bismillah* as part of Surat al-Fatiha and as an introduction to any other Sura besides it, and since it has also been proven through the avenue of "Ahlul Sunnah wal Jama'ah" that he used to go to extremes in reciting the *bismillah* audibly even in his inaudible prayers..., all this proves that it is included in the authentic Sunnah: whoever leaves it out abandons his obligation and invalidates his prayers. Acting contrarily to the Sunnah is nothing but misguidance;

"Whatever the Messenger gives you, accept it, and from whatever he forbids you, stay away" (Holy Qur'an, 59:7).

After all this, we have a great deal of criticism of the traditions related by the *sahabah* which contradict the Sunnah of the Prophet. This criticism is backed by several proofs some of which we have already stated in our previous researchers, and we will mention the others in our forthcoming ones. What is important in all of this is that we should know that "Ahlul Sunnah wal Jama'ah" follow the statements and emulate the actions of the *sahabah* due to the following reasons:

1. They believe that their statements and actions are a binding Sunnah.
2. They erroneously think that whatever the *sahabah* said and did never disagreed with the Prophet's Sunnah. The *sahabah* used to judge according to their own views then attribute the same to the Prophet so that they may be able to influence people and shelter themselves against the opposition of those who opposed them.

Ali ibn Abu Talib (peace be upon him) was their only opponent who tried his best during his caliphate to bring people back to the Sunnah of the Prophet by his statements, actions, and judicial decisions. Yet it was all in vain because they distracted him with crushing wars; he had hardly finished one war before they started another.

He had hardly finished the Battle of the Camel before they started the Battle of Siffeen. And he had hardly finished the Battle of Siffeen before they started the Battle of Nahrawan. Once he finished it, they assassinated him as he stood at the [Kufa] mosque for prayers.

Then Mu'awiyah came to power with the sole purpose of putting out Allah's light; so he tried his best to put an end to the Prophet's Sunnah which had been revived by Imam Ali (peace be upon him). He brought people back to the caliphs' innovations, especially those which he himself had initiated. He insulted Ali (peace be upon him) and cursed him so that nobody would mention him in anything other than infamy.

Al-Mada'ini states that a *sahabi* came once to Mu`awiyah and said, "O commander of the faithful! Ali died, and there is nothing you should be apprehensive of. Why don't you put an end to the custom of cursing him?" Mu`awiyah said, "No, by Allah, I shall not stop it till youths grow gray hair and till children grow old doing the same."

Al-Mada'ini says, "So they (Banu Umayyah) kept doing so for quite a long time, teaching their children at Qur'anic schools, as well as their women, servants, and slaves, to do likewise." Mu`awiyah succeeded a great deal in his plan to distance the Islamic nation, barring a few, from its *wali* and true leader, dragging them into antagonizing him and dissociating themselves from him.

He made falsehood appear to them as the truth and convinced them that only they were the followers of the Sunnah, and that whoever accepted them as the masters and followed in the footsteps of Ali was a Kharijite, one who introduced a *bid'at*.

If the Commander of the Faithful Ali, the great man that he was, used to be cursed from the pulpits, and if people sought nearness to Allah by cursing and condemning him, how do you think the treatment meted to the Shi'as who followed him was? These were deprived of their share of public money; their houses were burnt; they were crucified on palm tree trunks, and some of them were buried alive. There is no power nor might except in Allah, the most Exalted One, the Great.

Mu`awiyah, in my view, was a ring in the chain of the major plot and one of its chapters, but he more than anyone else succeeded in hiding the truth and turning facts upside down, bringing the nation back to its original *Jahiliyya* under the guise of Islam.

It is noteworthy here to point out that he was more shrewd than any of his predecessors among the caliphs. He was a skilled actor who could play his part extremely well: sometimes he would cry till he influenced the minds of those in his presence into thinking that he was one of the ascetics and sincere servants of Allah. And sometimes he would demonstrate his cruelty and arrogance to the extent that those around him would see him as one of the greatest atheists. A bedouin may mistake him for a messenger from Allah!

In order to complete our research, we can assess the extent of his cunning and shrewdness from a letter sent to Mu`awiyah by Muhammad son of Abu Bakr, and from his answer to it. We will also come to know from both letters facts which are indispensable to those who seek the truth.

MUHAMMAD IBN ABU BAKR'S LETTER TO MU'AWIYAH

'From Muhammad son of Abu Bakr to the sinner Mu`awiyah son of Sakhr:

Peace of Allah unto those who obey Him from one who is peaceful to whoever accepts only Allah as his Master.

In His Omnipotence, Greatness, Power and Might, Allah did not create the creation in vain, nor due to a weakness in Him, nor to a need to what He creates. Rather, He created His beings so that they may worship him. He let some of them sin while keeping others on the right guidance. Some of them He left to suffer, and to some He granted happiness.

Then He knowingly chose from them Muhammad to be the sole bearer of His Message. He selected him to receive His revelation and entrusted him to carry out His commandments. He sent him as His Messenger, bearer of glad tidings, and warner, to testify to the divine Books which were revealed before his time, and to guide people to uphold His injunctions.

So he invited people to accept his mission through wisdom and beautiful exhortation. The first to respond positively to his call, to obey him, to believe in him, to put his all at his disposal, and to be a Muslim, was his brother and cousin Ali ibn Abu Talib (peace be upon him).

He believed him with regard to the knowledge of the unknown; he preferred him over everyone else he loved; he protected him with his own life; he solaced him in every precarious situation; he fought those whom he had fought and sought peace with those to whom he was peaceful. He never fled when death seemed imminent out of his love for his life; he came out as one unmatched in prowess; nobody could ever come close to what he undertook.

I saw how you tried to reach his lofty status, though you are what you are, while he is the one who stood out above the rest as the foremost in the doing of anything good and in embracing Islam. His conviction was most sincere, his offspring the best among all people, his wife the best of all women, whose cousin was the very best, whose brother traded his life on the Day of Mu'tah[1] for the Pleasure of Allah, whose uncle is the master of martyrs on the Day of Uhud, whose father defended the Messenger of Allah and his mission, whereas you are the accursed and the son of the accursed. You and your father have never ceased plotting to undermine the religion of Allah, trying, both of you, to put out the light of Allah, rallying others behind you, spending your wealth and seeking the support of other tribes.

Thus did your father die, and in his footsteps are you now following. Those who testify against you are the very ones whom you seek to please, while those who resort to you are the pariahs from the remnants of parties, the leaders of hypocrisy, those who are the foremost in dissenting from the Messenger of Allah.

Those who testify for Ali, though his virtues are quite obvious and merits eternal, are his supporters whom Allah, the Most Exalted One, mentioned and praised in the Qur'an over all others from the Muhajirs and the Ansars: they are with him battalions and valiant defenders, protecting him with their words, always ready to spill their blood to protect his, finding the truth in following him and perdition in opposing him.

---

[1] Battle of Mu'tah. Refers to Ja'far ibn Abi Talib also known as Ja'far aṭ-Ṭayyar, who was martyred in the battle of Mu'tah.

Woe unto you! How dare you set yourself as an equal to Ali while he is the heir of the Messenger of Allah, his *wasi*, the father of his offspring, the first among the people to follow him, the very closest to him? He shares with him his secrets; he unfolds his affairs before him, while you are his enemy and the son of his enemy!

So enjoy your life as long as you can through the means of your falsehood, and let the son of al-As support your sinning, for your end seems to have come close, and your mischief seems to be waning: soon you will come to know who is to receive the lofty rewards!

And be informed that you are plotting against your own Lord Whose Might you do not fear, from achieving Whose Mercy you have despaired, and He will soon take you by surprise while you remain in the deluge of your conceit. And peace be with whoever follows the right guidance.'[2]

* * *

The above quoted letter written by Muhammad son of [first caliph] Abu Bakr contains irrefutable facts of interest to all seekers of the truth. It describes Mu`awiyah as a misguided and misguiding person, as an accursed and the son of an accursed man, and that he tries by all might and means to put Allah's light out, spending wealth to distort the creed, plotting against Allah's religion, and that he is the enemy of Allah and His Messenger who deals with falsehood assisted by Amr ibn al-As.

This letter also unveils the virtues and merits of Ali (peace be upon him) which nobody else could claim in the past nor can anyone achieve in the future. In fact, Ali ibn Abu Talib (peace be

---

[2] *Jamharat Rasaail al-Arab,* Vol. 1, p. 475. Al-Mas`udi, *Muruj al-Dhahab,* Vol. 2, p. 59. Ibn Abul-Hadid, *Sharh Nahjul Balagha,* Vol. 1, p. 283.

upon him) has more virtues and merits than what Muhammad ibn Abu Bakr has counted here, but what concerns us most in this chapter is the answer he received from Mu`awiyah ibn Abu Sufyan.

Such an answer will acquaint the seeker of the truth with what is hidden and plotted in history. We will uncover, once we read it, the threads of the plot that kept the caliphate out of the reach of its legitimate owner and that caused the nation to deviate; so, let us provide you with his answer.

MU'AWIYAH ANSWERS MUHAMMAD IBN ABU BAKR'S LETTER

From Mu`awiyah son of Sakhr to the one who faults his own father, Muhammad son of Abu Bakr:

Peace unto those who obey Allah.

I have received your letter wherein you state what Allah has indicated of His Greatness, Might, and Omnipotence, and what He bestowed upon the Messenger of Allah, in addition to a great deal of talk which you authored to your own liking and which faults you and is offensive to your father.

In it you stated the merits of the son of Abu Talib and his age-old feats and kinship to the Messenger of Allah, his having supported and solaced the Prophet in each and every precarious and perilous situation. Your argument against me was produced by you praising someone else rather than demonstrating your own merits; so, you should praise the Lord Who has deprived you of such merits and bestowed them upon someone else.

I and your father used, during the life-time of our Prophet, to recognize the merits of Abu Talib's son, and the fact that his feats were greater than ours. When Allah chose for His Prophet (upon whom be peace and blessings) that which He has with him, completing His promise to him, permitting his mission to supersede that of all others, making his argument the uppermost, Allah caused him (blessings of Allah be upon him) to die.

Your father and his Farooq were the first to snatch his right away from him and dispute with him regarding what rightfully belonged to him. This is something which they both agreed upon and for which they coordinated their efforts. Then they invited him to swear the oath of allegiance to them, but he slackened and was hesitant, so they harbored evil intentions against him and plotted to kill him. He, therefore, swore the oath of allegiance to them later on and yielded.

Then their third person, Uthman, stood up to follow their guidance and walk in their footsteps, whereupon you and your friend faulted him for doing so. You did so to the extent that [you caused] even those who went to extremes in sinning to covet his post. You both harbored evil intentions against him till you achieved your common goal.

So be on your guard, O son of Abu Bakr, for you will see the evil of your affair. And do measure your span according to your own measure: you will then neither equal nor parallel one whose vision weighs as much as a mountain. Do not incline to overpower him, for even the most far-sighted person cannot realize the limits of his patience.

It was your father who paved for him what he paved, building his domain. If our condition is sound, your father is the first to receive credit for it, but if it is oppression, then your father went to extremes in oppressing, and we all are his accomplices: It was his guidance that we followed and whose conduct we emulated.

Had it not been for what your father had done, we would not have disputed with the son of Abu Talib, and we would have surrendered to him. But we found your father doing so before us; therefore, we followed his example and emulated his deeds. Find fault with your father, then, for what he did, or refrain, and peace be with whoever returns to his senses, to the right guidance, and who repents.[1]

* * *

---

[1] *Jamharat Rasaail al-Arab*, Vol. 1, p. 477. Al-Mas`udi, *Muruj al-Dhahab*, Vol. 2, p. 60. The Mu`tazilite scholar Ibn Abul-Hadid, *Sharh Nahjul Balagha*, Vol. 1, p. 284.

We conclude from reading this reply that Mu`awiyah does not deny any of the merits and feats of Ali ibn Abu Talib, but he dared to oppose him only to follow the path of Abu Bakr and Umar. Without the latter, he would not have undermined Ali's status, nor would anyone else have. Mu`awiyah also admits that Abu Bakr was the one who had paved for the government of Banu Umayyah and who set the foundations of their authority.

We also understand from this letter that Mu`awiyah did not emulate the Messenger of Allah, nor did he follow his guidance, admitting that Uthman followed the guidance of Abu Bakr and Umar, and that he followed in their footsteps.

Thus does it become quite obvious to us that they all had abandoned the Sunnah of the Prophet, each following the *bid'at* of the other. Mu`awiyah did not even deny his being a misguided person who traded in falsehood. Nor did he deny the fact that he and his father were cursed by the Prophet...

In order to generalize the benefit for everyone, there is no harm in mentioning the letter sent by Yazid son of Mu`awiyah to Umar's son [Abdullah] which, though brief, drives to the same conclusion.

In his *Tarikh*, al-Baladhuri states the following:

Once al-Husayn ibn Ali ibn Abu Talib (peace be upon both of them) was killed, Abdullah ibn Umar wrote a letter to Yazid ibn Mu`awiyah saying: "The calamity has surely intensified, and so has the catastrophe. An event of a great import has taken place in the history of Islam. No day can ever be like the day when al-Husayn was killed."

Yazid answered him saying, "You, fool! We only came to homes improved, beds prepared, and pillows piled up, so we fought over them! If right is on our side, then we simply defended our own right. But if right belongs to others, then your father was the first to start such a tradition, confiscating for himself that which belonged to others."

* * *

In Mu`awiyah's answer to the letter he received from Abu Bakr's son, as is the case with Yazid's answer to the letter he received from Umar's son, we find the same logic and the same argument. By my life, this is a necessity sanctioned by conscience and realized by any rational person, and it does not need, in truth, any testimony from Mu`awiyah or from his son Yazid.

Had it not been for the usurpation by Abu Bakr and Umar of Ali's right, no such a tragedy would have taken place in the history of the Islamic nation. And had Ali ascended the caliphate following the demise of the Messenger of Allah and ruled the Muslims, his caliphate would have lasted till the year 40 A.H./660 A.D., that is, for thirty years.[2]

Such a period of time would have been sufficient to set the foundations of Islam in all its roots and branches, and he, peace be upon him, would have been able to implement the injunctions embedded in the Book of Allah and the Sunnah of His Messenger without anyone's distortion or personal interpretation.

When the caliphate, after Ali's demise, fell to the hands of persons other than the masters of the youth of Paradise, namely Imam al-Hasan and Imam al-Husayn, then to the remaining infallible Imams from his progeny (peace be upon them all), the government of the righteous caliphs would have continued for three full centuries.

After that, the unbelievers, the hypocrites, and the atheists would never have had any influence or existence. The earth would

---

[2] Abu Bakr, Umar, and Uthman died during the life-time of Imam Ali.

have been a different one, and the servants of Allah would also have been different; so, there is no might nor power except in Allah, the most Exalted One, the Great.

That which remains to be discussed is an objection to this hypothesis raised by some "Ahlul Sunnah wal Jama'ah" from two different angles:

FIRST: They say that what happened was something chosen by Allah, and that had Allah willed to let Ali and the Imams from his offspring (peace be upon them) lead the Muslims, it would have been so. And they always repeat saying: "Good is whatever Allah wills."

SECOND: They argue saying that had Ali become the caliph immediately after the Prophet and was followed by al-Hasan and al-Husayn, the caliphate would have turned hereditary, with sons inheriting their fathers, something the religion of Islam, which gave people the right of *shura*, does not sanction.

In order to respond and to remove the confusion, we would like to state the following:

FIRST: There is not a single proof that what happened was something desired and chosen by Allah; rather, arguments to the contrary are fixed in the Holy Qur'an and the Sunnah. The Qur'an, for example says,

"Had the people of the towns believed and feared (their Lord), We would have opened unto them blessings from the heavens and the earth, but they disbelieved, so We overtook them for what they were doing" (Holy Qur'an, 7:96).

The Holy Qur'an also states:

"Had they upheld the Torah and the Gospel and that which was revealed to them from their Lord, they would have eaten from above them, and from beneath their feet. Some of them keep to the

moderate course, while most of them are doers of evil" (Holy Qur'an, 5:66).

The Almighty also says,

"What would Allah do with tormenting you so long as you thank and believe in Him? And Allah is Appreciative, Knowing" (Holy Qur'an, 13:11).

All these clear verses convey the meaning that deviation, be it on an individual basis or on that of groups and nations, is something that comes from the latter, not from Allah.

There are proofs from the Prophet's Sunnah, too. The Messenger of Allah has said, "I have left among you the Book of Allah and my Progeny: so long as you uphold them (simultaneously), you will never stray after me." He has also said, "Let me write you a book beyond which you will never stray."

He has also said, "My nation shall be divided into seventy-three sects all of which, with the exception of one, will go to hell." All these sacred traditions convey the meaning that the nation strays due to its own deviation and reluctance to accept what Allah has chosen for it.

SECOND: Suppose the Islamic caliphate was hereditary, it is not as they conceive it, that is, the ruler oppresses his subjects then prior to his death installs his son and calls him the heir apparent to the throne, even when both the father and his son are sinners. Rather, it is a divine inheritance chosen by the Lord of the World from Whose knowledge nothing is excluded, not even the weight of a mustard seed. And it is concerns a good band selected by Allah Who granted it the Book and the wisdom in order to lead the people; He has said,

"And We made them Imams guiding (people) as We order them, and We inspired to them the doing of good deeds, the upholding of the prayers, and the payment of zakat, and they

worshipped Us" *(Holy Qur'an, 21:73).* Their claim that Islam does not sanction such a hereditary government, that it lets people apply shura, is false; it is not supported by facts or by history. Ironically, they fell exactly in the abominable hereditary system. Nobody took charge of the nation following the death of Imam Ali except the oppressors and usurpers who handed power over to their sinning offspring despite the will of the nation.

So which party is better: should the sinners who judge according to their own views and who submit only to their desires inherit it, or should the purified Imams whom Allah chose and from whom He removed all uncleanness, bestowing the knowledge of the Book upon them so that they might judge between the people with the truth and guide them to the right path and enable them to enter the Gardens of Eternity?

Allah has said,

"And Solomon was David's heir" (Holy Qur'an, 27:16).

I do not doubt that any rational person would choose anything but the second option, provided he is a Muslim! Since we are talking about the *status quo*, we cannot benefit from sighing over what has passed; so, let us resume the discussion of our topic to state the following:

Having succeeded in distancing the Commander of the Faithful from his post as caliph and in usurping the government for themselves, Abu Bakr and Umar belittled and insulted Ali, Fatima, and Ahlul Bayt, peace be upon all of them. It was then that Mu`awiyah's task, as well as that of Yazid, Abd al-Malik ibn Marwan and their likes, became very easy.

They both facilitated for Mu`awiyah and empowered him in the land till he remained the ruler of Syria for more than twenty years. He was never deposed. He attained power over the people, bending their necks to him and forcing them to do his bidding.

Then he handed the caliphate over to his son who, as he himself admitted (as cited above), found improved homes, spread beds, and pillows piled up; so, it was only natural that he should fight for such largesse and kill the fragrant flower of the Prophet without feeling remorseful. He had suckled the milk of his mother Maysoon which was filled with hatred towards Ahlul Bayt, and he grew up in the lap of his father who was accustomed to cursing and condemning Ahlul Bayt. No wonder, then, that he did what he did. Some poets admitted this same fact; one of them says: Had it not been for the swords sharpened by the *Khalifa* [3],

I would have announced interesting

Statements about Muhammad's offspring,

And that al-Husayn was killed on the Day of the *Saqifa*...

Any researcher investigating the government of Banu Umayyah will find credit for its establishment going to Abu Bakr and Umar. So is the case with the Abbaside and other ["Islamic"] governments as well. This is why we find the Umayyads and the Abbasides doing their best to laud Abu Bakr and Umar and invent virtues and attribute to them in order to prove their being most worthy of the caliphate. The Umayyads and the Abbasides simply realized that their legitimacy could not be justified unless the caliphate of Abu Bakr and Umar was legitimized, and unless they both are described as fair and just.

We also find all of them oppressing Ahlul Bayt for no reason except their being the rightful owners of the caliphate. They, and only they, threatened their existence and authority.

This is common knowledge with rational people who know the truth. You can see nowadays some Islamic governments headed by

---

[3] Arabic original of the word "caliph."

kings who have neither merits nor virtues except their being the offspring of kings, sultans, and emirs just as Yazid was an emir when his father Mu`awiyah was a king who forced his authority on the nation by coercion.

So it is not reasonable to expect the kings and princess of Saudi Arabia to love Ahlul Bayt and those who follow them. And it is not reasonable to expect Saudi kings and princes to hate Mu`awiyah and Yazid and the constitution they set up for the ascension of the throne as well as other institutions.

It is from the constitution established by Mu`awiyah and Yazid and the rest of Umayyad and Abbaside rulers that our contemporary monarchs derive their legitimacy and justify their continuity.

It is from here, too, that the custom of sanctifying and favoring the three caliphs came. They are always described as just, and they are always defended. Nobody is permitted to criticize them or find any fault with them because they are the foundation upon which all governments since the Day of the Saqifa were and will be established till Allah reigns as the Sole Ruler of the earth and everyone on it.

Upon such a basis do we come to understand why they chose for themselves the title of "Ahlul Sunnah wal Jama'ah" while labelling others as Rafizis or atheists. This is so because Ali and his Ahlul Bayt rejected their government, refused to swear the oath of allegiance to them, and argued with them on every occasion. The rulers, therefore, took to belittling and despising, cursing and condemning, killing and expelling them...

It is through loving Ahlul Bayt, according to the Holy Qur'an, that we can express our gratitude to Allah for having blessed us with His Divine Message. So, if they were meted with such insults and killing, no wonder, then, that their Shi'as and those who accept them as the masters and are guided through them are meted with such oppression, persecution, discrimination, insults and excommunication. The outcome: One who is rightful is turned into an antagonized pariah, while followers of misguidance become role models and masters obedience to whom is mandatory on everyone.

Hence, whoever accepted them as the masters and followed Ali is labelled as the follower of *bid`at*, whereas whoever accepted the mastership of and followed Mu`awiyah is called a follower of the Sunnah and consensus...!

All Praise is due to Allah Who granted us reason whereby we can distinguish between truth and falsehood, light and darkness, black and white, and surely my Lord is on a Straight Path.

"The blind and the seeing are not alike, nor are the darkness and the light, nor are the shade and the heat, nor are the living and the dead. Surely Allah makes whomsoever He pleases hear: you cannot make those in the graves hear." (Holy Qur'an, 35:19-22)
Surely Allah says the truth.

THE SAHABAH ACCORDING TO THE FOLLOWERS OF AHLUL BAYT

If we research the subject of the *sahabah* without prejudice or sensationalism, we will find the Shi'as viewing them as the Holy Qur'an, the Prophet's Sunnah, and reason view them. They neither regard all of them as unbelievers, as some extremists have done, nor do they accept all of them as equitable, as "Ahlul Sunnah wal Jama'ah" have done.

Imam Sharaf al-Din al-Musawi[1] says the following in this regard:

'Whoever researches our view with regard to the *sahabah* will find it the most moderate of views. We neither go to extremes in this regard as the *ghulat* have done, labelling them all as apostates, nor do we go to extremes in accepting them as trusted authorities as most [Sunni] Muslims have done. Those who attribute their perfection, as well as those who go to the opposite extreme and label them as apostates, are all in the same box.'

Sunnis are of the view that anyone who heard or saw the Prophet is absolutely equitable. They support their view from the tradition saying, `... whoever traversed or walked on the earth from them without any exception.' But as far as we are concerned, although we regard keeping company with the Prophet as a great honor, it, as is, does not render one infallible. Like all other men,

---

[1] His full name is Sharaf al-Din Sadr ad-Din al-Musawi. He is author of the celebrated book *Al-Muraja`at*. The translator of this book has translated it into English under the title: *Al-Muraja`at: A Shi`i-Sunni Dialogue*. It was published (hard cover edition only) in 1995 by Imam Hussain Foundation, P.O. Box 25/114, Beirut, Lebanon. Tr. This valuable book is available full text at: https://www.al-islam.org/al-murajaat-shii-sunni-dialogue-sharaf-al-din-al-musawi

the *sahabah* included equitable persons who are their scholars and greatest men, whereas some of them are hypocrites who committed crimes.

The condition of some of them is unknown; so, we rely on the equitable ones among them and accept them as our masters in the life of this world as well as in the life to come. As for those who oppressed the *wasi* and the Prophet's brother, as well as all those who committed crimes such as Hind's son [Abu Sufyan], the son of the genius, the son of "the blue woman," the son of Uqbah, the son of Arta'a, etc., and their likes, these have nothing to be honored for, nor does their *hadith* hold water. It is of an undecided nature, and we have to carefully scrutinize it.

"Such is our view with regard to the *sahabah* who narrate *hadith*. The Qur'an and the Sunnah are our argument to pack this view as explained wherever appropriate in our books that deal with the basics of jurisprudence. But the majority of Muslims have gone too far in sanctifying the *hadith* they hear from any *sahabi*, so much so that they swayed from moderation and sought their arguments from those who are good as well as from those who are bad, blindly emulating every Muslim individual who had heard or seen the Prophet. They resented others who differed from them in going to such extremes and went beyond all limits in denouncing them.

"How intense their denunciation of us when they find us rejecting the *hadith* of many *sahabah* whose integrity we publicly challenge or whose condition is not fully ascertained! While doing so, we simply follow the binding legislative obligation in verifying religious facts and looking for authentic Prophetic legacy.

"It is for this reason that they cast doubt about us, piling their accusations on us, charging us with unfounded charges, vying with one another to remain in ignorance about us. Had they recalled their wisdom and consulted the bases of knowledge and scholarship, they would have come to know that equity as a basic ingredient in all the *sahabah* cannot be proven. Had they delved in depth into the meanings of the Qur'an, they would have found it full of references to a number of *sahabi* hypocrites. Suffices you, for example, Surat al-Tawbah and Surat al-Ahzab."

Dr. Hamid Hafni Dawood, Professor of Arabic Literature and Head of the Department of Arabic at Ayn Shams University in Cairo says, "As for the Shi'as, they view the *sahabah* as they view others: they do not distinguish between them and between the Muslims who came later till the Day of Judgment."

The reason for that is their application of one set of rules whereby the deeds of the *sahabah*, as well as those of other generations that followed them, are measured. The mere quality of being a *sahabi* does not award anyone a particular merit except when one qualifies himself for such a merit and demonstrates his readiness to carry out the injunctions set by the one who introduced the Shari`a.

Among the *sahabah* are those who are divinely protected against sinning, such as the Imams who were blessed to be in the company of the one who introduced the Shari`a. These include Ali and his sons (peace be upon them). And among them are the men of equity who maintain a beautiful company with Ali following the demise of the Messenger of Allah.

Among the *sahabah* are those who are accurate in their *ijtihad*, while others among them erred in their *ijtihad*. Among them are those who sinned, those who turned atheists and whose views are uglier and more dangerous than those of the latter group. The circle of atheists includes the hypocrites and those who worshipped Allah only marginally. And among them were the disbelievers who never repented, as well as those who reneged after having embraced the Islamic creed.

This means that the Shi'as, who constitute a great portion of the Muslim population, place all Muslims in one balance without differentiating between a *sahabi*, a *tabi`i*, or anyone else. To be a *sahabi* is not to have immunity against wrong beliefs.

It is upon this strong foundation that they allowed themselves, out of their own *ijtihad*, to criticize the *sahabah* and to research the extent of their equity. They also permitted themselves to cast doubt about a number of *sahabah* who violated the conditions of such companionship and who deviated from the path of loving the Progeny of Muhammad.

Why not? The greatest Messenger, after all, has said, "I am leaving among you that which, so long as you adhere to them both, you shall never stray: the Book of Allah and my `itra*, my Progeny. They shall never part from one another till they rejoin me at the Pool [of Kawthar]; so, see how you succeed me in faring with them."

Upon this and similar *hadith*, they find many *sahabah* as having violated this *hadith* by oppressing Muhammad's Progeny, and by cursing some members of such Progeny; so, how can the honor of companionship be sound for such violators, and how can they be branded as equitable?

This is the summary of the view held by Shi'as in rejecting the equity of some *sahabah*, and these are the factual scholarly proofs whereupon they built their arguments.

Dr. Hamid Hafni Dawood admits somewhere else that to criticize the *sahabah* and to find fault with them is not a *bid`at* invented by the Shi'as alone. He goes further to say, "Since the beginning, the Mu`tazilites dealt with the same while discussing the issues relevant to the creed. They did not only criticize the *sahabah* in general, they even criticized the caliphs themselves. In doing so, they won supporters and opponents."

The Shi'a: The Real Followers of the Sunnah

The subject of criticizing the *sahabah* used to be confined, during the first centuries, to those who were deeply immersed in knowledge, especially Mu'tazilite scholars who were preceded in going in such a direction by the heads of the Shi'as and by the leaders who were enthusiastically supporting the Progeny of Muhammad.

I have already pointed out somewhere else that the scholars of Arabic, and Mu'tazilite mentors, were a burden on Shi'a leaders from the first Hijri century. Thereupon, the issue of criticizing the *sahabah* is the child-birth of following Muhammad's Progeny.

It was the result, not the nature, of Shi'ism. Those who followed the Progeny of Muhammad came to recognize the latter as having studied in depth all the branches of knowledge relevant to the creed due to their enjoyment of the sources of knowledge provided by the Imams of Ahlul Bayt who are the pristine source and the over-flowing spring from which Islamic scholarship is derived since the inception of Islam and till our time.[2]

I personally think that one who seeks the truth has to open the door for criticism and fault-finding; otherwise, he will remain veiled from such faults. This is exactly what "Ahlul Sunnah wal Jama'ah" have done: They have exaggerated in their belief in the equity of all the *sahabah* without researching the latter's conditions; they, therefore, remained to our time distant from the truth.

---

[2] This text was published on p. 8 and its following pages of the book titled *Al-Sahaba fi Nadar al-Shi'a al-Imamiyyah* (the Prophet's companions as seen by Imamite Shi'as).

THE SAHABAH ACCORDING TO AHLUL SUNNAH WAL JAMA'AH

As for "Ahlul Sunnah wal Jama'ah," these have exaggerated the "infallibility" of the *sahabah*, attributing justice and equity to all of them without any exception. They, thus, went beyond reason and recorded documentation in their resentment of anyone who criticized them or charged them with being unfair, let alone of their being sinners. Let us provide you with some of their statements so that you may realize how far they are from Qur'anic precepts and confirmed authentic Sunnah of the Prophet as well as what reason and common sense have already proven:

Imam al-Nawawi is quoted in *Sharh Muslim's Sahih* says, "The *sahabah*, may Allah be pleased with them, are all the best of people, the masters of the nation, and are better than those who succeed them.

They are all equitable and are role models in whom there is no blemish at all. Delirium is what those who followed them articulated, and residue are those besides them."[1]

Yahya ibn Ma'een says, "Anyone who vilifies Uthman or Talhah or any companion of the Messenger of Allah is an imposter who should not be quoted and who is cursed by Allah, the angels, and all mankind."[2]

Al-Dhahabi says, "A major sin is to abuse any of the *sahabah*; whoever discredits or abuses them forsakes the creed and reneges from the religion of Islam."[3]

---

[1] Muslim, *Sahih,* Vol. 8, p. 22.

[2] *Tahdhib al-Tahdhib,* Vol. 1, p. 509.

[3] Both pages 233 and 235 of al-Dhahabi's book *Al-Kabaair* (major sins) record this statement.

Abu Ya'li, the judge, was asked once about what he thought of one who abused Abu Bakr. He described such a person as *kafir*, apostate. "Should funeral prayers be performed for him?" he was asked. He answered in the negative. "How will it be dealt with his corpse, then," he was asked again, "especially since he used to testify that: There is no god except Allah?" His answer was: "Do not touch his corpse; just push it with wooden rods till you bury him in his hole."[4]

Imam Ahmad ibn Hanbal says, "The best of the nation after the Prophet are: Abu Bakr, then Umar, then Uthman, then Ali: they are all righteous caliphs who guided others to righteousness. Then come the *sahabah* of the Messenger of Allah next to these four men in being the best of the nation. It is not permissible for anybody to mention any of their faults, nor should anyone discredit any of them by pointing out his shortcomings or defects.

Whoever does any of that has to be disciplined and punished. He must not be forgiven; rather, he must be penalized and required to repent. So, if he repents, his repentance must be accepted, but if he persisted, he should be punished again then confined till he dies or retracts what he had said."

The Hanafi Shaykh Alaaud-Din al-Tarabulsi has said, "Whoever abuses any of the Prophet's *sahabah*: Abu Bakr, Umar, Uthman, Ali, Mu'awiyah, or Amr ibn al-As, by saying that they were misguided and apostates, must be killed. If he otherwise abuses them as people abuse one another, he should be severely punished."[5]

---

[4] This is recorded on p. 275 of the book titled *Al-Sarim al-Maslul*.

[5] This is recorded on p. 187 of *Mu'een al-Hukkam feema Yataraddadu baynal Khasmayn min al-Ahkam* (rulers' aid with regard to injunctions relevant to opponents).

Dr. Hamid Hafni Dawood briefly quotes such statements made by "Ahlul Sunnah wal Jama'ah" then comments thus:

Sunnis are of the view that all the *sahabah* are just and fair, that all are accepted as equitable even if their degree of equity varies from one person to another. Whoever labels a *sahabi* as apostate commits apostasy himself, and whoever labels him as a sinner sins. Whoever discredits a *sahabi does*, in fact, discredit the Messenger of Allah himself. The most critical Sunnis are of the view that whatever historical events went on between Ali (may Allah be pleased with him) and Mu`awiyah must not be discussed.

There are among the *sahabah* those who exerted *ijtihad* of their own and were accurate: these include Ali and those who follow his line. There are others among them who followed their own views and fell into error such as Mu`awiyah and Ayesha (may Allah be pleased with her) as well as those who followed in their footsteps.

Sunnis think that we ought to draw the line here and not discuss anyone's defects. They [Sunnis] were prohibited from abusing Mu`awiyah, since he was a *sahabi*, and they were quite strict in denouncing anyone who abused Ayesha, since she was the second mother of the faithful after Khadija and since the Prophet loved her most.

Anything beyond this ought not to be discussed but must be referred to Allah, Glory to Him. In this regard, al-Hasan al-Basri and Sa`id ibn al-Musayyab say, "Such were issues from which Allah kept our hands and swords clean; so, we have to purify our tongues as well." This is the summary of the views held by the

Sunnis with regard to the *sahabah* being just and equitable and what our stand should be.[6]

If the seeker of the truth wishes to further investigate the *sahabah* to find out who "Ahlul Sunnah wal Jama'ah" imply in the word "*sahabi*," he will realize that they grant this badge of honor to anyone who had seen the Prophet!

In his *Sahih*, al-Bukhari says, "Whoever kept company with the Messenger of Allah or saw him is one of his *sahabah*." Ahmad ibn Hanbal says, "The best of people, barring those who accompanied the Messenger of Allah during the Battle of Badr, is whoever kept him company for a year, a month, or a day, or who even saw him. He is respected proportionately according to the length of time he accompanied the Prophet."[7]

In his book *Al-Isaba fi Tamyiz al-Sahabah*, Ibn Hajar says, "Anyone who quotes one *single hadith* of the Prophet or even one word, or who has seen him and is a believer in him, is a *sahabi*. So is anyone who has met the Prophet believing in him then dies as a Muslim, whether he kept him company for a long or a short period of time, whether he quotes him or not, whether he has participated in a campaign with him or not, whether he saw him but did not meet him, or whether he could not see him due to certain obstacles."[8]

The vast majority of "Ahlul Sunnah wal Jama'ah" share this view. They label as *sahabi* anyone who saw the Prophet or was

---

[6] This statements continues from p. 8 to p. 9 of the author's book *Al-Sahaba fi Nadar al-Shi`a al-Imamiyyah* (the companions as viewed by Imamite Shi`as).

[7] This is stated on p. 51 of *Al-Kifaya* and also on p. 2 of *Talqeeh Fuhum Ahlul Athaar*.

[8] Ibn Hajar, *Al-Isaba*, Vol. 1, p. 10.

born during his life-time even if he had not reached the age of distinguishing right from wrong. There is no better proof than their counting Muhammad ibn Abu Bakr as one of the *sahabah* although when the Messenger of Allah died, Muhammad ibn Abu Bakr was only three months old...!

This is why we find Ibn Sa'd classifying the *sahabah* into five categories or, as he calls them, classes (*tabaqat*) in his renown book *Tabaqat ibn Sa'd*. Hakim Nishasapuri who wrote *Al-Mustadrak*, however, categorizes them into twelve classes as follows:

First Class includes those who accepted Islam prior to the Hijra, such as the righteous caliphs.

Second Class includes those who attended *Dar al-Nadwa*.

Third Class includes those who migrated to Abyssinia (Ethiopia).

Fourth Class includes those who attended the First *Aqaba* [allegiance swearing].

Fifth Class includes those who attended the Second *Aqaba*.

Sixth Class includes those who migrated to Medina following the Prophet's migration thereto.

Seventh Class includes those who participated in the Battle of Badr.

Eighth Class includes those who migrated after Badr and prior to the [treaty signing at] al-Hudaybiyyah.

Ninth Class includes those who participated in *Bay`at al-Ridwan*.

Tenth Class includes those who migrated after the Hudaybiyyah and prior to the conquest of Mecca such as Khalid ibn al-Waleed, Amr ibn al-As, and others.

393

Eleventh Class includes those who were called *"taleeqs"* by the Prophet.

Twelfth Class includes the youths and children of the *sahabah* who were born during the life-time of the Prophet such as Muhammad ibn Abu Bakr...

"Ahlul Sunnah wal Jama'ah," then, unanimously regard all the *sahabah* and the Imams of their four sects as just and fair. They unhesitatingly accept their traditions, and they do not permit anyone to criticize or discredit them.

Critics and verifiers of *hadith* have taken upon themselves to subject the traditionists and narrators to their own critique in order to classify their traditions and purify them from any impurity. Yet when they arrive at a *sahabi*, regardless of his "class" or age at the time of the death of the Prophet, they halt there and fall short of discrediting the traditions he narrates no matter how many doubts arise about them, and no matter to what extent they contradict reason and documentation, saying that the *sahabah* are not subject to criticism or discrediting, and that they are all just and fair!

This, by my life, is obviously the bending of the rules, something which reason and nature find as contemptible; it is not endorsed by scholarship, and I seriously doubt that today's educated youths accept such ludicrous innovations.

I do not know, nor does anyone else, where "Ahlul Sunnah wal Jama'ah" derived such views from. They certainly are foreign to Islam, a religion based on scientific evidence and convincing proofs. I wish I knew, and I wish one of them can bring me one single proof from the Book of Allah or the Sunnah, or even from logic, which convinces me that each and every *sahabi* was fair and just!

We, by the Grace of Allah, have come to know the solution of the mystery of such false views, and this we will explain in the forthcoming section. Seekers of the truth have, in turn, to uncover some secrets.

THE FINAL WORD IN EVALUATING THE SAHABAH

The *sahabah* are undoubtedly fallible human beings. Like all other humans, they have obligations and rights. Surely they are honored with being the companions of the Prophet so long as they respect and safeguard such companionship; otherwise, their penalty will be doubled because Allah's justice mandates that someone distant [from the Prophet] is not to be tormented as one who is near.

One who has heard the Prophet directly, saw the light of Prophethood, witnessed the miracles with conviction and was fortunate to be taught by the Prophet himself is not like one who lives in the post-Prophet period and who neither saw nor directly heard him.

Reason and conscience prefer a man who lives in our time and who respects the Book of Allah and the Sunnah and carries out their instructions over a *sahabi* who was contemporary to the Messenger of Allah, who kept him company, yet conviction did not penetrate his heart; he accepted Islam only to yield to the dictates of the time. He did not keep the Prophet's company in righteousness and piety as long as the Prophet lived. Once the Prophet died, such a *sahabi* reneged and reverted.

This is what the Book of Allah and the Sunnah of His Messenger sanction, in addition to what is sanctioned by reason and conscience, and by anyone who has some knowledge of the Holy Qur'an and the sacred Sunnah of the Prophet. Such a person does not doubt this fact, nor does he find any alternative for it.

One proof for this argument is the verse saying, *"O wives of the Prophet! Whoever of you commits an open indecency, its punishment will be increased doubly, and this is easy for Allah"* (Holy Qur'an, 33:30).

The Prophet's companions included believers who perfected their conviction as well as those whose conviction was quite feeble. Among them were those whose hearts did not surrender to conviction.

Among them were pious ascetics as well as reckless individuals who sought only their self-interests. Among them were gracious and equitable persons as well as mean oppressors.

Some of them were the believers who upheld righteousness as well as sinning transgressors. They included scholars who implemented what they learned as well as ignorant ones who invented *bid`ats*. Among them were sincere companions as well as hypocrites. Among them were those who violated their oaths, who strayed from the path, and who reneged.

Since the Holy Qur'an, the sacred Sunnah of the Prophet, and history stated all these facts and clearly explained them, the claim put forth by "Ahlul Sunnah wal Jama'ah" that all the *sahabah* were fair and just becomes nonsense which has no face value whatsoever because it contradicts the Holy Qur'an and the Sunnah. It contradicts history, reason, and conscience. It is nothing but fanaticism and a claim which cannot be proven, an illogical statement.

One who researches these matters may wonder about the mentality of "Ahlul Sunnah wal Jama'ah," one which contradicts reason, facts, and history. But when he reads about the roles the Umayyads played, and the methods the Abbasides employed, to firmly fix the foundations of this doctrine, I mean respecting all the *sahabah* and avoiding criticizing them or doubting their integrity, his amazement will then disappear.

He will no longer have the least doubt that the latter deliberately prohibited anyone from criticizing the *sahabah* so that those Umayyads would not be criticized or discredited, and so that the horrible actions they committed against Islam, the Prophet of Islam, and the nation of Islam, would not be revealed.

Abu Sufyan, Mu`awiyah, Yazid, Amr ibn al-As, Marwan ibn al-Hakam, al-Mughirah ibn Shu`bah, and Bisr ibn Arta'ah were all *sahabis* who ruled the Muslims. How could they, then, not prohibit any criticism of the *sahabah*? How could they not fabricate about them false traditions that label each and every one of them as just and fair so that such virtues would include them, too, and so that nobody would dare to criticize them or discuss their actions?

They label anyone among the Muslims who does so as *kafir*, apostate, sinner, issuing religious verdicts permitting his murder. They prohibit the washing and shrouding of his corpse which should be pushed with wooden pieces into the grave, as we have said above.

Whenever they wanted to kill the Shi'as, they would accuse them of verbally abusing the *sahabah*. What they mean by that is criticizing them and discrediting some of their actions, a reason which they deem suffices to kill and annihilate them.

They even went beyond that. Suffices one to ask about the meaning of *hadith* to be killed, and here is the proof:

In his *Tarikh*, the Baghdadi *khatib* (orator) states the following:

One *hadith* narrated by Abu Hurayra was once mentioned in the presence of Haroun al-Rasheed. It said, "Moses met Adam once whereupon he asked him, `Are you the one who had us dismissed from Paradise?'" A man from Quraysh who was present then asked, "When did Adam meet Moses?!" Al-Rasheed became very angry and said, "Saying too much and the sword go hand in hand; kill this atheist who doubts the *hadith* of the Messenger of Allah."[1]

When a man such as this one, who must have been a highly respected dignitary because he attended the meetings set up by al-Rasheed, was beheaded simply because he inquired about the place where Adam met Moses, do not ask me about a Shi`a who charges Abu Hurayra of being a liar based on the fact that the *sahabah*, headed by Umar ibn al-Khattab, falsify his *hadith*. Thus does the researcher understand the contradictions that crept into many *ahadith* as well as the many abominable and impossible matters and the obvious blasphemy.

All this happened because criticism or discrediting were taboo: they would lead one to perdition. Even if someone asked for an explanation so that he could reach the truth, and who is detected as inquisitive and researching, was undoubtedly put to death in order to serve as a lesson for others, so that nobody after him would dare to speak his mind.

They fooled people into thinking that anyone who raised doubt about the *hadith* narrated by Abu Hurayra or any other *sahabi*, be he a commoner among them, would be regarded as having discredited the Messenger of Allah. Thus did they place a halo on fabricated *ahadith* which a number of the *sahabah* invented after the death of the Prophet, so they became accepted facts.

Quite often, I used to argue with some of our scholars[2] that the *sahabah* did not adopt such sanctifying; rather, they themselves used to doubt each other's *hadith* whenever there is a contradiction with the Qur'an, and that Umar ibn al-Khattab had beaten Abu

---

[1] *Tarikh Baghdad*, Vol. 14, p. 7.

[2] The author here is referred to Sunni scholars with whom he used to argue before accepting Shi`a Islam. __ Tr.

Hurayra with his cane, prohibited him from narrating *hadith*, and even accused him of lying.

These scholars used to always answer me by saying: "The *sahabah* had the right to say to one another whatever they pleased; as far as we are concerned, we are not on their level to respond to them or criticize them."

I would say: "But, O servants of Allah! They [the said *sahabah*] fought one another, called each other *kafir*, and killed one another!" They would respond by saying: "They all are *mujtahids*: if one of them is right in his *ijtihad*, he receives two blessings, whereas if he errs, he receives only one. It does not befit us to discuss their affairs."

Certainly these scholars must have inherited such a doctrine from their fathers and forefathers, one generation from the other, so they were repeating it like parrots without contemplation or scrutiny.

Their Imam, al-Ghazali, had adopted such a view, one which he propagated among people, making himself the ultimate authority for Islam and Muslims. In his book *Al-Mustafa*, he says, "What is accepted by the ancestors and the posterity is that the justice of the *sahabah* is well known due to the fact that Allah, the most Exalted One, the most Great, has called them just and has praised them in His Book, and this is our conviction in their regard."

I wonder about al-Ghazali in particular and about "Ahlul Sunnah wal Jama'ah" in general when I read about their seeking from the Qur'an testimonies regarding the *sahabah* being fair and just, knowing that there is not a single verse in the Holy Qur'an which backs this claim.

On the contrary, there are many Qur'anic verses which deny the justice of the *sahabah*, which reveal their secrets, and which expose their hypocrisy. We have dedicated an entire chapter to discuss this topic in our book *Ask Those Who Know* from pp. 113 – 172. So, whoever wishes to research this subject further in order to become familiar with such facts should refer to this book. He will know what Allah and the Messenger say about them.

So that the researcher may come to know that the *sahabah* never dreamt one day of the status invented for them by "Ahlul Sunnah wal Jama'ah," he has only to read modern books as well as history books which overflow with their horrible deeds. They tell tales of how they called each other *kafir*, and how so many of them used to wonder whether they were among the *munafiqun*, hypocrites.

Al-Bukhari, for example, states in his *Sahih* that Ibn Maleeka met thirty of the companions of the Prophet who all dreaded being counted among the hypocrites, and none of them ever said that his conviction was to be compared with that of [arch-angel] Gabriel.[3] Al-Ghazali himself indicates in his book that Umar ibn al-Khattab used to ask Huzayfah of Yemen whether the Messenger of Allah mentioned his [Umar's] own name among the hypocrites of whose names he informed him.[4]

The statement of those who claim that there are no hypocrites among the *sahabah* is completely worthless when we come to know that the definition of a *sahabi* is the one we have already discussed above, that is, anyone who saw and believed in the Messenger of Allah, whether he met him or not.

Their phrase "and believed in" the Prophet, too, contains an exaggeration simply because all those who kept the Prophet company had articulated the *shahada*, and the Prophet accepted

---

[3] Al-Bukhari, *Sahih*, Vol. 1, p. 17.
[4] Al-Ghazali, *Ihyaa 'Uloom al-Din*, Vol. 1, p. 129. Al-Muttaqi al-Hindi, *Kanz al-Ummal*, Vol. 7, p. 24.

their superficial admission of faith, saying, "I have been ordered to judge what is apparent, and Allah will deal with one's innermost." As long as he lived, he never said to any of them, "You are a hypocrite, so I shall not accept your declaration of faith!"

This is why we find the Prophet calling the hypocrites "my companions" even while knowing their hypocrisy! Here is the proof:

Al-Bukhari states that Umar ibn al-Khattab asked the Prophet to have Abdullah ibn Ubayy, the hypocrite, beheaded. He said to him, "O Messenger of Allah! Let me strike the neck of this hypocrite with the sword!" The Prophet said, "Leave him alone; I do not want people to say that Muhammad kills his own companions."[5]

Some scholars among "Ahlul Sunnah wal Jama'ah" may try to convince us that the hypocrites used to be well known; so, we should not confuse them with the *sahabah*. This is impossible. Contrariwise, the hypocrites are among the *sahabah* with whose secrets only Allah, Glory to Him, is familiar. They may perform their prayers and they may fast, worship Allah and seek nearness to the Prophet through all means. Let us provide you with the proof:

In his *Sahih*, al-Bukhari indicates that Umar ibn al-Khattab on another occasion asked the Messenger of Allah to permit him to kill Dhul Khuwaysara when the latter said to the Prophet: "Be fair!"

But the Prophet said to Umar, "Leave him alone, for he has companions if one of you were to compare his prayers with that of theirs, he would find it inferior and would find his fast as well inferior to theirs; they recite the Qur'an which does not go beyond

---

[5] Al-Bukhari, *Sahih*, Vol. 6, p. 65, where the merits of the Qur'an and Surat al-Munafiqun are discussed. Ibn Asakir, *Tarikh*, Vol. 4, p. 97.

their throats. They leave the creed as swiftly as the arrow leaves the bow."[6]

I do not exaggerate if I say that most companions were not far from hypocrisy according to what is determined by many verses of the Holy Qur'an and according to the decisions of the Messenger of Allah embedded in many of his *ahadith*. In the Book of Allah, we come across verses such as these:

"He has brought them the truth, yet most of them are averse from the truth." (Holy Qur'an, 23:70)

"The dwellers of the desert are more [fierce] in disbelief and hypocrisy." (Holy Qur'an, 9:97)

"And from those who are round about you of the dwellers of the desert there are hypocrites, and from the people of Medina (too); they are stubborn in hypocrisy; you do not know them; We know them." (Holy Qur'an, 9:101)

It is noteworthy here that some scholars among "Ahlul Sunnah wal Jama'ah" try very hard to cover the truth. They interpret "dwellers of the desert" to mean that they were not among the *sahabah* but are meant to be the residents of the desert and the outskirts of the Arabian Peninsula. Yet we have found how Umar ibn al-Khattab, shortly before drawing his last breath, left his will to the caliph who would succeed him saying: "I urge you to be good to the dwellers of the desert, for they are the origins of the Arabs and the substance of Islam."[7]

So, if the Arabs' kinsfolk and the substance of Islam are the worst in disbelief and hypocrisy and it is best that they should not know the limits of what Allah revealed to His Messenger, then

---

[6] Al-Bukhari, *Sahih*, Vol. 4, p. 179.

[7] Al-Bukhari, *Sahih*, Vol. 4, p. 206.

there is no value attached to the statement made by "Ahlul Sunnah wal Jama'ah" claiming that the *sahabah* were all just and fair.

In order to shed more light, and so that the researcher may be convinced that the phrase referring to the dwellers of the desert, that is, bedouin Arabs, was meant to refer to the *sahabah* in general, the Holy Qur'an, after describing the bedouin Arabs as the worst in disbelief and hypocrisy, goes on to say:

"And of the dwellers of the desert are those who believe in Allah and the latter day and take what they spend to be (means of) nearness to Allah and the Prophet's prayers; surely it shall be for them means of nearness (to Allah); Allah will permit them to enter into His mercy; surely Allah is Forgiving, Merciful" (Holy Qur'an, 9:99).

As for what the Messenger of Allah had decided in the Prophet's sacred Sunnah, it is his following statement:

My *sahabah* will be taken to the fire [of hell], whereupon I shall plead: "O Lord! But these are my *sahabah*!" It will be said to me, "You do not know what they brought forth after you." I will say, "Then perdition should be the lot of all those who altered after me."[8]

Traditions like this one are numerous, and we have avoided quoting them seeking to be brief. Our objective, after all, is not to research the biographies of the Prophet's companions in order to cast doubts about their justice, for history has spared us such an undertaking. It testifies against some of them as having committed adultery, drunk wine, made a false oath, reneged from the creed, committed crimes against innocent people and betrayed the nation.

---

[8] Al-Bukhari, *Sahih,* Vol. 7, p. 209, in a chapter dealing with the Pool [of al-Kawthar].

We only wish to bring into focus the fact that to say that each and every *sahabi* was fair and just is a legendary myth invented by "Ahlul Sunnah wal Jama'ah" in order to cover the faults of their masters and heads from the *sahabah* who made many alterations to the religion of Allah, changing its injunctions with innovations which they themselves had invented.

We also wish again to prove that by embracing the doctrine of the *sahabah* being all just and fair, "Ahlul Sunnah wal Jama'ah" unveiled their real identity, the identity of seeking to please the hypocrites and to follow the *bid`as* they had invented in order to bring people back to the period of *jahiliyya*.

Since "Ahlul Sunnah wal Jama'ah" banned their followers from criticizing or discrediting the *sahabah*, closing the doors of *ijtihad* in their faces since the time of the Umayyad rulers and the period of inventing sects, the said followers inherited such a doctrine which they passed down to their offspring, one generation after another. Hence,

"Ahlul Sunnah wal Jama'ah" remained till this day prohibiting any discussion of the *sahabah* for whom they seek Allah's Pleasure, labelling as *kafir* whoever criticizes any of them.

The summary of this chapter is that the Shi'as, followers of the creed of Ahlul Bayt, place the *sahabah* in perspective; they pray Allah to be pleased with the righteous among them, and they dissociate themselves from the hypocrites and the sinners, the enemies of Allah and His Messenger, from them. They, hence, are the only ones who follow the true Sunnah because they loved those whom Allah love and the *sahabah* who are loved by the Messenger of Allah. They dissociate themselves from the enemies of Allah and of His Messenger who were the primary cause of the misguidance of the vast majority of Muslims.

HOW AHLUL SUNNAH WAL-JAMA'AH CONTRADICT THE PROPHET'S SUNNAH

In this chapter, we have to unveil to the researcher, in general terms, how "Ahlul Sunnah wal Jama'ah" practically contradict most of the Prophet's traditions. In contrast, we will explain how only the Shi'as are the ones who uphold the Sunnah of the Prophet. This is why we justify our use of the title of this book as *The Shi'as are Ahlul Sunnah*.

In this chapter, we wish to discuss the main issues which clarify for the researchers, more convincingly, the fact that "Ahlul Sunnah wal Jama'ah" violated the teachings of Islam with regard to all what the Qur'an decrees and what the Messenger decided in his sacred Sunnah. This caused the misguidance of those of this nation and the setback that befell the Muslims leading, in the end, to their backwardness and suffering.

In my belief, the reason for the misguidance is rendered to one major factor: love for this world. Did not the Messenger of Allah say, "Loving this world tops every sin"? Loving this world is characterized by loving power and authority: for the sake of achieving political power, nations have been ruined, countries and lands have been reduced to rubble, rendering man more dangerous than wild beasts. It is the same meaning to which the Prophet refers when he said to his companions, "I do not fear for you that you will associate someone with Allah; rather, I fear for you that you dispute with one another."

This is why there is a need to study the subjects of caliphate and Imamate, or what we call nowadays the Islamic government system. It led to the worst calamity and catastrophe for Islam and its followers, bringing them peril and agony, misguidance and annihilation.

1. ISLAM'S GOVERNMENT SYSTEM

"Ahlul Sunnah wal Jama'ah" are of the view that the Messenger of Allah did not specify who to succeed him, leaving this issue subject to mutual consultation among people to choose whoever they wanted. This is their belief with regard to the issue of caliphate. They have insisted upon it since the day the Prophet died till our time.

"Ahlul Sunnah wal Jama'ah" supposedly act upon this principle in which they believe and which they defend with all their might. But the research will reveal to us the fact that they did exactly the opposite. Regardless of the allegiance to Abu Bakr, which they themselves called a mistake the evil of which Allah spared them, it was Abu Bakr who invented the notion of the succession to the post of caliph, appointing, prior to his death, his friend Umar ibn al-Khattab as his successor.

At the time of his death, Umar ibn al-Khattab appointed Abdul-Rahman ibn Awf to choose one of five persons whom he recommended for the post of caliph, and to kill anyone who refused to accept the selected one.

When Mu'awiyah secured the post of caliph for himself, he put this principle of succession into practice, appointing his son Yazid ibn Mu'awiyah. Thus, the caliphate remained since that time being handed over from one promiscuous person to another, from one generation to another, each caliph appointing his son, brother, or relative, to succeed him.

So did the caliph since the inception of the Abbaside government till its dissolution. And so did the Ottoman caliphs from the time it was established till the period when the caliphate weakened and waned during the time of Kamal Ataturk in the present century.

"Ahlul Sunnah wal Jama'ah" represent such caliphate, or, say, those successive governments represented "Ahlul Sunnah wal Jama'ah" in all parts of the world, and throughout the Islamic history. This is why you can now see in Saudi Arabia, Morocco, Jordan, and all Gulf states rulers who act upon the theory of succession which they inherited from their "good posterity" who all belong to "Ahlul Sunnah wal Jama`ah."

Even if we suppose that the theory they uphold, the one saying that the Prophet left the issue for mutual consultation, and that the Qur'an endorses the concept of consultation, were accurate, they still opposed the Qur'an and the Sunnah. They turned the system of "democratic" consultation into a dictatorial monarchic hereditary system of succession.

But if we suppose that the Prophet had appointed Ali ibn Abu Talib to succeed him, as the Shi'as argue, "Ahlul Sunnah wal Jama'ah" would then be in clear violation of many texts of the Sunnah and contradict the Qur'an. This is so because the Messenger of Allah never did anything without the permission of his Lord. For this reason, you find them aware of the fact that this issue of mutual consultation is erroneous because the early caliphs did not implement it, nor did they act upon it.

They also feel the inaccuracy of the theory of succession to the caliphate, so you find them justifying it through *ahadith* such as the one saying, "Caliphate after me shall last for thirty years followed by a government of oppression," as if they want to convince others of their own conviction that government is for Allah to grant it to whomsoever He pleases, and that the kings and sultans were appointed by Allah, the most Exalted One, to rule people; so, obedience to them is obligatory.

This is a lengthy topic which drags us to the issue of destiny and predestination which we discussed in our book *To be with the Truthful*, a topic we do not wish now to return to. Suffices us here to bear in mind that "Ahlul Sunnah wal Jama'ah" are also called "Qadaris," believers in destiny, as they espouse.

The end result is that "Ahlul Sunnah wal Jama'ah" believe in the system of succession which they regard as conducive with the Shari`a not because the Messenger of Allah mandated it, or because he appointed his own successor, for they very strongly deny any such things, but only because Abu Bakr appointed Umar, and Umar appointed six persons, then Mu`awiyah appointed Yazid, and so on.

None of their scholars or Imams of the four sects ever claimed that the Umayyad or the Abbaside or the Ottoman government was in agreement with the Shari`a. Yet we find them rushing to swear their oath of allegiance, to support and brand their caliphs as "legitimate." Even most of them went as far as claiming that caliphate is legitimate for anyone who attains it by force or oppression, and they are not concerned whether he is righteous, a sinner, or a promiscuous, or whether he is an Arab, a member of Quraysh, a Turk, or a Kurd.

Dr. Ahmad Mahmud Subhi says the following in this regard, "The stand adopted by Ahlul Sunnah with regard to the issue of caliphate is to accept the status quo without endorsing or opposing it."[1] In reality, however, Ahlul Sunnah do support it. Abu Ya`li al-Farraa quotes Imam Ahmad ibn Hanbal saying, "The caliphate is fixed by winning, or by force, and it does not lack a contract."

According to Abdoos ibn Malik al-Attar, "If one wins by the sword and becomes caliph and is referred to as Commander of the Faithful, it is not legal for anyone who believes in Allah and the Last Day to spend his night without recognizing him as the Imam, be he a righteous man or a sinner." He builds this view on a

---

[1] He says so on p. 23 of his book *Nazariyyat Al-Imama*.

statement made by Abdullah ibn Umar saying, "We are with whoever wins."

Thus, "Ahlul Sunnah wal Jama'ah" become a pawn to this *bid`at*, the innovation of the issue of succession. They swear their allegiance to the winner and the oppressor regardless of the extent of his fear of Allah, piety, or knowledge, be he righteous or a sinner. This is proven by the fact that most *sahabah* who fought on the side of the Prophet against Mu`awiyah ibn Abu Sufyan in many battles ended up swearing allegiance to Mu`awiyah as the "commander of the faithful" after the Prophet's demise. They also accepted the caliphate of Marwan ibn al-Hakam whom the Messenger of Allah called *alwazgh* (the shiner), and whom he banished from Medina saying, "He shall not reside where I reside, whether alive or dead."

They even accepted the caliphate of Yazid son of Mu`awiyah to whom they swore the oath of allegiance and whom they called "commander of the faithful." When al-Husayn, grandson of the Prophet, revolted against him, they killed al-Husayn and his Ahlul Bayt in order to solidify the foundations of Yazid's government and to label it as legal.

Their scholars went as far as saying that al-Husayn was killed by the sword of his grandfather. Some of them write, even in this time and age, books dealing with the "facts" relevant to "the commander of the faithful Yazid ibn Mu`awiyah." All of this is done out of their support for Yazid's caliphate and as an indictment of al-Husayn who revolted against him.

If we know all of this, we have no choice except to admit that "Ahlul Sunnah wal Jama'ah" contradicted the Sunnah which they attributed to the Prophet and which they say mandated leaving the issue [of caliphate] for discussion and consultation among the Muslims.

As for the Shi'as, these upheld the concept of Imamate with one single view which is: "Allah and His Messenger appoint the caliph." Imamate according to them cannot be legitimate except through a text, and it cannot be legitimate except for one who is infallible, whose knowledge is the highest, who is the most pious, and who is the best.

They do not prefer one who is good over another who is better. This is why we find them first rejecting the caliphate of the *sahabah*, then rejecting the concept of the caliphate as envisioned by "Ahlul Sunnah wal Jama`ah."

Since the texts which the Shi'as produce with regard to the issue of caliphate enjoy a practical presence and a true authenticity even in the *Sahih* books of "Ahlul Sunnah wal Jama'ah," we have no choice except to admit that the Shi'as are the ones who actually upheld the authentic Sunnah of the Prophet.

Whether we say that the issue is to be resolved by mutual consultation (*shura*) or through texts referring to the issue of caliphate, only the Shi'as are right because the only person who stands out as the one who was appointed by such texts as well as by the *shura* is Ali ibn Abu Talib.

Nobody among the Muslims, be he a Shi`a or a Sunni, claims that the Messenger of Allah made any reference, even remotely, to the issue of hereditary succession. Nor does any Muslim, be he Sunni or Shi`a, claims that the Messenger of Allah said to his companions, "I have left your affair for *shura*; so, choose whoever you wish to succeed me."

We call upon them to produce even one single such *hadith*. So if they cannot do so, and they most surely cannot, they must go back to the confirmed Sunnah of the Prophet and to accurate Islamic history to derive guidance therefrom.

Or do they claim that the Messenger of Allah neglected to deal with this very important issue and did not clarify its features so that his nation might enter into a never-ending struggle and a blind dissension that all tear its unity apart and disunite it and cause it to deviate from Allah's Straight Path? We see in our times how corrupt and oppressive rulers take into very serious consideration the fate of their peoples after their own authority is over, so they appoint their successors whenever there is a vacancy; what, then, would you say about the one whom Allah sent as mercy for the whole world?!

2. TO CALL ALL THE "SAHABAH" EQUITABLE IS TO CONTRADICT THE CLEAR SUNNAH

If we take a look at the way the Prophet dealt with his companion and what he said about them, we will find him giving credit where credit is due. He is angered when Allah is angered and is pleased when He is pleased. The Prophet dissociated himself from any companion who went against the commandments of Allah, Glory to Him, as was the case when Khalid ibn al-Waleed killed Banu Juthaymah.

He also became angry with Usamah when the latter came to him seeking favor on behalf of a high class lady who stole something. It was then when he made his famous statement, "Woe unto you! Do you intercede regarding the trespassing over one of the boundaries set by Allah? By Allah! Had Fatima daughter of Muhammad stolen, I would have cut off her hand. Nations before you were annihilated because whenever a dignitary among them stole, they left him alone, but when a simple person stole, they would carry out the appropriate penalty."

We also find him sometimes blessing and seeking the pleasure of Allah for some of his sincere companions, supplicating for them, seeking Allah's forgiveness for them. And we also find him cursing some of them, those who insisted not to carry out his orders or simply took them lightly. For example, he said once, "The curse of Allah be on all those who lag behind Usamah's army" when they cast doubts about his nomination of Usamah to be their leader and who refused to join his army because he was too young.

We also find him explaining to people and not leaving them to be dazzled by some of the fake *sahabah*, saying about one of them, "He has companions if one of you were to compare his prayers with theirs, he would find it inferior, and he would find his fast as well to be inferior to theirs; they recite the Qur'an which does not go beyond their throats."

They leave the creed as swiftly as the arrow leaves the bow." He may even stop short of performing the funeral prayers for one of the *sahabah* who was martyred during the campaign of Khaybar on the side of the Muslims, revealing the truth about him and saying, "He fell short of discharging his responsibility in the cause of Allah." When they searched the belongings of that person, [stolen] Jewish beads were found among his items.

Al-Maroodi narrates to us saying that the Prophet felt very thirsty once during the campaign of Tabuk, whereupon the hypocrites said, "Muhammad tells the news of the heavens but does not know the way to water!" It was then that Gabriel descended to tell him the names of those who said so. The Prophet named them to Sa'd ibn Abadah who said to him, "If you wish, you can have them killed." The Prophet said, "I do not wish people to say that Muhammad kills his own companions. Rather, we will deal with them beautifully as long as they are in our company."[1]

The Messenger of Allah dealt with them just as the Holy Qur'an tells us. Allah was pleased with the truthful among them and wrathful with the hypocrites, renegades, and those who violated their oaths. And the Almighty cursed them in many sacred verses. We have dealt with this subject in full detail in our book *Ask Those Who Know* in a chapter titled "The Holy Qur'an Reveals Facts

---

[1] His statement: "I do not wish people to say that Muhammad kills his companions. Rather, we will deal with them beautifully, etc." contains an evident proof that the hypocrites were, indeed, among the *sahabah*. The claim put forth by "Ahlul Sunnah wal Jama'ah" that the hypocrites were not among the *sahabah* is rejected because this claim is contradicted by the statement of the Messenger of Allah who refers to them as his companions.

about some of the *Sahabah*." If anyone wishes to research this subject further, he should refer to the said book.

We will be satisfied by producing one example of what some hypocritical companions had done and which was exposed by Allah Who shamed those involved. They were twelve *sahabis* who sought to be excused [from meeting with the Prophet] due to their living far away, saying that they had no time to meet with the Prophet.

They, therefore, built a mosque so that they could perform the prayers on time. Can you see sincerity and loyalty greater than that? A servant of Allah spends huge sums of money to build a mosque out of his concern for performing the prayers on time, and a group of brethren united together under the roof of one mosque?

But Allah, Glory to Him, from Whom nothing is hidden in the earth or in the heavens, and Who knows where the eyes trespass and what the chests conceal, knew their innermost thoughts and what they were hiding, so He inspired to His Messenger about them and acquainted him with their hypocrisy saying,

"And those who built a mosque (only) to cause mischief, to promote unbelief, to cause dissension among the believers, and to lie in wait for whoever made war against Allah and His Prophet before; they will certainly swear: We did not desire aught but good, while Allah testifies that most surely they are liars." (Holy Qur'an, 9:107)

Since Allah is not shy about the truth, nor is His Messenger who used to frankly tell his companions that they would fight one another for the attainment of the good things in this life. He told them that they would follow in their misguidance the customs of the Jews and the Christians, one span at a time, one yard at a time, and that they would go back on their heels and renege. He also told them that on the Day of Judgment, they would enter the fire of hell; none of them except a few would be spared, those the Prophet described to be "as few as lost camels."

So how can "Ahlul Sunnah wal Jama'ah" convince us that all the *sahabah* were just and fair and that they all are in Paradise, that their injunctions are binding upon us, that their views and innovations have to be followed, and that anyone who discredits any of them abandons the creed and should be killed?!

It is a statement which even insane people reject, let alone the wise. It is a false statement, a calumny, something said to please the rulers, monarchs, by the evil and intruding scholars who follow them suit. As for us, we cannot accept such a statement at all so long as we have reason because that would be going against what Allah and His Messenger tell us. Anyone who does the opposite of what Allah and His Messenger decree is an apostate. It also clashes with reason and conscience.

We do not force "Ahlul Sunnah wal Jama'ah" to abandon or reject it, for they are free in believing whatever they want to believe, and they are the only ones who will be held responsible for the results and terrible outcomes of so doing.

But they must not label as *kafir* those who follow the Qur'an and the Sunnah in as far as the justice of the *sahabah* is concerned. They should say to the *sahabah* who do good: "You have done well," and to the ones who fell into error, "You committed something wrong and made a mistake." They ought to befriend the friends of Allah and His Messenger and dissociate themselves from the enemies of Allah and His Messenger.

Thus does it become clear that "Ahlul Sunnah wal Jama'ah" violated clear Qur'anic texts as well as clear texts of the Sunnah and followed the dictates of the Umayyad and Abbaside governments, discarding all juristic and rational criteria.

3. THE PROPHET ORDERS THE MUSLIMS TO EMULATE HIS `ITRAT WHILE SUNNIS OPPOSE HIM

In our past researches, we proved the authenticity of the Prophet's *hadith* known as *hadith al-thaqalayn*, that is, *hadith* of the two weighty things. It states the following:

I am leaving with you *al-thaqalayn*: so long as you uphold them, you shall never stray after me. They are: the Book of Allah and my `itrat*, my Ahlul Bayt. The Most Munificent, the most Knowing, informed me that they shall never part from one another till they reach me at the Pool.

We proved that this *hadith* is authentic and is consecutively reported by the Shi'as as well as by "Ahlul Sunnah wal Jama'ah" who record it in their *sahih* and *musnad* books. It is well known that "Ahlul Sunnah wal Jama'ah" left Ahlul Bayt behind their backs and turned their faces towards the Imams of the four sects whose authority was forced on the public by oppressive governments, the governments which, in turn, were supported by "Ahlul Sunnah wal Jama'ah" who swore to them their oath of allegiance.

If we wish to elaborate on this topic, we can say that "Ahlul Sunnah wal Jama'ah" are the ones who, led by Umayyad and Abbaside rulers, fought the household of Prophethood. If you, therefore, sift through their beliefs and books of *hadith*, you will find no traces whatsoever for the *fiqh* of Ahlul Bayt. You will find all their *fiqh* and *ahadith* attributed to the Nasibis who were the enemies of Ahlul Bayt and who fought them, such as Abdullah ibn Umar, Ayesha, Abu Hurayra, and others.

They derive half of their creed from Ayesha, the lady with the reddish complexion[1], while the major Sunni *faqih* is Abdullah son of Umar [ibn al-Khattab]. Islam's narrator, according to them, is Abu Hurayra, mentor of al-Mudeera, while the *taleeqs*[2] and their sons constituted their judges and the legislators of Allah's creed.

What proves this fact is that "Ahlul Sunnah wal Jama'ah" were not identified as such but were, as a whole, opponents of Ahlul Bayt since the day of the *Saqifa*, and they are the ones who conspired to usurp the caliphate from Ahlul Bayt and did their best to distance them from the nation's political stage.

The party known as "Ahlul Sunnah wal Jama'ah" was then formed to counter the Shi'as who rallied behind, supported, and followed the Imamate of Ahlul Bayt in obedience to the Qur'an and the Sunnah.

It is only natural that those who opposed the truth were the vast majority of the nation especially in the aftermath of dissensions and wars. Moreover, Ahlul Bayt could not rule the Muslims except for only four years, the period of Imam Ali's caliphate during which they distracted him with bloody wars.

As for "Ahlul Sunnah wal Jama'ah" who opposed Ahlul Bayt, they ruled for hundreds of years, and their government and authority spread far and wide to the east and the west. They had their say, their gold and silver. "Ahlul Sunnah wal Jama'ah," hence, are the "winners" because they are the rulers. The Shi'as, led by Ahlul Bayt, became the vanquished because they are the subjects, the oppressed, the displaced and the murdered.

---

[1] In Arabic, she is called al-humayraa which means: the woman the color of whose complexion is slightly red. __ Tr.

[2] These were the Meccans who remained heathen till the conquest of Mecca.

We do not wish to prolong the discussion of this subject beyond our desire to reveal the secrets of "Ahlul Sunnah wal Jama'ah" who opposed the Prophet's will and legacy which guaranteed guidance and protected against straying, whereas the Shi'as upheld the will of the Prophet, followed in the footsteps of his pure Progeny and tolerated in so doing a great deal of hardship and pain.

The fact is that such dissension and rebellion from the part of "Ahlul Sunnah wal Jama'ah" with regard to *al-thaqalayn,* versus the acceptance of the Shi'as of the same and their adherence thereto, surfaced from that particular Thursday which came to be known as the Day of Infamy when the Messenger of Allah asked them to bring him some writing material to write them something that would protect them against misguidance.

It was then that Umar took his most serious stand and refused the Prophet's request claiming that the Book of Allah sufficed them, and that they had no need for his `itrat. It was as though the Prophet was saying, "Uphold both *thaqalayn*: the Qur'an and the `Itrat," whereas Umar answered him with, "We are satisfied with only one of them: the Qur'an, and we have no need for the other." This is exactly the meaning of Umar's statement: "The Book of Allah suffices us."

Umar's statement represented the stand adopted by "Ahlul Sunnah wal Jama'ah" because prominent Qurayshi heads, represented by Abu Bakr, Uthman, Abdul-Rahman ibn Awf, Abu Ubaydah, Khalid ibn al-Waleed, Talhah ibn Ubaydullah, all stood up to support Umar's stand. Ibn Abbas said, "Some of them kept repeating what Umar said, while some others said, `Bring writing material to the Prophet so that he may write you something."

It was only natural that Ali and his followers, since that day, upheld the Prophet's will even though it was not written down, acting upon both the Qur'an and the Sunnah simultaneously. Their enemies, on the other hand, did not act even upon the Qur'an which they agreed to do in the beginning and whose injunctions they idled when they attained power and authority, following their own views, leaving the Book of Allah and the Sunnah of His Messenger behind their backs.

4. "AHLUL SUNNAH WAL JAMA'AH" AND LOVE FOR AHLUL BAYT

No Muslim doubts that Allah, Glory and Exaltation to Him, has imposed love for Ahlul Bayt, peace be upon them, as a the dues the Muslims have to pay in return for granting them Muhammad's Message and the blessings such Message contains for them. He has said,

"Say: I do not ask you for any reward for it except love for my kinsfolk" (Holy Qur'an, 42:23).

This sacred verse was revealed to require the Muslims to love the purified `Itrat of the Prophet who are: Ali, Fatima, al-Hasan and al-Husayn, according to the testimony of more than thirty references all of which are authored by "Ahlul Sunnah wal Jama'ah,"[1] so much so that Imam al-Shafi`i composed the following in this regard:

O household of Allah's Messenger! Loving you is an obligation Which Allah enjoined in the Qur'an, His Revelation.

Loving them is mandated by the Holy Qur'an; it is an obligation on all followers of Islam, as Imam al-Shafi`i admits. Loving them is the price we have to pay for receiving Muhammad's Message, as the text clearly indicates. Loving them is a form of worship whereby nearness to Allah, the Most Exalted One, is sought. Since the case is as such, why do not "Ahlul Sunnah wal

---

[1] Refer to the book *Ma`a al-Sadiqin (To be with the Truthful)* by the same author. It is available at: https://www.al-islam.org/be-with-truthful-muhammad-al-tijani-al-samawi

Jama'ah" have any regard for Ahlul Bayt? Why do they respect them less than they respect the *sahabah*?[2]

We have the right to ask "Ahlul Sunnah wal Jama'ah" this question. Rather, we challenge them to bring about one Qur'anic verse, or one *hadith*, making it compulsory on the Muslims to love Abu Bakr or Umar or Uthman or any other *sahabi*! No, they will never be able to do that. Never! On the contrary; the Qur'an contains numerous verses which point out to the lofty status preserved for Ahlul Bayt, thus preferring them over all other servants of Allah. And the Prophet's Sunnah contains many *ahadith* favoring Ahlul Bayt and placing them ahead of all other Muslims just as the leading Imam is preferred over those whom he leads, and just as a scholar is preferred over an ignorant person.

The Qur'an suffices us with this verse, the one mandating love for Ahlul Bayt discussed here, in addition to the *Mubahala* verse, the verse mandating the invoking of Allah's blessings unto the Prophet and his Progeny, the verse referring to the removal of all abomination from and the purification of Ahlul Bayt, the verse mandating their *wilayat* (mastership), the verse referring to their being chosen by Allah to receive His favors and to inherit the knowledge of the Book.

From the Prophet's Sunnah, we content ourselves with *hadith* al-thaqalayn (tradition of the two weighty things), the *hadith* comparing Ahlul Bayt to the ark of salvation, the status *hadith*, the *hadith* referring to the complete prayers unto them, the *hadith* of the guiding stars, the *hadith* describing Imam Ali as the gate of

---

[2] This is so because all "Ahlul Sunnah wal Jama`ah" favor Abu Bakr, Umar, and Uthman over Ali ibn Abu Talib. Since the latter is the master of the `Itrat and the best of Ahlul Bayt after the Prophet, "Ahlul Sunnah wal Jama`ah" place Ahlul Bayt in the second place in their esteem. They prefer over them the first *sahabah* to whom they refer as the "righteous caliphs."

knowledge, and the *hadith* numbering the Imams after the Prophet as twelve.

We do not wish to say that one third of the Qur'an was revealed in praise and counting the merits of

Ahlul Bayt, as some companions, such as Ibn Abbas, say, nor do we claim that one third of the Prophet's Sunnah praises and lauds Ahlul Bayt and attracts the attention of people to their virtues and merits as Imam Ahmad ibn Hanbal points out.

Suffices us from the Qur'an and the Sunnah what we have quoted from the *Sahih* books of "Ahlul Sunnah wal Jama'ah" to prove the preference of Ahlul Bayt over all other people.

After casting a quick look at the beliefs of "Ahlul Sunnah wal Jama'ah," at their books and behavior towards Ahlul Bayt throughout history, we will realize without any doubt that Sunnis opposed and antagonized Ahlul Bayt, that they unsheathed their swords to fight them, utilized their pens to belittle and abuse them. They have been doing so in order to raise the status of the enemies of Ahlul Bayt and of those who fought them.

One evidence should suffice to give us the convincing proof. As we have indicated above, "Ahlul Sunnah wal Jama'ah" were not identified by this name except during the second Hijri century. That was their reaction to the Shi'as who became loyal to and who followed the line of Ahlul Bayt. There is no trace or clue whatsoever in Sunni *fiqh* or rituals or beliefs indicating that they make any reference at all to the Prophet's Sunnah as narrated by Ahlul Bayt.[3]

---

[3] Nowadays, they claim saying, "We are more worthy of Ali and Ahlul Bayt from the Shi`as." If so, why did their scholars and the Imams of their sects abandon the fiqh of Ahlul Bayt and forgot it completely? They, instead, followed sects which they invented and for which Allah sent no

This happens despite the fact that the people of the house know best what their house contains, for they are the offspring and the progeny of the Prophet. Nobody could ever surpass them in their knowledge or deeds. For three centuries, they were present among the people. They held the reins of spiritual and religious leadership through their Twelve Imams who never differed in any issue with one another. Despite all of that, we find "Ahlul Sunnah wal Jama'ah" adhering to the four sects which were not created except in the third Hijri century, the sects wherein each Imam contradicts that of the other. Despite that, they left Ahlul Bayt behind their backs, antagonized them and fought all those who followed them. And they are still fighting them even in our day and time...

If we need another proof, we only have to analyze the stand of "Ahlul Sunnah wal Jama'ah" *vis-a-vis* the commemoration of the Day of Ashura, the ominous day when a corner of Islam was demolished, when the master of the youths of Paradise [and all the residents of Paradise are youths] and of the purified Progeny, offspring of the Prophet, and of the selected band of righteous from his believing companions were martyred:

FIRST: We will find them pleased with and supportive of those who killed al-Husayn. This must not surprise us, for all those who killed al-Husayn belonged to "Ahlul Sunnah wal Jama'ah." It is sufficient for us to know that the leader of the army appointed by Ibn Ziyad to kill Imam al-Husayn was none other than Umar ibn Sa'd ibn Abu Waqqas. "Ahlul Sunnah wal Jama'ah," therefore, invoke Allah to be pleased with all the *sahabah*, including those who killed and who were accomplices in the killing of Imam al-

---

proof. The Most Exalted One has said, "The most worthy among people of Ibrahim are those who followed him." As for those who did not follow him, they clearly are not worthy of him.

Husayn. They accept their *ahadith* which they label as "authentic." Nay! Some of them even consider Imam Husayn as a Kharijite because he revolted against the authority of "the commander of the faithful Yazid ibn Mu`awiyah"!

We have already indicated that the *faqih* of "Ahlul Sunnah wal Jama'ah" Abdullah ibn Umar had sworn his oath of allegiance to Yazid ibn Mu`awiyah and decreed disobedience to Yazid as *haram*. He said, "We are with whoever wins."

SECOND: We find "Ahlul Sunnah wal Jama'ah" throughout history, from the Day of Ashura till our time, celebrating the Day of Ashura and considering it as an Eid when they take out the *zakat* of their wealth to distribute to their children, regarding it as a day for blessings and mercy.

As if all this does not satisfy them, they now scandalize the Shi'as and criticize them for mourning al-Husayn. In some Muslim countries, they prohibit them from conducting the commemorative ceremonies of this tragic epic and attack them with their weapons, beating or killing some of them in the pretext of fighting innovations.

In reality, they do not fight innovations as much as they re-enact the roles played by Umayyad and Abbaside rulers who tried their best to obliterate the memory of Ashura and who went as far as desecrating and defacing the grave of Imam al-Husayn, prohibiting people from visiting it. They still want to put an end to that memory for fear people would come to know, and so would those who are ignorant, of the truth about Ahlul Bayt.

These would come to know what really happened and the faults of these folks as well as of those of their masters and leaders would then be unveiled. People will then come to know the difference between right and wrong, between a believer and a sinner.

Thus do we once again come to know that the Shi'as are, indeed, the ones who actually adhere to the Prophet's Sunnah because they have followed the Sunnah of the Prophet even with regard to grieving for and mourning the father of Abdullah, Imam Husayn. Confirmed traditions testify that the Prophet of Islam himself wept over the martyrdom of his grandson al-Husayn before it happened when Gabriel told him of al-Husayn's future martyrdom at Karbala. That was exactly fifty years before its occurrence.

We also clearly come to know that "Ahlul Sunnah wal Jama'ah" celebrate the Day of Ashura because they followed the "sunnah" of Yazid ibn Mu`awiyah and of Banu Umayyah who used to celebrate that day as the day when they achieved "victory" over al-Husayn. They celebrate putting out Imam al-Husayn's revolution which threatened their very existence. They regarded their "victory" as putting an end to anarchy, as they claim.

History tells us that Yazid and Banu Umayyah celebrated that day with a great deal of festivities when the severed head of al-Husayn and those of Ahlul Bayt who were taken captives reached them. They rejoiced and cursed the family of the Messenger of Allah and composed poetry.

The evil scholars among "Ahlul Sunnah wal Jama'ah" sought to please them, so they fabricated for them a number of "traditions" praising that Day. They told them that Ashura was the day when Allah accepted Adam's repentance, when the ark of Noah landed on the Jodi mountain, when the fire turned cool and peaceful unto Abraham, when Joseph was released from prison and when Jacob recovered his vision, when Moses obtained victory over Pharaoh, when a table of viands descended upon Jesus..., etc.!!!

All these are fabricated "traditions" which "Ahlul Sunnah wal Jama'ah" and their scholars and Imams have been repeating from the pulpits even in our day and time on the occasion of Ashura. All these are "traditions" which were manufactured by swindlers who put on the garb of scholars and tried to please their rulers by all means, selling their hereafter for the price of this short life, so their trade did not earn them any profit, and they shall be in the hereafter among the losers.

They went to extremes in telling lies, claiming that the Prophet migrated to Medina, and it so happened that the day when he reached it was the tenth of Muharram (Ashura). He found the Jews of Medina fasting, so he asked them the reason. They said, "This is the day when Moses won victory over Pharaoh," whereupon the Prophet, according to this fabrication, said, "We are more worthy of Moses than you." Then he supposedly ordered the Muslims to fast the ninth and the tenth of Muharram. This is nothing but a flagrant lie. The Jews live among us[4] and we never heard that they have an Eid during which they fast and which they call Ashura!

We may even wonder why our Lord made that day a blessed Eid for all His prophets and messengers, from Adam to Moses, with the exception of Muhammad for whom it was a day of tragedy, a day of mourning, a day of bad omen, a day when his offspring, his Progeny, were slaughtered as animals are slaughtered, when his daughters were taken captive... The answer is:

"He is not asked about what He does, while they shall be asked" (Holy Qur'an, 21:23).

"But whoever disputes with you in this matter, after the knowledge that has come to you, say: Come: let us call our sons and your sons, our women and your women, and ourselves and yourselves, then let us earnestly pray, invoking Allah to curse the liars." (Holy Qur'an, 3:61)

---

[4] The author is from Tunisia where a good number of Jews have been living for centuries. Tr.

5. "AHLUL SUNNAH WAL JAMA'AH" AND THE CURTAILED PRAYER

In a previous chapter, we quoted a verse referring to invoking Allah's prayers unto the Prophet and his progeny, and we also quoted its explanation as provided by the Prophet himself and how he taught people how to make a complete invocation, prohibiting them from using the curtailed one which Allah, the most Exalted One, rejects.

Yet we find a great deal of stubbornness from the side of "Ahlul Sunnah wal Jama'ah" who insist on eliminating any reference to Muhammad's Progeny from such an invocation. If they do reluctantly mention them, they include with them (in the invocation) the *sahabah* all of them. If you say before any of them: *Salla Allahu alaihi wa aalih* (Allah blesses him and his progeny), he will immediately understand that you are a Shi`a. This is so due to the fact that the complete invocation unto Muhammad and the progeny of Muhammad has become the identifying mark of only the Shi'as.

This is a fact which cannot be refuted. I employed it at the inception of my research, identifying each writer as a Shi`a whenever I find him saying *Salla Allahu alaihi wa alihi wa sallam* (Allah blesses him and his progeny and greets them all) after making a reference to Muhammad.

In its absence, I conclude that the writer is a Sunni. I also conclude that a certain writer is a Shi`a when he says: *Ali alaihis-salam* "Ali, peace be upon him," rather than *Ali karrama Allahu wajhah*, as is the case with Sunni writers.

From the complete invocation, I see how the Shi'as have followed the sacred Prophet's Sunnah *versus* "Ahlul Sunnah wal Jama'ah" who disobeyed the orders of the Prophet and did not honor them in the least. You find them all uttering the curtailed invocation, and when they feel obligated to add to it the reference to Muhammad's Progeny, they add to them the companions all of them without any exception so that they do not leave any merit or exclusive feat for Ahlul Bayt whatsoever.

All this has resulted from the stand adopted by the Umayyads *versus* Ahlul Bayt and to the enmity which they had against them, the one that in the end caused them to substitute the invocation to Allah to bless Ahlul Bayt with one invoking Him to curse them. They kept doing so even from the pulpits, forcing people to do so by all means.

But "Ahlul Sunnah wal Jama'ah" did not follow the Umayyads' custom of cursing Ahlul Bayt. Had they done so, the truth about them would have been revealed to the Muslims, and they would have been known as they are, and people would have dissociated themselves from them.

So they abandoned the custom of cursing and abusing Ahlul Bayt, keeping to themselves the animosity and hatred towards Ahlul Bayt. They tried their best to put their light out by raising the status of their enemies from the *sahabah*. For the latter they invented imaginary feats which have no relevance at all to the truth.

What proves this fact is that you can find "Ahlul Sunnah wal Jama'ah," even in our time, refraining from saying anything against Mu`awiyah and the *sahabah* who cursed Ahlul Bayt for eighty years. Rather, they invoke Allah to be pleased with all of them. At the same time, they label as *kafir* any Muslim who discredits any of the *sahabah*, issuing *fatawa* permitting his murder...

Some fabricators tried to add something else to the complete invocation, the one which the Messenger of Allah taught to his companions, another part, thinking that it would further undermine the status of Ahlul Bayt. One narrator quoted the Prophet saying, "Say: O Allah! Bless Muhammad, the Progeny of Muhammad, his wives and offspring." The researcher is of the view that this part was added in order to include Ayesha among Ahlul Bayt.

We say to them: If we, for the sake of argument, suppose that this "tradition" is authentic and that it implies the inclusion of the mothers of the faithful, the *sahabah* still have nothing to do with Ahlul Bayt! I personally challenge any Muslim to produce one proof from the Qur'an or from the Sunnah backing his view, for surely the heaven are more within his reach than that.

Both the Qur'an and the Sunnah have mandated all the companions as well as all other Muslims who follow those *sahabah* till the Day of Judgment to send blessings unto Muhammad and the Progeny of Muhammad. This by itself is a great status compared to which any other status falls short, and compared to which nothing else comes close.

Abu Bakr, Umar, Uthman, and all the companions of the Prophet, as well as all the Muslims of the world who are counted by the billions, do, indeed, invoke Allah to bless Muhammad and his Progeny whenever they make their *tashahhud*; otherwise, their prayers will be rejected by Allah, Glory to Him.

This is exactly the meaning of a verse of poetry Imam al-Shafi`i composed and the rough translation of which is as follows:

Suffices you (O Ahlul Bayt!) of a great import,

Whoever does not bless you, his prayer is void.

Al-Shafi`i was accused of the "crime" of being a Shi`a because of having said so. Henchmen of the Umayyads and the Abbasides accuse anyone of being a Shi`a if he blesses Muhammad and the Progeny of Muhammad or who praises them in a verse of poetry or points out to one of their feats.

At any rate, researching this subject is quite exhaustive, and it may be dealt with repeatedly in many books. There is no harm in repetition so long as it benefits the reader.

What is important is that we have come to know from this chapter that the Shi'as are the ones who follow the Prophet's Sunnah and that their prayers are complete and accepted even according to the views of those who oppose them. "Ahlul Sunnah wal Jama'ah," on the other hand, have violated in this regard the clear Sunnah of the Prophet, and their prayers are curtailed and are not accepted even according to the views of their own Imams and scholars.

"Or do they envy the people for what Allah has granted them of His grace? Indeed We have given Abraham's children the Book and wisdom, and We have given them a great kingdom." (Holy Qur'an, 4:54)

PROPHET'S INFALLIBILITY AND ITS IMPACT ON AHLUL SUNNAH WAL JAMA'AH

The belief that the Prophet was infallible is a topic about which Muslims differ with one another. It is, however, the only factor that makes it compulsory on the Muslims to accept the Prophet's injunctions without any discussion or argument, especially since they believe that he does not speak out of his own desire but conveys the revelation from His Lord. They, otherwise, would not believe that the Prophet's statements and injunctions, beyond the text of the Holy Qur'an, are binding; instead, they are matters relevant to his own *ijtihad*.

But if they do uphold such a belief, feeling convinced that all affairs are referred to Allah, and that the Prophet is only a means to convey and to explain such affairs, they would then be Shi'as. Many *sahabah* came to be widely recognized as having adopted such a conviction.

These are headed by Imam Ali, peace be upon him, who would not alter the Sunnah of the Prophet in the least, who regarded it as Allah's revelation; so, nobody can resort to his own personal view and *ijtihad* in the presence of the injunctions of Allah, Glory and Exaltation are His.

But if they believe that the Prophet is not infallible in his statements and actions, that infallibility is relevant only to the Holy Qur'an, and that besides all of that the Prophet is not different from any other human being: once he is right and once he is wrong.

If they uphold such a belief, they would be belonging to "Ahlul Sunnah wal Jama'ah" who say that it was alright for the *sahabah* and scholars to employ *itjihad*, even in the presence of the Prophet's statements and injunctions, and according to the dictates of the public interest, in the light of the circumstances, and according to the views of the ruler.

435

It needs no explanation that the righteous caliphs (with the exception of Imam Ali) did, indeed, follow their own personal views despite the presence of the Prophet's Sunnah. Then they went beyond that to apply the principle of *ijtihad* even in the presence of relevant Qur'anic texts. Their views, hence, came to be identified by "Ahlul Sunnah wal Jama'ah" as binding injunctions (*ahkam*) which they require all Muslims to abide by them.

We have already discussed the *ijtihad* of Abu Bakr and Umar in our book *To be with the Truthful* and also in *Ask Those Who Know*, and we may write a book dedicated in its entirety to this subject, if Allah pleases.

We have also come to know that "Ahlul Sunnah wal Jama'ah" add other types of *ijtihad* to the two major sources of Islamic legislation, namely the Qur'an and the Sunnah, including the "sunnah" of both shaykhs (Abu Bakr and Umar), and the *sahabi*'s *ijtihad*. All of this is the result of their belief that the Prophet was not infallible, that he used to use his own judgment, and that some *sahabah* used to correct his views and make amends for his mistakes [*Astaghfirullah!*].

This clearly shows that "Ahlul Sunnah wal Jama'ah" allege that the Prophet was a faulty person...

Whether they know it or not, they, therefore, permit anyone to contradict or disobey him. Neither the Shari`a nor reason obligates anyone to obey a faulty person. In other words, as long as we think that such an individual is liable to err, we do not have to obey him. How can we obey what is wrong?

It also becomes clear to us, in contrast, that the Shi'as believe in the absolute infallibility of the Prophet, enforcing obedience to him because he is, from their viewpoint, is infallible. It is not permissible, the Shi'as advocate, to disobey him under any circumstance. Whoever contradicts and disobeys him does, in fact, contradict and disobey his Lord. It is to this principle that the Holy Qur'an refers in many verses such as these:

"And whatever the Prophet gives you, accept it, and from whatever he forbids you, stay away." (Holy Qur'an, 59:7)

"And obey Allah and the Prophet so that you may be shown mercy." (Holy Qur'an, 3:132)

"Say: If you love Allah, follow me: Allah will (then) love you and forgive your faults, and Allah is Forgiving, Merciful." (Holy Qur'an, 3:31)

There are many other such verses which obligate the Muslims to obey the Prophet and not to contradict him because he is infallible and does not convey except what he is required by Allah, Glory to Him, to convey.

This by necessity proves the fact that Shi'as are the ones who uphold the Prophet's Sunnah because of their belief that the Prophet is infallible and that following him is incumbent upon each and every Muslim. It also proves that "Ahlul Sunnah wal Jama'ah" are distant from the Prophet's Sunnah due to their belief that the Prophet is fallible and that disobeying him is permissible.

"(All) people were a single nation, then Allah raised prophets as bearers of glad tidings and as warners, and He revealed with them the Book with the truth so that it might judge between people in whatever they disputed, yet none except the very people who were given it differed about it even after clear arguments had (already) come to them, disputing among themselves; so Allah guided by His will those who believed to the truth about which they disputed, and Allah guides whomsoever He pleases to the Right Path." (Holy Qur'an, 2:213)

WITH DR. AL-MUSAWI AND HIS "AUTHENTICATION"

I met a group of educated youths at the house of a Brother in Islam to whom I was linked with ties of kinship and childhood memories. The meeting took place at a Paris suburb during a banquet he held on the occasion of a long awaited birth of a son, a newborn with whom Allah blessed him after an extended period of hopeful anticipation.

Our discussion revolved around the Shi'as and the Sunnis. Most of those present were Algerians who were very enthusiastically in support of the Islamic revolution [in Iran]. They were criticizing the Shi'as, repeating well known age-old myths. They differed among themselves. Some of them were fair minded persons who said that the Shi'as were their brethren, whereas there were others who charged the Shi'as with every misguidance, even preferring Christians over them.

When we dealt in depth with the discussion and deduction, some of them kept making fun of me, saying that I was one of those persons who were deceived by the glitter of the Iranian revolution. My friend tried to convince them that I was a well-known researcher and author of many books dealing with this same subject.

One of them, however, said that he had the proof which could never be repudiated. Suddenly everyone stopped speaking. I asked him what that proof was. He asked me to wait for a few minutes. Then he quickly went to his adjacent house and came back carrying a book titled *Al-Shi`a wal-Tasheeh* (*Shi'as and Authentication*) by Dr. Musa al-Musawi. I laughed when I saw the book and said, "Is this the proof which cannot be repudiated?!" He turned to those present and said:

The author of this book is the greatest Shi`a scholar, one of the highest Shi`a authorities. He has a certificate in *ijtihad*; his father and grandfather are also scholars. Yet he recognized the truth and renounced Shi`ism, becoming one of Ahlul Sunnah wal Jama'ah. And I am confident that had this Brother (meaning myself) read this book, he would not have defended the Shi'as at all, and he would have come to know about what they hide and about their deviation.

Again I laughed and said to him, "So that you may know that I did, indeed, read it as a scrutinizing researcher, I will provide you, before everyone present here, the proof which cannot be repudiated from the book itself and which you have just brought!" He and everyone else present eagerly said, "Let us hear it from you."

I said, "I do not remember the exact page number, but I do remember the title very well which is `What Shi`a Imams say about the Righteous Caliphs.'" He asked me, "And what is wrong with it?" I said, "Look for it and read it before everybody, then I will explain to you the irrevocable proof it contains."

He found the chapter and read it to those present. Its summary is that Imam Ja`far al-Sadiq, peace be upon him, used to express pride at being a relative of Abu Bakr "al-Siddiq," saying, "Abu Bakr begot me twice." Those who quote this statement narrate saying that Imam al-Sadiq, on the other hand, used to discredit Abu Bakr.

Dr. al-Musawi comments by saying, "Is it rational for Imam al-Sadiq to brag about his grandfather [Abu Bakr] on one hand then discredits him on the other? Such talk is not coming from an ordinary ignorant person but from an Imam."

Everyone asked, "Where is the proof in all of this?! It sounds reasonable and logical." I said, "Dr. al-Musawi concluded from Imam al-Sadiq's statement that Abu Bakr begot him twice that he used to be very proud of his grandfather, but such a statement does not indicate at all that it contains any praise of Abu Bakr. Add to this the fact that Imam al-Sadiq was not a direct grandson of Abu Bakr but only his mother's grandfather was Abu Bakr. Keep in mind that Imam al-Sadiq was born seventy years after the death of Abu Bakr; so, he never saw him."

They said, "We do not understand what you mean by that." I said, "What would you say about someone who brags about his immediate grandfather, the father of his father, saying that he is the most knowledgeable man of his time, and that history never knew a match for him, then he says that he studied and learned from him: is it reasonable for us to expect him to discredit him after having thus praised him? Can a rational person brag about someone on one hand then call him *kafir* on the other?!" They all said, "No, this is not reasonable, and it cannot be."

I then said, "Read what is written on the first page of the book in your hand. You will see that Dr. al-Musawi is that same person!" He read the following:

I was born and raised at the home of the greatest leader of the Shi`a sect, and I studied and learned at the hands of the greatest scholar and religious authority the history of Shi`ism has ever known from the time of the Great Occultation till our time: He is the greatest Imam Sayyid Abul-Hasan al-Musawi about whom it is said, "He made people forget those before him and eclipsed those who came after him."

I said, "All Praise is due to Allah Who has manifested the truth through the words of al-Musawi himself!

He personally indicted himself when he wondered: `Is it rational for someone to brag about his grandfather on one hand then discredit him on the other? Such talk comes only from an ordinary ignorant person...' One who describes his grandfather with such great merits which did not combine in anyone else among genius scholars, claiming that he learned at his hands and derived his knowledge from him, then he turns to discredit him and his creed, cannot be anyone but an ordinary ignorant person."

Everyone lowered his head, whereas my friend and host felt excited and said, "Did I not tell you that Brother al-Tijani is an objective and logical researcher?!"

The person who had the book with him, and who was making the most noise, contemplated for some time then said, "Listen, Brother! Maybe Dr. al-Musawi came to know the truth after growing up and learning. Glory to Allah! Seek knowledge from the cradle to the grave!" I answered him by saying, "Had the case been as you say, Dr. al-Musawi should have disowned his grandfather and mentor who granted him his certificate of *ijtihad*, rather than his bragging about them and building an argument based on their testimony while, at the same time, unknowingly calling them *kafirs*. If I discuss all the topics he wrote about, I will show you wonders."

That meeting terminated after explanations and details provided about the nature of the confusion. Its results, by the Praise of Allah, were very positive: three persons saw the light of truth after reading my books.

Now I seize the opportunity to briefly present my kind readers with some of what I have written about this topic because the book titled *Al-Shi`a wal-Tasheeh* is effective wherever there are Wahhabis. The latter have the wealth and the influence in some areas; therefore, they may be able to influence some Muslim youths who are not familiar with the Shi'as and deceive them with this book. They may stop them from arriving at useful researches and may thus install a barrier between them and the truth they seek.

These opponents have used the book titled *Al-Shi`a wal-Tasheeh* by Dr. Musa al-Musawi as their argument against the Shi'as, printing millions of its copies and distributing them free of charge among educated youths through the efforts of authorities whose goals and objectives are very well known to the elite as well as to the commoners.

These naive people thought that they refuted the beliefs of Imamite Shi'as by publishing and distributing a book simply because its author is Ayatullah al-Musawi, a Shi`a, so that their argument would be built on citing someone from the Shi`a folks themselves. But these poor souls have overlooked many issues which they did not calculate and whose negative results they could not assess. The result: a great deal of self-inflicted harm.

Personally, I do not waste my time in rebutting Dr. Musa al-Musawi's lies with which he filled his book. I think that my book *Ma`a al-Sadiqin (To be with the Truthful)* contains convincing responses to his lies although it was written shortly before his own book and its context was simply to prove that Shi`a beliefs are all based on the Holy Qur'an and the authentic Sunnah of the Prophet, as well as the consensus of the Muslims, including "Ahlul Sunnah wal Jama`ah." We did not discuss any of their beliefs without proving it from the *Sahih* books of "Ahlul Sunnah wal Jama`ah."

It is thus proven that what Dr. Musa al-Musawi says is nothing but nonsense and allegations which are not based on any scientific proof or Islamic logic, and it discredits Ahlul Sunnah before all others.

It also is quite clear that those who promoted his book do not know much about Islamic facts, thus unveiling their own faults and ignorance.

All Shi`a beliefs the author of this book criticizes and which he uses to slander the Shi'as, are all, by the Grace of Allah, backed by the authentic books of "Ahlul Sunnah wal Jama`ah." The shame is not on the Shi'as but on Musa al-Musawi and "Ahlul Sunnah wal

Jama'ah" who do not know what their *Sahih* and *Musnad* books contain. Consider the following:

Reference to the subject of Imamate and to the *ahadith* saying that the successors to the Prophet are twelve and are all from Quraysh is not an invention of the Shi'as; it exists in Sunni *Sahih* and *Musnad* books;

The belief in Imam al-Mahdi, that he belongs to the purified Progeny of the Prophet, who will fill the earth with justice and equity after its being filled with injustice and oppression, is not a Shi`a invention but exists in the *Sahih* books of "Ahlul Sunnah wal Jama'ah."

Saying that Imam Ali ibn Abu Talib is the *wasi* of the Messenger of Allah is not a Shi`a invention but exists in the *Sahih* books of "Ahlul Sunnah wal Jama`ah."

The belief in and the practice of the concept of *taqiyya* is not a Shi`a invention; rather, it exists in the Holy Qur'an and is fixed in the Prophet's Sunnah, and all of this is backed by the *Sahih* books of "Ahlul Sunnah wal Jama'ah."

The belief in the legality of temporary marriage (*mut`a*) is not a Shi`a invention; rather, Allah and His Messenger permitted it whereas Umar prohibited it. This is proven by the authentic books of "Ahlul Sunnah wal Jama'ah."

The belief in the payment of the *khums* levied from profit earnings is not a Shi`a invention; rather, the Book of Allah and the Sunnah of His Messenger mandate it as the *Sahih* books of "Ahlul Sunnah wal Jama'ah" testify.

As for visiting the shrines of the Imams, this is not done by the Shi'as alone; "Ahlul Sunnah wal Jama'ah" visit the shrines of righteous *walis* and other good people, holding in their honor annual festivals and celebrations.

The belief in the *badaa* and that Allah obliterates or confirms whatever He pleases is not the product of the Shi'as' imagination; rather, it is confirmed in Bukhari's *Sahih*.

To combine the prayers in exceptional situations is not an invention of the Shi'as; it exists in the Holy Qur'an; it was practiced by the great Prophet, and it is confirmed by the *Sahih* books of "Ahlul Sunnah wal Jama'ah."

To believe in the obligation of prostrating on the dust and on the ground is not a Shi`a invention; rather, it was done by the Master of Messengers and the Seal of Prophets as testified by the *Sahih* books of "Ahlul Sunnah wal Jama`ah."

Besides these issues which Dr. Musa al-Musawi mentions in order to blow things out of proportions and to make a fuss, such as the rumor of the distortion of the Qur'an, "Ahlul Sunnah wal Jama'ah" deserve to be charged with it rather than the Shi'as, as we explained in our book *To be with the Truthful*.

To sum up, the book written by Dr. al-Musawi entirely contradicts the Book of Allah and the Sunnah of His Messenger. It contradicts the Muslims' consensus as well as the dictates of sound reason. A great deal of what al-Musawi resents constitutes religious obligations mandated by the Holy Qur'an and ordered by the great Messenger of Allah. These obligations, moreover, are agreed upon by all Muslims. One who denies them is an apostate according to the consensus of the Muslims.

If he means by "authentication" the altering of such beliefs and injunctions, he will then have committed *kufr* and abandoned Islam altogether, and all Muslims are required to denounce him.

He probably means by it the altering of his own personal beliefs from whose complexes he suffers. Such complexes clearly demonstrate that he really does not know anything about Shi`ism. Or he may have had a personal grudge against the Shi'as whom he considers to be responsible for the murder of his father who, as he says on p. 5 of his book, was slaughtered by a criminal in religious garbs as a ram is slaughtered. So he grew up since his childhood suffering from that complex, bearing grudge against the Shi'as without their having committed any sin.

He, therefore, directed his attention towards "Ahlul Sunnah wal Jama'ah" and shared their grudge and animosity towards the followers of Ahlul Bayt. He, in fact, never in reality belonged either to this party or to that. He did not know anything about the Shi'as except the lies circulated by their enemies. Nor did he know about "Ahlul Sunnah wal Jama'ah" except their Friday and congregational prayers, that is to say, if he ever attended them. If his objective is as such, then he ought to correct his corrupt beliefs whereby he differed from the consensus of the nation.

As he claims on p. 5 of his book, Dr. al-Musawi grew up and learned at the hands of the greatest leader and theologian known in the history of Shi`ism since the Major Occultation, namely his grandfather the greatest Imam Sayyid Abul-Hasan about whom it is said that "he made people forget those before him and eclipsed those who succeeded him." If such is the case, why did he not learn from him and adorn himself with his manners? Why did he not follow his guidance and nourish his mind with his knowledge?

Rather, we find him in his book deriding and ridiculing the beliefs of his grandfather, the Imam and the leading religious authority of his time for whom the history of the Shi'as never saw a match. All this proves that the al-Musawi was disobedient to his parents. Actually, his disobedience went beyond that to include calling his grandfather as well as parents *kafir*. Had the Shi'as been *kafir*, as al-Musawi sees them, then their authority and greatest leader who led them to *kufr* was none other than his own grandfather (who is surely clear of this accusation).

It is a shame beyond which there is no other shame that the grandson Musa al-Musawi should be ignorant of what his grandfather Abul-Hasan al-Musawi, may Allah have mercy on his soul, wrote in his book *Waseelat al-Najat* (the means to salvation). Yet the grandson claims that he learned and was tutored by grandfather!

And it is a great shame that a young Tunisian man who lives thousands of kilometers away from Najaf[1] should be more familiar with the book titled *Waseelat al-Najat*: he finds through it guidance to the facts relevant to Ahlul Bayt. In contrast, the grandson of the author of this book, who was born and who grew up in his house and was tutored by him [as he claims], never did.

What the greatest Imam Sayyid Abul-Hasan al-Musawi al-Isfahani (may Allah sanctify his soul) wrote in *Waseelat al-Najat* is contradicted and ridiculed by his grandson Dr. Musa al-Musawi. The latter regarded it as deviation from the path of Islam.

Yet logic says that if the doctrine of the greatest Imam and the religious authority, for whom the history of the Shi'as never found a match (as his grandson thinks), is sound and accurate, the doctrine of the grandson is apostasy and misguidance.

And had the doctrine upheld by Dr. Musa al-Musawi been sound and accurate, the doctrine of his grandfather should have been apostasy and misguidance. In the latter case, he has to disown him rather than brag about him and make such glowing reference to his being raised by him as he states in the Introduction to his book.

Through this argument and logic can the highly coveted certificate earned by Musa al-Musawi from al-Kashif al-Ghita be thrown out for the following reasons:

---

[1] Here, the author is referring to himself. Tr.

FIRST: The photograph he included in his book of a statement testifying to his having earned a high degree of Islamic *fiqh*, namely the degree of *ijtihad*, is no more than a license relevant to the traditions the student had learned from his teacher; it is given by mentors to most of their students. I personally have two such certificates: one from [the late] Grand Ayatullah Abul-Qasim al-Khu'i of Najaf, and the other from [the late] Grand Ayatullah al-Mar`ashi al-Najafi of Qum.

So, a certificate in narrating *hadith* is not an advanced degree in Islamic *fiqh* as Dr. Musa al-Musawi claims in order to fool the commoners among his readers who do not know the system and the stages relevant to the studies conducted at scholarly *hawzas*.

SECOND: The grandson of one of the greatest scholars, who feigns the ability to correct others, has betrayed the trust with which he was entrusted by his teacher and mentor who, al-Musawi claims, granted him the degree of *ijtihad*.

The late supreme religious authority and head of the scholarly *hawza* of al-Najaf al-Ashraf Muhammad al-Husayn al-Kashif al-Ghita has said the following with regard to the certificate a photo of which is published in al-Musawi's book: "I [hereby] grant him permission to quote the authentic traditions which I had myself learned from my great mentors and revered professors [and which I taught him]."

We have seen how al-Musawi rebuts and ridicules everything narrated by al-Kashif al-Ghita, the supreme religious authority and the head of the scholarly *hawza* who cites his great mentors and revered professors in his [al-Ghita's] book *Asl al-Shi`a wa Usuliha* (*Roots and Principles of the Shi'as*). In that book, the author states all the beliefs and injunctions to which the Shi'as adhere. So how can anyone compare the book titled *Al-Shi`a wal-Tasheeh* which his betraying student wrote with the book titled *Asl al-Shi`a wa*

Usuliha which the supreme religious authority Kashif al-Ghita wrote?

Since Kashif al-Ghita is the supreme religious authority and the head of the scholarly *hawza* at al-Najaf al-Ashraf, as al-Musawi admits on p. 158 of his book, and since al-Musawi brags about the lofty certificate he earned from him thirty years ago, why does not the junior student al-Musawi ridicule the beliefs of his great professor who taught him and, as he claims, granted him a lofty certificate?!

If the supreme religious authority and the head of the scholarly *hawza* Shaykh Muhammad al-Husayn al-Kashif al-Ghita is right and his beliefs are accurate, al-Musawi is then wrong and all his beliefs are false. Had the supreme religious authority been wrong and his beliefs inaccurate, so al-Musawi ridicules and rebuts them, then the latter should not have told lies to people and deceived them into thinking that he had earned his high certificate in Islamic *fiqh*, that is, the degree of *ijtihad*, from his holiness.

The beliefs of Musa al-Musawi are labelled as accurate only by the author himself who says so in his book. He lauds his grandfather Abu al-Hasan al-Musawi al-Isfahani as the greatest leader and theologian known in the history of Shi`ism since the Major Occultation. He brags of being the student of Kashif al-Ghita whom he describes as the man who granted him his "high degree." And he labels millions of Shi'as from the day of the Saqifa till our time as "*kafir*."

I had promised my Lord to examine every issue before judging it. I, therefore, read Musa al-Musawi's book *Al-Shi`a wal-Tasheeh* with all my faculties in the hope I might find in it what I had missed and complete what was lacking in my knowledge. But I found nothing in it except lies and contradictions and the denial of what is already confirmed by the text of the Holy Qur'an.

I even found it ridiculing the Sunnah of the Prophet and violating the consensus of the Muslims. I then realized that al-Musawi did not exert any effort to even read al-Bukhari's *Sahih* which is held by "Ahlul Sunnah wal Jama'ah" as the most authentic of all books. Al-Musawi, according to his book, wants the Shi'as to join the ranks of "Ahlul Sunnah wal Jama'ah" and thus forsake the commandments of Allah and His Messenger.

This "brilliant scholar" earned a "high certificate" in Islamic jurisprudence, namely that of *ijtihad*, at the age of twenty (Praise to Allah Who grants wisdom to whomsoever He pleases!) followed by a Ph.D. in Islamic Legislative System (Shari`a) from Tehran University in 1955. Do not forget that he was born in al-Najaf al-Ashraf in 1930. He also earned his Doctorate of Philosophy from Paris University (the Sorbonne) in 1959.

I say: Had he taken time to read only al-Bukhari's *Sahih*, a book regarded by "Ahlul Sunnah wal Jama'ah" as quite reliable, he would not have fallen in such a dilemma from which he will never find any exit except by sincerely repenting, and by returning to Allah. Otherwise, high degrees, attractive titles, and money spent to divide the Muslims will not avail him in the least. Allah, the most Exalted One, has said,

"Surely those who disbelieve spend their wealth (only) to hinder (people) from the way of Allah; so they shall spend it, then it shall be to them (the cause of) an intense regret, then they shall be overtaken; and those who disbelieve shall all be driven to hell so that Allah might separate the impure from the pure and put the impure upon one another and pile it up together then cast it into hell: These are the losers." (Holy Qur'an, 8:36-37)

His book, anyway, is full of self-contradictions in which any researcher stumbles. If al-Musawi finds himself qualified to correct the beliefs and *ahkam* of those who adhere to Shi`ism, I invite him to a televised interview and to a scholarly debate attended by any researcher or verifier who wishes to attend so that people may come to know after it who really needs to be corrected. This is what the Holy Qur'an calls for and what free thinking in the most civilized societies encourages so that the Muslims will see their affairs clearly and will cease charging some people, out of sheer ignorance, of being *kafir* then repent thereafter.

"Say: Bring your proof if you are truthful." (Holy Qur'an, 2:111)

One thing remains to state so that we may be fair to Dr. al-Musawi. It is the reference he makes in his book to these subjects for which he provides three major headings:

1. Self-flagellation during Ashura
2. The third part of *Shahada* (that Ali is a servant of Allah)
3. Terrorism

As for self-flagellation, it is not one of the doctrines of the Shi'as, nor is it a part of their creed. Rather, it is what some commoners do, and Shi'as are not the only ones who practice it. There are some Sunnis, particularly those who follow the [sufi] Aysawi *tareeqa*, which is well known throughout all of north Africa, who practice rituals more damaging to Islam's image than what some Shi'as do. Yet by practicing them they do not express their grief for the tragedy that befell Imam al-Husayn, nor for the suffering of Ahlul Bayt, peace be upon them.

We agree with the author's statement in his book in this regard, and we would like to work with him to remove this phenomenon from all Muslim lands. There are many sincere Shi`a scholars who prohibit such an abomination and try hard to put an end to it, as al-Musawi himself admits.

As for the third portion of the declaration of faith, that is, that Ali is a friend of Allah, al-Musawi himself knows very well that Shi`a scholars always say that it is not a part of the *azan*. If one says it with the intention of its being obligatory or with the intention of its being part of the *azan* or the *iqama*, both his *azan* and *iqama* will be void. Al-Musawi knows this fact very well, but he only wishes to make a fuss about anything that serves his suspicious objective.

Regarding terrorism, we categorically reject it just as Dr. al-Musawi rejects it. Yet it was not appropriate for Dr. al-Musawi to attach this horrible charge to the Shi'as, for the wave of terrorism which has stamped the past decade with its seal is an inevitable result of the ongoing struggle between the East and the West, the North and the South, the arrogant ones and the downtrodden, the usurpers and those whose lands and everything else were usurped.

Why does Dr. al-Musawi link drug traffickers to the Shi'as? History testifies that the Shi'as have been targeted throughout history by followers of all other sects, by various governments, and by the colonizers, yet they have always rejected terrorism in all its forms and shapes.

Why does al-Musawi not talk about the terrorism of Mu`awiyah and the assassinations which he staged to eliminate many Muslims and which culminated with poisoning Imam al-Hasan? He used to always assassinate his opponents from truthful believers with poison then says, "Surely Allah has hosts made of honey."

Are promoters of world Islamic movements, who have been described [by the enemies of Islam, including governments of Muslim countries] as "terrorists," in Palestine, Egypt, the Sudan, Tunisia, Algeria, Afghanistan, and even in Western countries, in the Pacific, in Ireland, and elsewhere, adhere to the Shi`a faith?!

If Dr. al-Musawi defines "terrorism" as the kidnapping of hostages or the rerouting then blowing up of airplanes, freedom fighters from the Palestinian people, who have been displaced and expelled by Israel after being forced out of their homes, are the ones who kidnapped hostages at the Munich stadium at the beginning of the 1972 Olympic sports and killed a number of Israeli participants in them.

They are the ones who rerouted some airplanes then blew them up. They did all of this in order to wake up the world's conscience and to introduce their case to the world and make them aware of the oppression inflicted upon them and the like of which humanity never saw throughout its entire history.

Al-Musawi bears witness that these are not Shi'as. If Dr. al-Musawi permits himself to be influenced by those who run the foreign news media and who try their best to attach this horrible accusation to the Shi'as because of the political stand and the extreme animosity of such media to the Islamic Revolution (of Iran), the same media apparatuses include on the top of their list of international terrorists Libya, Syria, and Iraq, and these are not necessarily Shi`a countries.

So why does Dr. al-Musawi specifically singles out the Shi'as when he discusses terrorism in his book? He himself says on p. 122 that the Shi`a government of Iran does not represent all the Shi'as of the world or even of Iran. If the case is as such, then Dr. al-Musawi has to correct his own concepts.

Thus do we do justice to Dr. al-Musawi and distinguish the truth from falsehood, the good from the bad.

We have proven to the kind readers the fact that all the beliefs upheld by Imamite Shi'as are accurate and sound because they are all derived from the Holy Qur'an and the Prophet's Sunnah. The attempts of those who have special interests, the trouble makers, the enemies of Allah, of His Messenger, and of Islam, to level false charges and to circulate false rumors in order to discredit the beliefs of those who uphold the Purified Progeny will fail and bear no fruit whatsoever. Allah, the Most Exalted One, has said,

"As for the scum, it passes away as a worthless thing; as for that which benefits people, it tarries in the earth; thus does Allah set parables." (Holy Qur'an, 13:17)

We plead to Him, the Glorified One, the most Exalted, to guide all of us and to enable us to achieve what He loves for us to achieve, to inspire to us the means of guidance, to remove His wrath from us, to dispel our agony with the presence of the Awaited One, and to hasten for us his reappearance. They see it distant, while we see it nigh.

And the last of our supplication is: "All Praise is due only to Allah, the Lord of the Worlds, and the best of prayers and the purest of salutations are unto the man who was sent as a mercy for all the worlds, our master and leader Muhammad and unto his righteous and purified Progeny.

GLOSSARY

Ahadith: plural of *hadith* (see below)

Ahkam: plural of *hukm*, a religious ruling, an injunction

Ansar: supporters, Muslims in Medina who supported Prophet Muhammad's cause

Aqeeq: carnelia stone

Ashura: the tenth day of the month of Muharram

Ayat: a Qur'anic verse; literally: a miracle

Bad'a: starting point, the very beginning of something, the onset

Bismillah: the pronouncement of *Bismillahir-Rahmanir-Rahim*

Bayt al-Mal: Islamic government's state treasury

Bid'a or *Bid'at:* an innovation in religion not based on the Qur'an or the Sunnah

Dinar: an Islamic (now Arab) gold currency varying in weight

Dirham: an Islamic silver currency weighing approx. 3.12 grams

Fajr: daybreak

Faqih: jurist, one who is knowledgeable in Islamic jurisprudence

Fatawa: plural of *fatwa*, a religious edict or decision

Fatwa: singular of *fatawa* (see above)

Fidya: blood money, montary compensation for either murder or a crime as serious as murder

Fiqh: the science of Islamic jurisprudence

Ghazwa: a military campaign, invasion in which Prophet Muhammad (s) participated.

455

Ghulat: plural of *ghali*, an extremist, one whose views and/or actions are excessive, the name of a renegade sect

Ghusul: ceremonial bath

Hadith: (singular; plural: *ahadith*) tradition, a statement made by Prophet Muhammad

Hafiz: singular of *huffaz*, one who learns and memorizes the entire text of the Holy Qur'an by heart *Hajib:* chamberlain, doorman

Hajj: Islamic pilgrimage to Mecca during the prescribed period

Halal: Islamically permissible, admissible, allowed

Haram: Islamically prohibitive, inadmissible, forbidden

Hawza: a university-type place for Islamic studies

Hijab: veil, curtain, barrier

Hijra: migration of Prophet Muhammad (P) and his supporters from Mecca to Medina

Huffaz: plural of *hafiz* (see *hafiz* above)

Ibtihal: supplication, invocation

Ijma`: a consensus view

Ijtihad: the degree one reaches in order to be qualified as a *mujtahid*, one who is capable of deriving religious decisions on his own

Imam: leader of an *ummah*, a group of people (small or big); he may be the one who leads others in congregational prayers, or a supreme relgious authority, or one of the Twelve Infallible Imams (as)

Iqama: the formal introduction to a daily prayer

Isnad: the method whereby one *hadith* is traced and in the end attributed to a *muhaddith*, traditionist, one who transmitted it the first time

Istihsan: highly recommending something to be acted upon, to be implemented, to be accepted as part of the creed

`*Itrat:* progeny (usually) of Prophet Muhammad

Jahiliyya: pre-Islamic period of ignorance

Janaba: uncleanness caused by seminal discharge

Jihad: a struggle, an effort exerted, or a war waged in defense of Islam

Kafir: infidel, apostate, atheist, one who does not believe in the existence of the Creator

Khalifa: caliph, supreme Islamic ruler

Khums: one-fifth of one's savings (now paid by Shi`a Muslims only) set aside from annual income

Khutba: lecture, sermon; a speech delivered on a specific occasion

Kufr: apostacy, infidelity, disbelief

Majlis: meeting or gathering held to commemorate certain religious occasion, mostly applied to those held during the month of Muharram or to recite the Fatiha for a deceased person; plural: *masalas*, places where people sit to meet on an important occasion

Maraji`:* plural of *marji` (see below)

Marji`: a high theological authority-referee whose religious edicts are followed others

*Marji`iyya:* the institute of following or imitating a marji` (see above)

457

Mawla: depending on its usage, it may mean either "master" or "slave," or it may mean one who is most fit for a specific position of honor and prestige. Derived from the adjective *awla* (one who is best qualified), it means: the person who is best suited to be the religious and temporal leader of all Muslims.

Mufti: a judge empowered to issue binding legal opinions relevant to the Islamic faith

Mujtahid: one who acquires the degree of *ijtihad* and thus becomes capable of deriving religious decisions on his own

Musnad: a compilation of traditions (*ahadith*) which are consecutively and chronologically traced to their transmitters

Mut`a: temporary marriage

Mutawatir: consecutively reported, traced by a perfect chronological chain of ascertained narrators of *hadith*

Nafl: also *nafila*: supererogatory, optional, non-compulsory, highly recommended act of worship

Najasa: uncleanness, impurity

Noor: divine or celestial light

Nubuwwah: the concept of prophethood or the belief in following a prophet

Qunoot: supplication performed usually during the second *rak'at* (see below)

Rak'at: unit of prayer. For example, fajr prayer has two *rak'ats*.

Ruku': Bowing down in prayer before prostration (*sajdah*)

Risala: published collection of religious rulings by a *marji`* (see above); literal meaning: letter, dissertation

Sahabah: (plural) companions of the Holy Prophet Muhammad (P)

Sahabi: singular of *sahabah* (see above)

Saheefa: tablet, scroll, parchment, a written document

Sahih: literally: authentic, correct, accurate; it is generally used to refer to the collection, group of collections, or book, of verified and authenticated *ahadith* of the Holy Prophet (pbuh)

Saqifa: a shed, a simply built structure with a roof (*saqf*)

Shahada: martyrdom, testimony

Shaykh: also *syakh*, an honoring title with many meanings; literally, it means an old man; in Islamic theology and philosophy, however, it is used to denote a mentor, professor, or scholar of a high calibre

Shari`a: Islam's legislative system

Shirk: polytheism, the belief in the existence of partners with God

Shura: the principle of mutual consultation, Islam's form of democracy

Sufi: an ascetic, a mystic

Sunan: plural of *sunnah*: a highly commended act of worship or way whereby a Muslim seeks nearness to Allah

Sura: a chapter of the Holy Qur'an

Tabi`i*: (singular:) one who accompanied for a good period of time and learned from a *sahabi*, a companion of the Holy Prophet Muhammad (pbuh); its plural is: *tabi`in

Tafsir: (singular): exegesis or explanation of Qur'anic verses; its plural is: *tafasir*

Takbir: the act of glorifying Allah by declaring in an audible voice: "Allaho Akbar!" Allah is Great!

Talbiya: the pronouncement of "*Labbayk!*" which means: "Here I am! At your service!"

Taleeq: An unconfined man of Mecca who remained heathen till the conquest of Mecca

Taqiyya: one's way of exerting precaution in order to save his life when it is in jeopardy, Shi'as' way of trying to survive against the presence of sure perils

Taqleed: the concept of following a *mujtahid* or an authority recognized as the *a`alam*, the most knowledgeable in Islamics

Taraweeh: prayers performed in congregation by Sunnis during the nights of the month of Ramadan

Tareeqa: a Sufi method of conducting rituals, a Sufi code of ritualistic religious conduct

Tawatur: consecutive reporting, the tracing of one particular *hadith* to its respective chronological chain of narrators

Tawhid: the concept of the absolute Unity of God, the belief that God is One and indivisible, One and Only God

Tayammum: the rubbing of the hands and the face with clean dust by someone who is either in the state of uncleanness or cannot find water or has no time to perform the ablution

Umra: the pilgrimage to Mecca during any time other than the prescribed (first ten) days of the month of Dhul-Hijjah

Usul: the basics of jurisprudence

Wahi: revelation through the medium of an archangel or divine inspiration

Wali: master, supreme authority combining in himself both temporal and religious authority

Wasi: trustee, executor of a will, regent, successor of a prophet

Wilayat: the following of a *wali* (see above)

Wudu: ablution

Zakat: Literally, it means "purification;" it is a compulsory 2.5% tax on one of three categories of wealth: 1) metal coins (gold, silver, etc.), 2) grain crops (barley, wheat, grain, rice, etc.), and 3) animals raised for food consumption. *Zakat* is somehow a complicated subject; for details, readers are advised to consult books dealing with *fiqh*. Among its types are: *zakat al-mal* (taxable wealth accumulated during one full year), and *zakat al-fitr* (a tax to be paid by the head of a household at the commencement of the fast of the month of Ramadan).

And surely Allah knows best...

BIBLIOGRAPHY

THE HOLY QUR'AN TAFSIR BOOKS

1. Al-Tafsir al-Kabir, by al-Fakhr al-Razi
2. Tafsir al-Tabari, by Muhammad ibn Jarir al-Tabari
3. Tafsir Ibn Kathir, by Ismail ibn Kathir
4. Tafsir al-Khazin, by Ali bin Ibrahim al-Khazin
5. Tafsir al-Suyuti, by Jalal al-Din al-Suyuti
6. Ahkam al-Qur'an, by Abu Bakr Ahmad bin Ali Al-Razi Al-Jassas
7. Tafsir al-Qurtubi, by Abu 'Abdullah Al-Qurtubi
8. Tafsir al-'Alusi, by Mahmud ibn 'Abdullah al-'Alusi
9. Tafsir Ghara'ib al-Qur'an, by Imam Hakim Nishapouri
10. Shawahid al-Tanzil, by al-Hakim al-Haskani
11. Al-Durr Al-Manthur Fi Tafsir Bil-Ma'thur, by Jalal al-Din al-Suyuti

HADITH BOOKS

1. Sahih al-Bukhari, by Imam Muhammad bin Ismail Al-Bukhari
2. Sahih Muslim, by Imam Muslim ibn al-Hajjaj
3. Sahih al-Tirmidhi, by Muhammad ibn 'Isa as-Sulami al-Tirmidhi
4. Sahih al-Nasa'i, by Ahmad ibn Shu'ayb Sinan al-Nasa'i
5. Sahih Ibn Majah, by Imam Muhammad bin Yazid Ibn Majah
6. Sahih Abu Dawud, by Imam Abu Dawud Sulayman ibn al-Ash'ath
7. Mustadrak al-Hakim, by Imam Hakim Nishapouri
8. Musnad al-Imam Ahmad, by Ahmad Ibn Hanbal
9. Sunan al-Darimi, by 'Abdullah ibn `Abd al-Rahman al-Darimi
10. Sunan al-Daraqutni, by Abul-Hasan 'Ali ibn 'Umar Daraqutni

11. Sunan al-Bayhaqi, by Abu Bakr Ahmad ibn Husayn al-Bayhaqi

12. Muwatta al-Imam Malik, by Imam Malik ibn Anas

13. Tanwir al-hawalik, by Jalal Al-Din Abu Al-Fadl 'Abd Al-Rahman Suyuti

14. Khasa'is al-Nasa'i, by Ahmad ibn Shu'ayb Sinan al-Nasa'i

15. Kanz al-'Ummal, by al-Muttaqi al-Hindi

16. Muntakhab Kanz al-'Ummal, by Ahmad ibn Muhammad Ibn Hanbal

17. Minhaj al-Sunnah, by Taqi ad-Din Ahmad Ibn Taymiyyah

18. Al-Jami' al-Saghir, by Jalal al-Din al-Suyuti

19. Al-Jami' al-Kabir, by Jalal al-Din al-Suyuti

20. Jam' al-Jawami', by Jalal al-Din al-Suyuti

21. Usul al-Kafi, by Muhammad bin Ya'qub al-Kulayni

22. Basa'ir al-Darajat, by Abu Ja'far Muhammad al-Saffar

23. Mizan al-I'tidal fi Naqd al-Rijal, by Shams al-Din Muhammad al-Dhahabi

24. Lisan al-Mizan, by Ibn Hajar al-Asqalani

25. Al-lu'lu' wa al-marjan, by Imam Muhammad bin Ismail Al-Bukhari

26. Manaqib al-Shafi'i, by Abu 'Abdullah Muhammad ibn Idris al-Shafi'i

27. Manaqib Ahmad ibn Hanbal, by Imam Ahmad ibn Hanbal

28. Musannaf al-Hidayah, by Burhan al-Din al-Farghani al-Marghinani

HISTORY BOOKS

1. Tarikh Ibn 'Asakir, by Ali ibn al-Hasan Ibn `Asakir al-Shafi`i

2. Tarikh Baghdad, by Abu Bakr Ahmad al-Shafi`i al-Khatib al-Baghdadi

3. Tarikh al-khulafa', by Ibn Qutaybah al-Dinawari

4. Tarikh al-khulafa', by Jalal al-Din al-Suyuti

5. Tarikh al-Mada'ini, by 'Ali ibn Muhammad al-Mada'ini

6. Tarikh al-Waqidi, by Abu 'Abdullah Muhammad Waqid al-Aslami

7. Tarikh al-Tabari (al-Kabir), by Muhammad ibn Jarir al-Tabari

8. Tarikh Ibn al-'Athir (al-Kamil), by Ali ibn Muhammad al-'Athir

9. Tarikh al-Mas'udi, by 'Ali ibn al-Husayn al-Mas'udi

10. Tarikh A'tham al-Kufi, by Ahmad bin Ali Ibn A'tham Kufi

11. Tarikh Abu al-Fida, by Abu al-Fida Isma'il Ibn 'Ali

12. Tarikh al-Ya'qubi, by Ahmad ibn Ja'far al-Ya'qubi

BIOGRAPHY BOOKS

1. Al-Isaba fi Tamyiz al-Sahaba, by Ibn Hajar al-Asqalani

2. Usd al-Ghabah fi Ma'rifat al-Sahabah, by Ali ibn Muhammad al-'Athir

3. Al-Tabaqat al-Kubra, by Abu 'Abdullah Muhammad ibn Sa'd

4. Tabaqat al-Fuqaha', by Ibn Zanjuwih al-Nasa'i

5. Tabaqat al-Hanabilah, by Muhammad Ibn Abi Ya'la

6. Al-Milal wa al-Nihal, by Muhammad al-Shahristani

7. Al-'Iqd al-Farid, by Ibn 'Abd Rabbih

8. Al-Sawa'iq al-Muhriqah, by Ibn Hajar Al-Haytami

9. Al-Bidayah wa al-Nihayah, by Ismail ibn Kathir

10. Tadhkirat al-Huffaz, by Shams al-Din Abu 'Abdallah Ibn al-Dhahabi

11. Yanabi' al-Mawaddah, by Sulayman bin Ibrahim al-Qunduzi al-Hanafi

12. Fara'id al-Simtayn, by Ibrahim b Muhammad al-Hamwini

13. Maqaddimah Ibn Khaldun, by 'Abd ar-Rahman ibn Muhammad ibn Khaldun

14. Zuhr al-Islam, by Ahmad Amin

15. Manaqib al-Khwarazmi, by Muwaffaq bin Ahmad al-Khwarizmi

16. Shahr Nahj al-balaghah, by Ibn Abi al-Hadid al-Mu'tazili

17. Sharh Nahj al-balaghah, by Muhammad 'Abduh

18. A'lam al-muqi'in, by Ibn al-Qayyim al-Jawziyyah

19. Ansab al-Aashraf, by Ahmad Ibn Yahya al-Baladhuri

20. Al-'Isti'ab, by Yusuf ibn Abdullah Ibn 'Abd al-Barr

21. Al-Riyad al-Nadirah, by Muhibb Al-Din Ahmad Ibn 'Abd al-Tabari

22. Siyar a'lam al-nubala, by Shams al-Din Abu 'Abdallah Ibn al-Dhahabi

23. Talkhis al-Mustadrak, by Shams al-Din Abu 'Abdallah Ibn al-Dhahabi

OTHER REFERENCES

1. Taqyid al-ilm, by Abu Bakr Ahmad al-Shafi`i al-Khatib al-Baghdadi

2. Jami' bayan al-'ilm, by Yusuf Ibn Abdullah Ibn 'Abd al-Barr

3. Al-Silah bayn al-Tasawwuf wa al-Tashayyu', by Kamil Mustafa al-Shaybi

4. Ma'alim al-Madrasatayn, by Allamah Murtaza al-'Askari

5. Al-Fitnat al-Kubra, by Taha Husayn

6. Tahdhib al-Tahdhib, by Ibn Hajar al-Asqalani

7. Ahmad ibn Hanbal, by al-Shaykh Abu Zuhrah

8. Usul al-fiqh, by al-Shaykh Abu Zuhrah

9. Mulakhkhas ibtal al-qiyas, by 'Ali ibn Ahmad Ibn Hazm

10. Al-Nasa'ih al-Kafiyah, by Abu al-Wafa Ali Ibn 'Aqil

11. Rasa'il al-Khwarazmi, by Muhammad bin 'Abbas Abu Bakr al-Khawarizmi

12. Al-Mu'jam al-Kabir, by Al-Qasim Suleiman bin Ahmed al-Tabarrani

13. Fath al-Qadir, by Muhammad ibn Ali ibn Abdullah al-Shawkani

14. Al-Muhalla, by Ibn Hazm al-Zahiri

15. Al-Fatawa al-Wadihah, by Muhammad Baqir al-Sadr

16. Sharh al-Mawahib, by Muhammad al-Zurqani

17. Al-Muraja'at, by Sharaf al-Din al-Musawi al-Amili

18. Al-Nass wa al-Ijtihad, by Sharaf al-Din al-Musawi al-Amili

19. 'Abqariyyat Khalid, by 'Abbas al-'Aqqad

20. Al-Ihtijaj, by Ahmad bin Ali bin Abi Talib al-Tabrasi

21. Abu Hurayrah, by Mahmud Abu Riyyah

22. Fath al-Bari, by Ibn Hajar al-Asqalani

23. Maqalat al-Islamiyyin, by al-Hassan 'Ali bin Isma'il al-Ash'ari

24. Ta'wil Mukhtalif al-hadith, by 'Abdulluh ibn Muslim ibn Qutaybah

25. Ghayat al-maram, by Hashim bin Sulayman al-Bahrani

26. Al-Imam al-Sadiq, by al-Shaykh Abu Zuhrah

27. Jamharat Rasa'il al-'Arab, by Ahmed Zaki Safwat

28. Al-Sahabah fi nazar al-Shi'ah al-Imamiyyah, by Hamid Hafni Dawood

29. Kitab al-Kaba'ir, by Shams al-Din Abu 'Abdullah Ibn al-Dhahabi

30. Kitab al-Sarim al-maslul, by Taqi ad-Din Ahmad Ibn Taymiyyah

31. Kitab mu'in al-hukkam, by Ali ibn Khalil Tarabulusi al-Hanafi

32. Kitab talqih fuhum al-'athar, by Abd al-Rahman Ibn al-Jawzi

33. Ihya' 'Ulum al-Din, by Muhammad ibn Muhammad al-Ghazali

34. Nazariyyat al-Imamah, by Ahmad Mahmud Subhi

35. Al-Imam al-Sadiq wal Madhahib al-Arba`a by Shiekh Asad Hayder

36. Al-Nasaih al-Kafiya, by Ibn Aqeel

37. Abqariyyat Khalid, by Abbas Mahmud al-Aqqad

38. Tasheeh al-I`tiqad, by Shaykh al-Mufeed

39. Thumma Ihtadayt, by the author
40. Ma 'a al-Sadiqin, by the author
41. Fas'alu Ahl al-Dhikr, by the author

INDEX

A

A'lam al-Nubala, 290, 291
A'lam al-muqi'in, 166
aam al-huzn, 281
Aaron, 53, 149, 235, 252, 259
Abbas Mahmud al-Aqqad, 275
Abbaside, 8, 23, 27, 35, 52, 53, 57, 92, 115, 119, 124, 130, 133, 164, 187, 359, 360, 384, 386, 393, 394, 402
Abd al-Malik ibn Marwan, 172, 195, 358
Abd al-Muttalib, 240, 317
Abd al-Rahman ibn Mahdi, 331
Abd al-Rahman ibn Yazid, 229
Abdoos ibn Malik al-Attar, 386
Abdullah ibn Abbas, 122, 127, 150, 306, 320
Abdullah ibn Awn al-Basri, 98, 201
Abdullah ibn Mas`ud, 122, 127, 229, 230
Abdullah ibn Ruwahah, 284
Abdullah ibn Saba, 26, 77, 94
Abdullah ibn Ubayy, 379
Abdullah ibn Umar, 10, 55, 56, 58, 65, 68, 69, 70, 71, 93, 111, 122, 126, 127, 171, 194, 195, 196, 197, 210, 214, 230, 253, 299, 300, 301, 302, 303, 305, 306, 307, 308, 310, 311, 312, 313, 314, 315, 316, 334, 354, 387, 394, 402
Abdullah son of Umar, 315, 395
Abdul-Rahman ibn Awf, 9, 43, 70, 94, 214, 226, 227, 250, 254, 255, 261, 262, 263, 265, 266, 279, 304, 384, 396
Abqariyyat Khalid, 275
Abu Bakr, 9, 10, 22, 27, 34, 35, 40, 43, 45, 46, 47, 48, 49, 50, 51, 52, 56, 63, 68, 70, 71, 72, 73, 74, 84, 88, 93, 105, 106, 117, 126, 127, 145, 157, 164, 165, 168, 171, 195, 196, 203, 209, 210, 214, 215, 216, 217, 218, 219, 221, 224, 226, 227, 228, 229, 234, 235, 240, 242, 250, 254, 256, 260, 261, 263, 265, 266, 268, 271, 272, 280, 284, 285, 286, 295, 299, 300, 301, 302, 303, 304, 313, 314, 317, 330, 333, 336, 340, 344, 350, 351, 352, 353, 354, 355, 358, 359, 368, 371, 372, 384, 386, 396, 399, 407, 410, 413
Abu Dawud, 69, 300, 314
Abu Dharr al-Ghifari, 52, 87
Abu Hanifah, 34, 59, 91, 102, 109, 115, 128, 140, 160, 173, 187, 188, 278
Abu Hurayra, 9, 65, 67, 68, 69, 111, 117, 144, 214, 288, 289, 290, 291, 292, 293, 294, 295, 296, 297, 298, 314, 335, 375, 376, 377, 394, 395
Abu Ishaq Ka`b ibn Mati, 144
Abu Ja`far al-Mansour, 8, 118, 119, 120, 121, 123, 124, 125, 126, 127, 130, 131, 132, 133

Abu Juhayfa, 66
Abu Sa'id al-Khudri, 62
Abu Sufyan, 30, 31, 37, 80, 93, 107, 128, 202, 210, 258, 270, 281, 282, 304, 344, 351, 363, 375, 387
Abu Talib, 97, 98, 107, 135, 204, 244, 251, 256, 258, 281, 283, 352, 353
Abu Thawr, 173
Abu Thuayb, 131, 132, 133
Abu Turab, 30, 94, 95, 272, 293
Abu Ubaydah Amir al-Jarrah, 44
Abu Ubaydah Amir ibn al-Jarrah, 94
Abu Ya'li al-Farraa, 386
Abu Yusuf, 115
Abul Fida, 265
Abul-Abbas al-Saffah, 57
Abul-Hasan al-Ash'ari, 115
Abyssinia, 371
Afghanistan, 425
ahkam, 103, 299, 323, 410, 423
Ahkamal-Qur'an, 230
Ahlul Bayt, 9, 10, 14, 23, 24, 26, 27, 30, 31, 32, 36, 57, 58, 65, 75, 77, 83, 84, 85, 86, 88, 89, 91, 96, 98, 102, 107, 108, 109, 110, 111, 116, 125, 135, 138, 139, 140, 143, 144, 146, 150, 154, 155, 157, 158, 163, 171, 176, 180, 181, 183, 198, 201, 202, 203, 204, 205, 206, 207, 208, 210, 252, 260, 273, 289, 301, 303, 313, 320, 321, 322, 328, 331, 333, 336, 338, 339, 358, 359, 360, 362, 366, 382, 387, 394, 395, 398, 399, 400, 401, 402, 403, 406, 407, 419, 420, 424
Ahlul Sunnah wal Jama'ah, 7, 8, 9, 10, 11, 18, 28, 34, 35, 36, 37, 48, 52, 55, 56, 58, 59, 64, 72, 74, 75, 77, 78, 79, 80, 82, 83, 85, 88, 90, 91, 92, 93, 95, 97, 101, 103, 107, 108, 127, 128, 129, 134, 138, 139, 140, 141, 142, 144, 147, 151, 152, 154, 156, 160, 161, 164, 166, 168, 170, 171, 174, 181, 183, 187, 188, 189, 194, 196, 198, 200, 201, 203, 204, 205, 206, 207, 208, 209, 210, 212, 213, 214, 216, 218, 225, 233, 239, 250, 261, 267, 269, 273, 275, 280, 281, 282, 285, 287, 289, 297, 298, 299, 301, 303, 304, 310, 311, 313, 315, 322, 323, 324, 325, 326, 327, 328, 329, 330, 331, 332, 333, 336, 338, 340, 341, 344, 345, 356, 360, 362, 366, 367, 369, 370, 372, 374, 377, 378, 379, 380, 381, 382, 383, 384, 385, 386, 387, 388, 392, 393, 394, 395, 396, 398, 399, 400, 401, 402, 403, 405, 406, 408, 409, 410, 411, 413, 416, 417, 418, 419, 422, 423
Ahmad Ameen, 134
Ahmad ibn Abdul-Aziz al-Jawhari, 40
Ahmad ibn Hanbal, 34, 52, 53, 54, 55, 58, 69, 88, 91, 97, 102, 104, 106, 107, 110, 111, 114, 115, 116, 126, 133, 163, 173,

174, 194, 203, 272, 273, 300,
301, 310, 314, 368, 370, 400
Ahmad in Ibn Abbas, 41
Al Bidaya wal Nihaya, 204
Al-`Iqd al-Fareed, 48
al-A`tal, 101
Al-A`tham, 253
al-Alusi, 233
Al-Awsat, 208
al-Awza`i, 168
al-Azhar, 80, 82, 83
al-Baladhuri, 265, 308, 354
al-Bayhaqi, 163, 229, 305
Al-Bayhaqi, 229, 304, 308, 314, 331
al-bid`a al-hasana, 117
Al-Bidaya wal Nihaya, 204, 205, 291
al-Bukhari, 39, 41, 49, 51, 55, 56, 63, 65, 66, 68, 69, 71, 87, 100, 104, 105, 118, 181, 194, 196, 216, 224, 241, 262, 263, 285, 295, 297, 300, 314, 315, 323, 334, 335, 343, 370, 379, 422, 423
al-Daraqutni, 208
Al-Daraqutni, 203
al-Darimi, 69
Al-Darimi, 331
Al-Daylami, 208
Al-Dhahabi, 104, 105, 145, 170, 203, 333, 334, 367
Al-Durr al-Manthur, 321
al-Fakhr al-Razi, 217, 326
Al-Fakhr al-Razi, 151, 326
Al-Fatawa al-Wadiha, 159
Al-Fitna al-Kubra, 237, 241, 244
Al-Fitnat al-Kubra, 235
Algeria, 425

al-Ghazali, 71, 377
al-Hasan, 21, 30, 31, 48, 49, 51, 76, 86, 87, 92, 97, 100, 101, 107, 136, 152, 187, 191, 232, 303, 320, 333, 337, 355, 356, 398, 422
al-Hasan al-Basri, 369
al-Husayn, 31, 48, 53, 58, 76, 84, 86, 92, 97, 100, 101, 136, 137, 152, 155, 187, 191, 231, 306, 333, 337, 354, 355, 356, 359, 387, 398, 401, 402, 403, 421, 422, 424
Al-Husayn, 243
Ali ibn Abu Talib, 30, 34, 35, 37, 38, 46, 47, 48, 49, 50, 52, 54, 59, 63, 65, 67, 68, 84, 85, 86, 88, 90, 94, 95, 96, 97, 100, 101, 107, 111, 126, 127, 128, 129, 134, 141, 144, 149, 152, 157, 160, 181, 184, 185, 187, 191, 194, 196, 201, 202, 204, 209, 226, 229, 230, 231, 241, 245, 247, 248, 252, 259, 260, 273, 280, 286, 289, 290, 294, 298, 299, 300, 301, 302, 303, 319, 321, 328, 330, 337, 341, 342, 345, 348, 350, 354, 385, 388, 399, 417
Ali ibn al-Jahm, 96
Al-Ihtijaj, 286
Al-Imam al-Sadiq wal Madhahib al-Arba`a, 134
Al-Imama wal Siyasa, 234, 254
Al-Imama wal-Siyasa, 250
Al-Isaba, 370
Al-Isaba fi Tamyiz al-Sahabah, 370
Al-Isti`ab, 271, 306

471

al-Jassas, 230
Al-Jihad wal Siyar, 41
Al-Kabaair, 367
Al-Kafi, 76, 323, 324
al-Kawthar, 136, 137, 139, 140, 381
Al-Khateeb al-Baghdadi, 173
al-Khawarizmi, 97, 100, 146, 204
al-Khayzaran, 97
al-Khidr, 87
al-khilafa al-rashida, 34
Al-Kifaya, 370
al-Kulayni, 323
Al-Kulayni, 76
Allama al-`Askari, 76
al-Mada'ini, 237
Al-Mada'ini, 345, 346
al-Mahdi, 24, 25, 100, 101, 123, 313, 417
al-Ma'mun, 57
al-marji` al-a`la, 184
Al-Maroodi, 391
Al-Maroozi, 173
Al-Mas`udi, 259, 320, 350, 353
al-milal wal nihal, 14, 43
al-Mu`tasim, 52, 53, 96, 115
al-Mudeera, 395
al-Mugheerah, 93, 275, 279
Al-Muhalla, 230, 310, 326
Al-Muraja`at, 82, 139, 149, 155, 362
al-Musayyab ibn Rafi, 172
Al-Mustadrak, 69, 195, 271, 371
Al-Mustafa, 377
al-Mutawakkil, 53, 57, 96, 97, 115, 204
Al-Muttaqi al-Hindi, 140, 378
Al-Muwatta, 74, 194, 210, 299

al-Nasa'i, 107, 139, 205, 251, 252, 300, 343
Al-Nasaih al-Kafiya, 195
al-Qadisiyya, 250
al-Qurtubi, 233
Al-Riyad al-Nadira, 284, 285, 337, 343
al-Saffah, 196, 197, 313
Al-Sahaba fi Nadar al-Shi`a al-Imamiyyah, 366, 370
al-saheefa al-jami`a, 75, 198
al-salaf al-salih, 77
Al-Saqifa, 40
Al-Sarim al-Maslul, 368
Al-Sawa`iq al-Muhriqa, 155, 208
Al-Sha`bi, 66, 309
al-Shafi`i, 34, 59, 91, 100, 102, 114, 128, 133, 134, 140, 173, 187, 218, 398, 407
al-Shaybani, 115
Al-Shi`a wal-Tasheeh, 412, 415, 421, 422
Al-Sihah al-Sittah, 205
Al-Sila bayn al-Tasawwuf wal Tashayyu, 94
al-Sirat al-Mustaqeem, 37, 82
Al-Sunan al-Kubra, 229
al-Suyuti, 139, 146, 164, 196, 321, 340
Al-Tabaqat al-Kubra, 330
al-Tabarsi, 286
al-Tabrani, 139, 208, 230
Al-Tafsir al-Kabir, 151, 204, 217, 326
al-Thaqalayn, 8, 76, 82, 139, 142
al-Tirmidhi, 76, 139, 163, 300, 309
Al-Waleed ibn Abd al-Malik, 53
al-Waqidi, 237

alwazgh, 387
al-Ya`qubi, 279
al-Zamakhshari, 100
al-Zubayr, 10, 48, 55, 70, 205, 214, 222, 240, 241, 242, 243, 244, 245, 246, 247, 248, 249, 251, 255, 262, 264, 265, 268, 306, 307, 308, 317, 318, 319, 320, 321
Am al-jama`ah, 303
Ameer al-Asab, 196
Amharic, 298
Ammar, 87, 94, 247, 248, 256, 273
Amr ibn al-As, 93, 112, 117, 251, 258, 350, 368, 371, 375
Anas ibn Malik, 329, 342
Anas ibn Qatadah, 340
Andalusia, 114
Ansab al-Ashraf, 265, 306
Ansar, 71, 173, 197, 227, 250, 253, 255, 262, 263, 294, 296, 303, 304, 306, 312, 428
Ansars, 45, 227, 302, 343, 349
apostasy, 18, 77, 170, 195, 217, 230, 278, 305, 307, 369, 420
apostates, 26, 33, 53, 60, 77, 170, 188, 248, 294, 311, 362, 368
Aqaba, 371
Arabian Peninsula, 115, 380
arjulakum, 151
arjulikum, 151, 152
ark of Noah, 154, 403
artificial insemination, 184
Ashura, 205, 206, 401, 402, 403, 404, 424, 428
Ask Those Who Know, 17, 28, 62, 87, 210, 268, 271, 297, 378, 391, 410

Asl al-Shi`a wa Usuliha, 421
Asmaa, 240, 317, 321
Ata ibn Yasar, 62
Ayatullah Abul-Qasim al-Khu'i, 421
Ayatullah al-Mar`ashi al-Najafi, 421
Ayatullah Muhammad Baqir al-Sadr, 158, 185
Ayesha, 9, 71, 72, 111, 205, 214, 233, 235, 236, 237, 240, 242, 251, 258, 268, 269, 270, 271, 272, 273, 290, 298, 314, 317, 318, 319, 334, 369, 394, 395, 407
azan, 210, 222, 314, 424

B

badaa, 417
Baghdadi *khateeb*, 375
Bahrain, 288
Banu al-Abbas, 88
Banu Ghanam, 244
Banu Hashim, 35, 234, 272, 320
Banu Juthaymah, 279, 390
Banu Ka`b ibn Luayy, 196, 313
Banu Makhzum, 275
Banu Sa`ida, 44, 45, 88, 104
Banu Taym, 234
Banu Umayyah, 56, 75, 88, 142, 197, 222, 223, 227, 228, 272, 273, 280, 292, 299, 303, 333, 341, 342, 346, 354, 359, 403
Banu Zuhra, 250, 261
Baqee, 295
Basra, 237, 238, 240, 241, 242, 243, 244, 318, 319

Battle of Badr, 64, 250, 334, 370, 371
Battle of Mu'tah, 349
Battle of Nahrawan, 345
Battle of Siffeen, 345
Battle of the Camel, 245, 268, 269, 317, 345
Battle of the Trench, 300
Battle of Uhud, 276, 337
Bay`at al-Ridwan, 371
bayt al-mal, 232, 241, 243, 244
bedouin Arabs, 381
bid`at, 107, 230, 241, 270, 361, 365, 387
bid`ats, 232, 339, 374
bid'at, 264, 273, 346, 354
Bilal, 242, 256
bismillah, 154, 329, 339, 341, 342, 344
Bismillahir-Rahmanir-Rahim, 340, 428
Black Thursday, 39
Britain, 17

C

Caesars, 59
Commander of the Faithful, 21, 55, 76, 95, 111, 126, 184, 191, 194, 196, 205, 226, 230, 241, 242, 245, 251, 253, 255, 260, 298, 299, 303, 312, 316, 342, 346, 358, 386

D

Dala'il al-Nubuwwah, 331
Dar al-Nadwa, 371
David, 276, 358
Dawood ibn Ali, 170, 171

Day of the Rahba, 344
Day of Uhud, 349
Dhul Khuwaysara, 379
Dhul-Fiqar, 337
Dhul-Noor, 337
Dhul-Noorayn, 9, 226, 295, 336, 337
Dictionary of Islam, 12
Dr. Ahmad Mahmud Subhi, 386
Dr. al-Musawi, 413, 414, 415, 418, 419, 424, 425, 426
Dr. Hamid Hafni Dawood, 364, 365, 369
Dr. Musa al-Musawi, 412, 415, 416, 418, 420, 421
Dr. Mustafa Kamil al-Shibeebi, 94
Dr. Sa`id Abd al-Fattah `Ashoor, 28

E

Eisawi, 120
Ezekiel, 336

F

Fadak, 46, 49
Fadl ibn al-Abbas, 290
faqih, 55, 110, 115, 116, 123, 133, 172, 184, 196, 210, 230, 311, 314, 340, 395, 402
farooq, 337
fatawa, 34, 75, 314, 406, 428
Fath al-Bari, 304, 312
Fatima, 31, 45, 46, 47, 48, 49, 136, 145, 146, 216, 221, 240, 252, 256, 285, 302, 337, 358, 390, 398

Fatima al-Zahra, 47, 48, 49, 145, 215, 221, 240, 285, 302
fatwas, 173
Fayd al-Qadeer, 208
fidya, 64
fiqh, 26, 83, 89, 108, 114, 115, 116, 118, 126, 128, 137, 157, 191, 299, 316, 320, 321, 323, 394, 400, 420, 421, 422, 434

G

Gabriel, 77, 184, 337, 378, 391, 403
Ghadeer, 45, 155, 204, 205, 234, 344
ghazwa, 241
ghulat, 362

H

Habib al-Najjar, 336
Haddab ibn Khalid al-Azdi, 62
Hajjaj ibn Yusuf al-Thaqafi, 112, 195
Hakim Nishasapuri, 371
halal, 241, 272, 321
Hamna, 257
Hamza, 31
Hanafi, 100, 101, 103, 128, 183, 368
Hanbali, 103, 110, 111, 115, 116, 128, 183, 200
Hanbalis, 14, 55, 58
Haqaiq an Ameer al-Mumineen Yazid ibn Mu'awiyah, 78
Hareez ibn Uthman al-Dimashqi, 98
Hareezi sect, 98
Haroun al-Rasheed, 57, 115, 375

Hasan al-Basri, 114, 168
Hawab, 242, 317
hawza al-'ilmiyya, 184
hijab, 64
Hijjatul Wada, 45
Hims, 144
Hish Kawkab, 237
Hudaybiyyah, 21, 22, 23, 71, 276, 371
huffaz, 308, 429
humayraa, 243, 395
Hunayn, 284
Husayn al-Radi, 149
Huzayfah, 152, 378
hypocrites, 47, 77, 89, 196, 327, 355, 363, 364, 374, 378, 379, 380, 382, 391

I

Ibn 'Abbas, 39
Ibn Abd al-Birr, 73, 271, 306, 331
Ibn Abd Rabbih, 48, 265
Ibn Abu Dawood, 114
Ibn Abu Thuayb, 114, 131, 132, 133
Ibn Abu Ya'li, 55
Ibn Abul-Hadid, 41, 150, 234, 235, 236, 238, 239, 245, 265, 266, 290, 291, 293, 318, 320, 350, 353
Ibn al-Athir, 139, 243, 343
Ibn al-Hadrami, 288
Ibn al-Qayyim al-Jawziyyah, 166
Ibn al-Sikkeet, 96
Ibn Aqeel, 195
Ibn Asakir, 140, 195, 196, 238, 309, 313, 379
Ibn Ayeenah, 41, 168

Ibn Hajar, 97, 98, 139, 154, 155, 201, 205, 208, 304, 312, 370
Ibn Hazm, 170, 230, 310, 326
Ibn Hazm al-Zahiri, 170
Ibn Jarir al-Tabari, 111, 205
Ibn Jarmooz, 246
Ibn Kathir, 73, 204, 205, 217, 233, 258, 259, 271, 291, 334
Ibn Khaldun, 108
Ibn Majah, 163, 305, 337
Ibn Maleeka, 378
Ibn Manzur, 28, 266
Ibn Mas'ud al-Ansari, 208
Ibn Qutaybah, 111, 118, 121, 123, 130, 131, 132, 203, 227, 234, 250, 251, 254, 290, 302, 309, 331
Ibn Sam'an, 131, 132, 133
Ibn Taymiyyah, 34, 59, 103, 111, 116
Ibn Ziyad, 401
Ibrahim, 66, 98, 202, 203, 207, 223, 224, 291, 401
Ibrahim al-Taymi, 66
Ibrahim ibn Ya'qub al-Jawzjani, 98, 202
ibtihal, 192
ihram, 314, 339
Ihyaa 'Uloom al-Din, 378
ijma, 161, 173, 312
ijtihad, 45, 46, 51, 74, 75, 88, 89, 92, 93, 103, 112, 146, 157, 168, 170, 171, 173, 181, 188, 198, 226, 227, 269, 277, 278, 279, 324, 327, 330, 364, 365, 369, 377, 382, 409, 410, 413, 415, 420, 421, 422, 423, 431
Imam Ahmad ibn Hanbal, 203, 386

Imam al-Awza'i, 331
Imam al-Baqir, 158, 187
Imam al-Hasan, 30, 192, 425
Imam al-Hasan ibn Ali al-Askari, 192
Imam Ali ibn Muhammad al-Hadi, 192
Imam Ali ibn Musa al-Rida, 57, 192
Imam al-Nishapouri, 341
Imam al-Shafi'i, 173, 207, 398
Imam Husayn, 23, 96, 402, 403
Imam Ja'far al-Sadiq, 65, 67, 69, 75, 76, 102, 133, 135, 158, 183, 278, 322, 413
Imam Ja'far ibn Muhammad al-Sadiq, 191
Imam Muhammad ibn al-Hasan al-Mahdi, 192
Imam Muhammad ibn Ali al-Baqir, 191
Imam Muhammad ibn Ali al-Jawad, 192
Imam Muhammad ibn Jarir al-Tabari, 204
Imam Musa ibn Ja'far al-Kazim, 191
Imam Muslim, 62, 251
Imam Sayyid Abul-Hasan al-Musawi al-Isfahani, 420
Imam Zain al-Abidin, 137
India, 12, 17
Islamic Republic of Iran, 17
Islamic Revolution, 426
Isma'eel, 91, 223, 224
Isma'eel al-Ash'ari, 91
isnad, 323
Israelites, 137
istihsan, 161, 173

istishab, 173
Itrat, 10, 139, 142, 143, 144, 150, 154, 203, 209, 394, 396, 398, 399, 430

J

Ja'far al-Iskafi, 291
Ja'far al-Sadiq, 109
Ja'far ibn Abd al-Wahid, 97
Ja'far ibn Muhammad, 134, 191, 229
Ja'far ibn Sulayman, 118, 119, 122
Ja'far al-Tayyar, 31
Jabir ibn Abdullah al-Ansari, 223
Ja'far aṭ-Ṭayyar, 349
jahiliyya, 27, 79, 125, 137, 180, 224, 253, 261, 286, 310, 382
Jahiliyya, 223, 346, 430
Jamharat Rasaail al-Arab, 350, 353
Jami' Bayan al-'Ilm, 331, 332
janaba, 290
Jesus Christ, 60
jihad, 60, 288
Jodi mountain, 403
Jordan, 385
jubbah, 291
Judaicas, 144
jurisprudence, 26, 83, 109, 122, 126, 212, 323, 363, 423, 428, 433

K

Ka'b al-Ahbar, 111, 144, 289, 291, 298
kafir, 115, 116, 153, 202, 230, 279, 309, 368, 375, 377, 378, 382, 393, 406, 414, 419, 422, 423
Kaisers, 59
Kamal Ataturk, 384
Kanz al-Ummal, 106, 140, 196, 208, 313, 334, 343, 378
Karbala, 96, 136, 191, 307, 403
Kashif al-Ghita, 420, 421, 422
Kenya, 17
Khadija, 369
Khalid ibn al-Waleed, 9, 214, 222, 275, 276, 279, 280, 283, 284, 287, 371, 390, 396
khandaq, 300
Kharijite, 30, 311, 333, 334, 346, 402
Kharijites, 201, 202, 310, 311, 332, 333, 336, 338
Khasais, 107, 139, 146
Khasa'is, 252, 337, 343
Khaybar, 49, 85, 235, 252, 300, 338, 391
khums, 46, 47, 417
Kitab al-'Ilm, 65, 66
Kufa, 195, 237, 240, 241, 250, 257, 293, 294, 345
kufr, 78, 128, 230, 418, 419

L

Layth ibn Sa'd, 114, 133
Lisan al-Arab, 28, 266
Lisan al-Mizan, 203, 205

M

Ma'al Sadiqin, 144, 163
Ma'alim al-Madrasatayn, 76
Ma'az ibn Jabal, 198
Mahmud Abu Rayyah, 290

Mahmud Shaltut, 82
majlis al-shura, 222
Major Occultation, 419, 422
Malik, 8, 34, 59, 74, 91, 102, 109, 114, 118, 119, 120, 121, 122, 123, 124, 125, 126, 127, 128, 129, 130, 131, 132, 133, 134, 140, 152, 173, 187, 188, 194, 210, 290, 299, 308, 340, 341, 342
Malik ibn Anas, 114
Malik ibn Nuwayrah, 280
Maliki, 34, 103, 115, 128, 183, 265
Malikis, 14, 58, 118
Mamlukes, 58, 88
Manaqib, 114, 133, 146, 173
Manaqib Imam Ahmad ibn Hanbal, 174
Mansham, 266
Maqalat al-Islamiyyin, 331
maraji, 183
marji`iyya, 187
Marwan ibn al-Hakam, 74, 94, 238, 246, 290, 308, 320, 375, 387
Marwan ibn Muhammad ibn Marwan, 56
Maryam, 192
Masjid al-Nabi, 250
mawla, 204
Medina, 29, 31, 43, 48, 67, 70, 73, 92, 118, 119, 122, 124, 130, 131, 134, 144, 173, 195, 196, 213, 231, 240, 241, 244, 250, 261, 271, 292, 293, 294, 303, 304, 307, 308, 319, 371, 380, 387, 404, 428, 429

Messenger of Allah, 16, 18, 21, 22, 26, 27, 29, 31, 35, 36, 39, 40, 41, 43, 46, 47, 48, 53, 56, 59, 62, 63, 64, 65, 67, 68, 69, 70, 71, 72, 74, 75, 76, 78, 79, 85, 86, 87, 88, 89, 90, 91, 92, 97, 102, 104, 105, 106, 111, 122, 134, 135, 137, 138, 139, 140, 145, 146, 149, 154, 157, 158, 163, 164, 165, 174, 177, 178, 179, 181, 184, 187, 189, 191, 194, 198, 199, 203, 205, 206, 207, 208, 209, 213, 215, 216, 217, 218, 219, 221, 223, 225, 226, 228, 229, 230, 231, 232, 233, 235, 237, 238, 240, 242, 243, 244, 246, 247, 251, 252, 253, 256, 257, 259, 268, 269, 270, 276, 277, 279, 280, 282, 283, 284, 285, 288, 289, 290, 291, 292, 293, 295, 296, 300, 304, 306, 307, 309, 310, 312, 313, 314, 315, 321, 322, 326, 328, 329, 330, 332, 333, 334, 337, 340, 341, 343, 349, 352, 354, 355, 357, 364, 367, 368, 369, 370, 371, 373, 376, 378, 379, 380, 381, 382, 383, 384, 385, 386, 387, 388, 389, 391, 396, 403, 406, 417, 418
Mina, 121, 229, 230, 322
Moguls, 58
Morocco, 385
Moses, 53, 72, 87, 101, 137, 149, 235, 252, 259, 324, 375, 376, 403, 404
Mr. Sale, 12
Mu`awiyah, 23, 30, 31, 37, 53, 56, 59, 60, 74, 77, 78, 80, 88,

93, 107, 112, 117, 128, 137, 138, 144, 146, 196, 197, 202, 205, 206, 210, 212, 213, 255, 256, 258, 259, 260, 270, 271, 272, 273, 281, 292, 293, 295, 298, 303, 304, 305, 306, 307, 311, 312, 313, 314, 315, 316, 333, 338, 344, 345, 346, 347, 348, 350, 351, 352, 354, 355, 358, 360, 361, 368, 369, 375, 384, 386, 387, 402, 403, 406, 425

Mu`een al-Hukkam feema Yataraddadu baynal Khasmayn min al-Ahkam, 368
Mu`tazilite, 100, 150, 239, 265, 353, 366
Mubahala, 192, 399
mufti, 82, 115, 118
Muhajirs, 45, 70, 227, 312, 349
Muhajirun, 173, 197, 227, 253, 255, 262, 263, 294, 296, 302, 303, 304, 306
Muhammad al-Samawi al-Tijani, 13
Muhammad ibn Abd al-Rahman, 174
Muhammad ibn Abd al-Wahhab, 34, 115, 116
Muhammad ibn Abu Bakr, 272, 371
Muhammad ibn Maslamah, 254
Muhammad son of Abu Bakr, 347, 348
muhyi al-Sunnah, 203, 204
Muhyyi al-Sunnah, 97
Mujaddid al-Sunnah, 116
mujtahid, 128, 183, 184, 429, 433
mujtahids, 159, 377

Muqaddimah, 108
Muruj al-Dhahab, 259, 350, 353
Musaylamah, 285
Muslim's *Sahih*, 39, 49, 60, 139, 252, 256, 269, 300, 304, 305, 334, 335, 340, 367
Musnad, 40, 69, 87, 104, 106, 107, 139, 208, 212, 272, 273, 302, 308, 310, 314, 416, 417, 431
Mustadrak, 69, 104, 107, 139, 140, 146, 243, 304, 337, 343
mut`a, 77, 223, 231, 320, 321, 330, 417
mut`at al-hajj, 222, 229
mut`at al-nisaa, 222
Mu'tah, 43, 283, 349
Mutamar al-Wahdah al-Islamiyya, 83
mutawatir, 76, 204

N

nafl, 222
Najaf al-Ashraf, 421, 423
Najdah ibn Amir, 310, 311
Nasibi, 115, 126, 201, 202, 203
Nasr ibn Ali ibn Sahban, 97
Nazariyyat Al-Imama, 386

O

organ transplantation, 184
Ottoman caliphs, 384

P

Pagans of Mecca, 22
Pakistan, 17
Palestine, 425

479

Pharaoh, 137, 337, 403, 404
Progeny of Muhammad, 207, 208, 209, 365, 366, 406, 407
Prophetic Sunnah, 50, 62, 73, 78, 84, 88, 92, 93, 139, 155
Prophet's Progeny, 28, 95, 112, 180, 210, 213, 299, 313

Q

Qasitis, 202
qibla, 79
qiyas, 161, 170, 173, 181, 198, 217, 219, 278, 279, 328
Quraysh, 22, 43, 69, 70, 75, 79, 87, 93, 100, 135, 136, 163, 180, 195, 223, 224, 240, 242, 261, 262, 263, 264, 266, 276, 277, 281, 291, 295, 336, 375, 386, 417

R

Rafidi, 110, 201
Rafizis, 338, 360
Raja ibn Haywah, 172
rak`ats, 229, 230, 270, 273
Ramadan, 78, 104, 433, 434
righteous caliphs, 34, 36, 52, 54, 55, 58, 62, 63, 74, 99, 110, 126, 161, 163, 164, 288, 301, 336, 355, 368, 371, 399, 410
Righteous Caliphs, 8, 9, 163, 191, 194, 413
risala, 158, 185
Ruqayya, 337

S

Sa`id ibn al-Musayyab, 369

Sa'd ibn Abadah, 391
Sa'd ibn Abu Waqqas, 9, 214, 250, 251, 252, 253, 254, 256, 257, 258, 259, 260, 261, 321, 401
sadd bab al-tharai, 161
Saeed ibn Jubayr, 41
Safiyya, 240
sahabah, 12, 22, 27, 35, 36, 39, 42, 43, 44, 45, 46, 47, 49, 50, 52, 59, 60, 62, 63, 65, 68, 73, 74, 80, 84, 91, 92, 102, 108, 110, 112, 122, 125, 126, 127, 129, 145, 146, 149, 152, 153, 154, 155, 161, 164, 166, 168, 169, 174, 200, 203, 207, 209, 210, 211, 212, 218, 227, 228, 229, 230, 231, 232, 240, 241, 243, 250, 256, 261, 277, 282, 288, 291, 293, 294, 298, 299, 300, 301, 302, 304, 314, 329, 330, 333, 336, 338, 341, 344, 345, 362, 363, 364, 365, 366, 367, 368, 369, 370, 371, 372, 373, 374, 375, 376, 377, 378, 379, 380, 381, 382, 387, 388, 390, 391, 392, 393, 399, 401, 405, 406, 407, 409, 410, 432
sahabi, 94, 152, 173, 229, 269, 297, 343, 345, 363, 364, 365, 369, 370, 372, 373, 376, 378, 382, 399, 410, 432
saheefa, 63, 65, 66, 67, 68, 69, 74, 75, 157
saheefa jami`a, 181
Sahih books, 21, 39, 48, 51, 64, 65, 100, 105, 143, 144, 208, 216, 225, 232, 251, 304, 330, 335, 388, 400, 416, 417, 418

Sahl ibn Haneef, 244
Salafis, 34
Saleem al-Din al-Bishri, 82
Salman al-Ahwal, 41
Saqifa, 44, 88, 104, 263, 359, 360, 395, 422, 432
Saudi Arabia, 34, 78, 360, 385
sawafi al-umara, 161, 172
Sayf-Allah, 336, 337
Shafi`i, 103, 109, 115, 128, 134, 155, 183, 407
Shafi`is, 14, 58
shahada, 262, 264, 378
Shahristani, 14, 43
shaqshaqi sermon, 257
Sharaf al-Din Sadr ad-Din al-Musawi, 82, 139, 362
Sharh Nahjul Balagha, 41, 257, 350, 353
Sharh Nahjul-Balagha, 234, 239, 245, 265, 266, 290, 291, 293, 318, 320
Shari`a, 8, 116, 160, 161, 166, 167, 168, 170, 171, 174, 176, 178, 180, 183, 185, 187, 278, 279, 280, 299, 315, 364, 386, 410, 423, 432
Shaykh Abu Zuhra, 110, 342
Shaykh Abu Zuhrah, 166, 167
Shaykh al-Islam, 116
Shaykh al-Mufeed, 323
Shaykh Muhammad Abdoh, 234, 257
shaykhain, 84
shaykhs, 84, 245, 302, 314, 343, 410
Shaykhs, 104, 146, 157, 226
Shi`a Ja'fari sect, 83
shirk, 111, 228

Shu`bah ibn al-Hajjaj, 291
shura, 55, 263, 265, 356, 358, 388
siddiq, 337
Solomon, 276, 358
son of Sakhr, 348, 352
Sudan, 425
Sufyan al-Thawri, 114, 168
Sufyan ibn Ayeenah, 229
Sufyan ibn Harb, 281
Sufyan ibn Umayyah, 257
Sulayman ibn Abd al-Malik, 74
Surat al-Ahzab, 154, 364
Surat al-Bayyinah, 321
Surat al-Munafiqun, 379
Surat al-Tawbah, 364
Sweden, 17
Sword of Allah, 275, 280, 283, 285
Syria, 30, 31, 144, 172, 272, 304, 358, 426

T

Tabaqat, 55, 73, 139, 172, 212, 223, 224, 235, 288, 294, 295, 305, 310, 312, 371
Tabaqat al-Fuqaha, 171
tabi`i, 174, 365
tabi`in, 161, 168, 432
Tadhkirat al-Huffaz, 73, 105, 114, 133, 145, 333, 334
Tafsir Ghara'ib al-Qur'an, 341
Taha Husayn, 235, 237, 240, 241, 244, 261
Tahdhib al-Tahdhib, 97, 98, 201, 367
talbiya, 228
taleeqs, 371, 395

Talhah, 9, 55, 70, 94, 205, 214, 233, 234, 235, 236, 237, 238, 239, 240, 241, 242, 243, 244, 245, 246, 249, 251, 255, 264, 265, 268, 307, 308, 317, 318, 321, 367, 396
Talkhis, 140
Talqeeh Fuhum Ahlul Athaar, 370
Tanweer al-Hawalik, 210
taqiyya, 77, 417
taqlid, 187
taraweeh, 104
Taraweeh, 218, 222, 433
Tarikh al-Khulafa, 121, 123, 130, 132, 146, 164, 196, 227, 250, 251, 302, 309
Tarikh Baghdad, 53, 168, 173, 174, 343, 376
tashahhud, 407
Tasheeh al-I`tiqad, 323
Tatars, 58
Ta'weel al-Ahadith, 290
Tawhid, 14, 339, 433
tayammum, 51, 222
thaqalayn, 112, 139, 394, 396, 399
Then I was Guided, 13, 28
Thomas Hughes, 12
Thursday Calamity, 39
To be with the Truthful, 17, 28, 87, 103, 144, 163, 329, 385, 398, 410, 416, 418
Tunisia, 25, 120, 404, 425
Twelfth Imam, 23, 157
Twelve Imams, 13, 14, 26, 87, 89, 100, 102, 137, 157, 181, 183, 185, 191, 313, 401

Two Weighty Things, 24, 28, 76, 104, 139, 140, 142, 147, 155, 189

U

Ubaydullah ibn Abdullah ibn `Utbah ibn Mas`ud. Abdullah, 39
ulama, 168, 323
Umar ibn Abd al-Aziz, 53, 57, 63, 64, 74, 75, 95, 164
Umar ibn al-Khattab, 9, 22, 23, 39, 40, 41, 42, 45, 48, 51, 56, 71, 73, 74, 84, 90, 104, 105, 144, 145, 197, 214, 216, 221, 223, 224, 226, 227, 233, 234, 240, 241, 250, 254, 261, 264, 280, 284, 285, 286, 289, 298, 299, 301, 304, 305, 315, 333, 334, 376, 378, 379, 380, 384
Umayyad, 23, 27, 53, 64, 74, 82, 92, 96, 146, 164, 187, 194, 197, 273, 327, 342, 344, 360, 382, 386, 393, 394, 402
Ummah, 27, 29, 32, 35, 42, 48, 73, 78, 88, 102
Umme Kulthoom, 261, 337
Umme Salamah, 259, 260
umra, 231, 242, 303
Uqbah ibn Abu Mu`eet, 261
Usamah, 43, 215, 216, 221, 254, 390
Usd al-Ghaba, 343
Usd al-Ghabah, 306
usul al-din, 91
Usul al-Kafi, 66, 322
Uthman, 9, 27, 34, 43, 50, 51, 52, 56, 68, 70, 74, 88, 93, 98, 105,

117, 126, 127, 164, 165, 195, 196, 197, 201, 202, 203, 209, 214, 226, 227, 228, 229, 230, 231, 232, 234, 235, 236, 237, 238, 239, 241, 243, 244, 250, 251, 254, 255, 257, 258, 261, 262, 263, 264,265, 266, 269, 270, 273, 294, 295, 299, 300, 301, 302, 303, 304, 313, 314, 318, 333, 336, 337, 340, 344, 353, 354, 355, 367, 368, 396, 399, 407
Uthman ibn Haneef, 243, 244

W

Wadeezah al-Himsi, 55
Wahab ibn Munabbih, 144
Wahhabi, 210
Wahhabis, 34, 415
Wahhabism, 116
Waleed ibn al-Mugheerah, 275
wali, 124, 149, 197, 272, 303, 310, 346, 433
Waseelat al-Najat, 419, 420
West Africa, 17
wilaya, 24

wudu, 151, 325

Y

Yahya ibn Ma`een, 367
Yamama, 280
Yanabi` al-Mawaddah, 101
Yanabi' al-Mawaddah, 100
Yasin T. al-Jibouri, 15
Yazid, 23, 74, 78, 88, 92, 136, 196, 197, 212, 213, 291, 305, 306, 307, 308, 311, 313, 333, 354, 355, 358, 359, 360, 375, 384, 386, 387, 402, 403
Yazid ibn Haroun, 291
Yemen, 144, 198, 378
Yusha`, 101
Yusuf, 86, 308

Z

Zahara al-Islam, 134, 135
zakat, 78, 145, 148, 215, 216, 221, 307, 357, 402, 434
Zayd ibn al-Haritha, 283
Zayd ibn Aslam, 62
Zoroastrian, 77

www.ingramcontent.com/pod-product-compliance
Lightning Source LLC
LaVergne TN
LVHW091652070526
838199LV00050B/2156